C000081585

USCG Project Evergreen V

Compilation of Activities and Summary of Results

AARON C. DAVENPORT, MICHELLE D. ZIEGLER, SUSAN A. RESETAR, SCOTT SAVITZ,
KATHERINE ANANIA, MELISSA BAUMAN, KARISHMA MCDONALD

This research was published in 2022.

Approved for public release; distribution is unlimited.

Preface

This report documents support by RAND Corporation's Homeland Security Operational Analysis Center (HSOAC) to the U.S. Coast Guard's Evergreen strategic foresight activity from July 2018 to July 2022. The report is a compilation of both Coast Guard and HSOAC activities, products, and jointly developed reports. The Evergreen Project has been a team effort consisting of staff from the Coast Guard Office of Emerging Policy (DCO-X), a core group of Coast Guard subject-matter experts (SMEs), and HSOAC researchers. The objective was to help the Coast Guard identify relevant topics, issues, areas of opportunity, and potential challenges that the service will likely face in the coming decades and to provide those to the transition team for the next commandant for consideration, thus posturing senior leadership to better bridge the gap between future challenges and near-term plans, which typically focus on the urgent needs of the present.

HSOAC analysts reviewed prior Evergreen activities, examined Coast Guard strategy-making and planning processes; adapted an approach for developing scenarios; narrated a set of exemplar global planning scenarios; supported workshops targeting diverse sets of SMEs; assisted with planning, facilitating, and capturing outputs from ideation exercises with target cohorts of service participants; published short documents on notable topics of interest identified during workshops; and aided the service in developing requirements and planning for a series of strategic games[1] to test new concepts of operations, set in specific future global scenarios. The series of focused workshops in the third year emerged from program engagements with the service's senior leadership, who provided the subject material and helped guide the team.[2]

This research was sponsored by DCO-X and conducted within the Strategy, Policy, and Operations Program of the HSOAC federally funded research and development center (FFRDC).

About the Homeland Security Operational Analysis Center

The Homeland Security Act of 2002 (Section 305 of Public Law 107-296, as codified at 6 U.S.C. AO 185) authorizes the Secretary of Homeland Security, acting through the Under Secretary for Science and Technology, to establish one or more FFRDCs to provide independent analysis of homeland security issues. RAND operates HSOAC as an FFRDC for the U.S. Department of Homeland Security under contract HSHQDC-16-D-00007. The HSOAC FFRDC provides the government with independent and objective analyses and advice in core areas

---

[1] A serious game is one used for training or analysis, not entertainment, whereas a wargame is often focused on conflict.

[2] The team consisted of USCG DCO-X staff, RAND/HSOAC researchers, diverse select cohorts of Coast Guard active-duty and civilian SMEs, and select senior leadership from the service's flag corps who helped guide the team.

important to the department in support of policy development, decisionmaking, alternative approaches, and new ideas on issues of significance. The HSOAC FFRDC also works with and supports other federal, state, local, tribal, and public- and private-sector organizations that make up the homeland security enterprise. The HSOAC FFRDC's research is undertaken by mutual consent with DHS and is organized as a set of discrete tasks. This report presents the results of research and analysis conducted under task order 70Z02318FM7P03200, Evergreen V.

The results presented in this report do not necessarily reflect official DHS opinion or policy. For more information on HSOAC, see www.rand.org/hsoac. For more information on this publication, see www.rand.org/t/RR-A872-2.

Summary

The U.S. Coast Guard (USCG) has spent the past 25 years trying to predict and understand the challenges and opportunities it will face in the next 25 years through Project Evergreen, its long-term strategic planning initiative. The aim of this effort is to identify emerging challenges and future trends that may alter the demand for USCG missions and the ability to perform them so that senior leaders can plan for the long term. In this report, we summarize the findings of Evergreen V—the most recent four-year initiative—run by the USCG Office of Emerging Policy (DCO-X) with support from the Homeland Security Operational Analysis Center (HSOAC), a federally funded research and development center operated by the RAND Corporation under contract with the Department of Homeland Security (DHS).

Year 1: Scenario Development

The HSOAC team designed and supported two workshops and wrote *Developing New Future Scenarios for the U.S. Coast Guard's Evergreen Strategic Foresight Program*, a research report that framed a more deliberate approach to developing scenarios in the Coast Guard's strategic foresight program.[1] The report developed the structure for how to create scenarios for robust strategic planning, and the workshops served to identify vulnerabilities and opportunities in Coast Guard strategies while implementing the scenario-based workshop concept.

Key Concerns from Earlier Evergreens	Improvements Made in Response
Scenarios should be robust and diverse rather than predictive. They should stress-test current plans, policies, and capabilities by helping workshop participants better articulate trade-offs that USCG will make today to address the wide variety of possible challenges that it may face in the future.	The Evergreen team improved the approach to scenario development in order to help participants articulate near-term trade-offs to address long-term challenges. The scenario development was analytically robust and created four diverse plausible futures, each of which was designed to exert various amounts of pressure on key drivers of Coast Guard missions.
Evergreen insights are underutilized. Evergreen participants generally valued the experience of considering long-range implications for Coast Guard operations, but Evergreen products and findings often did not directly influence Coast Guard decisionmaking due to different planning time horizons. This also makes it challenging to trace Evergreen's impacts.	The team began producing short summaries as well as deeper dives into topics of interest to make the findings more accessible, timely, and useful to Coast Guard decisionmaking. Senior leaders and specific offices were able to understand the themes, opportunities, and concerns raised in the workshops within weeks of the events and were better informed on complex topics that affect the service.

---

[1] Abbie Tingstad, Michael T. Wilson, Katherine Anania, Jordan R. Fischbach, Susan A. Resetar, Scott Savitz, Kristin Van Abel, R. J. Briggs, Aaron C. Davenport, Stephanie Pezard, Kristin Sereyko, Jonathan Theel, Marc Thibault, and Edward Ulin, *Developing New Future Scenarios for the U.S. Coast Guard's Evergreen Strategic Foresight Program*, Santa Monica, Calif.: RAND Corporation, RR-3147-DHS, 2020.

Years 2 and 3: Workshops and Communications

Using the approach to scenario development created in Year 1, HSOAC developed four possible "futures" for discussion in six workshops (called "Pinecones") held in 2019–2021. The scenarios were structured around five levers: geopolitics, economy, climate, technology, and society. Each scenario had distinct stressors and put varying amounts of pressure on drivers of demand for Coast Guard missions. This resulted in a spectrum of potential futures, ranging from a world characterized by rapid growth, innovation, and U.S.-led cooperation to one plagued by disasters, resource strains, and loss of global influence. The same scenarios, with slight modifications, were used in six subsequent workshops.

Driving Mission Demands in the Future

Below are highlights of the current and future trends, driven by various phenomena, that will ultimately converge to have a collective impact on the Coast Guard in the 2040 time frame. These are coupled with common themes raised by participants about how these trends could impact the service or what the service might consider in response.

Demographic shifts. Aging populations will affect recruiting pools and the profiles of those whom the Coast Guard rescues; population growth will intensify demand for Coast Guard services.

Technological shifts. The Coast Guard will use new technologies—but so will those whom USCG rescues, supports, partners with, regulates, and counters. The Coast Guard needs to dynamically adjust its operations to effectively use technology, make it interoperable with some technologies, and be able to counter others.

Workforce and work-arrangement shifts. As long-term employment shifts toward shorter-term engagements and independent contractual work, the Coast Guard may need to accommodate changing expectations and rethink how it recruits, develops, and retains talent.

Environmental shifts. Receding coastlines, more severe storms, rising water levels, and other climate effects will profoundly change demand for Coast Guard services and put its infrastructure at risk.

Changing patterns of energy production and usage. Shifts in the transport volume of coal, oil, and natural gas will affect the types of traffic and facilities that the Coast Guard will regulate and secure. The Coast Guard may also seek to reduce its own usage of fossil fuels.

Changing drug production, use, and legislation status. The types of illicit drug flows that the Coast Guard will need to address over the long term will vary based on policies, changes in demand, shifting sources, and how drugs are routed from their sources to consumers.

Geopolitical shifts. The rise of China, the resurgence of Russia, fragile state control in various regions, terrorist threats, and other geopolitical factors can alter the Coast Guard's emphasis on its various domestic and overseas roles.

Highlights of Key Themes from the Workshops

The Coast Guard will need to enhance its technical capabilities. These enhancements should help it actively share information with partners—international agencies, the Department of Defense, the intelligence community, state and local agencies, and the private sector; enhance collaboration with partners and allies that will become increasingly necessary due to increased demand signals in missions and geographic regions where authorities are shared; and improve its ability to more effectively deploy assets to meet mission demands.

Internal and external stakeholders need greater visibility and transparency. The Coast Guard will need to invest in its information technology systems to make actionable data accessible to analysts, decisionmakers, servicemembers, and external stakeholders. This approach will require a difficult change in culture, as well as substantial investment.

Grassroots innovation and enterprise integration can be at odds. The Coast Guard often develops novel solutions to meet its particular needs. But tailored solutions can hinder interoperability with other stakeholders and steepen the learning curve for personnel. Striking the right balance between innovation and standardization requires constant reappraisal.

There is a need for balance between centralized and distributed decisionmaking. Ensuring alignment across the service can increase interoperability and collective effectiveness, but individual commands also need to be able to tailor policies, approaches, and decisions to meet their specific needs, given their deeper awareness of their operational environment and issues.

There is an inherent tension between localization and the ability of units to deploy. Rooting units in a particular locale has advantages (e.g., connections with neighboring units and agencies, knowledge of an area), but units must be deployable to respond to short-term emergencies and long-term shocks, where localization can be a disadvantage (e.g., cost and effort of deploying; unfamiliarity with environment, agencies, and individuals). Recurring deployments to the same areas can enhance familiarity, but the efforts and costs associated with deployments may limit a unit's capabilities and experience in its home environment, as well as induce additional strain and burden.

The Coast Guard faces trade-offs between efficiency and resilience. Measures taken to make the service lean and efficient can backfire by making the Coast Guard less resilient and reducing its ability to surge. The Coast Guard needs to invest in skilled personnel, equipment, assets, and infrastructure to meet prospective crises, even if not all elements are used routinely.

The Coast Guard will need additional resources. The Coast Guard's budget will need to increase to address the expectation of more involvement abroad and the growing demand at home, as well as the increasing cost of equipment sustainment.

Year 4: Strategic Games

In Year 4, Evergreen shifted from workshops to strategic-level strategic games. Paratus Futurum (Ready for the Future) forced players to make distinct choices about mission priorities and investments to prepare for an uncertain future in which climate change, technological advancements, the U.S. economy, and global power competition shape the demand for USCG missions. There were two series of games: a virtual game for midgrade officers and civilian participants and another consisting primarily of senior officers. Participants probed the trade-offs that must occur to meet national and USCG priorities and to enable Coast Guard leadership to articulate a vision to the public, Congress, the Executive Branch, DHS, and the USCG workforce.

Game Play

Each team was assigned a unique scenario and corresponding strategic vision developed in a prior workshop. The game was intended to demonstrate how efforts to achieve the vision could be challenged by the need to make trade-offs among competing priorities. Game play proceeded as follows:

1. The game began in 2025. Each round represented a four-year period. Teams played three to five rounds, progressing to 2040 and beyond.
2. At the start of each round, each team received an intelligence brief on key trends for the next four years and a fixed number of "resource tokens." The tokens were used to prioritize ongoing missions, invest in longer-term capabilities for use in future rounds, or invest in operations and maintenance or facilities and infrastructure.
3. As in real life, investing in some capabilities also required "cultural" investment, such as institutional adaptation, new training, changes in talent management priorities and the desired attributes of recruits, and new types of equipment and organization and their integration costs. Teams could invest in cultural change to promote these new or changing efforts.
4. At the end of each round, challenging new events were introduced. Mission success depended on how well resources and investments were positioned in each region and an element of chance (a roll of the die).
5. The score reflected how the public, Congress, and the Executive Branch perceived success. The scores and additional domestic events determined the resource constraints for the next round.

Overarching Observations

- Several teams relied on the current, positive progress of the service to sustain operations, and their dominant strategy for the first round of game play was to invest in new capabilities. Notably, command, control, computers, communications, cyber, intelligence, surveillance, and reconnaissance (C5ISR) capabilities were uniformly identified as the priority investment
- The teams' early investment strategies almost universally accepted some level of short-term risk in traditional missions and often in culture to pay for future capabilities—but players pivoted back to domestic missions as game play progressed.
- Each team acknowledged the importance of investing in operations, maintenance, and facilities and was unwilling to take risks over several consecutive rounds of play.
- The concept of an adaptive force package emerged as a key approach for covering a broad range of missions.

- Ensuring mission success in the future while leveraging new technology and attracting and retaining a highly capable workforce will require investment in culture.
- Teams generally spread resources to cover mission demand signals contained in the intelligence briefs and relied on surge capability as insurance against plausible surprises.
- Domestic missions are enduring and fundamental to the Coast Guard, and the teams' resourcing decisions reflected that.
- Participants noted that while the principal Coast Guard mission set may not change, how missions are performed or accomplished may be different.

Abbreviations

AI	artificial intelligence
C5ISR	command, control, computers, communications, cyber, intelligence, surveillance, and reconnaissance
CNO	Chief of Naval Operations
CONOPS	concept of operations
CONUS	continental United States
DCO-X	Coast Guard Office of Emerging Policy
DHS	Department of Homeland Security
DMDU	decisionmaking under deep uncertainty
DoD	Department of Defense
DOTMLF+R/G/S	doctrine, organization, training, materiel, leadership, personnel, facilities plus regulations, grants, and standards
FFRDC	federally funded research and development center
HSOAC	Homeland Security Operational Analysis Center
IO	information operations
IT	information technology
MDA	maritime domain awareness
MTS	Maritime Transportation System
OCONUS	outside the continental United States
OMB	Office of Management and Budget
PPBE	planning, programming, budgeting, and execution
PWCS	ports, waterways, and coastal security
SAR	search and rescue
SME	subject-matter expert
USCG	U.S. Coast Guard

Contents

Figures and Tables

Figures

Tables

1. Introduction

The U.S. Coast Guard (USCG) has spent the past 25 years trying to predict the challenges and opportunities it will face over the next 25 years through Evergreen, its long-term strategic planning initiative. The aim of this effort is to identify emerging challenges and future trends that may alter the volume and types of demand for USCG missions, and/or the service's ability to perform missions so that senior leaders can plan for the future. This report details the findings of Evergreen V—the most recent initiative—and includes the key documents and activities that were produced to support it.

The service carries out 11 different statutory missions and must address both immediate requirements and future contingencies. Future changes to the operating environment in the physical, economic, social, political, and technological domains present additional stresses on service resources, in addition to changing or shaping the composition of the service itself. One way to aid decisionmaking in an uncertain future is by more effectively leveraging the Coast Guard's Project Evergreen strategic foresight initiative. Without weighing the long view of changes in the operating environment alongside current or nearer-term demands, the service will not have full awareness of what blind spots might exist in current strategies and plans. Being ready for the spectrum of challenges the future might bring requires thoughtful consideration of both the near and long terms and how change will affect the Coast Guard.[1]

Evergreen and the Importance of Strategic Foresight for the Coast Guard

Readiness to meet future emerging challenges is the overarching goal of Project Evergreen. These challenges can manifest in the form of capability gaps that may be articulated within the Joint Requirements Integration and Management System process. Other types of gaps may also exist, such as missing or disconnected strategies, inadequately formulated policies, or limiting practices related to the full spectrum of human resource management and workforce issues.

The USCG Office of Emerging Policy (DCO-X) runs Project Evergreen. DCO-X is responsible for foresight, long-term strategic planning, and forecasting, as well as supporting strategic senior leadership engagements. The office is focused primarily on understanding emerging challenges, analyzing how USCG can address them, and enabling the resulting findings to be incorporated into the wider strategic planning and budget processes.

Evergreen was established in 2003 to "infuse the Service with strategic intent."[2] It includes Project Evergreen, a scenario-based strategic foresight planning process used in various forms

---

[1] Tingstad, Wilson, et al., 2020.

[2] DCO-X Evergreen program briefing slides dated February 2021.

since its inception as Project Long View in 1996. DCO-X defines *strategic foresight* as a process that offers a decisionmaker a new perspective by testing explicit assumptions to bring about a new understanding that will inform organizational preparations for the future. Rather than focusing on specific plans for a specific future, strategic foresight looks at the opportunities, challenges, and possibilities across a variety of plausible futures.

Project Evergreen runs on a four-year cycle aligned with the change in Coast Guard commandant. Evergreen V kicked off in October 2018, with analytical contract support provided by HSOAC, a federally funded research center operated by the RAND Corporation. DCO-X restructured Project Evergreen, so that rather than providing a single major report for the incoming commandant, it instead delivers a series of more targeted reports based on scenario-based workshops with flag sponsors across the enterprise.

Evergreen V focuses on identifying the implications of potential global and regional changes on existing Coast Guard strategies, statutory missions, and near-term decisions 15–25 years in the future. DCO-X and HSOAC create future scenarios based on methods including data analysis and scholarly research. The scenarios are used during games and workshops called "Pinecones," in which Coast Guard personnel examine USCG and Department of Homeland Security (DHS) capabilities to perform missions in future operating environments and the potential implications of future trends and contingencies for the efficacy of near-term strategic decisions. The scenarios also help identify potential opportunities to ensure mission relevance.

In exploring and refining the direction of Evergreen V over the course of the project, HSOAC developed a logic model, shown in Figure 1.1. This logic model is based on documents, interviews, the HSOAC team's own experiences working with the Evergreen program, and feedback from Evergreen stakeholders. It was developed using a standard methodology that enumerates the *activities* performed as part of Evergreen, the *outputs* that result directly from those activities, and the higher-level *outcomes* to which they contribute.[3] As Figure 1.1 indicates, Evergreen entails developing analytically informed stressing scenarios and exploring those scenarios in the Pinecone workshops. The outputs include documenting the workshop results to inform the Coast Guard's evolution, deepening relationships with stakeholders outside the Coast Guard through the Pinecones themselves and subsequent discussions, and fostering long-term thinking in a service that is often heavily focused on its current operational demands. Evergreen ultimately provides outcomes and insights that help to inform leadership thinking, as well as various strategies and plans. It also enhances awareness of long-term challenges, both within and outside the Coast Guard, and contributes to a culture of addressing those challenges despite the perennial urgency of current operations.

---

[3] For more information on logic models and their development, see Scott Savitz, Miriam Matthews, and Sarah Weilant, *Assessing Impact to Inform Decisions: A Toolkit on Measures for Policymakers*, Santa Monica, Calif.: RAND Corporation, TL-263-OSD, 2017.

Figure 1.1. Logic Model Characterizing Evergreen

Activities > **Outputs**

Activities

- Identify chronic and acute stressors that can affect the Coast Guard and its operational environment
- Select which stressors to vary in the scenarios
- Develop scenarios around different levels of selected stressors and analysis of historical experiences and trends
- Conduct Pinecone workshops to analyze the impact of each scenario as a function of Coast Guard preparedness and the overall environment
- Summarize and analyze workshop findings
- Communicate findings

Outputs

- Briefings, short documents, posters, and in-depth reports on
  - long-term trends, challenges, and opportunities
  - assessments of scenario impact and potential mitigation measures
  - ideas and feedback from pinecone participants
- Fostering of partnerships and information exchanges with external and internal stakeholders (e.g. industry, other parts of DHS, DoD, other agencies, Congress, international partners, senior leadership, program managers, various commands, and operators)
- Organizational and individual exposure to long-term issues and anticipatory thinking, including a space for openly exploring ideas

Desired Outcomes

- Current and incoming commandants' leadership teams have
  - a set of identified service implications and strategic choices regarding future challenges and opportunities emerging from an analytical, structured process
  - timely, relevant, and insightful considerations to shape current and future Coast Guard policies and operations
- The Coast Guard develops better-informed strategies, plans, programs, policies, decisions, and investments to address the long-term needs of the service, based on
  - understanding of key drivers of change that take into account potential challenges, opportunities, and uncertainties over the next 15–25 years
  - an iterative strategic-planning process in continual dialogue with Evergreen to incorporate its ongoing findings
- Greater external and internal awareness of the Coast Guard's long-term challenges and opportunities, and how to address them
- The Coast Guard has a more long-term, comprehensive strategic culture that allows
  - broader perspectives on factors influencing the future Coast Guard and its operating environment
  - individuals to gain experience in long-term thinking at various stages of their careers

Over the course of the project, HSOAC research staff, who have diverse professional experience and analytic capabilities, supported DCO-X in all of these activities and outputs: engaging stakeholders in workshops; collecting insights regarding potential implications of ongoing and future trends and contingencies; identifying potential strategic challenges that may impact USCG's mission performance; describing potential future strategic challenges and global scenarios and a repeatable method for deriving them; and writing overviews of selected topics of relevance to Evergreen and summaries of workshop activities.

Figure 1.2 provides both the context and impact of the Evergreen program as envisioned by the Coast Guard. Evergreen is focused on supporting long-term strategic planning efforts at the doctrinal and policy level.

Figure 1.2. Evergreen Program Context and Impact

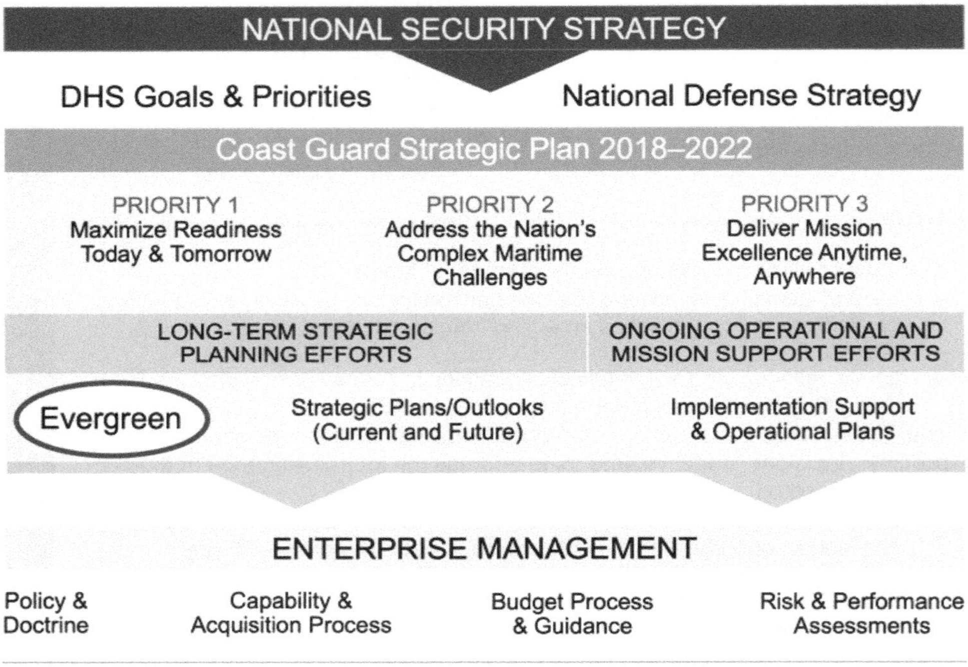

Source: Adapted from U.S. Coast Guard, *Coast Guard Strategic Plan: 2018–2022*, 2018.

Purpose and Organization of This Report

Since HSOAC began supporting Evergreen in 2016, the need to capture and document the Evergreen process and outputs has been voiced by the sponsor, several participants, and external stakeholders who benefit from Evergreen products and want to emulate the Coast Guard strategic foresight process. Prior to Evergreen V, there was no deliberate effort to publicize or publish Evergreen products. Continuous improvement, building upon past success, and learning from unsatisfactory outcomes become more challenging without a readily accessible repository of previous Evergreen work. Long-term institutional knowledge about Evergreen has been a historical challenge, given that active-duty personnel, including DCO-X staff, are typically reassigned every one to three years depending upon promotions, career opportunities, and the needs of the service. However, in recent years, Evergreen has gained a reputation and garnered interest from external stakeholders and interagency partners.

To respond to the need for greater documentation of Evergreen efforts, HSOAC developed this publicly releasable report, which is a compilation of Evergreen work. This report meets several of the service strategic foresight objectives, and new DCO-X staff and USCG program managers will benefit from a comprehensive compilation of activities and summary of results. HSOAC and DCO-X held lengthy discussions about this report's contents and organization and settled on presenting activities in chronological order with an introduction to orient an audience that may know little about the Coast Guard's strategic foresight effort. This report provides many of the documents produced by the Coast Guard and HSOAC in appendixes and links to lengthier documents online. For a summary of this report, visit www.rand.org/t/RBA872-1

Overall Approach and Methods

This section describes the work conducted in each year of Evergreen V in accordance with a program management plan that was jointly modified by the HSOAC team and DCO-X over the four years of performance.[4] Year 1 of the program included establishing a framework for scenario development and workshop execution; Years 2 and 3 included multiple workshops and the development of supplemental and output reports from the workshops; and Year 4 integrated games into the Evergreen portfolio and again included the development of supplemental reports. Figure 1.3 shows a timeline of Evergreen V reports, workshops, and games over the course of the four-year project.

Year 1: Creating a Framework for Effecting Change

The primary desired outcome for Year 1 of Evergreen V was generating a framework for how USCG might think about drivers of change that have the potential to impact demand for USCG operations and/or USCG's ability to execute missions in the next 15–25 years. HSOAC researchers reviewed documents, conducted interviews, analyzed historical data, and held a workshop with Coast Guard subject-matter experts (SMEs) to determine potential drivers of

---

[4] "Evergreen V: Project Management Plan," Homeland Security Operational Analysis Center, Strategy, Policy, and Operations Program, prepared for U.S. Department of Homeland Security, U.S. Coast Guard, Office of Emerging Policy (DCO-X), Modification 10, Santa Monica, Calif.: RAND Corporation, April 2021. Not available to public.

Figure 1.3. Timeline of Evergreen V Events and Products, 2018–2022

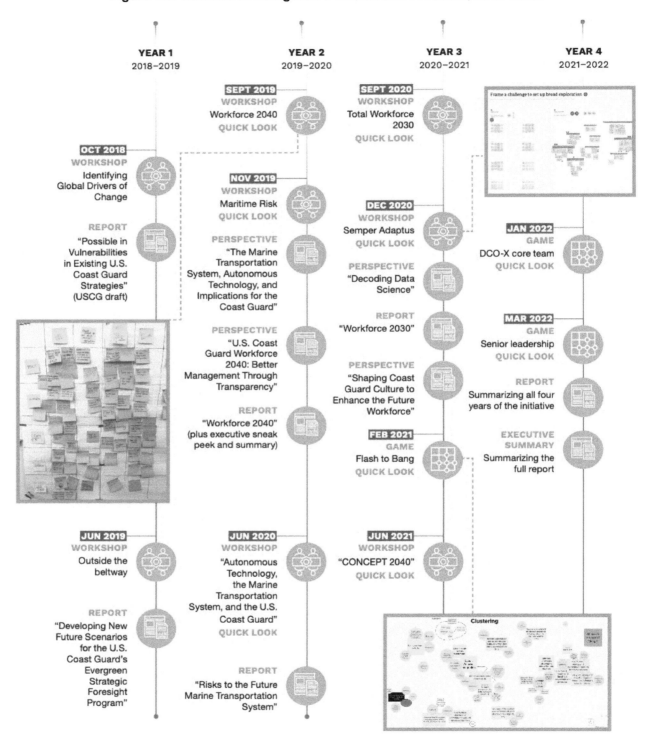

YEAR 1
2018–2019

YEAR 2
2019–2020

YEAR 3
2020–2021

YEAR 4
2021–2022

SEPT 2019
WORKSHOP
Workforce 2040
QUICK LOOK

SEPT 2020
WORKSHOP
Total Workforce 2030
QUICK LOOK

OCT 2018
WORKSHOP
Identifying Global Drivers of Change

REPORT
"Possible in Vulnerabilities in Existing U.S. Coast Guard Strategies" (USCG draft)

NOV 2019
WORKSHOP
Maritime Risk
QUICK LOOK

PERSPECTIVE
"The Marine Transportation System, Autonomous Technology, and Implications for the Coast Guard"

PERSPECTIVE
"U.S. Coast Guard Workforce 2040: Better Management Through Transparency"

REPORT
"Workforce 2040" (plus executive sneak peek and summary)

DEC 2020
WORKSHOP
Semper Adaptus
QUICK LOOK

PERSPECTIVE
"Decoding Data Science"

REPORT
"Workforce 2030"

PERSPECTIVE
"Shaping Coast Guard Culture to Enhance the Future Workforce"

FEB 2021
GAME
Flash to Bang
QUICK LOOK

JAN 2022
GAME
DCO-X core team
QUICK LOOK

MAR 2022
GAME
Senior leadership
QUICK LOOK

REPORT
Summarizing all four years of the initiative

EXECUTIVE SUMMARY
Summarizing the full report

JUN 2019
WORKSHOP
Outside the beltway

REPORT
"Developing New Future Scenarios for the U.S. Coast Guard's Evergreen Strategic Foresight Program"

JUN 2020
WORKSHOP
"Autonomous Technology, the Marine Transportation System, and the U.S. Coast Guard"
QUICK LOOK

REPORT
"Risks to the Future Marine Transportation System"

JUN 2021
WORKSHOP
"CONCEPT 2040"
QUICK LOOK

change in the Coast Guard.[5] The framework drew on disaster preparedness research that uses the concepts of resilience from both long-term, slow-burning issues (stresses) and sudden, large-scale disruptions (shocks). The process identified important drivers of change, and the resulting scenarios were meant to lay the foundation for a shift to an ongoing iterative strategic planning process, rather than treating each Evergreen cycle as distinct from the previous cycle. The preparation of scenarios in Year 1 formed the consistent foundation for the following three years of workshops.

The second key task was developing a reference document detailing the theory behind scenario development so that new broad planning scenarios can be developed for use in future Pinecone workshops. Scenarios linked potential stresses and shocks to impacts on the Coast Guard's ability to execute statutory missions and recover to baseline operations. The scenarios were used at subsequent Pinecone workshops and games as a way to help participants talk through potential challenges 15–25 years in the future and explore strategies to address them.

Scenario Development Methods

We grounded our proposed scenario development approach in two bodies of work that have strong academic foundations and have been used by a variety of practitioners to address similar challenges to those of the Coast Guard.[6]

First, we introduced the stressors-and-shocks framework (i.e., an assessment of how to address acute challenges in the context of chronic ones) as an approach for organizing and updating information about ongoing and future drivers of change that will affect operations and the service's internal considerations.[7] We adapted this way of thinking from the resilience community of research and practice because it provides a way to curate and focus the multidimensional and interconnected space of future change. This approach provided a structured and repeatable means of developing content for qualitative scenarios.

Second, we built and shaped the scenarios for use in the workshops using decisionmaking under deep uncertainty (DMDU) methods.[8] Briefly, DMDU methods are intended to address conditions of *deep uncertainty*, which are commonly defined as those in which (1) assigning probabilities to different futures or outcomes is difficult or impossible; or (2) decisionmakers, key stakeholders, and analysts disagree substantially about the likelihood of different futures or

---

[5] See Appendix B of this report, which contains the reports from Year 1 and provides greater detail regarding the specific methodology that was used and the documents and data that were reviewed. See also Tingstad, Wilson, et al., 2020.

[6] See Tingstad, Wilson, et al., 2020.

[7] Stressors-and-shocks frameworks have also been used in a number of other analyses, including to support disaster resilience and climate adaptation planning. See, e.g., Arup International Development, *City Resilience Framework*, prepared for the Rockefeller Foundation, April 2014, updated December 2015.

[8] Vincent A. W. J. Marchau, Warren E. Walker, Pieter J. T. M. Bloemen, and Steven W. Popper, eds., *Decision Making Under Deep Uncertainty: From Theory to Practice*, New York: Springer, 2019.

which drivers are most significant. Trying to project conditions decades into the future clearly falls into the realm of deep-uncertainty analysis. DMDU methods are a good fit for Evergreen because they seek to evaluate how approaches perform across multiple futures rather than trying to plan for one specific future. As a result, DMDU methods generally promote flexibility as part of the planning process. DMDU methods are usually designed to be used in participatory planning to help highlight trade-offs in future decisionmaking.

For specific information inputs to our scenarios, we relied on the sources and methods summarized in Table 1.1.

Table 1.1. Information Inputs to Evergreen Scenarios

Input Source	Link to Scenarios
Coast Guard workshop with planning games	Populated stressors-and-shocks framework
Strategic foresight literature	Initial material for planning games used in workshop
Coast Guard survey	Initial material for planning games used in workshop
Prior Evergreen and Long View reports	Initial material for planning games used in workshop; analysis of past lessons that helped shape scenario content and structure
Evergreen logic model	Analysis of past lessons that helped shape scenario content and structure
Coast Guard interviews	Analysis of past lessons that helped shape scenario content and structure
Coast Guard strategy and planning documents and guidance	Analysis of strategic planning processes and needed inputs that helped shape scenario content and structure
HSOAC team and internal SME reviews	Development of scenario families, scenario narratives (using stressors-and-shocks framework), and selected scenario-relevant shock narratives

Stressor-Based Scenario Families

While scenarios read as freeform narratives, they are built off of a carefully designed underlying structure. This structure serves to simplify some of the complexities of the world while maintaining a broad range of future possibilities. The methodology began by identifying two decision spaces that the Coast Guard is concerned with understanding in the future—namely, its workforce and its assets. These decision spaces were the starting point, but ultimately this year's work identified five major decision spaces that the Coast Guard is concerned with (geopolitics, economy, climate, technology, and society). Each of these decision spaces can be affected by multiple future factors, so we prioritized choices of key change dimensions (axes) based on expert judgment about which stressors were most relevant to the success or failure of workforce or asset objectives, respectively. The outcome of this process reduces the complex, causally rich decision space for each to two key change dimensions (axes).

Each axis makes up a range of futures that impact the objective, which can then be structured in a *scenario family*. A scenario family is a 2×2 matrix representing the interactions of two global stressors or trends, along with the universe of possible outcomes resulting from these interactions. Each cell in the matrix is a *scenario*. Together, the four cells allow for an exploration of the different configurations of opportunities and constraints that will likely affect Coast Guard decisionmaking.

An example of this approach is shown in Figure 1.4. In this scenario family, we looked at two stressors that will impact the Coast Guard workforce: We considered the competitiveness of a USCG career relative to other market drivers (such as the increase in shorter-term engagements and independent contract work, known as the "gig economy," or shifting retention norms), and we also considered the balance between having a workforce with specialized skill requirements versus more generalized skill requirements. By developing the scenarios using this underlying structure, we ensure that the two key change dimensions (axes) are explored in a simplified yet comprehensive range of futures.

Figure 1.4. Example of a Scenario Family for the Workforce Decision Space

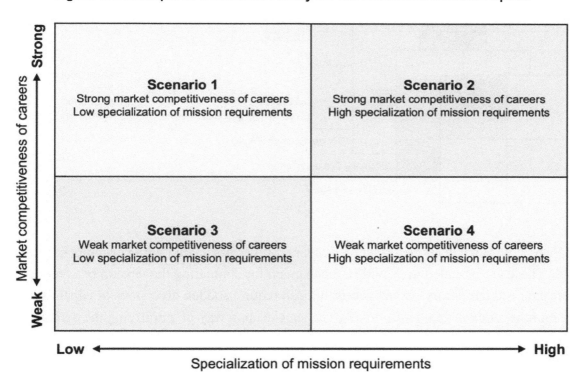

This example shows the tension captured in the range of futures: On one hand, demographic and educational changes could result in a smaller pool of available and capable labor; on the other, less competition for labor among comparable private-sector employers could make recruiting and retention easier for the Coast Guard. These conflicting stressor trends are combined into a scenario. Note that if quantitative data or models were available, DMDU methods (e.g., robust decisionmaking) could also define axes based on quantitative analysis.[9]

The above methodology discusses creating a scenario family across two key change dimensions (axes) focused on one objective (workforce). To capture a multidimensional future, the final set of future scenarios used in Evergreen workshops were developed around objectives that were identified as major drivers in the October 2018 workshop: geopolitics, economy, climate, technology, and society. Each of these objectives had a built-out scenario family, and the final future scenarios were built by combining cells from each scenario family into a narrative structure in Year 2, as shown in Figure 1.5.

Figure 1.5. Combining Scenario Families into a Single Multidimensional Future Scenario Narrative

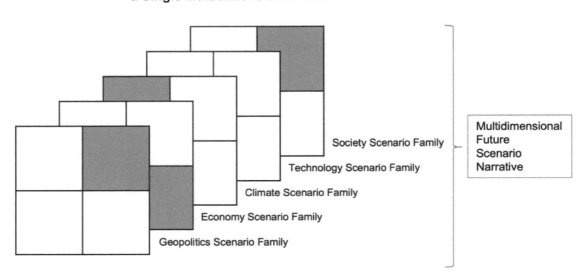

In Year 1, we also developed a set of *shock* narratives associated with particular scenario families. These are intended to provide a mechanism for simulating the tension between day-to-day demands and temporary perturbations that can require sudden diversions of capabilities for weeks, months, or even years to follow.[10] The shocks are a way of amplifying the demands on the Coast Guard in any particular stressor-based scenario.

At first glance, the use of 2 × 2 matrices seems similar to historical Evergreen analyses, which is one reason it was appealing (to provide continuity). However, there are several important differences. First, using the stressors-and-shocks framework to define dimensions

---

[9] Benjamin P. Bryant, and Robert J. Lempert, "Thinking Inside the Box: A Participatory, Computer-Assisted Approach to Scenario Discovery," *Technological Forecasting and Social Change*, Vol. 77, No. 1, January 2010, pp. 34–49.

[10] Conceptually, a perturbation might alter the operating environment over the long term. Examples include the 9/11 terrorist attacks and prominent hurricanes.

enables the development of complex change vectors. It also allows users to articulate different components and implications of change drivers and combine them (by selecting one scenario from each family) when it makes sense to do so for a particular decision.

Second, we separated shocks into a somewhat independent category of modular components that can be added to scenarios. This structural feature provides flexibility in the development of scenarios. Evergreen can focus on a response to particular situations through the inclusion of diverse shocks, or analyses can consider only day-to-day needs by not including shocks at all. Some scenarios might include shocks to gauge response capability or might instead introduce a perturbation to incorporate uncertainty about evolving future demands. Fundamentally, the relevance of a shock depends on whether the shock meaningfully interacts with current driver trends and influences the decisions at hand.

Years 2 and 3: Workshops and Communications

With a framework and future scenarios in hand, the second and third years of Evergreen V concentrated on conducting Pinecone workshops with personnel from DCO-X, communicating the findings, and further developing the concepts that resulted from the workshops. Workshops split participants into small groups, each of which was assigned a different scenario to discuss with the help of a facilitator and a note taker. After each workshop, a "Quick Look" synopsis summarized the findings from the scenario exercises. Then DCO-X and HSOAC selected a few key topics from the workshop that were fleshed out into short thought pieces, called "Perspectives," to give decisionmakers a brief introduction to the topics selected and key questions to consider. The specific workshops were dictated by DCO-X staff and planned throughout the Evergreen program cycle. (See Figure 1.3 for a list and sequence of the workshops.) In Year 1, DCO-X and HSOAC sponsored a shocks-and-stressors workshop and explored strategic challenges with USCG Pacific Area staff. Year 2 focused on future workforce challenges and marine transportation system risk. Year 3 also focused on workforce, service adaptation to technology, and addressing future mission demands in the Pacific and Arctic, as well as countering "gray-zone" competition.[11] In addition, preparations commenced for Year 4 game planning and developing and testing concepts of operations (CONOPS) for gray-zone competition.

---

[11] Competition in the gray zone is an underdeveloped area of U.S. strategy, planning, and synchronization of action, despite its wealth of advantages. The Center for Strategic and International Studies International Security Program has analyzed these threats and how the United States can best deter, campaign in, and respond to gray-zone approaches. Center for Strategic and International Studies, "Gray Zone Project," webpage, undated. See also Lyle J. Morris, Michael J. Mazarr, Jeffrey W. Hornung, Stephanie Pezard, Anika Binnendijk, and Marta Kepe, *Gaining Competitive Advantage in the Gray Zone: Response Options for Coercive Aggression Below the Threshold of Major War*, Santa Monica, Calif.: RAND Corporation, RR-2942-OSD, 2019.

Year 4: Strategic Games

In 2021–2022, the final project year, Coast Guard personnel participated in two games based on ideas generated in the prior years to test the validity and feasibility of the concepts and themes presented as well as the senior leadership team's affinity for them.[12] The games built on past Evergreen work and an HSOAC analysis of how the Coast Guard can effectively use gaming.[13]

One series of games was for midgrade officers and civilian participants, while the second primarily involved senior officers. Participants probed the trade-offs that must occur to meet national and USCG priorities and to enable Coast Guard leadership to articulate a vision to the public, Congress, the Executive Branch, DHS, and the USCG workforce.

A final report will evaluate the game outcomes, implications, and recommendations for the express purpose of helping to transition strategic planning to the next commandant and his or her leadership team.

Game Development

Games are widely used to better understand and prepare for a diverse set of challenges.[14] Gaming is very often associated with the U.S. Department of Defense (DoD), but many other types of organizations—governmental, commercial, nonprofit, and academic—use gaming to support decisionmaking or other functions.

"Gaming" is a generic term for a suite of structured, methodological approaches that can qualitatively (and occasionally quantitatively) support decisionmaking in many contexts. Games are interactive, rule-based, problem-solving exercises that include adjudication of outcomes. They can be played in formal or more relaxed settings and are typically supported by printed content, whiteboards, digital devices, software applications, and other communications tools.

While USCG employs some gaming-type approaches (largely informal), using games to inform strategic thinking is a new approach for the Coast Guard. Gaming offers a versatile approach to tackling a wide range of necessities for an organization such as the Coast Guard, ranging from concept development and strategic planning[15] to engagement and training. The Coast Guard must prepare for many types of contingencies and events that are complex and lack

---

[12] Julia Smith, Nathan Sears, Ben Taylor, and Madeline Johnson, "Serious Games for Serious Crises: Reflections from an Infectious Disease Outbreak Matrix Game," *Globalization and Health*, Vol. 16, Article 18, 2020.

[13] Abbie Tingstad, Yuna Huh Wong, and Scott Savitz, How Can the Coast Guard Use Gaming? Santa Monica, Calif.: RAND Corporation, PE-A148-1, 2020.

[14] See Tingstad, Wong, et al., 2020.

[15] See, e.g., Tingstad, Wilson, et al., 2020; Scott Savitz, Aaron C. Davenport, and Michelle D. Ziegler, *The Marine Transportation System, Autonomous Technology, and Implications for the U.S. Coast Guard*, Santa Monica, Calif.: RAND Corporation, PE-359-DHS, 2020; Susan A. Resetar, Michelle D. Ziegler, Aaron C. Davenport, and Melissa Bauman, *U.S. Coast Guard Workforce 2040: Better Management Through Transparency*, Santa Monica, Calif.: RAND Corporation, PE-358-DHS, 2020; Abbie Tingstad, Scott Savitz, Kristin Van Abel, Dulani Woods, Katherine Anania, Michelle D. Ziegler, Aaron C. Davenport, and Katherine Costello, *Identifying Potential Gaps in U.S. Coast Guard Arctic Capabilities*, Santa Monica, Calif.: RAND Corporation, RR-2310-DHS, 2018.

straightforward planning or training approaches and thus could benefit from gaming. For example, the Coast Guard's roles may change as the United States competes in the Indo-Pacific and Arctic regions. Crises can strain the service—as was seen during and after 9/11, the Deepwater Horizon spill, the 2010 Haiti earthquake, and the COVID-19 outbreak—as can extreme versions of traditional Coast Guard activities, such as responding to more frequent and intense hurricanes, or governance failures, such as the prolonged government shutdown in 2018–2019, which affected USCG funding. Even reexamining year-to-year needs to support the service's 11 statutory missions through processes such as planning, programming, budgeting, and execution (PPBE) requires an ability to anticipate problems and weigh different courses of action.

Since the late nineteenth century, gaming has been used for strategy development, training, and other purposes within DoD, where there is a large community of practitioners, senior leader interest, and educational opportunities offered by defense schools.[16] Various public and educational organizations as well as the private sector have employed gaming for responding to COVID-19 and other infectious disease outbreaks, emergency preparedness, humanitarian response, peacekeeping, critical infrastructure security, maritime security, threat analysis (e.g., nonstate actor use of drones), and even monetary policy.[17] Organizations that use gaming to support policy decisions, training, and other purposes are wide ranging and include the Federal Emergency Management Agency, the Cybersecurity and Infrastructure Security Agency, the Federal Reserve, and the Red Cross. Organizations that send participants to various interagency games include the Department of Energy, Department of Treasury, Federal Bureau of Investigation, other offices from the Department of Justice, and intelligence agencies.[18]

---

[16] See Yuna Huh Wong, Sebastian Joon Bae, Elizabeth M. Bartels, and Benjamin Michael Smith, *Next-Generation Wargaming for the U.S. Marine Corps: Recommended Courses of Action*, Santa Monica, Calif.: RAND Corporation, RR-2227-USMC, 2019, pp. 19–24; Peter Perla, *Peter Perla's The Art of Wargaming: A Guide for Professionals and Hobbyists*, John Curry, ed., Morrisville, N.C.: Lulu Press, 2012, pp. 64–65; U.S. Army Command and General Staff College, *Master of Military Science and Art (MMSA) Program Information*, Fort Leavenworth, Kans., undated.

[17] See Federal Emergency Management Agency, "Cyber Ready Community Game," webpage, 2020; Stephen Delahunty, "Banking Comms' 'Significant Role' Revealed in Cyber-Attack 'War-Game,'" *PRWeek*, October 30, 2019; Rex Brynen, and Gary Milante, "Peacebuilding with Games and Simulations," *Gaming & Simulation*, Vol. 44, No. 1, 2012, pp. 27–35; Smith et al., 2020; "Aftershock," PAXSims.Wordpress, webpage, undated; Simon Drees, Karin Geffer, and Rex Brynen, "Crisis on the Board Game—A Novel Approach to Teach Medical Students About Disaster Medicine," *GMS Journal for Medical Education*, Vol. 35, No. 4, 2018; American Red Cross, "The Disaster Game, or 'Lights Out!'" webpage, undated; Federal Reserve Bank of San Francisco, "Chair the Fed," webpage, 2020; Sylvan Lane, "'Chair the Fed' Makes Monetary Policy a Video Game," *The Hill*, September 15, 2016; Dan Solomon and Paula Forbes, "Inside the Story of How H-E-B Planned for the Pandemic," *Texas Monthly*, March 26, 2020; John Horn, "Playing War Games to Win," *McKinsey Quarterly*, March 2011; Mandiant, "Tabletop Exercise: Test Your Organization's Cyber Response Plan With Scenario Gameplay," *FireEye*, webpage, undated; Antony Zegers, *Matrix Game Methodology: Support to V2010 Olympic Maritime Security Planners*, Defence R&D Canada, Technical Report DRDC CORA TR 2011-016, February 2011; Charlie Hall, "The Art and Craft of Making Board Games for the CIA," *Polygon*, webpage, June 22, 2017; and Cyber and Innovative Policy Institute, *Defend Forward: Critical Infrastructure War Game 2019 Game Report*, Newport, R.I.: U.S. Naval War College, 2019.

[18] This is based on one recent tabletop exercise run by the RAND researchers on interagency cyber response.

In Chapter 6 and Appendix E, we offer a brief overview of gaming, a taxonomy for how it could intersect with Coast Guard needs, and a proposal for how the service might practically expand its use of gaming. In particular, we highlight the idea of gaming as a low-cost, scalable, structured scenario-based approach that can help gather information, aid decisionmaking, and promote learning at different echelons within the service.

2. History of Evergreen

> If companies want to make effective strategy in the face of uncertainty, they need to set up a process of constant exploration—one that allows top managers to build permanent but flexible bridges between their actions in the present and their thinking about the future. What's necessary, in short, is not just imagination but the institutionalization of imagination. That is the essence of strategic foresight....
>
> Nonetheless, few of the organizations that have conducted scenario-planning exercises in recent decades have institutionalized them as part of a broader effort to achieve strategic foresight. One of the rare exceptions is the U.S. Coast Guard, which describes its work with scenario planning as part of a "cycle of strategic renewal."[1]

Evergreen has its roots in the Long View project, initiated by the commandant's staff in 1998. Five 20-year scenarios were developed for exploration by a core team of participants. Each team developed strategies for operating in its assigned scenario. As academic Peter Scoblic observes,

> Many of the strategies weren't novel. But Long View allowed participants to think about them in new ways that [later] proved crucial in the post–September 11 world. In effect, Long View allowed the Coast Guard to pressure-test strategies under a range of plausible futures, prioritize the most-promising ones, and socialize them among the leadership—which meant that after the attacks, when the organization found its mission changing dramatically, it was able to respond quickly.[2]

According to multiple Coast Guard personnel whom we interviewed, Long View is credited within the Coast Guard with making execution of contingency plans after the terrorist attacks in 2001 and Hurricane Katrina in 2005 more effective, as well as with developing such Coast Guard strategies as using greater maritime domain awareness (MDA) for dealing with terrorism threats, merging maintenance and operations into sectors, and developing cross-agency partnerships. There is consensus that Long View made the logical argument for USCG becoming a geographically based organization so that USCG resources could be more responsive to sector and district needs.[3] While Long View was generally considered to be a success, an internal review identified a few weaknesses such as (1) the unstated assumption that the Coast Guard

---

[1] Peter Scoblic, "Learning from the Future," *Harvard Business Review*, July–August 2020.

[2] Scoblic, 2020.

[3] Tingstad et al., 2018.

would continue to be resource-poor and (2) the nonnegotiability of the commandant's support of the Deepwater program to modernize aging cutters and aircraft, which limited the creativity of the team.[4] Nevertheless, Long View demonstrated the nearer-term benefits of futures analysis, and the leadership decided to continue the exercise, renaming it "Project Evergreen" in 2003 to signify the continuous renewal of strategies and strategic intent.

While the focus of Long View was supporting strategy development, Evergreen I and II had a broader focus, which was to promulgate strategic intent throughout the Coast Guard. *Strategic intent* is a shared organizational understanding of where the service is headed and why it should move in that direction. The goal was for strategic intent not only to inform formal strategies and plans, but also to guide day-to-day activities. Evergreen III took a slightly different direction: It emphasized relying on SMEs to determine specific strategies and focused on identifying robust strategic needs for the service of the future. *Strategic needs* are those requirements that could put the service in a prepared and competitive position for future mission demands and can be used to inform decisions and planning at all organizational levels. Evergreen III also focused on supporting more "mid-term critical decisions."[5] Subsequently, Evergreen IV developed new scenarios to identify future needs of the Coast Guard and added topic-focused reports such as the Cyber Futures Report, the Arctic Initiative Report, and the Autonomous Systems Challenge Report, along with topic-focused workshops. Evergreen I ran from 2002 to 2005, Evergreen II from 2006 to 2009, Evergreen III from 2010 to 2013, and Evergreen IV from 2014 to 2015. Table 2.1 describes each phase up to the current Evergreen V.

Table 2.1. The Phases of Project Evergreen

Phase	Years	Focus
Evergreen I	2002–2005	Promulgate strategic intent throughout USCG to inform formal strategies and plans, and guide day-to-day activities
Evergreen II	2006–2009	
Evergreen III	2010–2013	Leverage SMEs to determine specific strategies and identify robust strategic needs for the service of the future
Evergreen IV	2014–2015	Develop new scenarios to identify future needs of the Coast Guard
Evergreen V	2016–2022	Strategic forecasting and gaming

For additional information, see Appendix F1, "Coast Guard Summary of Project Evergreen".

---

[4] U.S. Coast Guard, "Creating and Sustaining Strategic Intent in the USCG," Version 3.0, September 2013. Deepwater Program refers to the Coast Guard original acquisition plan and program for replacing the Service's aging fleets of ships and aircraft. See https://crsreports.congress.gov/product/pdf/RL/RL33753/63; https://businessofgovernment.org/sites/default/files/CoastGuard%20DeepPrgm.pdf.

[5] U.S. Coast Guard, 2013.

Structure and Process Cycles

Project Evergreen was designed to provide strategies and insights to inform the commandant's planning activities and to develop future leaders who can think and act strategically. It provides a unique opportunity to get beyond the "tyranny of the present" and consider how longer-term trends and potential surprise events could affect the Coast Guard so that it is better prepared for the future.

Evergreen is structured on a roughly four-year cycle to align with successive commandant planning. An iterative process is also essential for dealing with uncertainty when unpredictable changes—to national policy, security, geopolitical, technology, natural resources, and economic conditions—that alter the demands placed on USCG are to be expected. Thus, an iterative process is an inherent methodological element of planning for an uncertain world.

The basis for the Evergreen process is scenario-based planning. Scenarios themselves are not predictive tools, but rather represent plausible futures. A well-designed scenario stimulates deep, creative thinking and challenges participants to make difficult choices. Most, but not all, Evergreen cycles engaged a core group of participants who were assigned to "live" in a future scenario and develop strategies for success in that world. Strategies common to all scenarios were identified as robust.

Core team members had diverse technical and operational expertise and experience that was useful for identifying and understanding the effects of future trends on Coast Guard missions and for developing strategies to manage these effects. This diversity is considered a salient feature of the Evergreen process, which is consistent with research on innovative organizations that recommends utilizing formal or informal cross-functional teams that employ a systems view of the enterprise to break down barriers to creative problem-solving created by stove-piped functional organizations or mindsets.[6] The network of personnel established by the core members and other participants to assess trends, formulate strategies, and identify capability gaps was also a good avenue for promulgating the insights generated through the Evergreen process. Many team members were able to incorporate Evergreen material into their own planning activities.

Another feature of the Evergreen process is that it uses rigorous but relatively simple, understandable approaches that are scalable for different applications. The Evergreen team applies a human-centric design approach that begins with divergent-thinking exercises to identify challenges and opportunities presented by a given scenario and ends with convergent-thinking exercises to develop strategies for overcoming and leveraging the challenges and opportunities.

---

[6] Rosabeth Moss Kanter, John J. Kao, and Frederik Derk Wiersema, eds., *Innovation: Breakthrough Thinking at 3M, DuPont, GE, Pfizer, and Rubbermaid*, New York: Harper Business, 1997; John P. Kotter, *Leading Change*, Boston, Mass.: Harvard Business School Press, 1996; Debra Knopman, Susan A. Resetar, Parry Norling, and Irene T. Brahmakulam, *Systems of Innovation Within Public and Private Organizations: Case Studies and Options for the EPA*, Santa Monica, Calif.: RAND Corporation, DB-393-EPA, 2003.

Lessons Learned from Previous Evergreen Cycles

> Long View and Evergreen weren't designed to bring about a wholesale organizational shift from the operational to the strategic or to train the Coast Guard's attention primarily on the long term. Instead, the goal was to get its personnel thinking about the future in a way that would inform and improve their ability to operate in the present.

> Once participants began to view time as a loop, they understood thinking about the future as an essential component of taking action in the present. The scenarios gave them a structure that strengthened their ability to be strategic, despite tremendous uncertainty. It became clear that in making decisions, Coast Guard personnel should learn not only from past experience but also from imagined futures.[7]

A formal lessons-learned analysis identified the benefits and challenges of the Evergreen project.[8] Structured interviews with nearly 30 Evergreen participants reveal that Evergreen is a valuable activity for many reasons. Evergreen is an enterprise-wide analysis that captures input from a diverse group that has a breadth of expertise and experience levels from across somewhat stove-piped functional organizations. It provides a unique opportunity to examine and probe new ideas and operational constructs or question the status quo in a structured and "safe" setting. Discussions also force participants to confront hard choices about how to distribute limited resources across diverse geographic and mission demands while helping to build and substantiate the argument for why a particular policy change, strategy, or capability is essential to the future Coast Guard.

Interviewees noted a few instances in which Evergreen provided a framework for thinking through "what-ifs" or shocks in which simply walking through the response options was a form of contingency planning that ultimately improved the Coast Guard's response. For example, as noted earlier, individuals who had been involved in Long View and Evergreen felt they were better prepared for 9/11 and Katrina because they had plans derived from their Evergreen experience.

Individually, participants gained valuable insights on trends, shocks, and strategies for managing possible future maritime environments using a relatively simple but rigorous approach that can be easily scaled to and replicated in other settings. Interviewees overwhelmingly stated that this exposure permanently broadened their perspectives and appreciation for longer-term strategic trends that could affect the Coast Guard and caused them to think more strategically and consider uncertainty and risk—all of which would be useful in subsequent positions and leadership roles. These are especially valuable experiences, given the Coast Guard's operational tempo, which leaves relatively little time for training and reflection.

---

[7] Scoblic, 2020.

[8] The full discussion is documented in Tingstad et al., 2018.

Evergreen also faces several challenges. As mentioned, the program runs on a four-year cycle and is designed to inform the commandant's planning activities. However, without an established link to other Coast Guard planning processes, Evergreen has limited mechanisms to effect long-term change and is highly dependent on senior leaders' buy-in or interest in pursuing the identified strategies.[9] Furthermore, these effects are difficult to track since Evergreen's workshop discussions, the strategies that are developed, and the written reports often indirectly influence strategies and concepts without explicit attribution. Moreover, the effects on outcomes may not be immediate. For example, Evergreen may identify capability gaps that can't feasibly be addressed because of budget or technology issues; MDA is one area where this limitation is felt. In addition, cultural aspects of the Coast Guard, such as its consensus or operational focus, can impede or slow effects. However, Evergreen's value is in providing the analytic basis to determine what strategies to pursue and a rationale for why a capability is necessary. It is also helpful in socializing ideas before pursuing implementation and positions the Coast Guard to be ready and agile when opportunities are presented. The information generated from Evergreen can be used to communicate the risks or consequences of different paths for supporting national priorities to DHS, the Office of Management and Budget (OMB), or Congress. Indeed, OMB encourages the use of foresight planning for developing strategies and long-term goals.[10] It is also a practice that many large corporations and other federal agencies value.[11]

The other U.S. armed forces also recognize the importance of strategic foresight and have or had strategic study programs and strategic studies curricula embedded in several of their academic and leadership courses and majors. For example, for 35 years the Chief of Naval Operations (CNO) sponsored a strategic studies group that in recent years leveraged Evergreen futures as a backdrop for their innovation and strategic concept development. The mission of the CNO Strategic Studies Group was to "generate revolutionary naval warfare concepts" that could

---

[9] U.S. Coast Guard, 2013; U.S. Coast Guard, "EGIV Program Brief," 2014; and HSOAC structured interviews for Tingstad et al., 2018.

[10] Office of Management and Budget, "Circular No. A-11: Preparation, Submission, and Execution of the Budget," Washington, D.C.: Executive Office of the President, 2017.

[11] Scenario planning is used widely in industry, although its use has waxed and waned over time, even at the method's progenitor, Royal Dutch Shell. However, despite being an overhead function, its value in shaping strategic thinking continues to be recognized and maintained. See Angela Wilkinson and Roland Kupers, "Living in the Futures," *Harvard Business School Magazine*, May 2013. Although the analysis had limitations, a quantitative assessment of firm foresight analysis experience and market performance found that those firms engaging in foresight analysis generally had better sales growth. The authors note that these exercises can improve a firm's understanding of future environments and stimulate discussion of strategy. These exercises have greater effect when a cross section of business units is engaged in the process as opposed to relying on a report to stimulate an organizational response. See René Rohrbeck and Jan Oliver Schwarz, "The Value Contribution of Strategic Foresight: Insights from an Empirical Study of Large European Companies," *Technological Forecasting and Social Change*, Vol. 80, No. 8, 2013, pp. 1593–1606.

upset the existing order, were nonconsensual, and appeared to have great potential but that Navy organizations were not pursuing. Perhaps the greatest value of the CNO's group was that it forced upwardly mobile senior and junior officers to think and live outside their comfort zones in a less-structured innovative environment. It gave otherwise very tactical thinkers time to think strategically about innovative ideas and develop potential concepts for further consideration by the CNO. Senior fellows and staff were encouraged to support and kindle collaborative innovation and "accept disruptive thinking by young outliers, thereby expanding the pool of naval leaders who might be accepting of young innovators and their ideas in the future."[12]

The lessons-learned analysis found that Evergreen is an analytically rigorous approach for developing anticipatory strategy and strategic needs that can inform decisions and communicate risks and priorities. It provides a unique "space" to challenge the status quo and to consider how global trends may affect the service's operations and future needs and the associated risks from an enterprise-wide perspective. Moreover, it exposes personnel to structured strategic analysis methods and provides them with a greater understanding of how key global trends may affect the Coast Guard. Given that USCG has little capacity to prepare for an uncertain future, the modest investment in Evergreen's staff and financial resources provides a unique opportunity for staff development and an important organizational awareness of potential impacts of an uncertain future.

Developing Evergreen V

As the Evergreen team in DCO-X developed plans for Evergreen V, it sought to retain the successful practices from previous phases while trying new approaches to build or improve on some aspects previously identified in internal Coast Guard and HSOAC lessons-learned analyses.

First, the Evergreen team sought to address the feedback that previous scenarios did not always require participants to make hard choices, were sometimes too tactical in focus, or did not extend to over-the-horizon futures. In response to this feedback, the scenarios used for Evergreen V were developed by applying principles derived from a rigorous analysis of structured decision-analytic approaches. To enable easy access to the scenarios, corresponding vignettes were also developed for Evergreen V.[13]

Second, a concerted effort was made to use Evergreen workshops to support the longer-range planning and decisionmaking processes of senior leaders. A study of federal agency foresight planning activities highlights the general agreement that leadership involvement is essential to achieving successful outcomes.[14] To make Evergreen V more useful to senior leaders, the

---

[12] David Adams, Jeff Cares, Brett Morah, Albert Nofi, Antonio Sordia, and David Soldow, "SSG Served as an Innovation Incubator," *US Naval Proceedings*, Vol. 143, No. 4, April 2017.

[13] For more on this approach, see Chapter 4 in Tingstad et al., 2018.

[14] Joseph M. Greenblott, Thomas O'Farrell, Robert Olson, and Beth Burchard, "Strategic Foresight in the Federal Government: A Survey of Methods, Resources, and Institutional Arrangements," *World Futures Review*, Vol. 11, No. 3, 2019, pp. 245–266.

Pinecones exercises became more topically focused and scenario-driven so that they could produce robust strategies that address a senior leader sponsor's priority planning issue and questions. Also, "Quick Looks" were used to disseminate the workshop results in a timely manner, so that the ideas and initiatives could be developed further by the internal organization that is functionally responsible for the topic. In some cases, a topic was so vital to the future of the Coast Guard that a more in-depth "Perspective" was commissioned. Evergreen used games to further inform and support the incoming commandant's strategic planning. To maximize exposure to strategic forethought, these games were also designed to be scalable and replicable for future use in different contexts by various Coast Guard organizations.

Another key change from prior Evergreens is that a core team had provided the continuity necessary for an in-depth evaluation of each scenario's potential consequences for the Coast Guard, and the team was essential to the development of strategies for succeeding in the assigned future world. However, program management issues led the core team to disband when contracting issues caused the time commitment to become unmanageable. Furthermore, having a core team was less essential as Evergreen V pivoted away from focusing on a prolonged in-depth analysis toward experimenting with more frequent, intermediate products that could include wider participation and influence a broader audience of decisionmakers. Analytically, the emphasis was also shifted toward ideation and away from using consistent methods for generating data that could inform a more in-depth analysis of strategic choices. As a result, while some common themes emerged across all the Pinecones, a meta-analysis of the outputs is precluded because the workshops were structured differently.

3. Evergreen V: Year 1

During the first year of Evergreen V (2018–2019), the HSOAC team designed and supported two workshops and wrote a research report that created a framework for a more deliberate approach to developing scenarios for the Coast Guard's strategic foresight program. The report developed the structure for creating scenarios for robust strategic planning, and the workshops served to identify vulnerabilities in Coast Guard strategies while implementing the scenario-based workshop concept.

2018–2019

2 Workshops

- Identifying Global Drivers of Change
- Outside the Beltway

1 Report

Workshop: Identifying Global Drivers of Change

USCG Headquarters, October 22–23, 2018

The HSOAC team designed this workshop as a way to identify and prepare for possible vulnerabilities in existing USCG strategies. Prior to the workshop, HSOAC team members conducted structured reviews of Coast Guard strategy documents, interviewed SMEs regarding the development of Coast Guard strategies, generated a taxonomy of potential drivers of change, and helped inform the design of a Coast Guard–administered survey.[1] The HSOAC team then designed a workshop with Coast Guard participants that elicited feedback for two games regarding what types of potential future changes might be most important from a Coast Guard perspective and why.

Workshop: Outside the Beltway

Pacific Area Headquarters, June 5–6, 2019

This workshop aimed to identify a range of ways to prepare for future shocks and stressors that would affect the Coast Guard. Stressors included the accelerating decay of maritime infrastructure, impacts of climate change, a highly specialized U.S. job market, rapid technological expansion, intense public concern about data privacy, and increased cooperation with international partners. Shocks included various types of clashes among foreign competitors, including China, Japan, South Korea, India, and Indonesia, over-fishing in international waters

---

[1] See Appendix B of this report, which contains the reports and provides greater detail regarding the specific methodology that was used and the documents and data that were reviewed during Year 1 activities. For the full report, see Tingstad, Wilson, et al., 2020.

and a potential environmental disaster involving a collision of Chinese and Russian tank ships in the Bering Strait. Stressors included limited international cooperation, significant climate change impacts, and stagnating adoption of advanced technology. Participants discussed and ranked the importance of the shocks and stressors and identified different actions and policies the Coast Guard might consider to better prepare itself for these future scenarios.

HSOAC Report: *Developing New Future Scenarios for the U.S. Coast Guard's Evergreen Strategic Foresight Program*

For this report,[2] HSOAC analysts adapted an approach to developing future scenarios and used it to present example components of Coast Guard global planning scenarios related to the service's future readiness. These scenarios position Coast Guard leaders to better integrate slow-burning issues and problems that might only emerge down the road in their nearer-term decisionmaking. Without weighing the long view of changes in the operating environment alongside current or nearer-term demands, the Coast Guard will lack full awareness of potential blind spots in current strategies and plans. Being ready for the spectrum of challenges that the future might bring requires leaders to be mindful of how change will affect the Coast Guard in both the near and long terms.

> See Appendix B1 for the Research Brief.
>
> See Appendix F1, "Coast Guard Summary of Project Evergreen".

Themes, Trends, and Observations

The Year 1 work laid the groundwork for the next three years of Evergreen. The framework for future-scenario development based on systematic bracketing of uncertainties helps to ensure that the results of the scenario-based workshops are robust across a range of futures. In addition, the two workshops served as examples for how the Coast Guard might use scenarios to inform long-term strategic direction and allow servicemembers to gain experience with long-term strategic thinking.

Key findings from Year 1 work include the following:

Lessons from prior Evergreen activities can illuminate what has historically been valuable and what could be improved in the future. Generally speaking, Evergreen participants value the experience of considering the implications of longer-range future scenarios for Coast Guard operations and mission support. Because of the perpetual urgency of immediate operational needs, Evergreen scenarios and foresight activities have been limited in their ability to foster deliberation about long-term issues. Historically, products and findings from Evergreen activities

---

[2] Tingstad, Wilson, et al., 2020.

have not been directly used in some Coast Guard decisionmaking because of differences in planning time horizons. In many circumstances, this has also made it challenging to trace Evergreen's impacts.

The purpose, inputs, and outputs of Coast Guard planning (as part of PPBE) and the service's strategic library can shape Evergreen scenarios. Identifying potential needs for continued or additional decision support from Evergreen analyses helps focus the scenario content. The lack of a robust bridge between slow-burning or emerging future problems and near-term decision points presents both a challenge and an opportunity for Evergreen and speaks to the need for scenarios that enable discussion of trade-offs relevant in the near term even if the motivating problems might be longer in range. Strategies cover some stressors and shocks less densely than others, which can form important scenario inputs to stress-test current plans.

4. Evergreen V: Year 2

Using the approach to scenario development created in Year 1, HSOAC developed four possible "futures" for discussion in Pinecone workshops. The scenarios were structured around five levers: geopolitics, economy, climate, technology, and society. Each scenario had distinct stressors and shocks. This resulted in a spectrum of potential futures, ranging from a world characterized by rapid growth, innovation, and U.S.-led cooperation to one plagued by disasters, resource strains, and loss of global influence. The same scenarios, with slight modifications, were used in the subsequent workshops.

Briefly, the four scenarios set up the following futures for workshop discussion purposes:

Scenario 1: Beyond the Horizon. Subsidence and sea-level rise damage Coast Guard facilities and assets; China's aggression and footprint are growing, and the U.S. military increases its presence at sea; the U.S. debt is large, and maritime trade is increasingly efficient; port security is automated, and counterterrorism screening is highly effective and affordable; the U.S. population is increasing due to immigration and a baby boom; educational options are shifting, and military careers are more attractive.

Scenario 2: Steady Growth. Storm frequency and intensity are stable, but rapid ice melt in the Arctic opens access to the sea; global partnerships lead to a period of stability, as the United States increases its presence abroad to support maritime safety and global fisheries management; the economy is prospering, and green energy and hydrocarbons are in high demand; cryptocurrency use is on the rise, and space-based technology has improved navigation but also produced cybercrime risks; the United States is countering a virus from abroad, counter-drug efforts are increasing, and extended family support systems are the norm.

Scenario 3: Diverging Paths. Extreme weather damages the Midwest, South, and East Coast, and global fisheries are on the brink of collapse; Russia and the United States turn inward, while China takes a lead in the Arctic; Americans are prosperous, and the West Coast is an economic powerhouse; automatic security systems are efficient, but storm-response technology fails; more migrants pass through the United States on the way to Canada; the gig economy is on the rise.

Scenario 4: Increasing Disorder. Storms are intense and more frequent, and sea-level rise affects coastal operations; Russia establishes dominance in the Arctic, while China and Mexico team up for mutual economic gain; the U.S. dollar loses value, and the debt is large; electric car

2019–2020

3 Workshops

- Workforce 2040
- Risks to the Maritime Transportation System
- Autonomous Technology, the Marine Transportation System, and the U.S. Coast Guard

3 Quick Looks

4 Reports and Perspectives

and vessel technology matures, and drones grow more popular abroad; while Americans are more risk tolerant, a new strain of HIV increases demand for illegal drugs, and social support systems have weakened.

See Appendix A, "Future Scenarios and Workshop Design".

Workshop: Workforce 2040—Advantages, Challenges, Opportunities, and Strategic Needs

Yorktown, Virginia, September 9–12, 2019

This workshop focused on workforce challenges and opportunities for the Coast Guard in 2040. First, participants were surveyed about what they considered the most important drivers of change, and then they split up into three groups, each assigned to a different scenario. Participants considered the implications, challenges, solutions, and opportunities their respective futures presented to the workforce. They also proposed possible strategic solutions to the challenges that they discussed, which they conveyed to leadership from Coast Guard Human Resources, Force Readiness Command, and Mission Support–Personnel Readiness at the end of the workshop.

HSOAC Quick Look: Workforce Futures Workshop

A Quick Look summarized the discussion from the Workforce 2040 workshop. Most of the strategic needs that the groups identified belonged to one of three categories: information technology, evolving demands, or managing talent and accommodating the future workforce. Other key issues included compensation, the emergence of the gig economy, tensions between homeland-centric and global missions, increasing demand for Arctic and Antarctic activity, keeping up with technological innovations, and the future missions of the Coast Guard. Participants' proposed solutions looked at ways the Coast Guard could adapt existing practice and leverage new technologies to better recruit, accommodate, retain, and improve its workforce.

See Appendix D1, "Workforce Futures Workshop Quick Look".

HSOAC Perspective: U.S. Coast Guard Workforce 2040: Better Management Through Transparency

The Perspective[1] was informed by the discussions that took place at the Workforce 2040 workshop and the findings from empirical research on transparency. Like most employers, the Coast Guard will face personnel management challenges because of emerging technologies, changing demographics, and employment trends, such as the gig economy enabled by online platforms. The Perspective describes several ways in which the Coast Guard can effectively

---

[1] Reseter at al., 2020.

recruit and retain its future workforce by providing greater transparency in personnel management practices.

See Appendix C1, "Workforce 2040: Better Management Through Transparency".

Coast Guard Report: Workforce 2030

This report, written internally by the Coast Guard's DCO-X based on HSOAC-supported workshop activities and HSOAC-provided analysis, acknowledges the future challenges in personnel management that the Coast Guard will face. Resilience and flexibility of the force are at the heart of what has made the Coast Guard successful for over 200 years. An adaptive force will continue to be the service's greatest strength, but the environment the Coast Guard must navigate to build its force has changed dramatically since 2000. The rate of change will only accelerate. The fourth industrial revolution—the integration of the digital and physical worlds—is well underway, with deep implications for service missions and capabilities. Persistent demographic and social trends will fundamentally change the American population from whom the service recruits from and whom it serves. What worked in the past will not work in the future. The Coast Guard will be trying to retain its top talent in an increasingly competitive environment. Specialists such as cyberspace operators will be in high demand, but new needs may emerge that make a different set of skills the "new cyber." Rather than predicting how many of which specialty will be needed, *Workforce 2030* focused on creating a system that could generate the force that is needed, when it is needed. The Coast Guard must create a transparent talent management system that gives members greater control over their lives while still meeting the needs of unit commanders. Ensuring that the "talent" in the talent management system has the right skills will require changing the way the service thinks about training and preparing for a future of continuous learning. The success of these endeavors rests on establishing a data culture, enabled by robust, flexible, and interconnected information technology (IT) and data management systems.

See Appendix F2, "Workforce 2030".
See Appendix F3, "Workforce 2030 Executive Sneak Peek".

Workshop: Risks to the Maritime Transportation System

Maritime Risk Symposium, College State University of New York, November 14–15, 2019

This workshop was designed to address significant risks to the Maritime Transportation System (MTS) and approaches to managing those risks. Participants were split into four groups, each of which included a Coast Guard facilitator, a senior mentor to help shape the discussion, and a synthesizer to capture key themes and discussion. Each group was assigned one of the

2030 future scenarios. Group members discussed what they considered to be the greatest challenges, opportunities, and risks of their scenarios for the Coast Guard.

HSOAC Quick Look: Future Maritime Risk

This report summarized the following key takeaways from the workshop:

- Climate change may modify infrastructure and interfere with vessel navigation.
- Uncertainty regarding capacity demands throughout MTS may shift in unpredictable ways.
- MTS's broad response to risks is piecemeal and uncoordinated.
- The MTS workforce will handle new technologies and old ones simultaneously.
- MTS may lag behind private and illicit actors in adopting technologies.
- The potential for epidemics increases disease risks to the workforce.
- A rapidly changing Arctic will affect shipping, infrastructure, and operations.

See Appendix D2, Future Maritime Risk Quick Look.

HSOAC Perspective: The Marine Transportation System, Autonomous Technology, and Implications for the U.S. Coast Guard

In this Perspective,[2] the authors highlight key aspects of autonomous systems; their potential to affect MTS; and how these systems might shape the Coast Guard's associated roles, responsibilities, and capabilities. Legitimate actors, criminals, and attackers, as well as the Coast Guard and many of its partner agencies, will increasingly use autonomous systems. In the next decade and beyond, there will be a greater need for the Coast Guard to incorporate autonomous systems into its strategies, policies, CONOPS, and tactics.

See Appendix C2, "The Marine Transportation System, Autonomous Technology, and Implications for the U.S. Coast Guard".

Coast Guard Report: Strategic Threats to the Future Marine Transportation System

This report, written internally by the Coast Guard's DCO-X based on HSOAC-supported workshop activities and HSOAC-provided analysis, describes MTS as the backbone of the global economy. In the United States it is an integrated network of 25,000 miles of coastal and inland waters and rivers serving 361 ports. It supports over $5 trillion of economic activity each year and accounts for the employment of more than 30 million Americans. For the purposes of this workshop, MTS was considered in its broadest possible sense to include the companies, communities, and individuals who interact with the system, as well as the greater international maritime community. MTS of the future will be characterized by an explosion of complexity, driven by rapid technological and social change, with significant implications for the workforce

---

[2] Savitz, Davenport, and Ziegler, 2020.

and domestic governance. Almost every group in the Pinecones identified the failure to adapt MTS to a changing physical environment as the most significant long-term risk. Further, the erosion of the rules-based order and the governance regimes that rely on MTS is a direct threat to the ability of the maritime community to take any collective action on pressing challenges in MTS. While each risk is grave on its own, the intersection of these risks could create unprecedented challenges to the safety and security of MTS.

> See Appendix F4, "Strategic Threats to the Future Marine Transportation System".

Workshop: Autonomous Technology, the Marine Transportation System, and the U.S. Coast Guard

Remote, June 10–11, 2020

The goal of this workshop was to elicit insights and ideas from industry partners for best practices and standards to help MTS safely adopt emerging technologies, adapt them to increase efficiency and promote innovation, and do so voluntarily without regulation. This workshop focused on the internal waters MTS, and participants brought inland waterways experience and perspectives to the workshop. During this two-day workshop, participants identified future challenges and explored solutions that set standards for the marine industry and increased safety and efficiency through self-regulation. The workshop supported the ongoing Evergreen V work by brainstorming future concerns and potential solutions among a diverse group of experts. These inputs were used to generate several products to support USCG strategic decisionmaking.

HSOAC Quick Look: Emerging Technology and the Brown-Water Marine Transportation Industry

This summary highlighted the following key takeaways from the workshop:

- The competitiveness of the brown-water maritime industry[3] is sensitive to the availability of waterway infrastructure, waterway traffic management practices, environmental factors, and the global economy.
- Coast Guard–industry relations are more adversarial than desired, and industry is keenly interested in cooperation.
- There is a tension among three central regulatory desires: consultation, responsiveness, and consistency.
- Small regulatory changes can have disproportionate effects.
- Information technology is the primary focus in the industry due to the rapid pace of emerging cybersecurity threats, while the industry's expectations for autonomous vehicles are mixed.

---

[3] "Brown water" refers to inland or coastal waterways, especially when murky or colored brown by silt, sand, mud, and suspended particles or pollutants, as compared to open water or blue water that is clearer and contains fewer suspended solids.

- Technology adoption depends on many factors that affect individual owner-operators differently.
- Current regulations do not appear to consider relative risks and all available expertise, nor are there mechanisms for readily adapting rules to local or changing conditions.
- It is important to view the entire waterway as an integrated system.
- Coordination is key.

See Appendix D3, Emerging Technology and the Brown-Water Marine Transportation Industry Quick Look.

Themes, Trends, and Observations

Several key themes emerged from the Year 2 work, some of which build on observations from prior Evergreen cycles. We discuss the most important and most frequently mentioned themes in the first section, and minor themes in a second section.

Major Themes

The first major theme is the fact that largely independent trends, driven by various phenomena, will ultimately converge to have a collective impact on the Coast Guard in the 2040 time frame. These trends include

- *Demographic shifts.* Aging populations will affect both recruiting pools and the profiles of those whom the Coast Guard rescues, and gradually increasing populations (particularly along coastlines) will contribute to intensified demand for Coast Guard services. In addition, a larger share of the U.S. population will be composed of underrepresented groups that the Coast Guard has not adequately recruited and retained in the past.
- *Technological shifts.* There are multiple broad, rapidly advancing technology areas that can be used by the Coast Guard itself and by those whom it rescues, supports, partners with, regulates, or counters. Two of these are likely to have particularly strident impacts on the Coast Guard. The first is information technology (IT), including cyber defense, machine learning and other artificial intelligence (AI), and "big data," all of which are likely to be ubiquitous throughout the Coast Guard and the entities with which it interacts. The second is the expanding use of increasingly capable and autonomous unmanned vehicles in multiple domains (sea surface, undersea, air, and even ground). The Coast Guard needs to dynamically adjust its operations to effectively address the use of IT and unmanned technologies by others and to use technology to enhance its own efficiency and effectiveness. Other rapidly advancing technology areas that may have a substantial impact on Coast Guard operations include additive manufacturing and electronic attack/defense.
- *Workforce and work-arrangement shifts.* As society moves away from long-term employment toward shorter-term engagements and independent contractual work, the Coast Guard may need to rethink how it recruits, develops, and retains talent. The challenge of ensuring that it has the necessary talent will be exacerbated by the high demand for people with advanced skills in IT, unmanned systems, and other areas that the Coast Guard will need. The Coast Guard may also need to accommodate changing

expectations—accelerated by the COVID-19 pandemic—regarding the extent to which work needs to take place in an actual office during specified times.

- *Environmental shifts.* Receding coastlines, more severe storms, floods, rising water levels under bridges, droughts that impede shipping on inland waterways, long-term ecological disasters in other countries, reduced ice cover that is more mobile, thawing permafrost, and other impacts of climate change can have profound effects on the demand for Coast Guard services. They can also affect the Coast Guard's own fixed infrastructure, both on a chronic basis and in times of crisis. In addition, changing fisheries due to climate change and other environmental factors (such as maritime pollution and ocean acidification), coupled with increasing global demand for fish, can also affect demand for the domestic and international fisheries missions (Living Marine Resources [LMR] and Other Law Enforcement [OLE]).
- *Changing patterns of energy production and usage.* Changing volumes of maritime transportation of coal, oil, and natural gas will affect the types of traffic and facilities that the Coast Guard needs to regulate and secure. The Coast Guard will also need to oversee offshore wind power and possibly other types of renewable maritime energy, such as from the tides or waves, which will entail regulating and protecting facilities and managing traffic around them. In addition, the Coast Guard may also seek ways to reduce its own usage of fossil fuels in aircraft, vessels, vehicles, and fixed facilities.
- *Changing drug production, use, and legislation status.* The types of illegal drugs that Americans are consuming are evolving from cocaine to synthetic substances, even as marijuana is being decriminalized or legalized in some states and neighboring nations. The types of illicit drug flows that the Coast Guard will need to address over the long term will vary depending on policies, changes in demand, shifting source countries (including domestic production), and how drugs are routed via multiple domains from their sources to consumers.
- *Geopolitical shifts.* The rise of China, the resurgence of Russia, fragile state control in various parts of the Western Hemisphere and elsewhere, continuing domestic and international terrorist threats, and other geopolitical factors can alter the Coast Guard's degree of emphasis on its various domestic and overseas roles.

A second major theme that is related to many of these changes is the need for greater workforce flexibility throughout the Coast Guard. While the Coast Guard already evinces a high degree of flexibility in order to respond effectively to specific missions and has demonstrated an ability to adapt over the long term to sea changes such as 9/11 and the establishment of DHS, it also needs to be more flexible regarding its workforce. Today's relatively rigid approach to the Coast Guard workforce assumes that individuals join at a young age and remain for years or decades before permanently exiting; it also presumes that positions need to be filled based on rank, rather than skill sets. In response to changing societal expectations regarding employment, as well as the need to assign, reward, and retain people based on their skills, the Coast Guard needs to be more flexible about how it manages talent.

As just one example, given the rapid evolution of many skill sets related to IT and unmanned systems, the Coast Guard will need to continually offer opportunities for skilled personnel to receive specialized training, both to ensure that they are fully capable and to incentivize them to stay in the service. Their technology related skills will also need to be complemented by an increasing emphasis on strengthening the skills that only humans are likely to have in the next couple of decades, such as leadership, complex problem-solving, critical thinking, collaboration with the private sector and other agencies, and a holistic perception of overall needs and capabilities.

To characterize these changes, HSOAC developed another logic model that describes new approaches to recruitment, retention, and skills development, shown in Figure 4.1. As the logic model indicates, the Coast Guard may benefit from adjusting its policies, plans, procedures, cultural values, and rewards system over time to help it perform the activities listed in the second column of Figure 4.1 (many of which were cited above). These activities contribute to three distinct outputs: revolutionizing talent management, fostering continuous learning, and enabling a more data-driven culture. These outputs, in turn, contribute collectively to three higher-level outcomes: an overall workforce that is more technology-fluent, has more human-centric skills, and possesses the ability to develop new skills. These outcomes contribute to the culminating strategic goal: a workforce that is well positioned to meet future challenges.

A third, related theme from the workshops and documents was the extent to which the Coast Guard as a whole needs to more rapidly assimilate and address new technologies. Criminal outfits lack the encumbrances associated with layers of departmental and political oversight and may have ample quantities of cash, enabling them to employ technologies from advanced cyberweapons to unmanned vehicles more rapidly than the Coast Guard can develop countermeasures (using related or distinct technologies). The Coast Guard needs to be able to accelerate its own timelines for acquisition, training, and employment of new technologies to address emerging threats, and it must be able to work with the technologies used by private-sector entities and partner agencies. Such technologies can make the Coast Guard more effective, and in some cases are absolutely critical: For example, advanced and at least partly automated cyber defense will be a prerequisite for success in the next few decades. In addition, new technologies could potentially enhance the efficiency of an already highly efficient organization: For instance, automating some responsibilities (such as data entry, cursory data analysis, or generating standard data reports that do not require human inputs) could reduce personnel requirements. In addition, the use of unmanned systems in some contexts could obviate or reduce the costs associated with manned platforms: For example, unmanned aerial vehicles or low-cost satellite coverage could provide domain awareness that would otherwise require more costly manned aircraft. (A key caveat is that unmanned systems can still be expensive if they require numerous personnel for oversight and support; largely autonomous, high-reliability unmanned systems are most likely to circumscribe costs.)

Figure 4.1. Logic Model Characterizing Proposed Approaches to Recruitment, Retention, and Skills Development

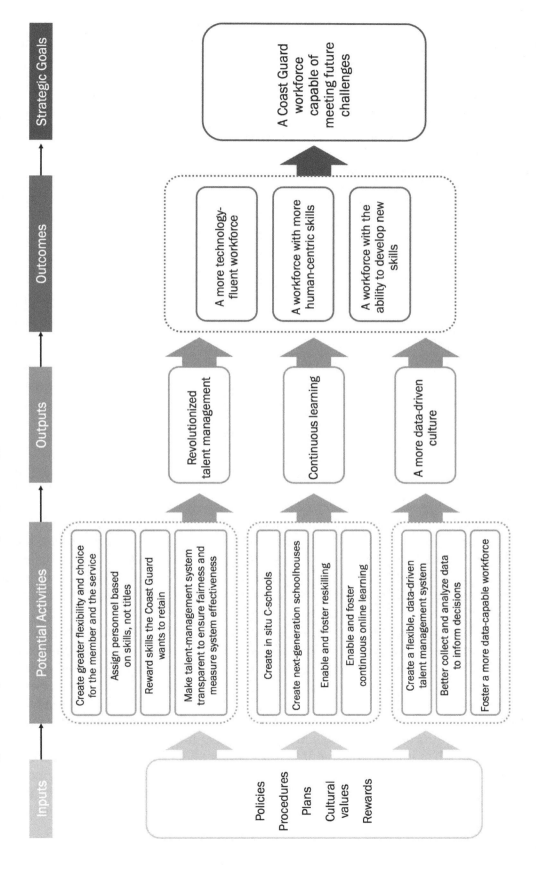

Finally, the Coast Guard's expanding geographic focus is a recurring theme that has been demonstrated on a number of occasions. While the Coast Guard has long operated far from the nation's shores, its personnel and assets have been focused primarily on domestic and Western Hemisphere issues in recent decades. In an era of great-power rivalry, the Coast Guard is increasingly being called upon to work alongside the Navy and Marine Corps in the U.S. Indo Pacific Command and elsewhere. Moreover, the Coast Guard's role in helping to address problems associated with weak states—such as counter-piracy, counter-smuggling, and fisheries protection—is likely to expand, with the Coast Guard both taking direct action and helping other nations' forces become more capable along shorelines ranging from western Africa to the central Pacific. In addition, increasing activity both in the Arctic and in Antarctica are contributing to further expansion of Coast Guard responsibilities.

The challenge for the Coast Guard is how to address all of these additional demands without creating capability and capacity shortfalls in the United States and nearby waters. The Coast Guard can potentially offset these shortfalls by rigorously demonstrating its need for additional resources to both Congress and DHS (increased resource needs will also likely be driven by other factors, mentioned in the bullet list above). To the extent that additional resources do become available, the Coast Guard would need to expand its size without diluting its culture. If more resources do not materialize, explicit acceptance of domestic risks may be necessary, while ensuring that DHS, Congress, and other stakeholders are made aware of this issue.

Minor Themes

Evergreen activities also raised many other considerations, although these were mentioned less frequently.

- *The criticality of sharing information with partners*, including international agencies, DoD, the intelligence community, state and local agencies, and the private sector. While this is self-evident, discussions underscored the extent to which this is not being taken seriously enough or adequately addressed by the Coast Guard. More effort is needed both to enhance technical capabilities to share information and to ensure that information is actively shared with these partners.
- *The inherent tension between localization and deployability of units.* There are advantages to having units rooted in a particular locale, including the strength of connections with other units and agencies in that environment, as well as extensive knowledge of that area. However, there is also a critical need for long-range deployability in response to acute shocks elsewhere that demand additional Coast Guard capabilities; in some cases, chronic needs in other locations may also require periodic deployments. Making a unit deployable requires efforts and costs, and actually deploying it increases those. A unit is also less effective when it is in an unfamiliar environment and interacting with agencies and people with whom it has not previously engaged. While recurring deployments to the same areas can enhance that familiarity, the efforts and costs associated with deployments may limit a unit's capabilities in its home environment, as well as diminish the extent of its experience in that environment and its engagement with partners there.

- *The need for balance between centralized and distributed decisionmaking*, which is an issue for many organizations. Ensuring alignment across the service can increase interoperability and collective effectiveness, but individual commands also need to be able to tailor policies, approaches, and decisions to meet their specific needs. The advent of modern communication technologies facilitates centralization, since higher levels of command have growing access to information from subordinate commands, but that information is not always matched by the deep awareness that a specific command has of its operational environment and issues.

- *The tension between grassroots innovation and enterprise integration.* Personnel throughout the Coast Guard are capable of developing novel solutions to the problems that they face, tailoring their efforts to meet particular needs. However, to the extent that individual commands develop their own solutions, they may hinder interoperability with other units and steepen the learning curve for personnel rotating into or out of those units. Striking the right balance between permitting innovation and seeking standardized, service-wide approaches requires a constant reappraisal of the merits of each in particular contexts.

- *Trade-offs between efficiency and resilience.* The service's limited resources relative to its missions and geographic scope make efficiency paramount, but minimizing redundancy can both make the Coast Guard more vulnerable to shocks (such as hurricanes that destroy shoreside infrastructure) while also limiting the Coast Guard's ability to surge in response to the effects of those shocks on others. There is a need for investing in skilled personnel, equipment, assets, and infrastructure to ensure that the Coast Guard can meet prospective crises, even if not all of these are used on a routine basis.

5. Evergreen V: Year 3

The four workshops held in Year 3 focused on how the Coast Guard can foster a workforce that is capable and ready to meet future mission demands (Total Workforce 2030), can strategically position itself to meet future challenges (Semper Adaptus), accelerate the time between the inception of an innovative idea and its implementation (Flash to Bang), and shape new strategic CONOPS for the Coast Guard to meet potential future threats (CONCEPT 2040).

2020–2021

4 Workshops

- Total Workforce 2030
- Semper Adaptus
- Flash to Bang
- Concept 2040

4 Quick Looks

3 Reports and Perspectives

Workshop: Total Workforce 2030

Coast Guard Headquarters, September 10–11, 2020

For this workshop, participants were presented with the four 2030 scenarios (described in Chapter 4; see also link below) and discussed the effects they might have on the Coast Guard and its members and how they could best prepare to handle them. Participants explored the future challenges for recruiting and retaining the workforce, including how to mitigate employment trends that work against the Coast Guard. The goal was to ensure that the Coast Guard has the workforce and cultural preparedness to address emerging global shifts and needs, including effective global presence and promotion of the rules-based order, and a more expeditionary force operating in austere, remote environments.

See Appendix A, "Future Scenarios and Workshop Design."

HSOAC Quick Look: Total Workforce 2030

This report summarized the following key takeaways from the workshop:

- developing greater visibility into enterprise-wide workforce demand and supply and establishing more responsive approaches for aligning them
- developing a broader range of workforce management tools to enable it to more quickly meet mission demands
- seeking policy, practices, and culture change to provide greater choice
- creating opportunities for continuous learning and leadership experiences to ensure the workforce retains knowledge, skills, and abilities essential for the mission
- expanding outreach and recruitment
- introducing more visible and enhanced messaging about the value proposition of working for the Coast Guard.

See Appendix D4, Total Workforce 2030 Quick Look.

HSOAC Perspective: Decoding Data Science: The U.S. Coast Guard's Evolving Needs and Their Implications

Like many large organizations, USCG has vast amounts of data that it could use to identify, predict, and solve pressing challenges. Data science could be valuable to the Coast Guard in a variety of domains, such as forecasting the resources needed for future trends in search-and-rescue missions, further automating aids to navigation, or automating fishery observations. In personnel areas, data science could help improve billet assignments, determine where to focus recruiting efforts, and boost employee retention. The Coast Guard has an opportunity to plot the path to determine service-specific uses, identify the strategy and driving mechanisms, and begin laying out a plan for the use of data science, which includes data collection, analysis, and management; AI; and machine learning. This Perspective outlines the role that data science can play in decisionmaking processes and provides a selected set of key questions and sensitivities for the Coast Guard to consider in developing its future usage of data science.

See Appendix C3, "Decoding Data Science: The U.S. Coast Guard's Evolving Needs and Their Implications".

Coast Guard Report: Total Workforce 2030

This report, written internally by the Coast Guard's DCO-X based on HSOAC-supported workshop activities and HSOAC-provided analysis, describes the capabilities and adaptability of the service's workforce as a key contributor to the success of the Coast Guard from its founding. During early engagements with hundreds of Coast Guard personnel and experts, the future workforce was a recurring, dominant concern.

The Coast Guard must be prepared to recruit and retain a capable workforce as demographic, social, economic, and technological trends advance and in some cases accelerate. To generate the force that is needed *when* it is needed, the Coast Guard must create a transparent and flexible talent management system that meets the needs of commanders while giving members greater control over their career paths. Integral to the talent management system of the future will be providing more diverse training opportunities and a reliance on a data-driven culture supported by robust data management systems.

See Appendix F2, "Workforce 2030".

Workshop: Semper Adaptus

Virtual, December 2–3, 2020

This workshop focused on the ways that rapid technical adaptation, rising globalization, evolving transnational criminal organizations, and environmental changes might fundamentally change how USCG operates. Participants discussed whether the Coast Guard would have the right capabilities and what strategic choices the service needs to make now to be ready. Participants split up into groups, and each group was assigned one of the four HSOAC-developed future scenarios. They were tasked with thinking about what implications their scenarios might have for the Coast Guard and what the service would need to do in the future to be prepared for future challenges and opportunities.

HSOAC Quick Look: Semper Adaptus

Key takeaways from the workshop include

- increasing visibility of the Coast Guard and its resource needs
- deepening and expanding relationships with other countries.
- collaborating more closely with other U.S. government partners
- ensuring that the Coast Guard can leverage technological advancements in a timely manner by pursuing policy and process change
- aggressively pursuing technological investments and organizational changes to improve data acquisition, analysis, dissemination, and application

See Appendix D5, Semper Adaptus Quick Look.

Coast Guard Report: Semper Adaptus

This report, written internally by the Coast Guard's DCO-X based on HSOAC-supported workshop activities and HSOAC-provided analysis, describes the Coast Guard as experienced in operating in a dynamic environment and adapting to changing national priorities and global trends, but it acknowledges that the service will face challenges from emerging technology and global competition that will have a deep impact on demand for the Coast Guard and on how it does business. The Coast Guard must create absorptive capacity for new technology through concerted integration campaigns, which may ultimately call on the service to change some of its structure and processes to reap the benefits of new systems and remain relevant as mission demands change. Preparing for shifting mission demand calls for futures-informed requirements that enable the Coast Guard to acquire adaptive capabilities to meet emerging needs and prepare for strategic surprise. The report identifies the most critical capability gap the Coast Guard faces as the ability to sense, collect, analyze, and share information in environments that range from permissive to austere.

See Appendix F6, "Semper Adaptus".

Perspective: Shaping Coast Guard Culture to Enhance the Future Workforce Culture

To cultivate an effective future workforce, the Coast Guard is purposefully considering ways to address culture change and reshaping its organizational culture. The service wants its 2030 workforce to have greater technological fluency and more human-centric skills, as well as the ability to develop new skills and capabilities. The Coast Guard's organizational culture—the behavioral norms and shared values consistently exhibited by its personnel—will play a critical role in creating an environment in which the workforce can put those skills into action. However, the service is increasingly concerned that the current policies for managing personnel, its homogeneous workforce, and the way it prioritizes specific skills could over time become barriers to fostering the workplace culture required to meet future challenges. Changing parts of the culture of a large, complex organization is difficult; doing so in the Coast Guard requires the service to address recruiting, training, retaining, and empowering the future workforce.[1]

> See Appendix C4, Shaping U.S. Coast Guard Culture Perspective.

Workshop: Flash to Bang

Virtual, February 23–35, 2021

This workshop explored what the Coast Guard needs to do and acquire in order to meet its anticipated future positioning. The workshop's objective was to answer the question: How can the service better capitalize on innovation and adapt more quickly? Participants were organized into the same four groups with the same future scenarios as in the Semper Adaptus workshop. They were tasked with identifying the major imperatives for change in each future scenario; categorizing the imperatives according to which Coast Guard mechanisms need to be activated to effect change; selecting three to five mechanisms USCG should prioritize; and discussing the implications the group's chosen priorities would have on USCG culture, mission support, and mission delivery. Teams then created a "causal layered analysis" of their ideas—juxtaposing the "way things are" now to the "way things might be" in the future by exploring specific ways that the service could make this transition, selecting the most important things the Coast Guard should work on, and considering the various barriers and opportunities implicated in their recommended priorities. The teams predicted several common future demands despite each group being assigned a distinct scenario representing divergent trends of key economic, geopolitical, technical, and environmental drivers.

> See Appendix A, Future Scenarios and Workshop Design.

[1] Michelle D. Zigler, Aaron C. Davenport, Susan A. Resetar, Scott Savitz, Katherine Anania, Melissa Bauman, and Karishma Patel, *Shaping Coast Guard Culture to Enhance the Future Workforce*, Santa Monica, Calif: RAND Corporation, PE-A872-1, 2021.

HSOAC Quick Look: Flash to Bang

This summary highlighted key takeaways from the workshop, including proposals for

- developing a commandant's Innovation Strategy, creating an Innovation Center of Excellence, and building a culture to implement both by creating an executive champion for innovation, including innovation as a criterion in decisionmaking, identifying innovation as a competency, and rewarding efforts to innovate
- pursuing a culture and acquisition process that maximizes asset flexibility by employing modular solutions, where the service views major assets as a platform or container for new technology
- integrating and prioritizing baseline technical proficiency into Coast Guard culture, beginning at enlisted and officer accession sources
- developing nimble, adaptive force packages that can be employed at home or abroad and using data and technologies to help inform rapid decisionmaking during contingency responses

See Appendix D6, Flash to Bang Workshop Quick Look.

Coast Guard Report: Flash to Bang

This report, written internally by the Coast Guard's DCO-X based on HSOAC-supported workshop activities and HSOAC-provided analysis, recognizes that USCG operates in a dynamic environment that requires operational flexibility and strategic adaptation to fulfill national priorities and keep pace with global trends. The report predicts that in the coming decades emerging technologies, strategic competition, and environmental challenges will compel the service to adjust resources and investments with a nimbleness that will require even more responsive business rules.

See Appendix D6, Flash to Bang Workshop Quick Look.

Workshop: CONCEPT 2040

Virtual, June 2–3, 2021

This workshop aimed to help shape new strategic CONOPS for the Coast Guard to meet potential future threats. Participants were organized into four groups and assessed the implications of the same future scenarios as in the previous workshops and then developed a CONOPS that met the demands of the scenario. The CONOPS included developing new goals and priorities to meet each individual future scenario. Resource, posture, and policy trades were also explicitly articulated in each CONOPS.

See Appendix F7, "Flash to Bang".

This summary highlighted the following key takeaways:

- USCG should use different operational paradigms enabled by new technologies to deploy human capital and assets to priority threats as they emerge both domestically and globally.
- USCG should pursue greater coordination and resource sharing with other U.S. agencies and foreign governments, particularly for improving MDA, interoperability and communications, and robust logistics support for overseas deployments.
- Greater international engagement will support foreign policy, security, and international maritime law enforcement missions.
- The Coast Guard should be prepared for the growing importance and frequency of operations in the Indo-Pacific and the Arctic.
- The service should pursue a technology-savvy workforce that has basic "cyber hygiene" skills and the organizational culture to embrace and utilize this expertise.
- Resource constraints will catalyze the Coast Guard and Congress to reconsider some of today's activities that may not be central to future Coast Guard mission requirements.
- USCG must position itself to acquire the budget needed to successfully perform its future missions and use political capital to ensure that necessary changes to asset laydown, resourcing and deployments, authorities, and so on are communicated widely and well understood both internally and externally.

See Appendix D7, CONCEPT 2040 Quick Look.

Themes, Trends, and Observations

Four major themes emerged from this year's workshops and analysis.

The first major theme was the need for the Coast Guard to have *greater visibility and transparency with external and internal stakeholders.* To effectively address the needs of the service and the nation at a time of rapid change, information about current shifts and trends needs to be made accessible to decisionmakers, and often to a wider audience, in relatively short time frames. For example, decisions about workforce policies and specific allocations of billets need to be informed by current data regarding required and available skill sets (regardless of how those skills were acquired); recruitment, retention, and individual goals; and demand signals from those the Coast Guard serves. At a tactical-to-operational level, increased visibility regarding all actors in the environment and the environment itself—sometimes termed "multidomain awareness"—can make forces more effective. Engagement with operational partners, DHS leadership, Congress, and the wider public is also strengthened by increased visibility and transparency regarding the Coast Guard. Partners' increased awareness of the Coast Guard's capabilities can enable them to work better with it, while wider knowledge of how the service's resource limitations circumscribe its capacity can inform public, DHS, and congressional debate. For example, when the Coast Guard gets increasing demand signals from DHS to focus on the Drug Interdiction, or from DoD to focus on the Defense Readiness mission, greater public recognition of the service's contributions can also potentially improve recruiting and retention.

There are two key aspects of increasing visibility and transparency within and beyond the Coast Guard. The first is investing in and using IT systems to make actionable data accessible to analysts, decisionmakers, and those who engage with external parties. As the Perspective on data science notes, there are opportunities for the service to apply existing and emerging technologies to collect and analyze data more efficiently and insightfully than before. The second key aspect is that this technological approach needs to be complemented by a cultural shift. The Coast Guard has traditionally had to rely on data sets that were less detailed, less accurate, and less timely, and transforming those data sets into actionable information could sometimes require substantial efforts. The result was that decisionmakers sometimes had to operate with considerably less information than might have been desired. As data and information flows improve and become more automated and timely, the Coast Guard can increasingly rely on them to help shape decisions, including at a more rapid pace. However, this requires that individuals and organizations develop confidence in those sources and discern how they can be used to support human judgment. This cultural shift will be bolstered by the increasing technological skills of Coast Guard personnel over time, making them more aware of the values and limitations of particular data sources and how they can be applied to complement their experienced judgment. Integral to this shift to data-driven decisionmaking is an increasing need to invest in cybersecurity systems and workforce capabilities.

A second major theme was the *need for enhanced collaboration with partners and allies*. While the Coast Guard has always worked closely with international, federal, state, and local partners, the need for collaboration is growing due to increased demand signals in missions and geographic regions where authorities are shared. For example, the Coast Guard is expected to conduct more of its operations outside U.S. waters and to operate alongside DoD more frequently in the coming decades. As the Coast Guard intensifies its work to counter smuggling, piracy, and unlawful fishing alongside its international counterparts, it needs to enhance collaboration both by liaising through personnel with a knowledge of those nations' languages, cultures, and agencies and by using accessible, appropriate communications technologies to ensure effective coordination and data sharing. The Tri-Service Maritime Strategy requires that the Coast Guard, Navy, and Marine Corps achieve a still-higher level of interoperability.[2] In varied scenarios— such as a joint patrol in East Asia or when the Coast Guard helps to secure a port that DoD is using—the services need to be hand-in-glove, particularly in the face of gray-zone challenges or hostile action. While the services already work well together, their disparities in size and the types of technologies that they use at any given time require that they relentlessly strive to ensure

---

[2] A senior member of the DCO-X staff was temporarily detailed to the U.S. Navy/U.S. Marine Corps staff team charged with assisting with drafting the Tri-Service Maritime Strategy and representing the Coast Guard equities. "U.S. Maritime Strategy: Advantage at Sea," *USNI News*, December 17, 2020.

interoperability over time and in different contexts. Additionally, greater collaboration can lead to an effective use of resources when investments in technology, data, or infrastructure are leveraged among partners. For example, as the service increases its operational presence in the Arctic and other regions globally, partnerships will be a critical means to access needed infrastructure and support services. The same holds true for accessing the latest technology or operationally relevant information. If done well, collaboration can facilitate more rapid adaptability to a changing environment and mission demand signals.

A third theme was the need to *enable the service to adopt innovative technology rapidly* to enhance its ability to more effectively deploy assets to meet mission demands. Technologies such as unmanned or autonomous vehicles, greater use of sensors and data analytics, and so on can extend the capabilities of Coast Guard assets and more effectively deploy them to meet changing mission needs. However, the Coast Guard must have processes in place to identify, acquire, field, and maintain new technologies more rapidly as they emerge. And it must have the ability to train a skilled workforce capable of using and maintaining new technologies as they are fielded. Technologies of the future may also free up valuable human capital, allowing members to focus on tasks that require higher-order cognitive or creative problem-solving skills, but the workforce will likely need higher overall technology literacy and must be able to acquire new technological skills in new and more varied ways.

The fourth and final theme was the need for *additional resources to address increased Coast Guard involvement abroad and growing demand at home*. The Coast Guard's operations far from U.S. waters are resource-intensive and rapidly increasing. At the same time, the demand for domestic operations—including in an increasingly open Arctic—are also expanding. Increasing coastal populations within the United States, rising frequency and intensity of natural disasters, and other factors are likely to contribute to rising long-term demand. The Coast Guard is also increasingly concerned with cybersecurity for MTS and the use of unmanned vehicles by both legitimate and hostile actors. Issues including drug trafficking, migration, and natural disasters are likely to expand the Coast Guard's role in nearby areas of the Western Hemisphere. While the Coast Guard may find some efficiencies, such as the use of unmanned vehicles and additive manufacturing to reduce costs, these will be partly offset by the need to attract and retain a more skilled workforce. If the Coast Guard is to engage more heavily with nations around the globe and on the high seas, while also fulfilling its missions domestically and in proximate areas of the Western Hemisphere, it needs to have the requisite assets and personnel. The previously cited need for visibility and transparency can help to communicate this issue to Congress and the public, and partners—notably DoD—and can vouch for the Coast Guard's contributions in ways that help it to achieve the capacity it needs to fulfill its growing responsibilities.

6. Evergreen V: Year 4

Gaming was the primary activity executed in Year 4. The main goal of the gaming effort was to support strategic discussion and engagement among senior leaders to inform the next four years of the Evergreen initiative.[1]

The game—played once by DCO-X personnel[2] and again by USCG senior leaders—was set in the same futures that have been utilized throughout Evergreen V. While the varied drivers create four distinctly different future scenarios, they all indicate that USCG will increasingly be asked to engage in gray-zone competition against adversaries and threats to support global maritime security. This will require USCG to expand its international role and presence. The service identified several broad questions to guide the gaming efforts, in response to calls from stakeholders to expand the Coast Guard's international maritime security engagement and reach beyond the current international operations planning. Some of these questions were as follows:

- What available capabilities do players apply to specific problems?
- How do adversary actions or unexpected circumstances affect decisionmaking?
- What trade-offs are players willing to make to achieve their objectives?
- How do alternative force structures affect USCG's ability to operate in forward theaters such as the Indo-Pacific and to bolster maritime security while still achieving domestic missions?

2021–2022

2 Games

- Office of Emerging Policy (DCO-X)
- USCG senior leaders

2 Quick Looks

1 Report

1 Executive Summary

---

[1] This chapter provides a compilation and overview of the gaming activities during Evergreen V. Additional follow-on Paratus Futurum gaming activities are planned during the first year of Evergreen VI. At the conclusion of all Evergreen V–related gaming activities, a final gaming report will be published (currently under development) during the first year of Evergreen VI. The gaming report will go into greater detail about the design, methodology, and analysis of the game outputs.

[2] DCO-X staff were augmented by a core team of SMEs who were previous participants in multiple workshops. Having USCG experts who were familiar with the Evergreen Program and the various scenarios improved the quality and efficiency of the gaming efforts.

Game Development

The objective of the game—named "Paratus Futurum," or "Ready for the Future"—was to facilitate discussions about alternate Coast Guard long-term institutional strategies. The game provided a sandbox in which USCG leaders could experience how a variety of USCG mission profiles and investment options might face challenges under different potential scenarios. All of the scenarios and events that were used to stress and explore the strategies were drawn from USCG-developed analysis and concepts that resulted from the first three and a half years of Evergreen V. Participants gained a better appreciation for how to think and talk about strategic options and trade-offs and will thus be in a better position to participate in future strategic decisionmaking and investment development activities.

Paratus Futurum focused at a strategic level on USCG's roles, missions, available resources, and potential adjustments to those resources through 2040 and beyond. The game's design forced players to make distinct choices about prioritizing missions and investments to prepare for an uncertain future when climate change, technological advancements, the economy, and the global competition for power all shape USCG demand. The game was intended to speak directly to the incoming commandant and to help Coast Guard leadership understand and experience the trade-offs that will likely occur to meet USCG priorities so that they can articulate a vision to Congress, the Executive Branch, DHS, and the workforce.

CONOPS that were developed during the Year 3 CONCEPT 2040 Pinecone provided the initial inputs for the Year 4 gaming effort. As discussed in Chapter 5, each of the four Evergreen core teams from the previous Pinecones developed a strategic CONOPS designed to confront their assigned future scenario. The decision context for the scenarios was framed around how the Coast Guard could rethink its operations and investments, given the evolving demand for various mission sets.

The four resulting concepts outlined distinct overarching strategic visions for the service, goals for service capabilities and capacities, and ideas for how the Coast Guard will compete on a global scale. During game play, the teams tried to work toward their assigned strategic vision by identifying how the service will resource any changes in mission prioritization by region, capabilities, capacity, investments, and culture. Because teams were not given enough resources to do everything, decisions about what risks to take and where to spend resources prompted thoughtful discussion and debate among participants.

Game Design Approach

Each turn began with an overview trend briefing highlighting a few key informational updates that introduced several scenario twists that posed significant dilemmas in various regions of the world. Players then discussed and decided where to allocate their limited resources to best position the service to achieve the assigned strategic vision and to prepare for events set out in the intelligence briefing.[3]

During the planning stage, participants outlined what course of action to take in the current turn and how that course would or would not carve a path toward their strategic vision. They decided what missions and investments to resource and what risks were acceptable, with an emphasis on the inherent trade-offs this entails. Participants had to balance competing priorities, address multiple challenges across operating areas, examine wider service implications, and allocate limited Coast Guard capabilities and resources, given anticipated government policies and priorities.

After resourcing choices were set, event cards (e.g., complicated disasters or aggressive behavior by adversaries) were revealed.[4] Teams received scores reflecting the extent to which their resourcing and investment decisions allowed the service to respond to the new events and whether stakeholders viewed the Coast Guard's response as successful.[5] In the subsequent turn, teams could revise investments and resources (e.g., adding or removing a resource token, or requiring resources to be allocated to a certain mission or region).

During discussion phases, a facilitator from the design team led the participants in examining the wider implications of their course of action and how the initial CONOPS did or did not prepare USCG to achieve its strategic goals, given the challenges of the future scenario.[6] The game identified the changes required for the Coast Guard to get from where it is to where it needs to be. This ranged from logistical and support considerations to personnel and training requirements to necessary shifts in institutional culture. Overall, the games had between three and five turns,[7] and each ended in a facilitated after-action discussion to examine players'

---

[3] Within this game and report, the term "intelligence brief" is a concise summary of the key pieces of information participants are presented with at the start of each turn; it should not be confused with a contemporary classified "intel" brief. Intelligence briefs can include global or regional trends, indicators of potential events, or specific updates about the scenario drivers, which will be expounded on in further detail in the forthcoming game report. These are a function of the game and not part of the intelligence aspect of C5ISR; needs and methods of intelligence gathering; or sharing among other militaries, agencies, or foreign partners.

[4] The event cards were preselected by the HSOAC team to cover a range of topics that had been identified repeatedly in previous Pinecones as difficult choices and trade-offs that would likely come in the near future. It was at facilitator discretion to adjust cards "on the fly" to best guide discussions based upon group dynamics.

[5] Scoring specifics (including the statistical reasoning for the scales and impacts of the scores) will be included in the full game report that will be completed at the completion of the Evergreen gaming activities that have been extended into Evergreen VI.

[6] Specifically, the implications for DHS's DOTMLPF+R/G/S framework.

[7] The number of turns played in a game is under the control and discretion of game facilitators. The purpose of this is to allow for flexibility of time in the case of rigorous and thoughtful, but expansive discussions, as well as to keep participants from knowing when the last turn will be, which would allow them to "game" the game and play to give themselves a favorable outcome.

thoughts about their choices, what those might mean for current and future leaders of the service, and how the game affected their thinking about current challenges and choices.

The initial design concept was subject to a change in response to lessons learned during internal testing by HSOAC researchers and pilots with the Pinecone core teams, and refinements were indeed made along the way. The game design was influenced by a host of practical elements outside of our analytic goals, including the venue where the game would be played, the number of participants, and the time available for game play.

Because of the COVID-19 pandemic, Paratus Futurum had to be designed to be played both virtually and in person. The game mechanics were developed conceptually so that it could be played virtually or as an in-person board game (Figure 6.1 shows the in-person board); for virtual purposes, the game space and game board utilized an online platform called Mural, which mirrored the physical play of the in-person game.[8] The game was designed so that it could be completed in one day or played across multiple days; this was done by including a significant and expandable range of scenarios and events that challenge the Coast Guard.[9]

Figure 6.1. Paratus Futurum Game Board

---

[8] Mural is a digital workspace that enables teams to collaborate visually and brainstorm solutions to challenges. Mural.com, undated.

[9] Paratus Futurum was designed with maximum flexibility and repeatability so that it could be played again for different groups of participants as the service sees fit. The proof of concept of the virtual play can open up additional participation where travel and site logistics might have hindered it. The planning for Evergreen VI currently includes two additional plays of Paratus Futurum in its first year.

The USCG sponsor sought to incorporate a large number of players.[10] To run the game and direct discussions, each team was led by two co-facilitators and played for a full day, with two teams playing per day over the course of two days. As with most Evergreen events, participants were encouraged to be collegial, creative, and collaborative. Participants used first names only and wore civilian clothing so that rank and formality did not hinder collaboration and creativity.

The gaming effort was divided into three stages:

1. A virtual game with some of the four Evergreen core teams from the previous Pinecones, supplemented members of DCO-X and with new players from a variety of backgrounds in the service, to gain a better understanding of gaming attributes, examine the game system, and reflect on the strengths and stresses in the respective concepts. We refined the concepts derived in the CONCEPT 2040 Pinecone to ensure they had the necessary elements to be utilized in future games and explored where and why strategic concepts diverged across teams.
2. An in-person game played by Coast Guard senior leaders to examine force design and global operating concepts. This game was intended to help inform future strategic planning efforts by the commandant's transition team.
3. A third phase will provide additional gaming options for USCG senior leaders, based on input from the new senior leadership.[11]

See Appendix D8, Paratus Futurum (Game 1).

See Appendix D9, Paratus Futurum (Game 2).

Overarching Observations from Game Play

A number of overarching observations can be drawn from the two rounds of games with Evergreen core teams and senior leaders; some were unique to the round, and others were in concurrence.

Observations from Round 1

The first round of Paratus Futurum was conducted virtually on January 11–12, 2022, with almost 30 Coast Guard personnel. Several overarching observations were derived from the game.

Teams relied heavily on their given scenario and strategic vision to guide resource allocation. Player decisionmaking hinged on the scenario, their operationalization of the strategic vision, and additional information provided in the intelligence briefs. These guidance documents provided the mission demand signals that were used to prioritize resource allocation. Such allocation was somewhat easier to do at the start of play, and most teams immediately

---

[10] Game participants included senior active-duty and civilian SME in key leadership positions (ranks O8 to E9), carefully chosen by DCO-X staff.

[11] In May 2022, DCO-X asked HSOAC/RAND to host up to two additional Paratus Futurum games during the first year of Evergreen VI, based on senior leadership feedback and the draft technical execution plan for Evergreen VI.

began making investments that would contribute to longer-term objectives. Most teams began with a discussion of which modernization investments would allow them to effectively meet the needs of their assigned future scenario (although one team did not focus as much on the scenario-driven capability needs and concentrated instead on investments that provided efficiencies or greater flexibility). They discussed what was essential for the strategy or scenario and then how to allocate any remaining resources, often focused on enduring CONUS missions. At times the intelligence briefs led to lively discussion and debates regarding how to balance more immediate needs with longer-term objectives. As game play progressed, players often revisited the scenario and strategic vision to take stock of where resources had been allocated, to remind themselves of the longer-term objectives, and to ensure that recent trends and events would not necessarily disrupt progress toward these objectives. Teams frequently examined where the most recent intelligence conflicted with the goals of the strategic vision. However, no team decided to update its strategic vision after discussing the intelligence briefs.

A strong focus on the demand signals associated with a scenario's strategic vision can open consideration for trade-offs and cuts traditionally considered to be unacceptable (e.g., search and rescue [SAR]) and the need to keep prioritizing them. Discussions about facilities investments were sometimes catalyzed by an intelligence brief, such as mitigating vulnerabilities to storms or improving quality of life to help recruiting and retention, but often investments were made because a player felt the investment was overdue or was a priority for Congress. At the end of the game, some players recognized that those decision trade-offs would have been significantly more challenging if they had not made early investments by accepting risk in mission areas.

Understanding the Coast Guard's role for a given mission in a region and the advantages the service provides were also inputs into resource allocation. Because missions can be performed in many ways, teams often debated exactly how missions might be operationalized to meet demand signals and what would constitute acceptable mission performance. Discussions also centered on allocating resources in ways that take advantage of the service's leadership, law enforcement, assets, or technical capabilities, while leveraging the capabilities of partners and allies (e.g., suggesting that the Navy had more capacity for humanitarian aid and disaster relief or that Arctic SAR could be done by partners with Coast Guard support) to efficiently use resources to meet the mission needs.

Understanding or articulating the value of marginal shifts in mission categorization was also challenging. For example, teams discussed how the Coast Guard might increase its involvement in defense operations to either supplement or complement the DoD mission, or whether MTS was best served by the ports, waterways, and coastal security (PWCS) mission or by the marine safety mission. What might be the Coast Guard's specific level of involvement or engagement in the mission, and how is this contribution measured or assessed? Another example centered on how to measure the contribution of increasing Coast Guard resources allocated to counterterrorism or marine-safety missions. Players recognized that "stretching the rubber band" or expanding Coast Guard roles across missions and regions has both short- and long-term costs. In a practical sense for game play, this sometimes made it more difficult to determine the value of adding resources to a regional mission or whether investing resources in longer-term capabilities or efficiencies would be of greater benefit. From a learning perspective, the discussions demonstrated that gaming creates an environment for substantive discussions about the Coast Guard, its institutional strategy, and the kinds of strategic trades that it must evaluate.

Homeland missions are enduring. Some teams' strategic visions focused on domestic issues, and some were focused on the "away game." All teams acknowledged that failure to execute homeland missions would affect stakeholder opinions and have deep political, and thus resource, consequences regardless of scenario. Teams also recognized that changes to Coast Guard authorities may be needed to alter missions or implement certain initiatives in response to new threats and demands. In contrast, they sometimes deemed deemphasizing overseas missions as less risky: The American public and Congress are less vested in overseas missions;[12] such missions are costly and pose risks to culture; and overseas priorities may ebb and flow with geopolitical events and Executive Branch goals. Early in the game the "away" vision teams were willing to take on some calculated risk for CONUS missions despite their importance, but as intelligence brief trends affected MTS, PWCS became a concern; or as climate-related issues increased during the game, the away teams put more resources back into CONUS, relying on their agility investment assets to respond to global demands. At the end of the game, each team had allocated significant resources to CONUS, regardless of whether their strategic vision was focused on the home or the away game.

Investment strategies for new capabilities were largely motivated by the efficiencies or agility they generate, allowing the Coast Guard to resource missions at a higher priority in the future. They were also motivated to satisfy the perceived needs of Congress and the Executive Branch (both of which must support new technology and facilities or administration strategy), although the emphasis teams placed on stakeholder interests varied. How new capabilities might be used creatively to increase mission performance was not central to the game and was thus only minimally discussed. Instead, teams focused on how these capabilities could be leveraged to free up resources for other priorities. For example, investing in unmanned autonomous systems and command, control, computers, communications, cyber, intelligence, surveillance, and reconnaissance (C5ISR) was motivated by the desire to either free up traditional assets that are difficult to sustain in remote locations or gain efficiencies that free up traditional resources for other priorities. Similarly, discussions about investing in expeditionary logistics often focused on keeping resources available in the next round, rather than enabling more independent or longer-duration operations. There was a reluctance to "fully commit" limited resources by investing in facilities or prioritizing missions to a high level without strong, enduring signals that doing so would result in efficiencies or technologies that reduce mission risk. In the final turn, teams' investment strategies were mixed: They either focused on near-term mission priorities and

---

[12] Public opinion score in Paratus Futurum refers to the United States only.

maximizing their stakeholder opinion score to "win" the game or invested in long-term capabilities to set the service up for future success.

Service culture considerations are a concern as the Coast Guard's focus and talent needs evolve. As teams made investments in technology or international capabilities that prioritized the "away game," they expressed concerns about the influence on Coast Guard culture. Some teams actively monitored the culture's status and used their tokens to lower the risk. Investments in culture were intended to support leadership, training, and other activities that sustain an effective or supportive culture, especially when adapting to new systems or operational paradigms. For others, institutional culture was an important but secondary consideration. There was also some discussion about redefining what it means to serve in the Coast Guardsman in the future, as demand for traditional skills wanes, new skills become more prominent, and changes in mission priority affect what life in the service looks like. For example, during one team's debate about SAR being deprioritized (or no longer a Coast Guard mission at all) and the service becoming more focused on defense and military operations, players were concerned with anticipating how these changes could influence the organization's identity and culture.

Observations from Round 2

The second round of games was conducted March 30–April 1, 2022 and drew more than 25 senior Coast Guard leaders to RAND's offices in Arlington, Virginia. Participants were urged by the event champion (the deputy commandant for mission support) to be bold as they help shape the thinking of the next leadership council and prepare today's Coast Guard for tomorrow. Several overarching observations were drawn from the game play, some of which were similar to round 1 choices, while others were unique—though none was in conflict or disagreement of round 1 themes.

Several participants relied on the current positive progress of the service to sustain operations, and their dominant strategy for the first round of game play was to invest in new capabilities. Notably, C5ISR capabilities were uniformly identified as the priority investment (consistent with the results of a parallel survey of strategic objectives), despite the resources and lead time required to realize the capability. Early investments were seen as enabling the Coast Guard to remain successful despite an uncertain future and to gain efficiencies that could be reinvested in future rounds. Some teams invested in desired capabilities without necessarily considering where they may be deployed, while others invested to cover specific regions and mission needs identified in the scenario and intelligence brief. In all cases, careful consideration and prioritization were given to investing in capabilities that efficiently extended the Coast Guard's presence while maintaining flexibility to adapt to changing conditions.

The teams' early investment strategies nearly universally accepted some level of short-term risk in traditional missions and often in culture to pay for future capabilities—but players pivoted back to domestic missions as game play progressed. Teams sought to meet future mission demand through investments in efficient or flexible assets such as expeditionary logistics, adaptive force packages, and unmanned systems. The specific focus of these investments varied by scenario and team. While all teams acknowledged the cultural costs of these investments, not all devoted resources to mitigate them. Before investments or resources were committed to a region, partner and ally capabilities were considered. Furthermore, teams were generally reluctant to commit to fixed assets such as a permanent forward operating base despite maintaining a long-term presence in a region after several rounds of game play. Even teams whose scenario and strategic vision were for globally distributed operations and had a significant focus on the "away game" eventually moved more resourcing back to CONUS missions once the investments that provided agile capability and capacity could be utilized overseas.

Teams acknowledged the importance of investing in operations, maintenance, and facilities, and were unwilling to take risk over several consecutive rounds of play. Yet these investments were not always made in the first round and frequently took a "back seat" to capabilities investments. Often the catalyst for operations, maintenance, and facilities investments was an intelligence brief specifying workforce trends that would make it harder for the Coast Guard to recruit and retain members or an intelligence brief that identified threats to facilities due to storms and other natural hazards. During rounds that teams did not make these investments, there was substantial reluctance to leave facilities or operations and maintenance at risk because they know the importance of these investments and had experienced times when the investment was not made.

The concept of an adaptive force package emerged as a key approach for covering a broad range of missions. The concept shifts the focus from platforms and their activity level to mission performance by bringing together capabilities and assets in a flexible manner for operations ranging from emergency management to international engagements. Adaptive force packages were used by all teams as "insurance" against unpredictable or varied mission needs and were deployed both domestically and abroad. Participants repeatedly offered the multi-mission role of Coast Guard organizations and platforms as a risk-mitigation strategy and, perhaps not surprisingly, gravitated toward investments that enabled multi-mission response (such as adaptive force packages and unmanned systems) over the more targeted investments of foreign area officers and law enforcement detachments. Multiple players said this shifted their thinking about service-wide planning and force allocation from assets and days to capabilities and goals.

Teams generally spread resources to cover mission demand signals contained in the intelligence briefs and relied on agile investment capability as insurance against plausible surprises. Only one team moved a mission to the highest priority level (an emergency management/disaster response mission in the Atlantic). Participants had lively discussions about SAR mission's importance to the Coast Guard identity and to public awareness and opinion of the service; SAR's role as an enabler for the capabilities and capacities needed for contingencies such as hurricane response; and SAR's influence over training, aircraft configuration, and stationing. When confronted with a challenge, teams generally weighed the likelihood of mission success with the consequence of inadequate response. Deploying an adaptive force package was the preferred surge method because it avoided tapping into future resources (although players noted the service's natural inclination is to surge regardless of resource trades). However, on several occasions, teams considered using surge options to gain favor with stakeholders in the hopes that this would improve resourcing in the future. While they often discussed the surge capability, players rarely if ever used it, as they deemed it was not worth the cost in resources or culture. In reality, the Coast Guard has always surged for immediate demand despite the costs. Participants noted that this discrepancy can surface only in an environment that encourages them to "play the way you think it should be done, and not as though you are representing how it will be done." Instead, teams relied on agility-focused investments and tried to place them in the appropriate region to be available if needed for a surprise in demand.

Investment in culture will be required to ensure mission success in the future while leveraging emerging technologies and attracting and retaining a highly capable workforce. The game explicitly recognizes that to accommodate new technologies and new ways of performing missions, Coast Guard leadership must commit resources and attention to adjusting training curricula and requirements, promotion and career pathways, deployment practices, and other organizational processes that comprise part of the service's culture. Players were aware of the importance of balancing investments in new capabilities with workforce culture. Some teams were very concerned about overextending culture and recognized that, while the workforce often embraces change, the rate of change needs to be actively managed. Teams varied in their tolerance of cultural risk during game play, but all acknowledged that change takes substantial time and resources and cannot be avoided for too long.

Domestic missions are enduring and fundamental to the Coast Guard, and this was reflected in resourcing decisions. Participants expressed that the Coast Guard's purpose is saving lives, helping people, and facilitating safe and prosperous maritime trade in support of the economy. Though these missions were often left at risk due to resource constraints, participants noted that these missions are what historically and currently distinguishes the Coast Guard and allows it to satisfy the expectations of the Executive Branch, Congress, and the public. This branding defines and drives recruiting, retention, and capabilities development. As a result, resource allocation considered the asymmetric risks of performing poorly in these missions. Demand for capabilities overseas fluctuates with geopolitical developments and changing national priorities, necessitating an adaptable force when resources are limited. Participants also sought to prioritize missions that used the service's specialized capabilities abroad for roles that added value to DoD or complemented the perceived capabilities of partners or allies. After several rounds of game play, teams tended to shift resources back to domestic missions regardless of scenario, relying on their agile investments to respond abroad as needed.

Participants noted that while the principal Coast Guard mission sets may not change, the way in which they are performed or accomplished may be different. For example, new opportunities to leverage new technologies such as unmanned autonomous systems (air, surface, or submersible) or to engage service providers from the private sector may change the service's activities. Furthermore, while USCG operations facilitate trade and maintain safety, other mechanisms, such as funding grants or developing industry standards, have historically been used for these purposes.

Did the Game Change Participants' Perspectives?

One of the Coast Guard's stated objectives for the game was to see if it affected participants' choices about which strategic objectives were most important for the commandant to consider. To answer this question, we used a modified Delphi exercise,[13] which is a structured elicitation process designed to help groups reach a consensus or draw out additional information about where there is disagreement.[14] The exercise asked participants to rate the strategic objectives (synthesized from previous Pinecone workshops in Evergreen V) along two dimensions: anticipated level of impact and implementation difficulty. In a modified Delphi exercise, SMEs are asked to provide inputs (or assess the strategic objectives, in this case). This process was conducted in three steps: (1) a survey that asked participants to rate strategic objectives issued before game play, (2) a discussion of the results during game play and the play of the game itself, and (3) a repeat survey after game play.

The game's impacts were evident in several participant comments enumerated below:

- "The game showed us the shocks that could affect CONUS if we focused all of our efforts OCONUS [outside the continental United States]. We'll need more resources if we want to maintain our effectiveness [in] CONUS while projecting force into OCONUS regions."

---

[13] The Delphi method, developed by the RAND Corporation in the 1950s in the field of operations research, is used to approach a consensus among a group of expert participants through a series of controlled iterative steps. The Delphi method is particularly useful when empirical data are not available. It has three key features: It is anonymous, it is iterative, and it provides a statistical group response where the group opinion is an aggregate of individual opinions on the final round of the Delphi. See N. C. Dalkey and O. Helmer, *An Experimental Application of the Delphi Method to the Use of Experts*, Santa Monica, Calif.: RAND Corporation, RM-721/1, July 1962; N. C. Dalkey, *The Delphi Method: An Experimental Study of Group Opinion*, Santa Monica, Calif.: RAND Corporation, RM-5888-PR, 1969; T. Gordon and O. Helmer, *Report on Long-Range Forecasting Study*, Santa Monica, Calif.: RAND Corporation, P-2982, 1964; Kathryn Fitch, Steven J. Bernstein, Maria Dolores Aguilar, Bernard Burnand, Juan Ramon LaCalle, Pablo Lazaro, Mirjam van het Loo, Joseph McDonnell, Janneke Vader, and James P. Kahan, *The RAND/UCLA Appropriateness Method User's Manual*, Santa Monica, Calif.: RAND Corporation, MR-1269-DG-XII/RE, 2001; S. L.-T. Normand, B. J. McNeil, L. E. Peterson, and R. H. Palmer, "Eliciting Expert Opinion Using the Delphi Technique: Identifying Performance Indicators for Cardiovascular Disease," *International Journal for Quality in Health Care*, Vol. 3, No. 2, 1998, pp. 247–260; Dmitry Khodyakov and Christine Chen, *Nature and Predictors of Response Changes in Modified-Delphi Panels*, Santa Monica, Calif.: RAND Corporation, EP-68427, 2020.

[14] This section provides an overview of the modified Delphi analysis done as part of the Paratus Futurum game. For a more in-depth look into the exact process, strategic objective, and statistical analysis, please see the forthcoming report on the Paratus Futurum game.

- "After playing the game it seems that the Coast Guard will need more subject matter experts and less jack-of-all trade types. It may help retention but may not be as positive for the service."
- "The game showed us that we need the talent to make the technological leaps [in unmanned systems] and special skills to operate in OCONUS locations long term."
- "The game made me think of MTS in an entirely different way. The increase in possible automation and goods moving through the ocean means we will want to lead from the front."
- "Lots of game investments in systems that require IT. Modernizing now allows the CG to take advantage of so many systems that make our teams much more efficient."
- "More impactful based on the game but about as hard as I originally thought."

Common Themes in the Two Rounds of Panels

In addition to evaluating participant responses from each game by individual panel, the responses were examined in aggregate, which revealed several common themes.

- Each panel consistently indicated—both before and after completing the game—that the most significant strategic objectives revolved around technology such as IT infrastructure upgrades, data integration, and unmanned systems.
- The combined panel results revealed that several personnel/human resource objectives were also critical. These included creating a flexible talent management system, taking organizational risk, and developing a workforce more prepared for more (and longer) deployments to overseas regions, as well as the language and cultural skills needed for more assignments focusing on diplomacy and other aspects of international engagement.
- Some of the most difficult objectives to implement were creating a flexible talent management system, integrating data, rapidly growing the service, taking a deliberate role in the modernization of MTS, and committing resources overseas while accepting risk for CONUS missions. Participants remarked that "seeing the whole board" through the events of the game made them think about some of the strategic objectives differently.
- The game participants consistently identified funding/resources and cultural inertia as the greatest barriers to the implementation of any strategic objectives.

Game Value to Participants

Paratus Futurum participants actively participated in the discussions, successfully immersed themselves in their assigned scenario and concepts of operation, and made resource allocation decisions aligned with those priorities. Participants noted that the game revealed the importance of sticking to a strategy—and "perhaps militant adherence" to strategy—even when other events occur. This takeaway suggests that a robust strategic vision that is communicated and understood broadly can be a powerful means to guide investment.

Participants also discovered that some level of risk is acceptable and that random events will happen but may not necessarily have significant, negative consequences. Players felt that including culture considerations in the game design made the decision trades more realistic and that the game helped them better understand the potential second-, third-, and fourth-order effects of geopolitical trends, which may not be initially apparent. These insights could be especially helpful for senior leadership.

Additionally, participants from both the virtual and in-person games remarked that the ability to participate and actually play the game was far more effective than a briefing or a discussion would have been. Being able to step away from their assigned office or unit, leaving rank at the door, and being challenged to "be bold" in this low-risk environment allowed them to engage in trade-off discussions and strategic choices in a way they had not previously experienced—and that should be experienced and not just read about or be briefed on.

Finally, and perhaps most often mentioned, the game gave participants a greater appreciation for the strategic risks and budget constraints across the entire Coast Guard mission set. Participants could probe the implications of various futures in a collaborative setting, which allowed them to leave behind their individual mission focus, escape their siloes, and become immersed in decisions that require trading off strategic risks among the mission areas amid resource constraints. Participants also repeatedly mentioned that exposure to this type of thinking and gaming should start much earlier in the career progression, as often those who are making trade-off decisions are confronting that sort of strategic thinking for the first time. The service has indicated that games that are specifically developed for various service programs and applications have both great utility and potential to enhance strategic thinking and foresight across the entire USCG enterprise.

7. Conclusion

Looking back at Evergreen V, we take stock of this multiyear program to build upon the success of previous Evergreen efforts and to give the service's strategic planning process greater visibility, relevance, and utility.

We view Year 1 as the critically important starting point because the scenarios that were developed served as the scene-setters or futures for subsequent strategic foresight activities. Early Pinecone workshops elicited what types of potential changes might be most important and why, and identified future shocks and stressors that would have the most profound effect on the service and its missions. A secondary but important outcome of all Evergreen activities was introducing the application of strategic foresight to service personnel who had never been exposed to the strategy. The majority of participants appreciated the opportunity to exercise strategic thinking and collaborate in a team setting outside the rank structure.

In Year 2, the Evergreen team built on the scenario development in Year 1 by leveraging those futures in a series of workshops. Select service members participated in strategic foresight exercises about future workforce challenges, future risks to MTS, and the implications of emerging technologies to the Coast Guard operating environment. The HSOAC and DCO-X Evergreen project teams worked in a collaborative fashion, synchronizing activities and analytical support to maximize impact.

Year 3 built on the earlier workshops, refining the approach and gaining greater senior leadership participation in the Evergreen process. As the primary strategic decisionmakers, senior leaders functioned as guides, mentors, and primary consumers of Evergreen outputs. The diverse mix of senior and junior SMEs who participated had an opportunity to share their perspectives through structured ideation exercises. Workshop participants formed teams or focus groups charged with tackling various challenging subjects informed by a specific future scenario. Their input was captured in reports and communications with strategic planners at the program and enterprise level and in some cases was used to facilitate senior leader strategic planning events, which had the further effect of directly elevating Evergreen's impact within the service. Due in part to the past and present commandants' strategic focus on future workforce and in part to geopolitical and domestic events during Evergreen V, human resource and culture became recurring themes across multiple workshops. Under the broad rubric of technology, data science also emerged as a future opportunity and challenge with implications for future decisionmaking and mission execution.

Year 4 brought all these exercises together in a way that was designed to be informative for the incoming commandant. In developing the first Coast Guard game, Paratus Futurum, the team pulled together the wide range of challenges and opportunities identified by Pinecone participants across a global span and allowed service leaders to engage the opportunities and challenges in such a way that they could experience what the trade-offs might be and how the strategic objectives might affect an uncertain future. The eight teams that played Paratus Futurum found much common ground in prioritization, investments, and level of risk acceptance, despite being assigned four substantially different futures and strategic objectives.

While the current phase of Evergreen is ongoing, a few factors have contributed to the success and influence of Evergreen V. One is the program's agility to adapt to external and internal requirements and requests, such as moving to online workshops during COVID-19 restrictions or adjusting products to better reach the intended audience. As illustrated by the many documents compiled in this report, Evergreen has embraced "short-and-sweet" product communication, allowing the program to draw attention to multiple findings from the Evergreen Pinecones in a timely manner, while at the same time broadly disseminating materials to a diverse audience. Finally, Evergreen has used a dual approach of focusing on topics of interest to senior leaders and exposing future leaders to strategic foresight planning to earn support and interest from both senior Coast Guard leadership and the lower ranks. This made it an invaluable resource across the entire service. This current phase of Evergreen has adapted to the times and the needs of the Coast Guard, ensuring the current and future relevance of the program.

The central question that emerged from many of the workshop discussions with Coast Guard personnel and service stakeholders was, "What force will we need in 2030?" Major themes emerged from the collective Pinecones, including a perceived future need for

- skill sets related to technological fluency in an increasingly technologically oriented work environment
- human focus in a world of increasing automation, autonomous systems, and AI, and
- skill stacking, or developing and applying many different skill sets during one's career.

Related to the future workforce, workshop participants were also asked, "What investments do we need to make now to meet future needs?" Emerging concepts centered on shifting from "human resource" management to "talent" management with a focus on flexibility and choice. This focus includes providing the workforce of the future with a range of opportunities to serve—such as options to leave and return to the service and greater flexibility for members caring for dependents—and increased transparency in human resource management, improved expectation management, and greater personal control over one's career.

Based upon joint HSOAC/DCO-X analysis of the Pinecone outputs and workshop outcomes over the course of Evergreen V, we found four main sets of drivers that will likely affect the future Coast Guard and require the entire organization to adapt: changing workforce culture, rapid technological developments, climate change, and geopolitical dynamics.[1] The implications of the many drivers of change discussed in this conclusion and throughout the report are enduring across the scenarios used during the Evergreen V cycle. We elaborate on the drivers of these

---

[1] The societal driver that was previously identified in Year 1 was not carried forward through the subsequent workshops.

themes and the implications for the Coast Guard in the sections below, then discuss overall takeaways.

Demographic and Cultural Themes

Drivers

The U.S. population is changing in ways that affect both the Coast Guard's potential workforce and its responsibilities. The population's rapid aging results in smaller cohorts of potential recruits relative to the overall population and increasing family-care responsibilities for the working-age population.[2] The aging of the population also influences its geographic distribution: Many older Americans are choosing to live close to the water and/or in warm southeastern states where hurricanes are prevalent.[3] Moreover, a growing percentage of young Americans—including a majority of people under the age of 18—come from ethnic and racial communities that have generally been underrepresented in the Coast Guard.

The culture of work is also evolving. This has been a gradual process since the mid-twentieth century, when a large percentage of the population had the same employer for decades or even an entire career. Across society, employment relationships are becoming more transient and more distant, which the extent of teleworking during the pandemic may have intensified. Although it is too soon to be certain, the pandemic may also permanently influence the culture of work. People are reexamining their relationships with work, family, and communities in ways that may make them less committed to long-term employment with a single employer.

The intense political divisions within American society, should they continue, may also shape the willingness of individuals to embrace the Coast Guard's ethos of service. While there have always been doubts about whether emerging generations will want to serve their country, today's fractured political landscape and deeply rooted disagreements may discourage people from feeling motivated to do so.

Implications for the Coast Guard and Potential Coast Guard Responses

- *Increased efforts to recruit underrepresented minorities and women are necessary to ensure the sustainability of the service.* A Coast Guard that remains primarily white and male will be too small and culturally homogenous to address the needs of the nation.
- *The growth of populations in areas that are subject to hurricanes or routine flooding and where recreational boating is common will increase demand for the SAR mission.* The fact that many of these people will be older means they will be more challenging to rescue when necessary.

---

[2] The median age has increased from 28 in 1970 to 38 today; the percentage of the population over the age of 65 rose from 10 percent to 17 percent over that period and is still rising rapidly. See Erin Duffin, "Median Age of the Resident Population of the United States from 1960 to 2020," Statista, webpage, undated.

[3] This migration to the Southeast has been a continuing trend for the last half-century. Overall, 38 percent of Americans live in that region, compared with 31 percent in 1970. Florida has gone from having 3.3 percent of the U.S. population to 6.4 percent over the same period.

- *The Coast Guard will need to adjust to an employment environment in which people are less willing to commit to long-term career relationships, and fewer of them may be moved by the Coast Guard's sense of purpose.* They may also be less willing to periodically relocate based on the service's needs because of their own needs or those of older relatives. The Coast Guard will most likely need to be more accommodating of the widespread desire for part-time remote work.

- *A workforce that includes more civilians, reservists, and auxiliary personnel relative to active-duty personnel may help the Coast Guard acquire the numbers and the specific talents it needs,* without pushing away people who are hesitant to undertake the commitment of active-duty service or do not meet the service entry requirements. The Coast Guard can also increase flexibility with respect to entering and leaving the service; for example, "stitched careers" give people more freedom and can prevent the permanent loss of their skill sets to the service. The Coast Guard's "up-or-out" human resources policy and statutory time limits on active-duty service can arbitrarily prevent competent and experienced workers from continuing to serve.

Technological Themes

Drivers

Information technology—combined with advancements in sensor technologies and including such diverse areas as AI, big-data analytics, and cyber defense—will continue to grow in importance. Information flow, much of it automated, will be central to organizational success. Unmanned and (increasingly) autonomous systems will also be operating in multiple domains and in growing numbers, often with high-quality sensors and communication capabilities on board. Technology areas such as additive manufacturing (3-D printing) and low-cost commercial satellites are also rapidly increasing in capability and availability.

These technological trends will affect the Coast Guard in three key respects. First, the Coast Guard can—and in some cases, must—use these technologies as they become more pervasive. Second, the Coast Guard needs to interact with other entities that use these technologies (e.g., private companies and individuals, other parts of DHS, DoD, other federal agencies, state and local law enforcement, and international partners). Third, the Coast Guard will need to counter malefactors' use of these technologies in its Drug Interdiction, Migrant Interdiction, Defense Readiness, and PWCS missions.

Implications for the Coast Guard and Potential Coast Guard Responses

- *Technological advances will drive future workforce needs, such that almost all personnel will need to have a basic level of familiarity and comfort with the use of technology and data, particularly IT and data analytic methods.* In addition, demand will increase for technology specialists, particularly within IT, but also in other areas.

  Achieving a universal basic level of technology fluency will require a combination of enhanced recruiting criteria and a modest amount of training. Specialists will be needed to handle the Coast Guard's own usage of emerging technologies; to interact with the private companies, individuals, and partner agencies that use them; and to understand how to counter their use by adversaries. Developing a pool of technology specialists requires a talent management system that fosters their recruitment, retention, training, and continued intellectual and career growth through opportunities to learn from experience. More fluid career paths and rebalancing of the force away from active-duty personnel can also aid in retaining people with in-demand technology skill sets.

As some processes are automated, Coast Guard personnel will increasingly need human-specific strengths, such as thinking critically, defining and solving complex problems, building partnerships, collaborating with a team, and engaging in leadership. These critical-thinking and interpersonal skills are hard to teach and to measure. To cultivate them, the talent management system needs to emphasize mentorship, training where appropriate, and recruitment and promotion for these skill sets. *Increasingly, positions will need to be filled based on the technological and human skill sets that are required, rather than specified by rank.*

- *A more data-driven Coast Guard can use automatically collected data sets and automated routine analysis to inform human analysis and decisionmaking.* Commanders will be able to make decisions armed with additional information that they previously would not have had—not as a substitute for human judgment, but as a powerful, pervasive complement to it. When needed, commanders will be able to use this additional information to help communicate their decisions to external stakeholders and to inform those stakeholders about Coast Guard needs.

- *The rapid and accelerating pace of technological advances will require the Coast Guard to be more willing and able to integrate new technology over shorter time spans and be more innovative in ascertaining how it can best employ that technology.* The Coast Guard may need to automate data collection and integration and then have personnel who can analyze those data sets help inform decisions at multiple levels of command. Coast Guard usage of emerging technology can make some missions and support functions easier. For example, the shift to virtual aids to navigation can reduce the need for physical devices that need to be emplaced and maintained. Increasingly autonomous unmanned vehicles will be able to conduct parts of some missions with limited human oversight, thereby lowering risks and costs. In some cases, they can add capabilities by operating where humans cannot. The 3-D printing of spare parts—or even unmanned vehicles—on demand can reduce logistical timelines, storage requirements, and costs.

- *The use of emerging technology by malefactors can impose additional capability and capacity demands on the Coast Guard.* Regulation of private entities' cyber defenses will become increasingly important in protecting MTS. Countering the use of unmanned vehicles for smuggling or terrorist attacks will require additional Coast Guard efforts.

Environmental and Economic Themes

Drivers

Climate change affects the Coast Guard in multiple ways. The fixed infrastructure of the Coast Guard and those whom it regulates and supports are vulnerable to a host of risks: more frequent and severe storms, receding coastlines, rising water levels under bridges, routine low-level flooding, wildfires in select locations, droughts that cause groundings on inland waterways, more mobile ice cover, increased calving of icebergs, and thawing permafrost. These can also increase demand for Coast Guard missions such as SAR, marine safety, marine environmental protection, and aids to navigation/waterway management. Demand for icebreaking, iceberg monitoring, and ice-dam clearance may increase as midwinter shipping on the Great Lakes becomes more viable and the Arctic becomes more accessible. Around the globe, the Coast Guard may also be forced to operate in increasingly harsh environments—such as the aftermath of more frequent humanitarian assistance/disaster relief events both domestically and overseas—that will stretch its assets and resources.

Climate change is only one of several environmental trends that will likely increase demand for Coast Guard services. Worldwide population growth, together with rising incomes, will increase demand for fish and may also increase pollution. While fossil-fuel consumption for combustion may decline, the use of copious chemicals for fertilizers, manufacturing, and other purposes will rise. Ecosystem damage due to pollution, overfishing (with especially destructive fishing methods), and climate change will curtail the supply of fish. All these factors will intensify demand for other law enforcement, living marine resources, marine safety, and marine environmental protection missions. The growth of offshore wind energy, and perhaps tidal or wave-energy facilities, will create new regulatory demands for the Coast Guard, as will the growing use of lower-carbon natural gas, much of which will be liquefied along shorelines and transported by tankers.

Economic and environmental factors will also influence maritime migration and drug-smuggling patterns. Central America, the Caribbean, and the northern portions of South America are experiencing more frequent and intense natural disasters and chronic environmental damage. At the same time, these regions are not experiencing the rising incomes seen in developing parts of Asia, and in some cases, incomes were falling even before the pandemic. The transition of COVID-19 from a pandemic to an endemic disease may further curtail economic opportunities in developing nations with large youth populations and low rates of vaccination. People in affected countries may try to reach the United States by sea, perhaps in mass movements. They may be inclined to contribute to drug production and smuggling, particularly if their governments are unable or unwilling to counter such activity due to their weakened economies. An increasing divergence between a growing U.S. economy and the weaker economies of some neighbors to the south will increase not only the financial motivation to smuggle drugs northward but also the U.S. population's demand for illicit substances. Collectively, these factors will likely increase demand for the Migrant Interdiction and Drug Interdiction missions.

Implications for the Coast Guard and Potential Coast Guard Responses

- *The Coast Guard's own infrastructure will increasingly be subject to both chronic and acute degradation by climate change.* To maintain the Coast Guard's future infrastructure, higher levels of investment in resilience measures and possible adaptation will be needed.

- *Environmental and economic changes are likely to increase demand for the Coast Guard across most of its statutory missions.* The Coast Guard will need to increase its capacity accordingly. While technological advances can help to reduce the personnel requirements and costs associated with increasing capacity—for example, autonomous unmanned aircraft or commercial satellites can provide overhead imagery that would otherwise require manned aircraft—this will not eliminate the need for a larger Coast Guard to address the substantial increase in demand across various missions and geographic areas.

Geopolitical Themes

Drivers

In an era of great-power competition, DoD and the nation seek an increasingly global Coast Guard. Combatant commanders around the world want the unique strengths and capabilities that the Coast Guard can provide. These include its combined Title X and Title XIV authorities; its ability to work effectively with smaller navies and coast guards; its ability to engage with local communities and the private sector; its skills in dealing with SAR, fisheries, pollution, smuggling, and sovereignty; and the way it presents itself as an inherently benevolent service. Positive perceptions of the Coast Guard, relative to other U.S. services, can play an important role from an information operations (IO) perspective. The Coast Guard's regional expertise in Latin America, the polar regions, Pacific island nations, and elsewhere is also in high demand. Finally, its skills in protecting assets in ports and confined waterways are important in a world where sudden attacks, far from the scene of combat, can greatly impair military capabilities.

Implications for the Coast Guard and Potential Coast Guard Responses

- *The Coast Guard requires more capacity to conduct additional operations overseas while still maintaining responsibility for its missions at home.* Not all of this capacity growth needs to take the form of physical assets, since deployable teams of Coast Guard personnel can often have a valuable impact in helping other nations improve their own capabilities. For example, providing periodic maintenance support or training in tactics may enable another nation's coast guard to more effectively secure its maritime environment. However, deploying to another nation without a cutter, aircraft, or other highly visible asset may diminish the IO effect of engagement. Perceptions matter.
- *The Coast Guard needs to be increasingly savvy regarding both the technical and human aspects of IO.*
- *As the Coast Guard operates more overseas, the partnership and interpersonal skills that were cited above will be particularly critical.* These skills will need to be complemented by linguistic and cultural expertise for different regions. The Coast Guard will need to ensure that the workforce develops these skills and that it retains the people who have them by providing rewarding training and opportunities, much as it should for people with specific technical expertise.

Recommendations for Service Leadership

Although the drivers spanned four categories (demographic and cultural, technological, environmental and economic, and geopolitical), not all recommendations that emerged from them fit neatly into those categories. Instead, the following recommendations address the scale and investments of the future Coast Guard, its management of talent, and its use of technology.[4]

Scale and Investments of the Coast Guard

- The Coast Guard needs to grow more rapidly than the U.S. population as a whole. This is driven by four key sets of factors:
  - environmental changes, such as climate change and the depletion of global fisheries, which will increase demand for Coast Guard services
  - increasing populations, including large numbers of older people, living in coastal and hurricane-prone areas
  - growing technological capabilities of malefactors, which make Coast Guard missions that counter active opponents harder
  - increasing national and DoD demand for the Coast Guard to play a greater role overseas without a corresponding diminution of domestic responsibilities.
- The Coast Guard will also need to invest more in its physical infrastructure, due to climate change inducing both chronic damage (e.g., routine low-level flooding in some areas) and a greater urgency to reduce a large backlog of infrastructure improvements and deferred maintenance, as well as acute events (e.g., increased frequency and severity of hurricanes and other natural disasters).

Talent Management

- The Coast Guard must redouble efforts to recruit and retain both underrepresented minorities and women. This is imperative to meet future demand.
- It must ensure that all personnel have a basic ability to work with IT, data analytics, and other advanced technologies, through a combination of enhanced recruiting criteria and training.
- The service must also increase the number of technology specialists across a range of fields. These people can be recruited and retained despite extensive demand for those skills by
  - intensifying efforts to provide them with rewarding training and experiences, thus contributing to their intellectual and career growth
  - opening opportunities based on skills, not necessarily rank
  - providing incentives for them to stay.
- As the Coast Guard assumes more global responsibilities, it should provide a similar mix of training, experiential opportunities, and incentives to ensure a growing linguistically and culturally skilled workforce.

---

[4] These recommendations reflect a consensus of HSOAC researchers and DCO-X staff, based on collaborative analysis of Pinecone outcomes through a series of internal workshops and meetings conducted during the spring and summer of 2021.

- It should foster greater critical-thinking and interpersonal skills through mentorship, training opportunities, and incentives (promotional and otherwise). This will enable humans to more effectively do the tasks that machines cannot, such as building partnerships and making complex decisions with incomplete information.
- Because positions overall will increasingly need to be filled based on skill sets, rather than on rank, the Coast Guard should offer greater flexibility in entering, departing, and reentering the service, particularly for people with in-demand skill sets. Stitched careers can enable the Coast Guard to acquire and retain the skills and numbers that it needs.
- The balance among active-duty, reserve, civilian, and auxiliary personnel may need to be adjusted to enlarge the latter three categories and provide greater mobility among all four.
- The service should also reduce the frequency with which personnel are reassigned to different locations, take individual preferences into greater account, and consider being more accommodating of part-time telework.

Technology

- The Coast Guard should use emerging technology in areas such as IT, unmanned systems, 3-D printing, and low-cost commercial satellites to increase capabilities and capacity, while reducing personnel requirements and costs.
- The Coast Guard should also develop more skills in these technology areas so that it can interact effectively with the parties that it supports, regulates, and partners with, since they will increasingly use those technologies.
- Given rapid technological change, the service should develop processes to integrate new technologies more expeditiously and innovatively than in the past.
- The Coast Guard should also be made more data-driven than in the past by using automated data collection and some degree of automated analysis, followed by human analysis and assessment. This method—automated data collection and analysis that complements and supports human judgment—can result in better-informed decisions that improve the service's effectiveness at multiple levels, while reducing risks and costs. It can also make the reasoning behind decisions easier to articulate and communicate to external stakeholders, such as DHS and Congress.
- As the Coast Guard conducts more overseas operations and as IOs become increasingly important, the service will need to be more technically capable to execute these operations.

The rapid pace of technological change; the increasing potential for sudden, accelerating climate change; and other rapidly changing geopolitical dynamics suggest that pursuing agile and adaptable planning and resourcing systems are also strategies that could better position the Coast Guard to prepare for whatever the future might hold.

Finally, because the purpose of strategic foresight planning is to consider a range of potential goals and actions and their potential outcomes in the future, there is inherently a considerable amount of uncertainty in this endeavor and in the trends discussed in this report. This uncertainty suggests that the Coast Guard needs to continue to ensure agility and adaptability of its planning and resourcing systems, that it should revisit these trends and potential futures periodically, and that the strategic foresight planning enabled by Evergreen V will continue to be a valuable asset to the Coast Guard.

Appendix A. Future Scenarios and Workshop Design

This appendix contains scenarios that were developed in January 2020 for discussion during the Pinecones games in years two, three, and four of Evergreen V. The documents present various fictional scenarios that USCG might face in the future, each reflecting a different perspective on what climate, geopolitics, the economy, technology, and society might look like in the year 2030. In each of the settings, participants were divided into four groups, and each group received a different scenario to discuss and suggest solutions to head off challenges the service may face. The same scenarios were used for Pinecones throughout the last three years of Evergreen V.

Each scenario has two versions: a full description (labeled "read-ahead" in this appendix), which was sent to participants before each Pinecone, and a one-page summary, which was available for quick reference during the workshops themselves.[1]

Contents

---

[1] All references to media sources in the future scenarios are purely hypothetical.

PROJECT EVERGREEN V
FUTURE SCENARIO 1: BEYOND THE HORIZON

WHAT DOES THE WORLD LOOK LIKE IN 2030?

Climate
Subsidence and sea level rise cause problems in the mid-Atlantic
Record hurricane damage impacts Coast Guard assets

Geopolitics
Growing Chinese aggression and footprint
Increased U.S. military presence at sea

Economy
Large U.S. debt
Increasingly efficient maritime trade

Technology
Security at ports is automated
Counter-terrorism screening is now highly effective and affordable

Society
Immigration and a baby boom boost population
Educational options are shifting
Military careers are attractive

Clockwise from upper left: Kswinicki via Getty Images; Japan Maritime Self-Defense Force; Aurelio Antonio via Getty Images; Vera Petrunina via Getty Images; Metamorworks via Getty Images

SCENARIO 1: BEYOND THE HORIZON

Today is September 10, 2030. A lot has changed.

Geopolitics

Increasing Chinese aggression and footprint
U.S. increases military presence at sea

China's investments in maritime infrastructure, including large ports and international canal widening, have continued to spread within the Indo-Pacific region. Billed as the maritime "Silk Road," investments to create access to ports (in Myanmar, Pakistan, Sri Lanka, and Djibouti, among others) and other infrastructure running from the Chinese mainland to East Africa has expanded to include additional infrastructure in and around the South China Sea (including in Cambodia, the Philippines, and Malaysia). While China's use of these ports remains exclusively commercial, some shipments are escorted at

times by military vessels when crossing through areas prone to piracy. This has provided China with the justification it needs for establishing an ongoing naval presence throughout Asia, including established bases in multiple nations. These developments have raised tensions with the U.S. and its allies in the region because of the belief that the Chinese may be using this as a mechanism to gain further military control over key maritime shipping routes. Regardless of Chinese intent, this activity has increased the number of unplanned encounters between U.S. and Chinese Naval and commercial vessels.

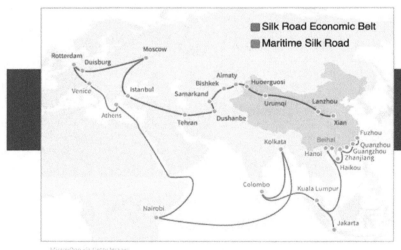

MARITIME SILK ROAD:
The modern Silk Road includes ports all over Indo-China and extending into Africa.

MicrovOne via Getty Images

This scenario was generated by HSOAC-RAND in support of the U.S. Coast Guard's Project Evergreen V. This is not a forecast, but one of many plausible potential futures. It was developed by combining major drivers of change and imagining their potential interactions and outcomes. (*Updated January 2020*)

HS AC
HOMELAND SECURITY
OPERATIONAL ANALYSIS CENTER

2

SCENARIO 1: BEYOND THE HORIZON

Geopolitics (continued)

Biz
Wire

California
insists
China deal
is legal

The Light
Too close for comfort

U.S. and Chinese patrol boats nearly collide in Bay of Bengal

A deal struck between the state of California and the Chinese government began making its way through U.S. federal courts in 2027. The agreement would enable the Chinese to pay for green upgrades to the Ports of Long Beach, Los Angeles, Richmond, and Oakland in exchange for access to the same technology for developing and upgrading China's yet undisclosed expansions to the maritime silk highway.

The official position of the U.S. is that China has steadily been chipping away at other countries' sovereignty in the region. The U.S. also takes exception to China's implication that California is looking west to become part of the maritime silk highway. The U.S. Navy has begun stepping up security patrols in international waters off the coasts of Somalia, Yemen, Pakistan, India, Myanmar, Thailand, as well as by the Strait of Malacca. This quickly threatens to squeeze the service's resources, which have also been dedicated to patrolling distributed U.S. Marine Corps expeditionary locations in the Philippines and Vietnam. Agents of the Chinese government are believed to have broached security at these remote locations. Increased maritime vessel traffic has led U.S. forces abroad to participate in search and rescue and environmental cleanups. There have not been major vessel accidents in U.S. waters, but analysts say the maritime transportation system is at close to the maximum capacity that it can expect to operate without major incidents.

3

SCENARIO 1: BEYOND THE HORIZON

Economy

Large U.S. debt

Increasingly efficient maritime trade

U.S. diplomatic bargaining power has become somewhat hampered by the economic reality that U.S. national debt to China is increasing. Global markets experienced substantial volatility in 2024-2027 as China threatens on-and-off to sell a substantial portion of its U.S. treasuries. The U.S. feared an economic downturn, especially since growth has been stagnant, in part because of the total government debt, which now looms at a record 120% of GDP. Large military expenditures, intended to counter rising China and address instability elsewhere, have fueled the increase in U.S. debt. Although China has managed to find new markets for exports throughout southeast Asia and into Africa, it still

needs the U.S. to import its goods, and thus ultimately stops short of a large sell-off of U.S. treasuries.[1]

Maritime trade has accelerated within and through the Indo-Pacific and California. The proliferation of real-time business analytics, human-assisted machine decisionmaking, robotics, and commercial drones has multiplied the timeliness and efficiency of maritime transport for just-in-time manufacturing. Maritime vessel traffic (increasingly autonomous) has doubled, including oil tankers and cargo vessels going through the Strait of Malacca.

TODAY'S HEADLINES

The Gazette

THE JOURNAL

Natural gas flows at capacity via Maritime Silk Road

GLOBAL ECONOMY

Nigeria just keeps growing; who will get the economic advantage?

API

National debt hits a record

[1] What this means for the Coast Guard in 2030: Confidence in the U.S. economy has dropped and the economy is experiencing a strong downward trend. Fewer people are investing in the market, interest rates are down, people are expecting to retire later and have lower income levels during retirement. Unemployment is up and military and Coast Guard careers are especially attractive because of relative stability and job security.

4

SCENARIO 1: BEYOND THE HORIZON

Technology

Subsidence and sea level risk causing problems in the mid-Atlantic

Record hurricane damage impacting Coast Guard assets

Security has been largely automated at port facilities, with use of biometrics fully replacing Transportation Worker Identify Cards (TWIC) for port employees. Paperless bills of lading are on the rise; ports like Los Angeles-Long Beach, New York-New Jersey, and Boston are experimenting with digital ledger formats.

Biometrics have also advanced to a state where they can be used to identify unusual and suspicious behavior with remarkable accuracy. Public places and facilities such as ports have increasingly installed surveillance upgrades that enable security personnel to identify individuals before they engage in disorderly conduct. This type of technology is available to law enforcement to help cue action when actors display malicious intent. There have been a number of small-scale terrorist attacks thwarted with this technology, which has allowed anti-terrorism efforts to be more effective while simultaneously decreasing the amount spent on counterterrorism. This technology is also being applied to the drug interdiction mission initiatives, with positive results. It is predicted that drug interdiction efforts and spending will also drop as the technology matures and the Coast Guard relies more upon biometrics and other advances in identity management. Surveys suggest that the general public is embracing this type of surveillance activity as a means for enhancing security in cities that continue to grow.

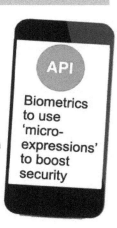

API

Biometrics to use 'micro-expressions' to boost security

Climate

Subsidence and sea level risk causing problems in the mid-Atlantic

Record hurricane damage impacting Coast Guard assets

THE DAILY

Port of Houston is rebounding 7 years after Hurricane Margot

U.S. maritime installations have begun flooding with greater frequency. A combination of sea level rise and subsidence meant that the mid-Atlantic region has suffered from sustained tidal flooding and periodic limited access to facilities. To maintain access and capability, several Coast Guard small boat stations from New Jersey to South Carolina within one mile from of the coast plan to move inland by 2035. So far, only 10% of Coast Guard stations have relocated. The other 90% of facilities routinely suffer some degradation in operational readiness during high tide cycles and storm surge.

Hurricanes in 2023, 2025, and 2026 produced record damage in southeastern Texas (including Houston), southern Louisiana, and Virginia, respectively. As a result of these three hurricanes, $8 billion worth of damage was done to Coast Guard facilities and assets. The facilities and assets have yet to be replaced.

5

SCENARIO 1: BEYOND THE HORIZON

Society

Large U.S. debt
Increasingly efficient maritime trade

Austerity measures such as rolling back healthcare and social services spending have become important issues ahead of the 2032 presidential election. In particular, Medicare, Medicaid, and veteran healthcare spending face deep potential cuts. In addition, people with insurance through their employers and the self-insured have begun paying much more out of their own pockets. The desire for better health-care coverage becomes a major determinant in people's career decisions.

To the surprise of demographers, the U.S. population has begun growing younger, reversing the aging population of previous decades. This was due to two factors: a change in immigration laws led to a vast increase in immigration levels in the early 2020s—primarily of young adults, some of whom are coming with children. Easier rules for legal immigration meant there has been a large dropoff in illegal immigration. The population growth in the U.S. is also due to a baby boom among millennials and Generation Z, reflecting the fact that childcare became free from birth onwards in 2022, funded by the federal government. The result is that U.S. population has grown faster than it had in decades, and immigration has swelled the

The Tribune
Bankrupt CSU Dominguez Hills, UC Merced join growing list of closures

ranks of the workforce. The percentage of the population that is employed has begun to grow.

At a time of perceived national vulnerability, many young adults have become interested in joining military services to contribute to their country. Service careers have also gained attractiveness for their longevity and medical benefits.

Additionally, the cost of education has continued to increase, so many parents whose children attend universities want them to choose high-earning career paths to recoup the costs of their educations. However, a large percentage of young people have been sufficiently deterred by the high cost of universities that they are seeking alternative educational credentials, such as "IT bootcamps" and massive open online courses (MOOCs). The result is that many universities have closed.

As a result of population growth and the popularity of military service careers, the Coast Guard is inundated with more applications than ever. The number of applicants with college degrees is at an all-time low.

6

A2. Scenario 1: Beyond the Horizon Summary

PROJECT EVERGREEN V

FUTURE SCENARIO 1: BEYOND THE HORIZON

TODAY IS SEPTEMBER 10, 2030. A LOT HAS CHANGED

Geopolitics

The U.S. is in direct competition with Chinese influence ushered in by its maritime "Silk Road" project. China has used investments to create access to ports across the Asia Pacific, East Africa, and most recently the West Coast of the U.S. This move has been used as justification to increase the use of Chinese military vessels to conduct freedom of navigation patrols and anti-piracy operations. The increase in maritime trade has also elicited a U.S. response that has spread thin American naval assets. Analysts say that maritime transportation system is close to maximum capacity.

Economy

The diplomatic bargaining power of the U.S. is hampered by the increasing U.S. national debt to China. The total government debt looms at a record high of 120% of Gross Domestic Product. Although China has expanded its consumer market, it still depends on the U.S. market to purchase its goods, which prevents China from selling off U.S. treasuries. New technologies have increased the rate and scale of maritime trade, and vessel traffic (increasingly autonomous) had doubled.

Climate

Climate-related change such as rising sea levels and increased hurricanes and storms have affected Coast Guard infrastructure and facilities. To escape the rise in sea level and the resulting sustained tidal flooding, various Coast Guard facilities are relocated inland; those that have yet to be moved cannot reliably perform duties at high tide. Several hurricanes in the Gulf of Mexico and along the eastern seaboard have caused billions of dollars' in damage to Coast Guard facilities and assets, many of which have yet to be repaired or replaced.

Technology

Technology has had a significant impact on how the Coast Guard conducts security and law enforcement operations. The advanced used of automation in port facilities has seen biometrics replace traditional identification cards. Advanced surveillance systems in ports have been implemented to identify actors displaying malicious intent. These new systems have been successful in thwarting terrorist attacks and preventing criminal behavior. Surveys suggest the general public is embracing this type of surveillance activity.

Society

The dynamics and demographics of U.S. society have changed significantly based on national policy development and implementation. Immigration reform has caused a vast increase in immigration levels in the early 2020s, bringing in a younger population with a higher birth rate. The federal funding of childcare has caused a baby boom among millennials and generation Z. As a result, the U.S. population has grown faster that it has in decades. Because of a perceived national vulnerability and the pivot to technical skills-based jobs, young adults express a greater interest in joining the military. The Coast Guard is inundated with more applications than ever before.

---

[1] What this means for the Coast Guard in 2030: Confidence in the U.S. economy has dropped and the economy is experiencing a strong downward trend. Fewer people are investing in the market, interest rates are down, and people are expected to retire later and have lower income levels during retirement. Unemployment is up because of the slower economy, and military and Coast Guard careers are especially attractive because of relative stability and job security.

PROJECT EVERGREEN V
FUTURE SCENARIO 2: STEADY GROWTH

WHAT DOES THE WORLD LOOK LIKE IN 2030?

Climate
Storm frequency and intensity remains stable
Rapid ice melt in the Arctic opens access to the sea

Geopolitics
Global partnerships lead to a period of stability
U.S. increases presence abroad to support maritime safety and global fisheries management

Society
U.S. works to avoid a virus from abroad
Drugs are out; counter-drug efforts are in
Extended family support systems are the norm

Technology
Space-based technology has improved navigation but has also come with risks
Cryptocurrency use is on the rise

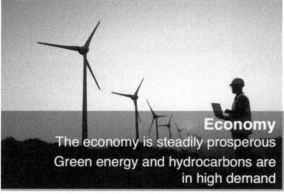

Economy
The economy is steadily prosperous
Green energy and hydrocarbons are in high demand

Clockwise from upper left: Pglam via Getty Images; Kondor83 via Adobe Stock; Imgorthand via Getty Images; BulentBARIS via Getty Images; aapsky via Getty Images

SCENARIO 2: STEADY GROWTH

Today is September 10, 2030. A lot has changed

Economy

The economy is steadily prosperous
Green energy and hydrocarbons are in high demand

The U.S. has entered a stable period of economic prosperity. The boom in hydrocarbons continues, and the market for green technologies has started to expand as the U.S. grows more urban, engineering solutions improve, and the U.S. public has demanded more resilience for the energy grid. More installations are built to capture wave and wind energy in coastal areas, including within the Great Lakes. Locations near existing shore infrastructure are popular due to access to services and land availability. Some small-to-medium sized ports have downsized or have begun renting space out as shipping operations become more efficient. As more dual-purpose transportation and energy sites are considered, decision-makers struggle with how to integrate these different types of infrastructure where usages conflict.

TODAY'S HEADLINES

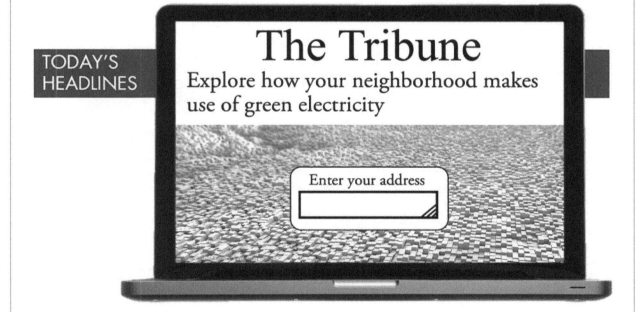

The Tribune

Explore how your neighborhood makes use of green electricity

Enter your address

This scenario was generated by HSOAC-RAND in support of the U.S. Coast Guard's Project Evergreen V. This is not a forecast, but one of many plausible potential futures. It was developed by combining major drivers of change and imagining their potential interactions and outcomes. (*Updated January 2020*)

HOMELAND SECURITY
OPERATIONAL ANALYSIS CENTER

2

SCENARIO 2: STEADY GROWTH

Climate
Storm frequency and intensity remains stable
Rapid ice melt in the Arctic opens access to the sea

The predicted increase in storm strength and frequency has not come to fruition in the past decade, and global storm damage rates remains steady, although scientists say there is a possibility for increasing storm intensity and frequency in the next decade.

The largest climate-related global changes can be seen in the Arctic, as the Arctic ice melt continues at an unprecedented rate. Strong global demand for oil and gas, intense Arctic ice melt, and improvements in deep sea drilling technologies have improved the economic viability of hydrocarbon fields under the Arctic Ocean. All five Arctic Ocean-adjacent states—Canada, Denmark (via Greenland), Norway, Russia, and the U.S.—have agreed through diplomatic discussions that cooperation between them helps all stakeholders gain the most from this economic windfall. China's interest in the Arctic has not abated, but China has been obliged to operate within the diplomatic guidelines for Arctic Observers expanded by the Arctic Council in 2023. This compliance has been managed primarily by Russia and Canada—China's two primary partners in the region.

China has continued to access Russian energy resources and is increasingly shipping cargo via the northwest and northeast sea routes. These are open to semi-autonomous cargo ships taking pre-set routes from March until November. Russia and Canada primarily manage these routes, paying a portion of commercial fees to Norway, Greenland, and the U.S. to maintain continuity of safety and stewardship when these ships venture closer to their respective maritime domains. Among other benefits, these funds have fueled Alaska's economy. To increase the length of the shipping season and accommodate predicted increases in traffic, the Coast Guard received approval to build ten more ice breakers. So far, there have been no major incidents in U.S. Arctic waters, but there have been three accidents with loss of life and one minor oil spill in Russian waters in the past decade. Funds have been allocated to increase SAR and environmental protection capabilities in the U.S. Arctic, but the tyranny of distance remains problematic.

TODAY'S HEADLINES

Alaska Today

Northern Sea Route tariffs fund Alaskan universities

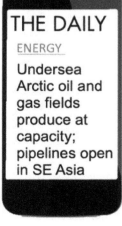
THE DAILY

ENERGY

Undersea Arctic oil and gas fields produce at capacity; pipelines open in SE Asia

3

SCENARIO 2: STEADY GROWTH

Geopolitics

Global partnerships lead to a period of stability
U.S. increases presence abroad to support maritime safety and global fisheries management

The U.S. has a strong presence abroad, and commitment to alliances and partnerships—particularly NATO—has allowed the U.S. to lead the world into a period of global stability.

The U.S. increasingly works with partners along heavily used historical shipping areas to maintain freedom of movement. The U.S. is increasing its presence—focusing on safety and sea lane stewardship—around the South China Sea (though the U.S. has avoided the Taiwan Strait), Gulf of Aden, Gulf of Oman, and Persian Gulf, and Brazil's largest ports of Itajui and Tubarao. As part of its increased presence, the U.S. has partnered with the Philippines, Malaysia, Indonesia, Tanzania, and Brazil to share its new space-based advanced AToN technology. This increased presence and technology sharing has been welcomed internationally, as the global maritime shipping community has experienced five years of all-time-low accident numbers.

Increased U.S. maritime presence in Southeast Asia and the Middle East countries has been tolerated somewhat more than theorists predicted in the early 2020s due to U.S. contributions to protecting fisheries and limiting the transport of illegal catch, including through trans-shipment. After a series of studies predicted catastrophic effects of over-fishing and climate change on fisheries by 2035, many fish-producing and -consuming countries around the world agreed to find new ways to work together to preserve this valuable food source for the now 10 billion people predicted to inhabit the planet by 2050. Governance alliances for global fisheries management are currently in development, with over 75% of coastal nations participating.

TODAY'S HEADLINES

API

Asia birth rates still dropping

The Gazette

Fish fraud on the rise: Farmed seafood sold as 'luxury' wild fillets

SCENARIO 2: STEADY GROWTH

Society

U.S. works to avoid a virus from abroad

Drugs are out; counter-drug efforts are in

Extended family support systems are the norm

The market for recreational drugs has not expanded; in fact, marijuana legalization has been scaled back. Many states have moved to limit the number, locations, and hours of dispensaries, and a cultural shift means smoking marijuana is seen with disdain, as smoking cigarettes once was. The U.S. government is making a dent in the opioid crisis that peaked in number of deaths and prescriptions in 2019. This required not only working closely with patients, care providers, and legal drug manufacturers, but also stifling illegal trafficking of opioids into the U.S., primarily from Russia via staging points in Venezuela. Despite less recreational drug use, counter-drug campaigns are well-funded because of the strong anti-drug culture.

A series of scandals in 2026 revealed that some American women have sold frozen human eggs to Asian countries, where demand is on the rise. Ships became the most common way to transport frozen eggs, where they were easy to hide in containers of legal cargo. The demand for healthy human eggs was driven by the outbreak of a virus causing mass sterilization and birth defects among some Asian populations. U.S. ports of entry continue to be on high alert for passengers who may carry the virus. The handful of cases that occurred in the U.S. have been contained. Assiduous efforts are made to interdict all U.S.-bound travelers from Asia who appear to be infected. However, the virus has spread to a substantial population in Panama, and there have been a number of cases in Costa Rica and Colombia. Due to both fear of the virus and its impact on local economies (particularly tourism), growing numbers of migrants from Costa Rica, Panama, and Colombia are seeking to enter the U.S. via Mexico. The Coast Guard has already detained a handful of boats carrying migrants from these nations near U.S. shores, and personnel performing this mission are increasingly concerned about exposure to the virus via pre-symptomatic carriers.

Prosperity and growing social acceptability of remote work has helped families move geographically closer together and has contributed to a decline in divorce. Extended family support systems have become the norm, and jobs that require relocating are less popular. Prospects for a "gig" economy have declined, with temporary work viewed as risky and low income. While this has created some incentives for young people to join military services, both they and their parents are highly concerned about the risks of injury or death that service careers may pose.

TODAY'S HEADLINES

THE JOURNAL

RI and Connecticut re-criminalize recreational marijuana

Biz Wire

Just 10% of Americans seek jobs in gig economy as temp work takes a dive

5

SCENARIO 2: STEADY GROWTH

Technology

Space-based technology has improved navigation but has also come with risks

Cryptocurrency use is on the rise

Smart contracts fueled by blockchain technology have helped manage growing demand for moving materials and goods around the world by increasing the efficiency of the shipping industry. Many organizations within maritime industries are moving toward more distributed decisions and operations for digital security, and toward greater responsiveness to local conditions and needs. U.S. flagged vessels have been required to install navigation system upgrades to support electronic aids to navigation, which will be the global standard by 2032. However, the "digitization" of the maritime industry has spurred increases in cyber piracy in the maritime domain. Hackers seeking ransom money disrupt ships' navigation systems and electronic tools and/or deny networks and systems used at ports until payments in digital currency are received.

In 2026, hackers may have begun testing a cyber weapon using a "back door" vulnerability built into digital navigation infrastructure that jams virtual buoys so that all operators can see on their screens is noise. Decentralization of the tech industry has enabled more multi-national partnerships and cooperation that has led to technology advances and proliferation, but it has also made it harder to detect nefarious activities by state and non-state actors alike.

Cryptocurrency has become very popular for international trade, but its vulnerability to hackers has caused a handful of risk-averse major U.S. companies to require precious metals be used for international trade, and heavily armed vessels carrying the metals have begun to traverse the oceans.

TODAY'S HEADLINES

API

Hackers hit Facebook's crypto cash yet again

The Light
Space is open for business

Will NASA need some interagency partners to manage it?

PROJECT EVERGREEN V

FUTURE SCENARIO 2: STEADY GROWTH

TODAY IS SEPTEMBER 10, 2030. A LOT HAS CHANGED

Geopolitics

The U.S. has a strong presence abroad, enabled by its commitments to significant partnerships such as NATO. These partnerships have allowed the U.S. to lead the world in a period of global stability. The U.S. has increased its presence forward focusing on safety and sea lane stewardship. The U.S. has partnered with several key countries to share advanced space-based AToN tech resulting in an all-time five-year low of maritime accidents. The U.S. has also contributed to the preservation and regulation of global fish stocks, enabling cooperation with nations all over the world.

Economy

The U.S. is in a period of stable economic prosperity. The development of the hydrocarbon industry, green tech, and a trend towards urbanization has allowed the U.S. to work on resilience for the energy grid. Efficiency and automation allowed some small to medium sized ports to downsize and rent out space for other infrastructure.

Climate

Climate-related predictions such as increased frequency and strength of hurricanes and storms have not occurred, and storm damage remains steady. The ice melt in the Arctic has increased at an unprecedented rate, resulting in more energy production through drilling and trade with the use of Arctic sea routes. The Arctic Council has managed to cooperate to develop this region as a trade route, setting guidelines for continuity of safety and stewardship. This increased usage of the Arctic has resulted in more funding allocated for environmental response, search and rescue capabilities, and ice operations.

Technology

Technology has increased the efficiency of the shipping industry through the implementation of electronic aids to navigation of U.S.-flagged vessels. The digitization of this industry is not without complications. Cyber piracy has allowed vulnerable systems to be hijacked and held for ransom until payments in digital currency are received. Cryptocurrency is now very popular for international trade, but due to its vulnerability to hackers some U.S. companies rely on precious metals for trade, resulting in heavily armed vessels carrying these metals.

Society

The nature of U.S. society has seen significant changes in how the family system organizes itself. Since remote work has become more socially acceptable, families have moved geographically closer together, resulting in extended family support systems and fewer divorces. The use of illegal drugs in the U.S. is unpopular, and drug use has been scaled back through effective campaigns. Counter-drug initiatives are well funded because of the strong cultural support for the anti-drug movement. A virus in Asia has resulted in mass sterilization and birth defects, which created a U.S. market for illegally selling frozen human eggs. The virus that caused these reproductive defects has popped up in other locations in Central and South America.

PROJECT EVERGREEN V
FUTURE SCENARIO 3: DIVERGING PATHS

WHAT DOES THE WORLD LOOK LIKE IN 2030?

Climate
Extreme weather damages
Midwest, South, and East Coast
Global fisheries are on the brink of collapse

Society
More migrants travel to Canada via US
Gig economy is on the rise

Geopolitics
Russia, U.S. turn inward
China takes a lead in the Arctic

Technology
Automatic security systems are
efficient but come with risks
Storm response technology fails

Economy
The U.S. prospers overall
West Coast's economy is a powerhouse

Clockwise from top left: EEI Tony, Juanmonino, swisshippo, uschoofs, KOHb, all via Getty Images

SCENARIO 3: DIVERGING PATHS

Today is September 10, 2030. A lot has changed

Geopolitics

Russia, U.S. turn inward
China takes a lead in the Arctic

Economic difficulties within Russia and a series of popular protests against cost of living, increased taxation, and "revised" health benefits result in a freeze of defense expenditures, as the Russian leadership tries to maintain peace at home and fears for its hold on power. China is frustrated by Russia's sudden turn inwards and looks to expand its options for international partners. The U.S. has limited its role abroad as it also focuses its resources inward.

China is changing international norms in a direction that serves its interests, especially in the Arctic. This convinces it to multiply diplomatic channels and efforts to "fit in" with international organizations such as the IMO and consider changing them from the inside. China is also increasing its economic investments with Arctic nations in order to gain a diplomatic and economic advantage in the Arctic. The U.S. is interested in rare earth reserves in Greenland, but a sudden decrease in the pace of Arctic warming has left these resources more difficult to extract than anticipated. The U.S. does not have equivalent capacity to operate in the Arctic, and China and Russia have a strong regional advantage.

TODAY'S HEADLINES

The Gazette

China hopes to gain advantage by investing in Arctic nations

API
President West lists domestic priorities

This scenario was generated by HSOAC-RAND in support of the U.S. Coast Guard's Project Evergreen V. This is not a forecast, but one of many plausible potential futures. It was developed by combining major drivers of change and imagining their potential interactions and outcomes. (*Updated January 2020*)

HSOAC
HOMELAND SECURITY
OPERATIONAL ANALYSIS CENTER

SCENARIO 3: DIVERGING PATHS

Economy

The U.S. prospers overall
West Coast's economy is a powerhouse

TODAY'S
HEADLINES

The Light

California signs deal with China for rare earth elements

Biz Wire

Machines alleviate ports' labor shortage

The West Coast of the U.S. has been extremely prosperous in the last decade, although periods of extreme drought continue. Jobs in advanced technology have become more common, and it has become difficult to find manual labor. The region has prospered through its continued development of applications for automating basic human tasks.

A conglomerate of companies in California that comprise 92% of the state's economy has struck deals with Chinese state-owned enterprises to gain access to more rare earth elements to further develop computing and communications technologies. In an unprecedented move, the state of California has been acting as a proxy for the California conglomerate. This diplomatic and economic deal is struck following a more limited U.S.

presence in southeast Asia and promises to share some technologies with China.

Rapid economic growth has increased Gross Domestic Product (and tax revenues). The national debt has come down due to increased productivity throughout the labor market.[1] Digital infrastructure is centralized in urban areas, which increases the draw of people to cities, especially at the coasts. The combination of economic prosperity and increased coastal population has led to a surge in popularity for recreational boating and ocean-based extreme sports and fitness challenges. A recent multi-day "100-mile sea kayak ironman" between Charleston and Myrtle Beach left many competitors in need of rescue for exposure, dehydration, and exhaustion.

[1] What this means for the Coast Guard in 2030: The US is entering a period of economic prosperity and stability. Employment rates are up, median household incomes are up, government spending and funding for the Coast Guard is high but not at the cost of increasing national debt.

3

SCENARIO 3: DIVERGING PATHS

 Climate

Extreme weather damages Midwest, South and East Coast

Domestic and global fisheries are on the brink of collapse

The northern jet stream has increasingly started to meander and experience stalled Rossby waves, which are bends in this "air river" that get stuck in place for days at a time. This has led to unusual geographic patterns in low- and high-pressure systems.

Intense rainstorms have battered the upper Midwest from March through November for the last three years, resulting in extreme flooding in the Great Lakes as well as in the Des Moines, Mississippi, Missouri, Ohio, and Platte Rivers. At the same time, the Great Plains states and the southeastern U.S. have experienced repeated wintertime Derecho storms, resulting in hurricane-force winds, thunderstorms, and flooding in areas around the Arkansas, Missouri, and Rio Grande Rivers, and around the ports of Baltimore, Norfolk, Savannah, and Tampa. Storms have caused multiple hazardous material dispersions from cargo ships on the Atlantic seaboard.

THE DAILY

Midwest, Mid-Atlantic prepare for Derecho storms and rainstorms

Some fisheries have migrated northward. However, slower-than-expected sea ice melt means that fish cannot be extracted from northern waters at rates that meet rising global and U.S. demand for sea-based protein. Illegal fishing, both domestic and internationally, is on the rise as quality fish become more rare.

 Technology

Automatic security systems are efficient but come with risks

Storm response technology fails

Applications designed to digitally manage storm response and recovery are not secure and massively fail due to cyberattacks that appear intended to confuse U.S. authorities while foreign agents smuggle drugs and humans into the U.S. through disrupted ports.

The ports of Los Angeles-Long Beach, Portland, and Seattle are on the road to becoming "minimally manned." Security, for example, is fully automated using two-factor authentication that leverages biometrics and implanted microchips that have replaced the Transportation Worker Identity Credential (TWIC). Analysts at

centralized facilities can monitor both maritime and road traffic to and from the port and leverage new electronic bills of lading. This new technology seems to be improving security and reducing costs, but the West Coast has not experienced major storm activity. Crime in recently storm-battered communities has skyrocketed. "Climate criminals" have begun positioning themselves to steal property based on weather pattern predictions; there have been large-scale break-ins at multiple port facilities after storms, causing a spate of Hollywood movies on the subject.

4

SCENARIO 3: DIVERGING PATHS

Society

More migrants travel through US to reach Canada

Gig economy is on the rise

The increasingly erratic climate has started a global trend of "climate refugees." Significant damage from climate-related disasters means the U.S. is not seen as a "climate sanctuary," but many migrants travel through the U.S. to reach Canada, which has had fewer climate impacts.

As families disperse, fewer people are nearby to help elderly relatives. This has increased the market for professional caregivers and pressure on hospitals to provide comprehensive care for the elderly. The large number of elderly Americans in U.S. Midwest and Southeast storm areas complicates relief efforts.

Improved health-care coverage has rapidly increased self-employment since individuals are no longer seeking employer coverage. Moreover, the provision of a low basic income for all—$1,000 per month for every person—has given people more confidence and flexibility. Many people of all ages, but particularly those under 40, are excited at the prospect of doing work on their own terms: they like the freedom of working for the clients whom they prefer, and to do so largely when they want. The result has been a blossoming "gig economy," as people seek independence over the stability of a consistent job, let alone an enduring career.

TODAY'S HEADLINES

API

50% of Americans are self-employed

The Tribune

America's elderly often homeless after disasters

DISASTER: Hundreds still without shelter months after storms

Jed Smith (above) and Patty Rice (left) both became homeless after the recent flooding.

5

PROJECT EVERGREEN V
FUTURE SCENARIO 3: DIVERGING PATHS

TODAY IS SEPTEMBER 10, 2030. A LOT HAS CHANGED

Geopolitics

the U.S. and Russia have a limited presence abroad because of their decisions to focus more on domestic issues. In Russia's absence China has worked within international organizations such as the IMO to assert influence and change norms from the inside. China is the now the predominant force of political and economic influence for the Arctic.

Economy

The U.S. is in a period of stable economic prosperity with huge gains seen on the West Coast through the emergence of large conglomerates. Efficiency and automation have made manual labor jobs increasingly rare. Through increased productivity in the labor market, the national debt has come down significantly resulting in the rapid growth of the U.S. GDP.[1]

Climate

Climate abnormalities have caused unusual patterns in high- and low-pressure systems. Significant storms across the Midwest and in the Mississippi basin have led to extensive flooding for the past several years. Flooding from storms has caused hazardous material spills at major East Coast ports. Illegal fishing has been on the rise, both domestically and internationally.

Technology

Technology has increased the efficiency of the shipping industry through the implementation of automation in major ports on the West Coast. Programs designed to manage storm response have been largely unsuccessful due to cyber attacks. These attacks have been used by foreign agents to smuggle drugs and humans in through U.S. disrupted ports. This criminal activity is not limited to foreign agents but also U.S. citizens termed "climate criminals" who have conducted large scale break in and robberies in port facilities after storms.

Society

The U.S. has seen significant increases in migrants crossing the homeland en route to Canada to relocate to an environment with a less erratic climate. Growing geographic dispersion of families has left an aging population with fewer care options, spurring an increase in caregiving jobs. With improved access to healthcare and a universal basic income, more Americans are moving toward working less traditional and less consistent jobs in the "gig economy," which allows for increased flexibility.

---

[1] What this means for the Coast Guard in 2030: The US is entering a period of economic prosperity and stability. Employment rates are up, median household incomes are up, government spending/funding for the Coast Guard is high but not at the cost of increasing national debt.

PROJECT EVERGREEN V
FUTURE SCENARIO 4: INCREASING DISORDER

WHAT DOES THE WORLD LOOK LIKE IN 2030?

Climate
Intense, frequent storms
Sea level rise impacts coastal operations

Geopolitics
Russia establishes Arctic dominance
China and Mexico team up for mutual economic gain

Technology
Electric car and vessel technology matures
Drone use up abroad

Economy
The dollar loses value
Large US debt

Society
Americans more risk tolerant

New strain of HIV means more demand for illegal drugs

Social support systems weaken

Clockwise from top: Stormtalk via Wikimedia; Yuri Acrus via Getty Images; Solvod via Getty Images; Nadia via Getty Images; SeppFriedhuber via Getty Images;

SCENARIO 4: INCREASING DISORDER

Today is September 10, 2030. A lot has changed

Geopolitics

Russia establishes Arctic dominance
China and Mexico team up for mutual economic gain

Russia works to establish its position as the strongman in the Arctic and extend its "near abroad" to America's doorstep. Russia has fully operationalized its dual-purpose military and civilian infrastructure along the Northern Sea Route and charges tariffs for shipping through the region.

Russia becomes increasingly assertive with its Arctic neighbors, threatening to pull out of the Barents Euro-Arctic Council and unilaterally denouncing the 2011 treaty delimiting its border with Norway in the Barents Sea. Pro-Russian media sources, and occasionally the Russian government, periodically claim that the U.S. violated the 1867 agreement by which it purchased Alaska, demanding that Russia be compensated. A series of incidents on and near Svalbard involving "fishermen" who might be in fact Russian military makes Norway increasingly nervous. Norway reaches out to its NATO allies to obtain a formal commitment on their part that they would consider an attack on Svalbard to be an attack on Norway, which would trigger the collective defense clause of the Atlantic Treaty.

TODAY'S HEADLINES

API

Last US troops exit Jordan

Alaska Today

Russia redefines 'near abroad' to include Alaska

The U.S. focuses more internally as hurricanes and other storms repeatedly batter coastlines, especially in the Gulf of Mexico, southeast, Caribbean, Hawaii, and Alaska. However, in 2026, the U.S. realized that disengaging from global affairs leaves a void for others to fill. China has continued to fund infrastructure projects in North and South America and is now offering lucrative trade deals in exchange for gaining a military foothold. China sought connections with Mexico in particular. The trade treaty that the two countries concluded has increased their exchanges, in value, by 300 percent. China-built infrastructure has earned Mexico City the nickname of "Shanghai of the Americas," and Mexico becomes a leader in the region in various industries, including the production of electric cars.

This scenario was generated by HSOAC-RAND in support of the U.S. Coast Guard's Project Evergreen V. This is not a forecast, but one of many plausible potential futures. It was developed by combining major drivers of change and imagining their potential interactions and outcomes. (*Updated January 2020*)

HSOAC
HOMELAND SECURITY
OPERATIONAL ANALYSIS CENTER

2

SCENARIO 4: INCREASING DISORDER

Economy

The dollar loses value

Large US debt

The dollar is no longer the dominant currency globally; its role was eroded by the relative rise of China (whose yuan is now dominant) and accelerated by a series of successful hacks of U.S. banks that led to counterfeit digital dollars proliferating. China is able to effectively leverage its majority ownership of U.S. debt, which has grown to 116% of Gross Domestic Product, in great-power competition. With encouragement by Russia, China suggested in 2027 that it will start to sell off treasuries if the U.S. attempts to interfere with its activities with Russia in the Arctic and South America. World markets continued to be shaky following this news, and the U.S. economy stagnated further. The depressed U.S. economy has meant a large drop off in immigration pressures, as other regions of the world offer more economic opportunity.

Ships have begun to move freely through much of the Eurasian Arctic from March until late November. Much of the surface vessel traffic consists of small semi- or fully-autonomous cargo vessels. Autonomous shipping began as a joint venture by China and Russia. The Arctic has become the only place in the world where autonomous vessels regularly operate due to safety concerns raised through the International Maritime Organization (IMO) and by maritime insurers. There has been a moderate increase in the presence of (non-autonomous) fishing vessels, tourist ships, and pleasure craft. Tanker traffic rose from a small baseline in the early 2020s but is experiencing limited growth due to a shaky decline over the past several years in global consumption of hydrocarbons.

The refocusing of U.S. military budgets has made additional funds available to support maritime infrastructure upgrades and disaster recovery. The U.S. will have three new icebreakers online by 2033 and, thanks to advances in space technology, communications systems in the Arctic have been established for even the most remote regions. The Coast Guard is increasingly seen as a critical organization on multiple fronts, and Congress has fully funded all Coast Guard budget requests during the past five years.

TODAY'S HEADLINES

The Gazette

Economy continues to stagnate

API

US set to buy 3 new icebreakers

3

SCENARIO 4: INCREASING DISORDER

Climate

Intense, frequent storms
Sea level rise impacting coastal operations

THE DAILY

Great Lakes area preps for more tornados

Rising sea levels and intensifying storms throughout the year have resulted in massive needs for infrastructure repair and recovery. A series of intense tornadoes ripped through the Great Lakes in 2026, destroying a large amount of shore infrastructure there, in addition to harming people, homes, and businesses. Port complexes and coastal military installations in Louisiana, Houston, Virginia, and Seattle (among others) frequently find themselves underwater during seasonal storm surges, and often face moderate flooding even in the absence of storms, limiting access to the ports and assets.

At the same time, worsening drought conditions have contributed to declining populations in parts of the western United States. Water rationing has become particularly severe in California, and the collapse of the state's agricultural economy has caused a mass exodus.

Technology

Electric car and vessel technology matures
Drone use increases abroad

Biz Wire

Malaysia unveils faster, more fuel-efficient e-Ship

Collaborative engineering research by Japan and India has developed large, long-lasting batteries, such as those that can be utilized to power vehicles and vessels. Isuzu and Tata were among the first to take advantage of these technologies in 2025, which has drastically reshaped offerings for fully electric vehicles. These companies have helped proliferate these cars in southeast Asia, where they continue to be in high demand due to intensifying adverse effects of air pollution on human health and well being.

Tsuneishi Shipbuilding and Malaysia Marine and Heavy Engineering have been partnering with Port-Liner and Rauma Marine Constructions to build a series of all-electric cruise ships, ferries, cargo ships, fishing boats, and patrol boats. Electric ship technology is slowly being adopted worldwide, particularly in Asia and Europe. In 2028, the U.S. government began an analysis of alternatives for replacing many of its smaller military vessels with e-ships.

Small "drone" boats or unmanned surface vessels—primarily used by criminal organizations to transport illegal goods and by law enforcement to surveil ports—have been proliferating rapidly since the early 2020s. Russia pioneers the large-scale use of autonomous surveillance vessels in the Bering Strait to monitor vessel traffic and environmental conditions, including early warning of fuel spills and whale movements into shipping lanes.

4

SCENARIO 4: INCREASING DISORDER

Society

US population more risk tolerant

New strain of HIV means illegal drug demand increasing

Social support systems weaken

Animal-rights activists have contributed to a cultural change regarding perception and treatment of animals. At the same time, plant-based substitutes for fish and meat have become inexpensive and highly palatable. As a result, U.S. consumption of both fish and meat has plummeted.

An increasing ability to monitor human productivity at scale has produced convincing results that work periods should not exceed four hours. The U.S. has followed New Zealand, Japan, and Sweden in transitioning to a "split shift" economy in which workers take substantial breaks between two four-hour work periods per day. Many organizations have begun to favor a system for splitting shifts that also enables 24-hour operations where remote work—increasingly accepted in society—is the norm. More Americans have embraced temporary employment than ever before. Temporary employment is most common among Americans under 25 and those over 50 as they seek partial retirement.

The younger public in the U.S. has become very excited about autonomy, including using autonomous boats for recreation. Autonomous boating in the U.S. becomes popular for international visitors as well as domestically. Ocean-facing as well as inland water harbors and marinas are in the process of expanding and upgrading to handle the volume of demand and rapidly evolving technology. Areas like the Salton Sea in California, Rend Lake in Illinois, and Onondaga Lake in New York that were previously allowed to decay are being refurbished as new water resort areas. Incidents involving passenger injuries, wildlife collisions, and fuel spills suggest that regulations are unevenly followed in this emerging industry.

The Light

HOW WORK HAS CHANGED

Remote, split-shift work catches fire	Temp work is replacing retirement

Embracing the digital environment has also led to an erosion of social connections between people. Cohabitation—rather than marriage—and single-parent households are on the rise. This, combined with a greater tolerance for risky behavior and the devastating effects of storms on housing and employment, has led to more poverty, especially among families with small children.

A drug-resistant form of HIV has appeared and is spreading rapidly as riskier sexual behaviors have become more common. Military services are struggling over the question of how to reach recruitment goals despite a large percentage of the teenage population testing positive for the new form of HIV. The illegal drug trade has seen a surge in demand for "miraculous" HIV cures from abroad that have gained traction on social media. Many of these imported drugs are laced with lethal substances.

5

A8. Scenario 4: Increasing Disorder Summary

PROJECT EVERGREEN V
FUTURE SCENARIO 4: INCREASING DISORDER

TODAY IS SEPTEMBER 10, 2030. A LOT HAS CHANGED

Geopolitics

The U.S. has left its role as an influencer of global affairs. In its absence, Russia has become the predominant force in the Arctic, where it controls all maritime traffic and has a significant system of infrastructure to support civilian and military operations. China has heavily invested in Mexico, causing Mexico to become a leader in various industries, including electric car production.

Economy

U.S. prosperity is declining as the yuan replaces the dollar as the dominant global currency. Effectively leveraging its majority ownership of U.S. debt, China has threatened to sell U.S. treasuries if the U.S. interferes with its foreign policy.[1] The U.S. economic downturn has caused immigration to drop significantly. The lack of U.S. presence in the Arctic has allowed China and Russia to establish a joint venture operating autonomous shipping in the northern sea lanes. This autonomous shipping has yet to become popular worldwide because of the IMO's safety concerns. Because of the limited defense budget, Congress has increasingly seen the Coast Guard as critical on multiple fronts and has fully funded its budget requests for the past five years.

Climate

As a result of climate change, sea levels have been on the rise, more frequent storms have caused significant damage at port complexes and military installations, causing a need for infrastructure repair and recovery. More frequent drought in the western United States has caused water rationing, the collapse of California's agriculture economy, and a mass exodus of the state's population.

Technology

Collaboration between Japan and India has led to significant advances in battery technology, resulting in the growth of the electric car and even the electric shipping industry. Asian shipbuilding firms have capitalized on this emerging tech to create cruise ships, car ferries, cargo ships, fishing boats, and patrol boats using electric powertrains. The U.S. military is even considering replacing smaller military vessels with electric platforms. Autonomous "drone" boats have been a recent trend used by criminal organizations to move goods and people.

Society

Americans are eating more plant-based substitutes for meat and fish. The U.S. labor market has seen traditional workdays transition into smaller blocks with more freedom for people to work "on demand"; because of this, remote work is very popular. The traditional family unit is less common, and co-habitation in place of marriage is the norm. More risky social behavior has resulted in an outbreak of drug-resistant HIV in the younger population. Access to illegal drugs that offer "miracle cures" is a significant concern as some products are laced with harmful substances. The HIV outbreak has also made recruiting for the Coast Guard and armed forces challenging.

---

[1] What this means for the Coast Guard in 2030: The U.S. economy is in a depression/recession period. The U.S. is no longer an economic world leader. Investments in U.S. markets are at an all-time low. Unemployment is up, and household income is down.

SCENARIO 1

Evergreen Times

Vol. 30, Edition 10,950   TUESDAY, SEPTEMBER 10, 2030 $3.50

Japanese, S. Korean Coast Guard Vessels Collide

Injuries and fatalities unknown; both nations send warships to disputed islands

The ships were near the disputed Dokdo Islands. (likaJzuchiN via Wikimedia)

SEA OF JAPAN—South Korean and Japanese coast guard vessels collided today near the disputed Dokdo Islands (which Japan calls the Takeshima Islands) in the Sea of Japan. In a dramatic escalation of a month-long standoff, both countries are racing to send warships.

Neither vessel is in immediate danger of sinking, and casualties are unknown. Japan and South Korea are also sending coast guard vessels and civilian vessels to tow the damaged ships home.

At the same time, three Chinese warships are rapidly approaching the Japanese-administered Senkaku Islands (which China calls the Diaoyu Islands) in the East China Sea, joining Chinese "maritime militia" vessels that have been circumnavigating the islands for a week.

The U.S. Coast Guard's base in Okinawa and U.S. Navy forces in the region are struggling to respond to the emerging crisis. Both are already strained by frequent standoffs with Chinese maritime forces and fishing fleets in the South China Sea, the Taiwan Strait, and around the Senkaku Islands. The result has been low morale and high stress levels among personnel. Many leave the Coast Guard after a tour in Okinawa—or even before deploying—and say they would rather draw on their blended retirement accounts than endure the posting.

The high tempo of operations is believed to have contributed to a recent series of fatal accidents traced to operator errors that stemmed from personnel shortfalls, stress, and sleep deprivation, as well as maintenance backlogs for the cutters, boats, helicopters, and fixed-wing aircraft stationed in Okinawa. That families can't join service-members on Okinawa is also widely held to contribute to the stress.

INSIDE

Coast Guard officer shoots 7 in East Africa

A Coast Guard officer who had complained of stress from pirates, standoffs with hostile Yemeni forces, and the harsh environment at the Djibouti station shot seven co-workers. *Page 2*

USCG still lacks facilities 3 years after Hurricane Velma

After Hurricane Velma's unprecedented devastation to the Gulf Coast, the Coast Guard can't meet all mission requirements due to a lack of appropriate facilities and coastal infrastructure. *Page 9*

Free childcare created a baby boom—and it's paying for itself

Critics of the federally funded childcare program argued it would cost more than it provides, but the initial data points to good news for the economy as more dual-income families are flush with disposable income despite record birthrates. *Page 27*

Automation in ports means smooth sailing for international trade

Ports are following the overall trend of using more surveillance technologies. The shipping industry reports fewer delays and greater efficiency despite concerns about privacy. *Page 32*

Evergreen Times

Vol. 30, Edition 10,951   WEDNESDAY, SEPTEMBER 11, 2030 $3.50

Disasters devastate western Alaska

Thousands affected by quake, landslides, and tsunami near Bering Strait

ANCHORAGE—A magnitude 8.4 earthquake triggered tsunamis and landslides in western Alaska last night. Some villages in the Bering Strait region appear buried or submerged.

Immediate damage from the earthquake itself was limited, but landslides buried large parts of some villages, particularly in regions where permafrost had thawed in recent years. A tsunami swept through the region about an hour later, easily overtopping the eroded coastline. Satellite imagery shows coastal villages mostly or entirely underwater.

Casualties and survivors are unknown. Many fishermen and two cruise ships were offshore at the time, and their status is also unknown due to damaged communications infrastructure throughout the region.

The Coast Guard station in Nome appears to have sustained substantial damage, and debris on roadways appears to be impeding the ability of personnel to get to the station itself. Some Coast Guard personnel may also have sustained injuries or may be caring for injured family members.

In addition to the station at Nome, Coast Guard assets in the Bering Sea, at the station in Utqiavik (formerly

The earthquake ruptured roadways near Nome, Alaska. (Rob Witter/USGS)

Barrow) and in Kodiak are rushing to provide relief, but because of the vast distances involved, it will take hours to reach the region by air and days by sea.

Despite the increase in Arctic shipping, fishing, and tourism, the Nome and Utqiavik stations are known for their reduced numbers of personnel, with many individuals taking on multiple roles. For example, Station Nome's lone

Russian-speaker was also the only person certified to perform aircraft maintenance at temperatures below -20 degrees.

Both are known as "divorce stations" because personnel there frequently separate from their spouses, likely stemming from the stressful environment. These stations also have the highest percentage of personnel failing drug tests of any units in the Coast Guard.

INSIDE

U.S. Coast Guard cutter hits mine in N. Europe

Infrared satellite imagery reveals a Russian trawler discarding large items in the area hours before the cutter escorting Estonian ships in the Baltic Sea struck the mine. *Page 5*

Green energy boom bolsters U.S. economy

The ReNEW Stock Index reaches record highs for the fifth consecutive quarter. High upfront investments appear to be paying long-term dividends. *Page 7*

Cyber pirates target S. Korea's digital currency

Korea's Department of Currency Cyber Security claims to have thwarted the attack, as risk-wary investors halt $350 billion of international trade. *Page 22*

'Family Block' hits home with extended families

The trend of extended families growing closer —both in relationships and geographically— continues as developers create a new product: the "Family Block." *Page 29*

Evergreen Times

Vol. 30, Edition 10,952 THURSDAY, SEPTEMBER 12, 2030 $3.50

Hurricane Mark leaves flooding, chemical spills, theft in its wake

Flood waters take over the streets in Hoboken, NJ. (Photo: NJ National Guard)

HOBOKEN—Hurricane Mark walloped New Jersey over the weekend. Flooding from storm surge and heavy rains reached record highs, leaving tens of thousands of homes and businesses flooded.

The most damage was sustained in Cape May, where the Coast Guard station was completely washed away. "We managed to evacuate in time to prevent any Coast Guard casualties," one source said, "But we can't do any search and rescue missions. We've had to call on the Navy for support because all East Coast Coast Guard resources are busy with their own regional storm response."

Three major chemical spills along the coastline have compounded the difficulty in rescue efforts. Chemical plants have storm and flood resilience requirements, but Hurricane Mark was a Category 6. Resiliency requirements are designed for an upper limit of a Category 5, but Hurricane Glenda in 2025 established Category 6 as the new "worst case" hurricane. The extent of the hazmat spills is unknown, but the governor of New Jersey has recommended evacuations within a 100-mile radius of the spills, despite limited road access at this time.

Finally, "climate criminals" have struck again, targeting ports in New Jersey and stealing high value containers of goods. These foreign actors wait on the high seas until the storm has passed, and then enter U.S. territorial waters to target ports. These opportunists take advantage of the largely automated port security systems that have been knocked out.

This relatively new form of crime has caused over $10 billion in losses in the past year alone, and security experts are struggling to secure facilities against these bad actors.

INSIDE

China 'effectively owns' the Arctic's shipping routes, Congress finds

An investigative panel on the nation's ability to maintain freedom of the seas finds that only China has the capabilities required to operate in the Arctic year-round. China is now the de facto "owner" of the Arctic. *Page 5*

Conglomerates in California drive surge in GDP, as debt loads drop

As automation and technology developed in California drive an increase in GDP, the national debt drops for the third year in a row. *Page 22*

With universal health coverage, gig economy soars and traditional "9-to-5s" lose appeal

Without the requirement of a healthcare benefit, today's workers demand more engagement and fulfillment, greater flexibility, longer vacations, and happier work environments. *Page 29*

TODAY'S WEATHER
Morning rain and high clouds in the afternoon.
High: 68 | Low: 52

Evergreen Times

Vol. 30, Edition 10,953   FRIDAY, SEPTEMBER 13, 2030 $3.50

Coast Guard Evacuates Americans from Mexico

U.S. Coast Guard personnel evacuate Americans from a resort in Mexico (above). Skirmishes occur in the streets during the coup (right).

Photos: USCG and Ederl.mx via Wikipedia

After coup, U.S. officials fear the effort will be seen as a military operation that belies nation's hands-off approach

Mexico's overnight coup d'etat has created a series of crises for the U.S. Coast Guard. With funding for the Department of Defense at an all-time low, it is up to the Coast Guard to manage the evacuation by sea of an estimated 3 million Americans living in or visiting Mexico.

Coast Guard cutters, boats, and drones are involved in the urgent effort, as are Law-Enforcement Detachments.

Officials are concerned that the Coast Guard's heavy involvement in the evacuation gives the appearance that the United States has abandoned its "hands off" foreign policy strategy. Pro-coup forces have reacted to the Coast Guard as an enemy force, including jamming signals used by the Coast Guard's drone fleet, which relies on the Coast Guard's constellation of low-earth orbit satellites.

The demands of the surge are stressing nearly the entire Coast Guard, ranging from asset operators to satellite-imagery analysts, as officials struggle to send a message that this is not a military engagement.

--- INSIDE ---

U.S. debt is a liability as China hardens stance

As the dollar plummets, China is hardening its stance against U.S. troops abroad. Personnel are being recalled from U.S. military installations in Korea and Japan. *Page 5*

Shared bathwater is the new normal in California

As drought continues, California considers water rationing, causing many families to embrace sharing bathwater and replacing lawns with gravel. *Page 10*

Gas stations close as gas vehicle sales hit new low

With over 90 percent of commercial, personal and military vehicles running on electricity, gas stations are soon to become a relic of a bygone era. *Page 29*

20-hour 'time blocks' improve productivity

More people are working fewer hours in shorter "time blocks" as flexible and remote work take hold. What happens when a field can't meet this new norm? *Page 29*

Appendix B. HSOAC Report Summaries

This appendix contains two summaries of *Developing New Future Scenarios for the U.S. Coast Guard's Evergreen Strategic Foresight Program*, the HSOAC report (written in Year 1 of the Evergreen V project and published in 2020) that developed the future scenarios used during the Pinecone workshops. To read the full report online, please visit https://www.rand.org/pubs/research_reports/RR3147.html

Contents

B1. "Developing New Future Scenarios for the U.S. Coast Guard's Evergreen Strategic Foresight Program" Research Summary

An FFRDC operated by the RAND Corporation under contract with DHS

Developing New Future Scenarios for the U.S. Coast Guard's Evergreen Strategic Foresight Program

Developing New Future Scenarios for the U.S. Coast Guard's Evergreen Strategic Foresight Program

ABBIE TINGSTAD, MICHAEL T. WILSON, KATHERINE ANANIA, JORDAN R. FISCHBACH, SUSAN A. RESETAR, SCOTT SAVITZ, KRISTIN VAN ABEL, R. J. BRIGGS, AARON C. DAVENPORT, STEPHANIE PEZARD, KRISTIN SEREYKO, JONATHAN THEEL, MARC THIBAULT, EDWARD ULIN

www.rand.org/t/RR3147

RESEARCH QUESTIONS

- What lessons (good and bad) from the Coast Guard's Evergreen strategic foresight initiative's 20-year history can shape future analytic support to service strategy making and planning?
- How can scenario development be structured to better posture the Evergreen initiative to meet broader Coast Guard strategy-making and planning needs?
- What types of scenarios bridge the gap between future challenges and near-term plans, which typically focus on the urgent needs of the present?

KEY FINDINGS

- Lessons from prior Evergreen activities can illuminate what has historically been valuable and what could be improved in the future. Generally speaking, Evergreen participants value the experience of considering the implications of longer-range future scenarios for Coast Guard operations. Because of the perpetual urgency of immediate operational needs, Evergreen scenarios and foresight activities have historically been limited in their ability to foster deliberation about long-term issues. Products and findings from Evergreen activities have not historically been directly used in some Coast Guard decisionmaking because of differences in planning time horizons. In many circumstances, this has also made it challenging to trace Evergreen's effects.
- The purpose, inputs, and outputs of Coast Guard planning (as part of Planning, Programming,

future problems and decision points in the near term represents both a challenge and an opportunity for Evergreen and speaks to the need for scenarios that enable discussion of trade-offs relevant in the near term even if the motivating problems might be longer range. Strategies cover some stressors and shocks less densely than others, which can form important scenario inputs to stress-test current plans.

RECOMMENDATIONS

- Frame Evergreen scenarios with the decisions they are intended to support.
- Use a stressors-and-shocks framework, which has its conceptual roots in a large body of academic and applied resilience work, to systematically compile, review, and update information about future trends and contingencies that could stress the Coast Guard in decision-relevant ways.
- Employ the concept of scenario families to summarize different types of futures subject to changes along a common set of trends; distinct families can be combined to create a richer scenario narrative.
- Add various types of compatible shocks to scenario narratives that present additional challenges for the Coast Guard and, in particular, simulate the tension between day-to-day demands resulting from stressors with sudden resource-consuming perturbations.
- Consider opportunities for incorporative quantitative, along with qualitative, information into Evergreen scenarios.

HSOAC is a federally funded research and development center (FFRDC) operated by the RAND Corporation under contract with the U.S. Department of Homeland Security (DHS). The HSOAC FFRDC provides the government with independent and objective analyses and advice in core areas important to the department in support of policy development, decisionmaking, alternative approaches, and new ideas on issues of significance. The HSOAC FFRDC also works with and supports other federal, state, local, tribal, and public- and private-sector organizations that make up the homeland security enterprise. RAND is a research organization that develops solutions to public policy challenges to help make communities throughout the world safer and more secure, healthier and more prosperous. RAND is nonprofit, nonpartisan, and committed to the public interest. For more information, visit www.rand.org/hsrd/hsoac.

B2. "A Novel Approach for Supporting the U.S. Coast Guard's "Evergreen" Strategic Foresight Program" Executive Summary

RAND CORPORATION

ABBIE TINGSTAD, MICHAEL T. WILSON, KATHERINE ANANIA, JORDAN R. FISCHBACH, SUSAN A. RESETAR, SCOTT SAVITZ, KRISTIN VAN ABEL, R. J. BRIGGS, AARON C. DAVENPORT, STEPHANIE PEZARD, KRISTIN SEREYKO, JONATHAN THEEL, MARC THIBAULT, EDWARD ULIN

A Novel Approach for Supporting the U.S. Coast Guard's "Evergreen" Strategic Foresight Program

Executive Summary

KEY FINDINGS

■ **Lessons from prior Evergreen activities can illuminate what has historically been valuable and what could be improved in the future.** Generally speaking, Evergreen participants value the experience of considering the implications of longer-range future scenarios for Coast Guard operations. Because of the perpetual urgency of immediate operational needs, Evergreen scenarios and foresight activities have historically been limited in their ability to foster deliberation about long-term issues. Products and findings from Evergreen activities have not historically been directly used in some Coast Guard decisionmaking because of differences in planning time horizons. In many circumstances, this has also made it challenging to trace Evergreen's effects.

■ **The purpose, inputs, and outputs of Coast Guard planning (as part of Planning, Programming, Budgeting, and Execution) and the service's strategic library can shape Evergreen scenarios.** Identifying potential needs for continued or additional decision support from Evergreen analyses helps focus scenario content. The lack of a robust bridge between slow-burning or emerging future problems and decision points in the near term represents both a challenge and an opportunity for Evergreen and speaks to the need for scenarios that enable discussion of trade-offs relevant in the near term even if the motivating problems might be longer range. Strategies cover some stressors and shocks less densely than others, which can form important scenario inputs to stress-test current plans.

The U.S. Coast Guard has an important opportunity to lead in the use of foresight methods for security-related strategic planning. The Evergreen Program, managed since 1998 by the Office of Emerging Policy (DCO-X), provides a mechanism for officers, enlisted, and civilians in different areas to explore future worlds and contingencies that will test the Coast Guard. This process explores how decisions made now will affect prevention and response under challenging, new conditions. The Homeland Security Operational Analysis Center (HSOAC) was asked by DCO-X to assess Evergreen successes and areas for improvement.

Evergreen has proven valuable in at least two important ways. First, some difficult futures explored using foresight have become relevant in the near term. For example, Evergreen scenario-based analysis highlighted key challenges in terrorism response shortly before 9/11 and, more recently, have spurred an Arctic strategy update to help drive planning in an evolving region. Second, Evergreen activities have provided leaders, planners, and operators a chance to anticipate and learn from problems and opportunities in a simulated environment.

Evergreen approaches to strategic foresight activities must evolve with Coast Guard needs and the increasingly complex suite of global trends and changes. A key finding from past foresight activities is that these did not always tee up relevant debates or clearly support decisions. HSOAC drew from literature on resilience planning and decisionmaking under deep uncertainty to adapt an Evergreen scenario development approach that limits these issues. The approach follows three basic methodological steps:

1. Frame and focus scenarios and subsequent analyses using a decision for context.
2. Compile information about global trends and specific contingencies affecting the operating environment.

3. Develop scenario families (representing intersections of key trends), layer them together to create distinct futures, and add contingencies to simulate resource-intensive events.

Using this approach results in decision-relevant multidimensional scenario narratives that can be supplemented with quantitative data as available. Examples in the report focus on workforce changes, technology needs, and resources. An appendix displays example scenarios used in Evergreen workshops during fiscal years 2019 and 2020, which expand on the material in the main body of the report. The broader scenario framing within a specific set of trends and contingencies preserves a sense of which were selected for analysis (why) and which were not (why not) that allows for better interpretation of foresight results.

Foresight can be a valuable tool for Coast Guard strategic planning and training. A structured, updated approach to designing scenarios will help make Evergreen results more relevant and compelling to decisionmakers.

The Coast Guard's Strategic Framework

Source: U.S. Coast Guard, Coast Guard Strategic Plan: 2018–2022, Washington, D.C., November 2018b, p. 8. As of June 16, 2019: https://www.uscg.mil/Portals/0/seniorleadership/alwaysready/USCG_Strategic%20Plan__LoResReaderSpreads_20181115_vFinal.pdf?ver=2018-11-14-150015-323

A Summary of Example Evergreen Scenarios

The scenarios that the authors developed are novel in the context of Coast Guard decision analysis in several ways. First, the authors deliberately scoped the scenarios to specific topics of interest to Coast Guard decision-makers. In this sense, the scenarios are outputs of, rather than inputs to, a strategic foresight process. Second, the authors' concept of scenario families maps Coast Guard strategic choices along key axes of change that are most relevant for decisionmaking. Third, the authors designed narratives for shocks that can be layered on top of complex future worlds constructed from the scenario families.

Scenario Family	Stressor-Based Scenario	Example Shock
Workforce: Each scenario represents a type of Coast Guard workforce future realized by 2040 given possible market competitiveness of careers and specialization of Coast Guard mission requirements.	• Captain's Got a New Gig: Focus moves from specialization to a successful recruitment strategy with reliance on a temporary and part-time workforce. • Up or Overboard: Missions are more specialized, and the service successfully recruits and develops skilled service members. • Try Switching to Aux: The Coast Guard has problems competing in the labor market to meet the capacity for a generalist workforce. • Silicon Sloop Slump: The Coast Guard prefers a highly trained and experienced workforce, eroding the personnel pipeline.	• Putting All Our Magnets in One Basket: A geomagnetic storm coupled with a cyberattack requires a response; there is a lapse in navigation capability; a fuel shortage ensues. • Quarantine Quagmire: Disease outbreaks and wildfires occur; port security needs increase at home and abroad.
Asset: Each scenario represents a sort of future emphasis placed on Coast Guard assets by 2040, given the pace of climate change impacts and rate of technology adoption.	• Sensing a Pattern: Artificial intelligence and automation technologies aid mission execution in a world with limited climate disruptions. • Shocks and Struts: Rapid technological change fosters unanticipated advances that help meet needs in a rapidly changing climate; climate change threatens supply chains. • Humdrum Doldrums: The rate of technological change and the pace of climate effects are low. • Things Go to 11: High impacts from climate change produce challenges; technological change and adoption levels are low.	• Oil and Water Don't Mix: A vessel spills oil in Arctic waters as hurricanes batter the Gulf of Mexico and the United States contends with an emerging security issue. • Al Sur de la Frontera: An earthquake devastates Mexico, leading to humanitarian and immigration crises and a lapse in security.

3

An FFRDC operated by the RAND Corporation under contract with DHS

The Homeland Security Act of 2002 authorizes the Secretary of the Department of Homeland Security (DHS), acting through the Under Secretary for Science and Technology, to establish one or more federally funded research and development centers (FFRDCs) to provide independent analysis of homeland security issues. The RAND Corporation operates the Homeland Security Operational Analysis Center (HSOAC) as an FFRDC for DHS under contract HSHQDC-16-D-00007.

The HSOAC FFRDC provides the government with independent and objective analyses and advice in core areas important to the Department in support of policy development, decisionmaking, alternative approaches, and new ideas on issues of significance. The HSOAC FFRDC also works with and supports other federal, state, local, tribal, and public- and private-sector organizations that make up the homeland security enterprise. The HSOAC FFRDC's research is undertaken by mutual consent with DHS and is organized as a set of discrete tasks.

The information presented in this report does not necessarily reflect official DHS opinion or policy.

For more information on this publication, visit www.rand.org/t/RR3147.

RR-3147/1-DHS (2020)

About This Report

This report documents support by Homeland Security Operational Analysis Center (HSOAC) to the U.S. Coast Guard's Evergreen strategic foresight activity. The objective was to help develop scenarios that postured Evergreen to better bridge the gap between future challenges and near-term plans, which typically focus on the urgent needs of the present. HSOAC analysts reviewed prior Evergreen activities, examined Coast Guard strategy-making and planning processes, adapted an approach for developing scenarios, and narrated a set of exemplar global planning scenarios. Although the scenario development process and resulting example scenarios focused on a Coast Guard planning context, the approach and considerations described in this report might be useful to other organizations with long-range planning needs.

This research was sponsored by the Coast Guard Office of Emerging Policy and conducted within the Strategy, Policy, and Operations Program of the HSOAC federally funded research and development center (FFRDC).

Appendix C. HSOAC Perspectives

This appendix contains expanded short thought pieces to give decisionmakers a brief introduction to selected key topics and questions to consider from the workshop.

Contents

May 2020

SUSAN A. RESETAR, MICHELLE D. ZIEGLER, AARON C. DAVENPORT, MELISSA BAUMAN

U.S. Coast Guard Workforce 2040

Better Management Through Transparency

L ike most employers, the U.S. Coast Guard will face personnel management challenges because of emerging technologies, changing demographics, and employment trends, such as the rise of online platforms and the
gig economy.[1] But participants in a Coast Guard Evergreen V workshop,
Workforce 2040, discussed several ways in which technology could also help the
Coast Guard effectively recruit and retain its future workforce by providing greater
transparency in personnel management practices. Workforce 2040 is among Coast
Guard efforts to retain its top talent in an increasingly competitive environment.
The Office of Emerging Policy engaged hundreds of Coast Guard personnel and
experts as part of a rigorous process to identify the biggest drivers of change for the
service in the coming years, and the need to focus on the future workforce emerged
as one of the most important.

The workshop, conducted by the Coast Guard Office of Emerging Policy
on September 10–12, 2019, at the Yorktown, Virginia, training center, presented
the approximately 35 participants with four possible futures that served as the

HS AC
HOMELAND SECURITY
OPERATIONAL ANALYSIS CENTER

An FFRDC operated by the
RAND Corporation under
contract with DHS

backdrop for each workshop group to tease out emerging and potential future challenges to Coast Guard operations. Participants came from a variety of Coast Guard fields, specialties, and organizations.

Inspired by the emphasis on transparency at the workshop, this Perspective focuses on more-widespread information-sharing practices and greater transparency in recruiting and workforce management decisionmaking. The Perspective integrates findings from empirical research on transparency with the insights from workshop participants into the future challenges and overall employment trends that work against the Coast Guard.

Transparency in personnel management refers to practices that offer visibility and knowledge into how personnel management processes work, as well as the outcomes they generate. When an organization effectively provides it, transparency can influence the perceived fairness and efficacy of both process and process outcomes to the benefit of individuals and institutions. An individual gains the necessary information to make better career decisions and might feel a greater sense of engagement and job satisfaction than when dealing with a less transparent organization. An institution benefits when transparency improves employees' commitment to the organization, job performance, and morale.[2] For example, through transparent processes, the Coast Guard could generate data (based on stated and revealed preferences) to help service members and leaders alike better understand career progression paths, along with the options for deviations from these paths and their effects. This approach enables leadership to set and adjust priorities, resources, policies, and guidance. It also allows service members to better understand how their assignment choices and preferences could affect their careers.

The Coast Guard has an opportunity to reap these benefits by improving transparency in personnel management areas, such as recruitment and hiring, compensation, performance assessment, assignments and rotations, and promotions. Recruitment, the assignment process, and the promotion process were specific areas of interest for workshop participants. The first steps toward increased transparency are identifying the areas with the greatest need for transparency and potential for benefits, then assessing what information and actions are necessary and feasible given data availability, privacy, security, legal, and cost concerns. Moreover, transparency is more than simply providing information; it means ensuring that information is received, understood, and interpreted correctly, builds knowledge of the process, and provides an accurate and complete picture. As the Coast Guard explores greater transparency in personnel management, these nuances must be considered with the full spectrum of costs and benefits to the service and its members.

An institution benefits when transparency improves employees' commitment to the organization, job performance, and morale.

2

Transparency: Definitions, Practices, and Key Coast Guard Considerations

Essentially, transparency is achieved when complete, quality information about how a process works, and the results the process generates, is provided in a way that ensures that the information will be interpreted correctly. *Institutional transparency in personnel management systems* refers to information and communication practices, policies, and procedures and training and management methods that provide clarity into overall workforce policies, management and decision processes, and process outcomes. Transparent systems provide enough quality information to leaders (who set policy), commanders (who direct service members) and supervisors (who direct civilians), and the workforce so they understand how the processes work and what results are produced.[3] The U.S. Office of Personnel Management defines *transparent* as having useful information about workforce management readily available while protecting privacy and security concerns.[4] The right level of transparency can improve both institutional and individual decisions because all involved understand processes and outcomes more clearly. Transparency can improve employees' job satisfaction, organizational commitment, productivity, and work performance by providing a level of accountability for process fairness, equity, and merit. According to the World Economic Forum, several industries indicate that providing transparent career paths, opportunities, and salary information while maintaining leadership accountability is an important part of the solution to eliminating gender bias.[5] Additionally, technology advancements that facilitate greater access to information

are becoming the norm. The Society for Human Resource Management has reported that, as members of the workforce become increasingly comfortable with having access to all kinds of information in their daily lives, they will expect greater access to personnel management systems to enable career decisions.[6] For the Coast Guard, this could mean an increased expectation that an individual service member could see how their preferences for the next billet might influence their potential for advancement or how selecting a nonstandard assignment (such as a short tour) might affect their progression.

Lack of transparency can lead to misconceptions or negative attitudes about a process that carry over to job satisfaction and performance. Sometimes personnel might *perceive* a process as lacking in transparency when the real issue is a lack of knowledge about the process or data regarding its outcomes. This is why transparency, rather than simply offering data, can require many forms of communication to ensure that the information has been received and understood and is trusted.[7]

A 2014 *Harvard Business Review* article presented an in-depth review of successful "game-changing" talent management strategies. Researchers chose three businesses that were purpose-driven, performance-oriented, and principle-led and concluded that a faithful connection between how a company presents itself and what it truly values creates authenticity. Subsequently, the authors pointed out, "Authenticity paves the way for transparency. When employees know what it takes to perform, develop, grow, and succeed, they trust that their company is a meritocracy."[8] More tactically, employees in transparent organizations align their individual performance with

3

107

> [T]ransparency requires finding the proper balance between providing enough information . . . and protecting the privacy of individuals.

organizational goals and with the incentive structures of the transparent personnel system in order to thrive.

Participants Identified Four Key Considerations About Transparency for the Coast Guard

Transparency is created when quality information is intentionally provided and delivered in a manner that is understood and enables the information consumer to act on it.[9] When planning for greater transparency, the Coast Guard should consider several issues:

- **In practice, transparency requires finding the proper balance between providing enough information to planners, supervisors, and the workforce to be useful and protecting the privacy of individuals.** For example, in previous RAND Corporation work, researchers found that organizations take different approaches to providing information on poor employee performance. Some simply describe the process for handling poor performance, while others publicize the number of suspensions, demotions, and removals, aggregated to maintain privacy.[10]

- **Transparency occurs on a continuum, with information provided at various levels of an organization.** If the purpose of the information is to monitor an issue and make course-correction changes, perhaps only the organization's leaders need granular information. On the other hand, if the purpose of the information is to demonstrate that a process is fair and equitable and enables individual action, broader distribution might be warranted.

- **To ensure that information is useful and trustworthy, transparency requires that the information be provided in a timely, accurate, complete, and instructive manner.** The greatest benefit to personnel comes from presenting data and information in the context of the larger personnel management system. This context helps address concerns about the perceived fairness of both the process and the outcomes it produces, which are related to employee attitudes and behaviors.[11] For example, providing the number of performance improvement plans for poor performers does not convey any ongoing actions to address the performance deficiencies, nor does it indicate the outcomes of these plans, such as an employee's decision to stay or leave.[12] However, it can provide context to show how many poor performers exist or the extent to which leadership is taking action to correct unsatisfactory performance. There is also a balancing of providing the right amount of information to demonstrate that processes are effective and equitable and providing so much information that people learn to "game the system," leading to unintended and undesirable behaviors. Recall that a well-positioned transparent process will align organizational objectives with individual objectives.

- On a cautionary note, poorly implemented efforts to promote transparency—for instance, information that is inappropriately framed or hard to understand—can be counterproductive if these efforts lead to misinterpretation or misperception.[13] In addition, greater transparency does not provide a simple solution to chronic management issues.[14]

Providing greater transparency essentially comes down to ensuring that personnel understand how the system works (i.e., the policies, procedures, and criteria that are applied) and providing opportunities for them to see that the system is fair and generates the desired outcomes. Disseminating this information requires a portfolio of actions, including the presentation of concise and comprehensive data; communications, such as briefings, reports, emails, and web-based content; management practices; and training opportunities. One example of a personnel management program that uses multiple methods to increase transparency is the U.S. Department of Defense's Civilian Acquisition Workforce Personnel Demonstration Project (AcqDemo), a demonstration program that tests alternative personnel management procedures for the acquisition corps. It provides training to supervisors and other personnel to increase their familiarity with the demonstration program. It also explains career fields and expectations,

forming the basis for using common factors for assessing employee performance. At the beginning of a performance period, each supervisor meets with each of their employees to discuss job expectations to ensure that all employees are aware of and understand the factors that tie their duties to the organization's mission. During that time, periodic meetings serve as checkpoints to provide actionable feedback. Finally, if an employee believes that the results of the assessment do not accurately reflect their contributions, they can offer input into the performance process or utilize a grievance process.[15] As this example suggests, achieving greater transparency can require a suite of activities.

Several Personnel Management Areas Are Ripe for Improvement

Where might the Coast Guard look for opportunities to provide greater transparency in workforce planning and personnel management? As part of the Human Capital Strategy released in 2016, the Coast Guard identified three priorities on which to focus:

- **mission** needs that focus on the processes that determine the Coast Guard's requirements for people and competencies
- **service** needs that focus on the development of military members and civil servants to meet mission demands
- **people** needs that focus on supporting the individual and their career objectives fairly and equitably.[16]

These needs—establishing data-driven personnel requirements, developing a proficient and diverse workforce, and supporting individual decisionmaking and growth—can provide a road map for areas to consider for providing greater transparency into Coast Guard personnel management processes, starting with recruitment and hiring, compensation, performance assessment, assignments and rotations, and promotions. These areas align well with the issues raised at the scenario-based Evergreen workshops and observations of Coast Guard personnel management processes, which include the following:

- **The assignment process is not well-understood, nor can the results always be reconciled with Coast Guard guidance.** Although guidance documents for the assignment process provide some information, they lack specific criteria and rules, as well as details about the process itself. For example, the sense is that assignments are determined using an unpublished set of "business rules" that favor some billets and categories of people, but it is unclear overall how decisions are made. Other services have identified the assignment process as an area of focus. Both the Army and the Navy experimented with more-visible, market-like assignment processes—the Green Pages (2010–2012) and Data-Enabled Talent Management (2015–2017) programs, respectively—and the Coast Guard might consider reviewing the results.[17]
- **The board and panel process can be ambiguous, particularly to the many members who have not served on a board or panel.** Although promotion boards and assignment panels have commandant guidance that is published, it is considered a guideline and, therefore, not compulsory. This leads to many questions about what aspects of diversity, for example, addressed in that guidance might or might not have been part of the criteria that the board or panel used in its decisionmaking process. The value of every board or panel establishing its own process (within legal and policy limits) must be weighed against whether increased visibility or transparency adds value and demystifies the promotion board and assignment panel process. One option to increase visibility on the process overall is piloting improved communications with the publication of board guidelines, process, and instructional memoranda, along with more-detailed data on selection decisions.
- **Some cultural biases influence the perception of process fairness and efficacy.** For example, waivers to the assignment policy are available for families with special needs (e.g., disability, medical conditions), but workshop attendees noted that these requests are not always encouraged in some operational communities. The Coast Guard has initiated two studies to understand the effects that gender and race have on representation, retention, and performance;[18] additional research could yield further insight into the biases of the Coast Guard personnel system.
- **Better information is needed on idealized versus actualized career pathways.** Some guidance exists for career pathways in theory, but little information is available on whether these pathways are valid in practice. Additionally, little is known about the effects of deviating from a traditionally successful pathway (although some research has established the correlation between service on certain large vessels and positive enlisted career outcomes).[19]

When uncommon opportunities arise during the assignment process, service members are often making best guesses or attempting to crowdsource scuttlebutt on what the different options might indicate, what sort of long-term effects an option might have on advancement likelihood, and how to rank choices to game the process.

Moving Forward Involves Weighing the Benefits Against the Costs

The Coast Guard can expand transparency by determining where the benefits are most promising when weighed against the potential costs. This could involve

- assessing the areas of personnel management in which leaders want greater transparency and visibility to inform institutional decisionmaking and planning today and in the future
- surveying Coast Guard personnel to determine where they want greater transparency. For example, how might additional data inform individual decisionmaking? What aspects of the personnel management system are perceived as unfair, confusing, or ambiguous—and where would more transparency help change those perceptions and improve worker satisfaction, retention, morale, and performance?
- determining which perceptions are due to a lack of transparency or a lack of knowledge about a process, because the remedies differ. If lack of transparency is the reason for this perception, then making more information available on process and process

outcomes is one solution. However, if lack of knowledge is the reason, potential solutions could involve meetings with leadership or additional training to ensure that available information is received and understood.

The results of the above exercise could be triaged and analyzed to determine how greater transparency can lead to better decisions in the specific personnel management areas identified. Ideally, processes should be well defined with established criteria and have accessible data on outcomes (or the potential to generate some). The Coast Guard will need to answer several questions: What information needs to be collected to provide greater transparency? What benefits do we expect to see? What policy or procedural changes, training, documentation, or other communications need to change? In other words, what suite of actions must be in place to provide greater transparency?

The next phase would be to consider the potential challenges of greater transparency. Some key questions in this phase include the following:

- Are the existing processes reproducible or definable?

Ideally, processes should be well defined with established criteria and have accessible data on outcomes. . . .

- Do data exist, or are they feasible to gather?
- Are there cultural or legal barriers to greater transparency (e.g., a perceived loss of flexibility or greater vulnerability to criticism)?

The Coast Guard could learn from previous experiments with greater transparency in Department of Defense programs and personnel assignment processes.

The 2016 Human Capital Strategy notes that more analysis is needed to determine the appropriate balance between system predictability and flexibility:

Analysis of facts, data, and stated assumptions influence decisions and policies. This information provides a degree of transparency and predictability that instills trust and produces better decisions in the Coast Guard's and member's best interests, but the HR [human resource] system must have flexibility to adjust to specific circumstances unique to each situation.[20]

Conclusion

The purpose of this Perspective is to introduce greater transparency as one approach for ensuring that the Coast Guard leverages new opportunities to remain relevant and competitive in the changing workplace environment. Improved predictability, greater confidence in the system, and a clearer understanding of the consequences of their choices are some of the many merits transparency could bring to the people of the Coast Guard. Additionally, leadership gains key insights into the organization's plans and policies and their effects on the depletion, sustainment, and growth of the current and future workforce. For example, transparency can help provide the data to model the consequences and effectiveness of potential changes to policies, thus helping to inform decisionmaking processes. These data and information can also be used for analysis to create alerts and other early indicators to serve as warnings about declines in retention, critical talents or skills, or readiness, which are among the most-challenging workforce concerns.

Determining where and how to effectively pursue transparency in ways that are the best fit for the service and its people requires analysis of opportunities, drawbacks, and costs. This analysis can start with a survey of leadership and the workforce that proceeds in parallel with an assessment of available data and information. Example questions include the following:

- Given the changing dynamics in the workplace in addition to Coast Guard goals, what does Coast Guard leadership see as the critical components of a transparent personnel management system?
- What does leadership hope to accomplish through greater transparency (e.g., elimination of inequities and biases, facilitation of career pathways, improved workforce planning capability)?
- On what personnel management processes does the workforce want more information and clarity, and how would that additional information and clarity improve recruiting, engagement, and retention?
- What system investments would be required to achieve these desired states?
- What is the anticipated effect of greater transparency in these particular areas, and is any system or process available to measure and report on that effect?

- What are the drawbacks or trade-offs of each point of transparency?
- How would the process be implemented and sustained to ensure that information is adequate, interpreted correctly, understood, and communicated in a way that ensures that the needs of the mission, the service, and the people are being addressed?

Through exploring opportunities to provide greater transparency in Coast Guard personnel management processes, the Coast Guard can leverage new ways of managing the workforce and new sources of information to remain competitive in the future work environment.

Notes

[1] *Gig economy* refers to a labor market characterized by the prevalence of short-term contracts and freelance work rather than salaried employment. Even with a "modest" influence on the number of workers engaged in part-time work, the gig economy is influencing the nature of work, as well as expectations among workers, particularly those within the age cohorts eligible for Coast Guard service. For comparison, see Lawrence F. Katz and Alan B. Krueger, "Understanding Trends in Alternative Work Arrangements in the United States," Cambridge, Mass.: National Bureau of Economic Research, Working Paper 25425, January 2019.

[2] Roy Maurer, "Leveraging Transparency Is the Future of HR," Society for Human Resource Management, September 23, 2016; Harvard Business School Analytic Services, *The Impact of Employee Engagement on Performance*, Harvard Business School Publishing, September 2013; Yochi Cohen-Charash and Paul E. Spector, "The Role of Justice in Organizations: A Meta-Analysis," *Organizational Behavior and Human Decision Processes*, Vol. 82, No. 2, November 2001; Mary A. Konovsky, "Understanding Procedural Justice and Its Impact on Business Organizations," *Journal of Management*, Vol. 26, No. 3, 2000; Rebecca Hawk, "5 Benefits of More Transparency in Your Workplace," American Society of Association Executives, undated; TINYpulse, "7 Vital Trends Disrupting Today's Workplace: Results and Data from 2013 TINYpulse Employee Engagement Survey," undated (survey data from 2013).

[3] Laura Werber, Paul Mayberry, Mark Doboga, and Diana Gehlhaus Carew, *Support for DoD Supervisors in Addressing Poor Employee Performance: A Holistic Approach*, Santa Monica, Calif.: RAND Corporation, RR-2665-OSD, 2018.

[4] U.S. Office of Personnel Management, "What Is Transparency in the Context of Open Government?" undated.

[5] World Economic Forum, *The Future of Jobs: Employment, Skills and Workforce Strategy for the Fourth Industrial Revolution*, January 2016.

[6] Maurer, 2016.

[7] Laura Werber, Lindsay Daugherty, Edward G. Keating, and Matthew Hoover, *An Assessment of the Civilian Acquisition Workforce Personnel Demonstration Project*, Santa Monica, Calif.: RAND Corporation, TR-1286-OSD, 2012; Cohen-Charash and Spector, 2001; Konovsky, 2000.

[8] Douglas A. Ready, Linda A. Hill, and Robert J. Thomas, "Building a Game-Changing Talent Strategy," *Harvard Business Review*, January–February 2014.

[9] Andrew K. Schnackenberg and Edward C. Tomlinson, "Organizational Transparency: A New Perspective on Managing Trust in Organization–Stakeholder Relationships," *Journal of Management*, Vol. 42, No. 7, 2016, pp. 1784–1810.

[10] Werber, Mayberry, et al., 2018.

[11] Transparency addresses concerns about procedural justice (the perceived fairness of the process through which an outcome was obtained) and distributive justice (the perceived fairness of the outcome itself), both of which are related to employee attitudes and behaviors (Cohen-Charash and Spector, 2001, and Konovsky, 2000, as cited in Werber, Mayberry, et al., 2018.

[12] Werber, Mayberry, et al., 2018.

[13] Bennett Conlin, "The Pros and Cons of Salary Transparency," *Business News Daily*, updated October 2, 2018.

[14] Sarah Greesonbach, "The Pros and Cons of Transparent Corporate Cultures," *Glassdoor*, December 1, 2016.

[15] Werber, Daugherty, et al., 2012.

[16] U.S. Coast Guard, "Human Capital Strategy," January 2016.

[17] Office of Economic and Manpower Analysis, U.S. Army, *Army Green Pages: Proof-of-Concept Pilot Report—Using Regulated Market Mechanisms to Manage Officer Talent*, West Point, N.Y.: U.S. Military Academy, version 11, December 15, 2012; Caroline Baxter, Brad Carson, Steven Deal, Kelsey Greenawalt, Daniel Madden, Joshua Marcuse, Morgan Plummer, and Lloyd Thrall, "Force of the Future," Office of the Secretary of Defense, 2015, pp. 32 and 41.

[18] See Kimberly Curry Hall, Kirsten M. Keller, David Schulker, Sarah Weilant, Katherine L. Kidder, and Nelson Lim, *Improving Gender Diversity in the U.S. Coast Guard: Identifying Barriers to Female Retention*, Santa Monica, Calif.: RAND Corporation, RR-2770-DHS, 2019, and Kimberly Curry Hall and Kirsten M. Keller, RAND Corporation, communication with the authors about their ongoing research into holistic study and analysis for recruiting and retention of underrepresented populations, 2019–2020.

[19] Jennie W. Wenger, Maria C. Lytell, Kimberly Curry Hall, and Michael L. Hansen, *Balancing Quality of Life with Mission Requirements: An Analysis of Personnel Tempo on U.S. Coast Guard Major Cutters*, Santa Monica, Calif.: RAND Corporation, RR-2731-DHS, 2019.

[20] U.S. Coast Guard, 2016, p. 29.

References

Baxter, Caroline, Brad Carson, Steven Deal, Kelsey Greenawalt, Daniel Madden, Joshua Marcuse, Morgan Plummer, and Lloyd Thrall, "Force of the Future," Office of the Secretary of Defense, 2015.

Cohen-Charash, Yochi, and Paul E. Spector, "The Role of Justice in Organizations: A Meta-Analysis," *Organizational Behavior and Human Decision Processes*, Vol. 82, No. 2, November 2001, pp. 278–321.

Conlin, Bennett, "The Pros and Cons of Salary Transparency," *Business News Daily*, updated October 2, 2018. As of November 5, 2019:
https://www.businessnewsdaily.com/11077-pros-cons-salary-transparency.html

Curry Hall, Kimberly, and Kirsten M. Keller, RAND Corporation, communication with the authors about their ongoing research into holistic study and analysis for recruiting and retention of underrepresented populations, 2019–2020.

Curry Hall, Kimberly, Kirsten M. Keller, David Schulker, Sarah Weilant, Katherine L. Kidder, and Nelson Lim, *Improving Gender Diversity in the U.S. Coast Guard: Identifying Barriers to Female Retention*, Santa Monica, Calif.: RAND Corporation, RR-2770-DHS, 2019. As of February 9, 2020:
https://www.rand.org/pubs/research_reports/RR2770.html

Greesonbach, Sarah, "The Pros and Cons of Transparent Corporate Cultures," *Glassdoor*, December 1, 2016. As of November 5, 2019:
https://www.glassdoor.com/blog/the-pros-and-cons-of-transparent-corporate-cultures/

Harvard Business School Analytic Services, *The Impact of Employee Engagement on Performance*, Harvard Business School Publishing, September 2013. As of January 28, 2020:
https://hbr.org/sponsored/2016/04/the-impact-of-employee-engagement-on-performance

Hawk, Rebecca, "5 Benefits of More Transparency in Your Workplace," American Society of Association Executives, undated. As of January 28, 2020:
https://www.asaecenter.org/association-careerhq/career/articles/talent-management/5-benefits-of-more-transparency-in-your-workplace

Katz, Lawrence F., and Alan B. Krueger, "Understanding Trends in Alternative Work Arrangements in the United States," Cambridge, Mass.: National Bureau of Economic Research, Working Paper 25425, January 2019. As of February 9, 2020:
https://www.nber.org/papers/w25425

Konovsky, Mary A., "Understanding Procedural Justice and Its Impact on Business Organizations," *Journal of Management*, Vol. 26, No. 3, 2000, pp. 489–511.

Maurer, Roy, "Leveraging Transparency Is the Future of HR," Society for Human Resource Management, September 23, 2016. As of October 30, 2019:
https://www.shrm.org/resourcesandtools/hr-topics/talent-acquisition/pages/transparency-future-hr-glassdoor.aspx

Office of Economic and Manpower Analysis, U.S. Army, *Army Green Pages: Proof-of-Concept Pilot Report—Using Regulated Market Mechanisms to Manage Officer Talent*, West Point, N.Y.: U.S. Military Academy, version 11, December 15, 2012. As of February 9, 2020:
https://talent.army.mil/wp-content/uploads/pdf_uploads/PUBLICATIONS/Green-Pages-Proof-of-Concept-Pilot-Report.pdf

Public Law 107-296, Homeland Security Act of 2002, November 25, 2002. As of May 12, 2019:
https://www.govinfo.gov/app/details/PLAW-107publ296

Ready, Douglas A., Linda A. Hill, and Robert J. Thomas, "Building a Game-Changing Talent Strategy," *Harvard Business Review*, January–February 2014. As of January 20, 2020:
https://hbr.org/2014/01/building-a-game-changing-talent-strategy

Schnackenberg, Andrew K., and Edward C. Tomlinson, "Organizational Transparency: A New Perspective on Managing Trust in Organization–Stakeholder Relationships," *Journal of Management*, Vol. 42, No. 7, 2016, pp. 1784–1810.

TINYpulse, "7 Vital Trends Disrupting Today's Workplace: Results and Data from 2013 TINYpulse Employee Engagement Survey," undated (survey data from 2013). As of January 28, 2020:
https://www.tinypulse.com/resources/
employee-engagement-survey-2013

U.S. Coast Guard, "Human Capital Strategy," January 2016. As of January 27, 2020:
https://www.work.uscg.mil/Portals/6/Documents/PDF/
CG_Human_Capital_Strategy.pdf

U.S. Code, Title 6, Domestic Security; Chapter 1, Homeland Security Organization; Subchapter III, Science and Technology in Support of Homeland Security; Section 185, Federally Funded Research and Development Centers. As of May 12, 2019:
https://www.govinfo.gov/app/details/USCODE-2017-title6/
USCODE-2017-title6-chap1-subchapIII-sec185

U.S. Office of Personnel Management, "What Is Transparency in the Context of Open Government?" undated. As of January 20, 2020:
https://www.opm.gov/FAQs/QA.aspx?fid=f342 4e21-72f6-40de-a0be-
7223a357a6b7&pid=f453c352-becb-4059-9ae1-bb20f139faeb

Wenger, Jennie W., Maria C. Lytell, Kimberly Curry Hall, and Michael L. Hansen, *Balancing Quality of Life with Mission Requirements: An Analysis of Personnel Tempo on U.S. Coast Guard Major Cutters*, Santa Monica, Calif.: RAND Corporation, RR-2731-DHS, 2019. As of February 9, 2020:
https://www.rand.org/pubs/research_reports/RR2731.html

Werber, Laura, Lindsay Daugherty, Edward G. Keating, and Matthew Hoover, *An Assessment of the Civilian Acquisition Workforce Personnel Demonstration Project*, Santa Monica, Calif.: RAND Corporation, TR-1286-OSD, 2012. As of February 9, 2020:
https://www.rand.org/pubs/technical_reports/TR1286.html

Werber, Laura, Paul Mayberry, Mark Doboga, and Diana Gehlhaus Carew, *Support for DoD Supervisors in Addressing Poor Employee Performance: A Holistic Approach*, Santa Monica, Calif.: RAND Corporation, RR-2665-OSD, 2018. As of February 9, 2020:
https://www.rand.org/pubs/research_reports/RR2665.html

World Economic Forum, *The Future of Jobs: Employment, Skills and Workforce Strategy for the Fourth Industrial Revolution*, January 2016. As of February 9, 2020:
https://reports.weforum.org/future-of-jobs-2016/

Acknowledgments

We would like to acknowledge RAND colleagues Laura Werber, Katherine Tiongson, Michael J. Mazarr, and Phillip Carter, who provided valuable source materials and insightful comments that helped shape our thinking and enriched the discussion.

About This Perspective

This Perspective documents support by the Homeland Security Operational Analysis Center (HSOAC) to the U.S. Coast Guard's Evergreen project. Founded in 1996, Evergreen is the Coast Guard's strategic foresight initiative, which has historically run in four-year cycles and uses scenario-based planning to identify strategic needs for the incoming service chief. In 2019, Evergreen was restructured in order to best support executive leaders in their role as the Coast Guard's decision engines. The project objective is to help posture the Coast Guard to better bridge the gap between future challenges and near-term plans, which typically focus on the urgent needs of the present. HSOAC analysts reviewed Evergreen activities, examined Coast Guard strategy-making and planning processes, adapted an approach for developing scenarios, and narrated a set of exemplar global planning scenarios. The individual Perspectives that resulted from this project reflect themes and specific subjects that have emerged from a series of workshops that were conducted with subject-matter experts and were identified as areas of particular interest for senior leadership strategic planning activities and emerging policy development.

This research was sponsored by the U.S. Coast Guard Office of Emerging Policy and conducted within the Strategy, Policy, and Operations Program of the HSOAC federally funded research and development center (FFRDC).

The RAND Corporation operates HSOAC under contract to the U.S. Department of Homeland Security (DHS). RAND is a research organization that develops solutions to public policy challenges to help make communities throughout the world safer and more secure, healthier and more prosperous. RAND is nonprofit, nonpartisan, and committed to the public interest. For more information, visit www.rand.org/hsrd/hsoac.

About the Authors

Susan A. Resetar is a senior operations researcher at the RAND Corporation. Her research focuses include personnel issues, workforce staffing, disaster recovery, climate change, collaboration, military installation management, and strategic planning using both quantitative and qualitative methods. She has an M.S. in operations research.

Michelle D. Ziegler is a technical analyst at the RAND Corporation. Her research focuses include U.S. Army logistics, disaster recovery, U.S. Coast Guard capability and capacity analysis, and cooperation and domain awareness in the Arctic. She has an M.S. in astronomy.

Aaron C. Davenport is a senior policy researcher at the RAND Corporation. His research focuses include border and maritime security, emergency preparedness and response, occupational health and safety, and national security strategy. He is a graduate of the U.S. Coast Guard Academy and retired Coast Guard senior officer with security assistance, search-and-rescue, and law-enforcement experience. He has an M.S. in environmental sciences, with a certificate in industrial hygiene and a minor in hazardous materials.

Melissa Bauman is a communications analyst at the RAND Corporation. She helps researchers make their complex findings accessible to a sophisticated audience of lawmakers, journalists, and practitioners. She has a B.A. in journalism.

HSOAC
HOMELAND SECURITY
OPERATIONAL ANALYSIS CENTER

An FFRDC operated by the
RAND Corporation under
contract with DHS

The Homeland Security Act of 2002 (Section 305 of Public Law 107-296, as codified at 6 U.S.C. § 185) authorizes the Secretary of DHS, acting through the Under Secretary for Science and Technology, to establish one or more FFRDCs to provide independent analysis of homeland security issues. The RAND Corporation operates HSOAC as an FFRDC for DHS under contract HSHQDC-16-D-00007.

The HSOAC FFRDC provides the government with independent and objective analyses and advice in core areas important to the department in support of policy development, decisionmaking, alternative approaches, and new ideas on issues of significance. The HSOAC FFRDC also works with and supports other federal, state, local, tribal, and public- and private-sector organizations that make up the homeland security enterprise. The HSOAC FFRDC's research is undertaken by mutual consent with DHS and is organized as a set of discrete tasks.

The information presented in this Perspective does not necessarily reflect official DHS opinion or policy.

For more information on this publication, visit www.rand.org/t/PE358.

PE-358-DHS

May 2020

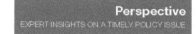

Perspective
EXPERT INSIGHTS ON A TIMELY POLICY ISSUE

SCOTT SAVITZ, AARON C. DAVENPORT, MICHELLE D. ZIEGLER

The Marine Transportation System, Autonomous Technology, and Implications for the U.S. Coast Guard

The Defense Science Board Task Force on the Role of Autonomy in DoD [U.S. Department of Defense] Systems defines *autonomy* as "a capability (or a set of capabilities) that enables a particular action of a system to be automatic or, within programmed boundaries, 'self-governing.'"[1] Autonomy is rarely absolute. Rather, it is on a spectrum extending from no autonomy (in which a system's decisions and actions are completely controlled by humans) to full autonomy (which requires no human involvement). Most autonomous systems lie somewhere in between.

At the outset, we need to distinguish between autonomous systems and unmanned vehicles. The two sometimes overlap but are not synonymous. Most civilian unmanned vehicles currently in use are remotely controlled by humans and have little or no autonomy, while the degree of autonomy for military

HSOAC
HOMELAND SECURITY
OPERATIONAL ANALYSIS CENTER
An FFRDC operated by the
RAND Corporation under
contract with DHS

unmanned vehicles varies. The most-commonly used unmanned vehicles at this time are unmanned aerial vehicles. An unmanned aerial system (UAS) includes an unmanned aerial vehicle, its potential payload, and the command-and-control system. Autonomous systems in other domains include unmanned ground vehicles (UGVs), unmanned surface vehicles (USVs), and unmanned under-sea vehicles (UUVs). Although an autonomous system can be a vehicle—even an inhabited one in which the occupant exerts no control—it can be also be a fixed system that makes decisions with little or no human input (e.g., autonomous systems that immediately respond to cyberintrusions or deconflict vessel traffic).

Gradations of autonomy have been established for different applications; for example, the ability of civilian cars to drive themselves is delineated on a 0–5 scale.[2] For some autonomous systems, the roles of humans have also been characterized (e.g., "in the loop" and "on the loop"). Managing a system with a moderate degree of autonomy is often particularly challenging. A human might perceive a system's autonomous capabilities as greater than they are or might become passive through boredom—factors that have contributed to autonomous-vehicle fatalities. Alternatively, a human might attempt to interfere in a system's decisionmaking, hindering its effectiveness and potentially overwhelming it with inputs.

The level of trust that humans grant an autonomous system will increase as autonomous capabilities grow, leveraging other parts of emerging information technology, such as improved sensors, machine learning, "big data," and artificial intelligence. Future autonomous capabilities, leveraging that trust, will likely change many aspects of the Marine Transportation System (MTS) while presenting new workforce, regulatory, legal, and operational challenges for the U.S. Coast Guard.

Background: Evergreen Workshop Recurring Themes

This Perspective builds partly on the Evergreen Pinecone workshop on future threats to the MTS, which was held in November 2019, in conjunction with the annual Maritime

> A human might perceive a system's autonomous capabilities as greater than they are or might become passive through boredom. . . . Alternatively, a human might attempt to interfere in a system's decisionmaking, hindering its effectiveness and potentially overwhelming it with inputs.

2

Risk Symposium. The workshop involved about 70 participants from the Coast Guard, academia, government agencies, and the maritime industry and was conducted over two half-day sessions at Maritime College, State University of New York. Participants were split into four groups, each of which was given a plausible state of the world in 2030. Members of the group then noted key opportunities and challenges for the Coast Guard stemming from that state of the world, as well as implications with an ambiguous potential impact on the Coast Guard. They then grouped these items into a series of clusters, each of which related to an overall risk. The risks were assigned relative values in terms of their importance for the MTS and the level of difficulty associated with addressing them. Each group then focused on a particular risk that was both important and difficult, describing its potential evolution and key implications, and shared these insights with the other groups.

Several recurring themes throughout the workshop have implications for the future of the MTS, some of which relate to autonomous systems:

- **differential paces of technological adoption**, given that private-sector companies and illicit actors might adopt novel technologies more rapidly than government agencies do because they have greater funding and organizational agility. These technologies include advances in autonomous systems that operate in the maritime domain, which could put response and regulatory agencies at a disadvantage in the timely completion of appropriate planning, regulatory, legal, and operational responses to developments.
- **workforce competence** because personnel must be capable of handling both advanced and legacy

technologies, as well as partially autonomous systems. This affects the ability to recruit and retain personnel with those technological skill sets that are in increasingly high demand.
- **uncertainty about capacity demands throughout the MTS** as sources, destinations, quantities, and types of goods evolve. It is unknown how the industry will adapt and whether government agencies will be able to keep pace with the speed of technology as cargo ships, work boats, and port facilities become more automated.
- **climate change** altering the physical environment, potentially making obsolete some aspects of systems' and humans' environmental knowledge over time. Climate change can also damage infrastructure. In some cases, the response to climate change might also entail the use of physical barriers to protect shorelines, but these barriers can themselves impede navigation.
- **governance challenges** as nations aim to address technological, economic, and environmental changes without imposing conflicting policies that hinder activities in the MTS or pose new unintended, unanticipated risks
- **increased disease risks** due to denser populations of people and livestock, greater mobility, overuse of antibiotics, climate change, and diminished international cooperation
- **increased Arctic activity** due to greater accessibility to and maritime activity in that region, even as land infrastructure becomes harder to build and maintain because of climate effects, such as thawing permafrost and coastal erosion. Indigenous

communities might be affected by rapid changes to habitats and resulting sources of food. The commercial and tourist use of Arctic shipping routes could increase the need for rescue capabilities.

Key Trends in Automation

Several important trends in autonomous systems could have meaningful effects on the future MTS and the Coast Guard's role in it:

- **increased numbers and capabilities:** Advances in autonomy will likely continue, and capabilities will become available to more actors. Autonomous systems will increasingly be used by those the Coast Guard assists, regulates, counters, and encounters, as well as by partner agencies and the Coast Guard itself.
- **multisystem autonomous operations:** Technologies that help multiple autonomous systems coordinate their behaviors are emerging. Autonomous systems need to be able to coordinate not only with each other but also with manned or remotely controlled systems; they also need to interact with their physical environments (e.g., animals, winds or currents, and obstacles).
- **multidomain autonomous operations:** For the past couple of decades, unmanned-vehicle advances have been most concentrated in the air domain. However, unmanned and increasingly autonomous vehicles are emerging on the water's surface, under the water, and on land. Autonomous vehicles will increasingly interact across domains, and some

individual vehicles will be able to operate in more than one of them.
- **human–machine interfaces:** There is a critical need to ensure that humans and autonomous systems understand each other's behavior and decisions in ways that reduce risk. Although the algorithms underlying autonomous systems are known, the interactions between machine and environment can lead to unexpected results. Although there are rapid advances in human–machine interfaces and efforts to better convey to humans what is happening, the growing complexity of machines (including autonomous ones) makes this a continuing challenge.
- **increased miniaturization:** Capacities for energy harvesting and storage will grow, even as the corresponding devices shrink. Sensors, information technology hardware, and other systems are also shrinking, increasing payload ratios for unmanned vehicles, including those operating autonomously.
- **increased importance of data sciences:** Because of increasing numbers of sensors and growing volumes of traffic, the amount of information associated with the MTS is also growing. At the same time, the ability of data sciences—such as big data, machine learning, and artificial intelligence—to analyze and act on these data sets is also increasing. This requires a critical evaluation of the viability of complex multimission autonomous platforms versus that of simpler platforms that cooperate with one another, given the challenges of communicating and interpreting large amounts of data. As data sciences advance over time, they will shape choices about

the right mix of autonomous capabilities within the Coast Guard.

In addressing how autonomous systems affect the MTS, the Coast Guard will most likely confront the following issues over various timelines:

- In the **near term (zero to five years)**, the Coast Guard can work to develop policies and limited technological changes to address current and emerging developments. It can also lay the groundwork for the introduction of more-advanced technologies and for policies to address the use of those technologies by others.
- In the **medium term (five to ten years)**, the Coast Guard can work on selecting technologies to incorporate into its capabilities, developing appropriate policies and plans, and finding both technological and nontechnological solutions to challenges posed by autonomous systems.
- For the **long term (ten to twenty years)**, the Coast Guard can be thinking creatively about emerging opportunities and threats involving autonomous systems, taking into account not only technological advances but also changes in the operational environment and other contextual factors. For example, it can seek to improve recruitment, training, and retention of people with particular skills relating to the operation and maintenance of autonomous systems.

The Impact of Autonomous Systems on Coast Guard Roles, Statutory Missions, and Mission Enablers

In this section, we review ways in which the Coast Guard will likely be dealing with autonomous systems in the MTS in the context of its operational roles and statutory missions. In addition, we address the broader category of mission enablers, as well as opportunities and challenges in the near term and further into the future. As autonomous systems become more capable and cost-effective, the Coast Guard could use them in a variety of contexts.

Maritime Safety

The maritime domain is particularly challenging for autonomous vehicles. Autonomous USVs operating on a moving surface, subject to forces from above and below, must be able to adhere to the Convention on the International Regulations for Preventing Collisions at Sea, 1972, and to avoid collisions with vessels that might not be obeying those regulations.[3] These vehicles also need to avoid capsizing or having accidental allisions with fixed infrastructure.[4] Autonomous UUVs need to operate without access to electromagnetic information (e.g., the Global Positioning System) because of the attenuation of electromagnetic energy underwater, while navigating in a complex, dynamic, three-dimensional environment. Autonomous systems have not yet caused a major accident in the MTS, although the Coast Guard needs to anticipate and address the potential. For example, if two large USVs collide in a major shipping channel, the Coast Guard will have to work

- **Defense Readiness:** Implications here are the same as those for Ports, Waterways, and Coastal Security, although requiring more consideration of how autonomous systems could interoperate with U.S. Department of Defense systems, particularly during contingencies.

Maritime Stewardship

Overall, autonomous systems could potentially facilitate the efficient movement of goods and people through the MTS while also reducing resource costs and helping to ensure the continuity of the MTS. The Coast Guard missions affected are

- **Ice Operations:** There are applications for autonomous systems in support of polar and domestic icebreaking operations. UASs or light UGVs preceding icebreakers could observe ice conditions to support safe ship navigation. UASs could also be used in support of the International Ice Patrol, reducing costs in identifying and tracking icebergs in lieu of predictive methods and time-consuming, potentially hazardous manned missions.
- **Living Marine Resources:** Autonomous fishing could bring unprecedented changes to the fishing industry in the ways in which fish are caught, processed, and brought to the market, requiring some commensurate level of monitoring and regulation enforcement. It could also result in a dramatic reduction in the number of injuries and fatalities associated with manned commercial fishing, routinely regarded as one of the most-hazardous occupations. UASs and USVs could be used to monitor closed areas and to observe vessels and their behaviors.
- **Aids to Navigation (ATON):** Through the use of UASs, the Coast Guard could monitor the physical condition of ATONs and, through exchange of information with self-diagnostic technology on the ATONs, could reduce the use of limited resource hours and potentially the future need for manned maintenance activities at sea, which is regarded as both dangerous and arduous work.
- **Marine Environmental Protection:** Spill responses are inherently dangerous missions. They often occur in remote and unforgiving terrain, where this risk is magnified. Real-time aerial views provide site evaluation, hazard identification, and responder orientation. With expanding payloads, potential mission-set opportunities increase dramatically, such as through remote air monitoring and infrared cameras. Autonomous systems could mitigate or eliminate significant hazards. UASs for spill assessment and response could provide commands with a rapid and clear operating picture while simultaneously acting as a force multiplier for responders. A UAS operating on a spill site could identify the source, determine the extent of impact, and direct response efforts, allowing the prioritization of resources and personnel. These capabilities could translate into increased recovery rates and reduced impacts to the marine environment. UASs, USVs, and UUVs could monitor spills. USVs could deploy cleanup materials into the water or recover contaminants. Handheld autonomous tools could be used in tight spaces on a ship to observe possible

to prevent obstruction of the channel, even in the absence of personnel aboard either vessel with whom to coordinate.

The Coast Guard missions affected in terms of maritime safety are

- **Search and Rescue:** UASs can serve as more-numerous and cost-effective search assets than manned aircraft.[5] Those with sufficient payloads could drop beacons to facilitate rescue and provide supplies for those in danger. In addition, USVs could enable conscious victims to be brought to shore. Some could be stationed offshore for long periods, then respond when alerted, arriving faster than a boat coming from shore and relieving the safety concerns of having manned aircraft in reduced-visibility, high-seas, and high-wind conditions.
- **Marine Safety:** UASs could help the Coast Guard observe possible safety risks: Handheld autonomous systems (e.g., small snake-like or crawling systems) could get into confined spaces to detect possible risks, greatly reducing the safety concerns about having humans enter confined spaces—concerns that have plagued the marine industry.

Maritime Security

Remotely controlled UASs are already being used by criminals to monitor, interfere with, and bypass law-enforcement agencies. These systems are hard to counter through electronic or kinetic means; moreover, unless they are captured, it is hard to definitively attribute them to particular individuals or organizations. As technology advances, smugglers will increasingly be able to use autonomous unmanned vehicles to gain situational awareness, to reduce risks and costs, and to interfere with Coast Guard operations (e.g., by jamming key frequencies, creating distractions, or colliding with Coast Guard assets). The relevant Coast Guard missions are

- **Ports, Waterways, and Coastal Security:** UASs could monitor for possible threats, and visible UASs could deter them. USVs could physically interdict possible threat vessels and, with appropriate sensors, monitor for undersea threats. Unmanned vehicles could also cue humans and, when authorized, use force.
- **Migrant Interdiction:** Visible UASs and USVs near shorelines could deter illegal migration. They could also aid in tracking vessels, communications, and rescue operations.
- **Drug Interdiction:** UASs could provide situational awareness less expensively than manned platforms can. In large areas, UASs could be launched from and recovered by USVs that would also provide power and conduct maintenance diagnostics. (Tethered balloons or UASs could also be used by USVs to achieve altitude in a fixed location, without the complexity of launch and recovery.) Visible, audible UASs could be used to induce compliance (for example, ordering a vessel to stop). With human authorization, UASs could eventually employ warning shots and disabling fire against noncompliant vessels. USVs that linger in the environment could also be used to physically interdict drug vessels when needed and remain undetected thanks to their small size. With the right sensors, USVs could help detect semisubmersible or submersible threats.

6

123

violations or aid in inspection and investigation of marine casualties.

- **Other Law Enforcement:** UASs and USVs could monitor key areas or particular vessels. If visible, they could also contribute to deterrence.

Mission Enablers

Autonomous technologies could also enable missions by improving critical functions:

- **logistical support:** Having autonomous delivery vehicles could cut personnel requirements and reduce the logistical challenges of offshore supply operations by, for example, potentially increasing on-station time.
- **training:** Autonomous vehicles could reduce personnel requirements and costs for training by serving as noncompliant vessels or vessels in distress, targets for use of force, towing, underway replenishment, refueling, and other multivessel operations.

- **command, control, communications, computers, intelligence, surveillance, and reconnaissance:** Because attackers are likely to use rapid, algorithm-based capabilities for cyberattacks, the Coast Guard will likely need similarly rapid and automated capabilities to defend its networks. The Coast Guard could use autonomous fixed systems to coordinate operation of unmanned vehicles that are providing communications and intelligence, surveillance, and reconnaissance capabilities, as well as to coordinate among manned and unmanned platforms. It will also need to partner with other government entities for their unmanned assets. However, using autonomous systems also creates vulnerabilities: The "cyberattack surfaces" of systems grow with increasing autonomy and complexity. The Coast Guard should anticipate diverse types of cyberthreats, including those involving insider elements. It also needs to address electronic warfare threats, such as jamming and spoofing.

Commercially available hobby UASs can already be a menace by interfering with flight operations, monitoring law enforcement, or illicitly moving small amounts of drugs; in the future, they will become more autonomous, more numerous, and more capable.

Other Challenges and Opportunities

Regulation

As addressed in the *Maritime Commerce Strategic Outlook*, "The Coast Guard must promote a shift from a rules-based regulatory structure in the maritime environment to a risk and principles-based regulatory structure to keep pace with emerging issues and technology advancements, such as electronic and autonomous systems."[6] The Coast Guard already faces remotely operated UASs, primarily owned by hobbyists and regulated by the Federal Aviation Administration, operating in the MTS. Even if the Federal Aviation Administration were to retain primary regulatory oversight of UASs, the Coast Guard will be responsible for regulating commercial and recreational use of other unmanned vehicles, including USVs, UUVs, and even UGVs (the latter primarily in port environments), that could create safety hazards. As a result, the Coast Guard will need to develop policies and protocols for preventing unsafe or unlawful behaviors, including licensing, certification, and countermeasures against unauthorized usage. Commercially available hobby UASs can already be a menace by interfering with flight operations, monitoring law enforcement, or illicitly moving small amounts of drugs; in the future, they will become more autonomous, more numerous, and more capable. It is even possible that, in a few decades, autonomous USVs will be delivering goods or conducting commercial fishing, requiring further regulation. Meanwhile, the Coast Guard has the advantage of being a leader in the international maritime community to help shape standards and guidelines on autonomous systems.

Response

Autonomous systems have not yet caused a major accident or security breach in the MTS, although the Coast Guard needs to anticipate and address such threats. For example, if two large USVs collide in a major shipping channel, the Coast Guard will need to prevent obstruction of the channel, even in the absence of personnel aboard either vessel with whom to coordinate.

Law Enforcement

Remotely controlled UASs are already being used by criminals to monitor, interfere with, and bypass law-enforcement agencies. The use of these systems is hard to counter through electronic or kinetic means; moreover, unless these systems are captured, it is hard to definitively attribute them to particular individuals or organizations. As technology advances, smugglers will be increasingly able to use autonomous unmanned vehicles to gain situational awareness, to reduce risks and costs, and to interfere with Coast Guard operations (e.g., by jamming key frequencies, creating distractions, or colliding with Coast Guard assets). As autonomous USVs and UUVs become more capable, and autonomous smuggling UASs become harder to discern amid large numbers of innocuous UASs, the Coast Guard will have to find ways to address these new and increasing threats.

Partnerships

If the Coast Guard is to effectively monitor this emerging technology in the maritime environment, the importance of creating, maintaining, and improving information sharing and relationships with interagency partners and the maritime industry will only continue to grow. Federal, state, local, international, and private-sector partners are beginning to use autonomous systems in a variety of capacities. The extent to which such systems are used and the degree of autonomy they have will likely increase over time. For these reasons, the Coast Guard will increasingly need to interact with other entities' autonomous systems. For example, when responding to an oil spill, the Coast Guard might interact with other agencies' autonomous UASs that are being used to monitor the situation; in time, it might also interact with private-sector USVs that contribute directly to cleanup.

In the next decade and beyond, the Coast Guard will increasingly need to incorporate issues relating to autonomous systems into its strategies, policies, concepts of operations, and tactics.

Conclusion

In this Perspective, we have briefly highlighted key aspects of autonomous systems and their potential to affect the MTS, as well as how they might shape the Coast Guard's relevant roles, responsibilities, and capabilities. Autonomous systems will increasingly be used by legitimate actors, criminals, and attackers, as well as by the Coast Guard and many other partner agencies. In the next decade and beyond, the Coast Guard will increasingly need to incorporate issues relating to autonomous systems into its strategies, policies, concepts of operations, and tactics.

Further Reading

The literature about autonomous systems and their prospective applications is voluminous and growing. In addition to the works cited in this Perspective, the interested reader can consult the following publications.

Gonzales, Dan, and Sarah Harting, *Designing Unmanned Systems with Greater Autonomy: Using a Federated, Partially Open Systems Architecture Approach*, Santa Monica, Calif.: RAND Corporation, RR-626-OSD, 2014. As of January 14, 2020:
https://www.rand.org/pubs/research_reports/RR626.html

Martin, Bradley, Danielle C. Tarraf, Thomas C. Whitmore, Jacob DeWeese, Cedric Kenney, Jon Schmid, and Paul DeLuca, *Advancing Autonomous Systems: An Analysis of Current and Future Technology for Unmanned Maritime Vehicles*, Santa Monica, Calif.: RAND Corporation, RR-2751-NAVY, 2019. As of January 14, 2020:
https://www.rand.org/pubs/research_reports/RR2751.html

Peters, John E., Somi Seong, Aimee Bower, Harun Dogo, Aaron L. Martin, and Christopher G. Pernin, *Unmanned Aircraft Systems for Logistics Applications*, Santa Monica, Calif.: RAND Corporation, MG-978-A, 2011. As of January 14, 2020:
https://www.rand.org/pubs/monographs/MG978.html

Savitz, Scott, Irv Blickstein, Peter Buryk, Robert W. Button, Paul DeLuca, James Dryden, Jason Mastbaum, Jan Osburg, Phillip Padilla, Amy Potter, Carter C. Price, Lloyd Thrall, Susan K. Woodward, Roland J. Yardley, and John M. Yurchak, *U.S. Navy Employment Options for Unmanned Surface Vehicles (USVs)*, Santa Monica, Calif.: RAND Corporation, RR-384-NAVY, 2013. As of January 15, 2020:
https://www.rand.org/pubs/research_reports/RR384.html

Schmid, Jon, "The Diffusion of Military Technology," *Defence and Peace Economics*, Vol. 29, No. 6, 2018, pp. 595–613.

Notes

[1] Defense Science Board, *The Role of Autonomy in DoD Systems*, task force report, Washington, D.C., July 2012.

[2] See Jennifer Shuttleworth, "SAE Standards News: J3016 Automated-Driving Graphic Update," SAE International, January 7, 2019.

[3] International Maritime Organization, Convention on the International Regulations for Preventing Collisions at Sea, 1972, adopted October 20, 1972.

[4] The U.S. Navy's Sea Hunter USV program is working to address many of these challenges. See, for example, Joseph Trevithick, "Navy's Sea Hunter Drone Ship Has Sailed Autonomously to Hawaii and Back Amid Talk of New Roles," *The Drive*, February 4, 2019.

[5] Jeremy M. Eckhause, David T. Orletsky, Aaron C. Davenport, Mel Eisman, Raza Khan, Jonathan Theel, Marc Thibault, Dulani Woods, and Michelle D. Ziegler, *Meeting U.S. Coast Guard Airpower Needs: Assessing the Options*, Homeland Security Operational Analysis Center operated by the RAND Corporation, RR-3179-DHS, 2020.

[6] U.S. Coast Guard, *Maritime Commerce Strategic Outlook*, October 2018, p. 29.

References

Defense Science Board, *The Role of Autonomy in DoD Systems*, task force report, Washington, D.C., July 2012. As of March 2, 2020:
https://apps.dtic.mil/docs/citations/ADA566864

Eckhause, Jeremy M., David T. Orletsky, Aaron C. Davenport, Mel Eisman, Raza Khan, Jonathan Theel, Marc Thibault, Dulani Woods, and Michelle D. Ziegler, *Meeting U.S. Coast Guard Airpower Needs: Assessing the Options*, Homeland Security Operational Analysis Center operated by the RAND Corporation, RR-3179-DHS, 2020. As of April 21, 2020:
https://www.rand.org/pubs/research_reports/RR3179.html

International Maritime Organization, Convention on the International Regulations for Preventing Collisions at Sea, 1972, adopted October 20, 1972. As of March 2, 2020:
http://www.imo.org/en/About/Conventions/ListOfConventions/Pages/COLREG.aspx

Shuttleworth, Jennifer, "SAE Standards News: J3016 Automated-Driving Graphic Update," SAE International, January 7, 2019. As of February 11, 2020:
https://www.sae.org/news/2019/01/sae-updates-j3016-automated-driving-graphic

Trevithick, Joseph, "Navy's Sea Hunter Drone Ship Has Sailed Autonomously to Hawaii and Back Amid Talk of New Roles," *The Drive*, February 4, 2019. As of March 2, 2020:
https://www.thedrive.com/the-war-zone/26319/usns-sea-hunter-drone-ship-has-sailed-autonomously-to-hawaii-and-back-amid-talk-of-new-roles

U.S. Coast Guard, *Maritime Commerce Strategic Outlook*, October 2018. As of March 2, 2020:
https://www.dco.uscg.mil/Our-Organization/Assistant-Commandant-for-Prevention-Policy-CG-5P/Marine-Transportation-Systems-CG-5PW/Maritime-Commerce/

11

About This Perspective

This Perspective documents support by the Homeland Security Operational Analysis Center (HSOAC) to the U.S. Coast Guard's Evergreen project. Founded in 1996, Evergreen is the Coast Guard's strategic foresight initiative, which has historically run in four-year cycles and uses scenario-based planning to identify strategic needs for the incoming service chief. In 2019, Evergreen was restructured in order to best support executive leaders in their role as the Coast Guard's decision engines. The project objective is to help posture the Coast Guard to better bridge the gap between future challenges and near-term plans, which typically focus on the urgent needs of the present. HSOAC analysts reviewed Evergreen activities, examined Coast Guard strategy-making and planning processes, adapted an approach for developing scenarios, and narrated a set of exemplar global planning scenarios. The individual Perspectives that resulted from this project reflect themes and specific subjects that have emerged from a series of workshops that were conducted with subject-matter experts and were identified as areas of particular interest for senior leadership strategic-planning activities and emerging policy development.

This research was sponsored by the U.S. Coast Guard Office of Emerging Policy and conducted within the Strategy, Policy, and Operations Program of the HSOAC federally funded research and development center (FFRDC).

The RAND Corporation operates HSOAC under contract to the U.S. Department of Homeland Security (DHS). RAND is a research organization that develops solutions to public policy challenges to help make communities throughout the world safer and more secure, healthier and more prosperous. RAND is nonprofit, nonpartisan, and committed to the public interest. For more information, visit www.rand.org/hsrd/hsoac.

About the Authors

Scott Savitz is a senior engineer at the RAND Corporation. Much of his research focuses on how to improve the effectiveness and resilience of operational forces, as well as the impact of reallocating resources among those forces. He has a PhD in chemical engineering.

Aaron C. Davenport is a senior policy researcher at the RAND Corporation. His research focuses include border and maritime security, emergency preparedness and response, occupational health and safety, and national security strategy. He is a graduate of the U.S. Coast Guard Academy and retired Coast Guard senior officer with security assistance, search-and-rescue, and law-enforcement experience. He has an MS in environmental sciences, with a certificate in industrial hygiene and a minor in hazardous materials.

Michelle D. Ziegler is a technical analyst at the RAND Corporation. Her research focuses include U.S. Army logistics, disaster recovery, U.S. Coast Guard capability and capacity analysis, and cooperation and domain awareness in the Arctic. She has an MS in astronomy.

HS**O**AC

HOMELAND SECURITY
OPERATIONAL ANALYSIS CENTER

An FFRDC operated by the
RAND Corporation under
contract with DHS

PE-359-DHS

C3. "Decoding Data Science: The U.S. Coast Guard's Evolving Needs and Their Implications"

June 2020

Perspective
EXPERT INSIGHTS ON A TIMELY POLICY ISSUE

AARON C. DAVENPORT, MICHELLE D. ZIEGLER, ABBIE TINGSTAD, KATHERINE ANANIA, DANIEL ISH, NIDHI KALRA, SCOTT SAVITZ, RACHEL LIANG, MELISSA BAUMAN

Decoding Data Science

The U.S. Coast Guard's Evolving Needs and Their Implications

Like many large organizations, the Coast Guard has vast amounts of data that it could use to identify, predict, and solve pressing challenges. Data science could be valuable to the Coast Guard in a variety of domains, such as forecasting the resources needed for future trends in search-and-rescue (SAR) missions, further automating aids to navigation, or automating fishery observations. In personnel areas, data science could help improve billet assignments, determine where to focus recruiting efforts, and boost employee retention.

The Coast Guard has an opportunity to plot the path to determine service-specific uses, identify the strategy and driving mechanisms, and begin laying out a plan. This Perspective outlines the role that data science can play in decisionmaking processes and provides a selected set of key questions and sensitivities for the Coast Guard to consider in developing its future usage of data science.

Data science uses elements from many disparate fields and includes such methodologies and concepts as artificial intelligence (AI), big data, and machine learning (ML). *Data science* refers to the processes through which data are collected,

HS AC
HOMELAND SECURITY
OPERATIONAL ANALYSIS CENTER

An FFRDC operated by the
RAND Corporation under
contract with DHS

129

manipulated, analyzed, and understood. Data science takes huge, complex, and dynamic arrays of data and distills them into patterns and trends, enabling organizations like the Coast Guard to glean valuable insights into personnel, processes, and procedures.

To harness the power of data science, an organization needs the right data, the right people, and the right culture willing to understand the new information and insights and factor them into decisionmaking processes. Employing data science is not without costs or risks, so it is critical that an organization develops its plans and milestones to align to its strategies, priorities, and goals. Small-scale, proof-of-concept work using a variety of data science techniques and currently available data are underway in various areas of the Coast Guard, the U.S. Department of Defense, other government agencies, and the private sector. The broad employment of data science applications across an organization is evolving and maturing but is not so new as to require navigating uncharted waters.

Data Science Explained in Brief

Data science is an umbrella term covering an expansive field of approaches to and techniques for collecting, manipulating, analyzing, and understanding data. Something akin to this science has existed since humans developed the need for data and the ability to track them for various applications. Both the presence of big data and the ability to manipulate them relies on computers and other technological advances (e.g., the internet) that they have helped enable. Whereas *big data* once referred to data

sets that were too large to be housed on a single laptop, it now includes large and complex data sets, often with unstructured data and mixed media, such as video, images, numbers, and raw text. Although some of the mathematics and basic mechanisms behind data science have existed for decades, this field has recently gained increasing public, private, and government attention. The proliferation of high-density networks (social and otherwise) have generated dramatically more data, increasing the availability and proliferation of big data. Computing power has increased to the point at which complex algorithms to analyze and infer meaning from data can be more widely employed. The final piece is the use of the insights and information derived from the data analytics to support decisionmaking.

2

Within data science are two principal categories:

- *data management:* defining, collecting, storing, and presenting measurements of relevant characteristics. This can be thought of as capturing and cultivating data.
- *data analysis or analytics:* systematically using qualitative or quantitative methods (or a combination of these) to describe and evaluate patterns within data ("Data Analysis," undated).

Both categories require the development and deployment of policy, practices, and infrastructure for using data science and data analysis and analytics to support decisionmaking and for addressing the challenges that their use might present (e.g., protecting privacy and preventing hacking).

One example of the data value chain was developed by IBM. Figure 1 illustrates the nine levers that IBM identified as having significant influence on an organization's ability to gain value from data and analytics.

These nine levers fall into three categories, as described in Table 1 (Balboni et al., 2013).

Taking the time to work through mechanisms to integrate data analysis across the organization, ways to support the development and implementation of strategy, what technology will be required, and how data science

FIGURE 1

Nine Levers That Influence the Ability to Derive Value from Data and Analytics

Enable: Basis for big data and analytics

Source of value	Measurement	Platform
Actions and decisions that generate value	Evaluating impact on business outcomes	Integrated capabilities delivered by hardware and software

Drive: Needed to realize value

Culture	Data	Trust
Availability and use of data and analytics	Data management practices	Organizational confidence

Amplify: Boosts value creation

Sponsorship	Funding	Expertise
Executive support and involvement	Financial rigor in analytics funding process	Development and access to skills and capabilities

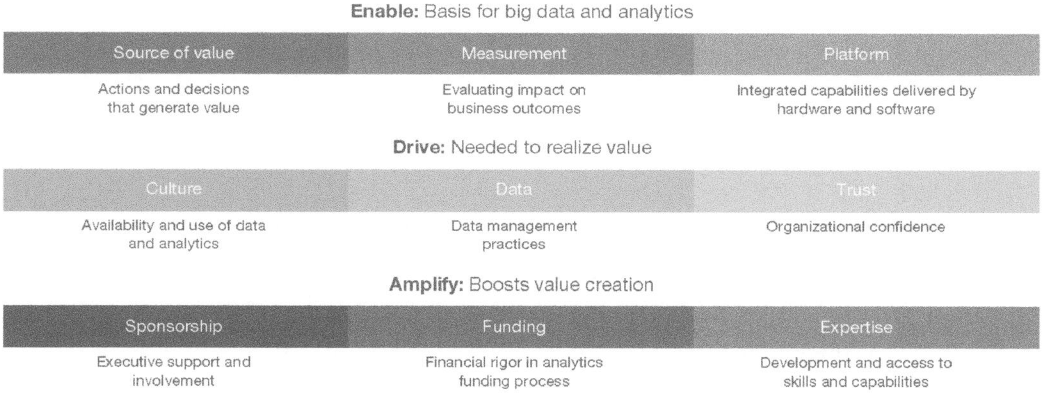

SOURCE: Balboni et al., 2013, p. 4.

3

TABLE 1

Categories of the Nine Levers That Affect an Organization's Ability to Derive Value from Data

Mechanism Category	Function	Example
Enabling	Create the foundation for data analytics and big data use within organizations.[a] By aligning the data strategy with the enterprise strategy, leadership establishes the organizational direction for analytics.	Metric or platform. For example, to promote the strategic goals of equality and diversity, the Coast Guard might want to analyze racial or gender bias in its performance review system; an enabling mechanism would be modification of the existing database of performance review data to allow statistical analysis of differences in evaluations.
Driving	Push an organization from analytic discovery to value creation.	Culture, data, trust, or strong governance and security so that data will be valued as a decisionmaking tool. An example of a driving mechanism for the Coast Guard would be developing a billet assignment optimization model that ensures that billets are filled with the correct skills and informs service members which assignments are most likely to support their desired career trajectories.
Amplifying	Generate the energy and capabilities necessary to translate the results of data analysis into actions that positively affect the organization.	Expertise or funding. An example of a Coast Guard amplifying mechanism would be decisionmakers applying data analytic investments across all missions and requirements.

[a] Balboni et al., 2013.

can help the Coast Guard execute its missions will provide senior leadership with tools to integrate data analytics into its culture and processes.

Data Science Terminology

Some terms, such as *AI*, *ML*, and *big data*, are often used interchangeably because clear definitions were lacking as data science techniques quickly evolved and became more mainstream. Table 2 summarizes some of the key terms associated with data science, although some definitions lack consensus and the relationship between terms is not always clearly delineated. Each term is a field of study in and of itself, with entire careers focused on expertise in just one area. However, in this Perspective, we generally discuss data science as a whole to avoid prescribing a particular path or solution, given that it is still unknown which analytic tools and aspects of data science the Coast Guard will employ. "A Deeper Dive: Types and Examples of Data Analysis," later in this Perspective, ventures into a few of these niche areas to highlight examples, possibilities, and challenges. Figure 2 illustrates the relationships between some of these concepts.

Big data and ML have delivered impressive results in a wide variety of use cases, including financial models that help investors make better decisions, image analysis that monitors the effects of climate change, and natural-language processing that turns spoken words into

TABLE 2

Definitions for Some Key Data Science–Related Terms

Term	Definition
Data science (Provost and Fawcett, 2013)	Umbrella term for a field of study and practice centered on a broad set of approaches and techniques that enable information and knowledge to be derived from data sets
Data analysis ("Data Analysis," undated)	Act of systematically employing qualitative or quantitative approaches (or a combination of these) to describe and evaluate patterns within data
Data conditioning, curation, and normalization (Boyer et al., 2015)	Steps taken to "clean" data sets so that data analytic processes (such as mining) can be more easily utilized
Data mining (Provost and Fawcett, 2013)	Using technology to extract information and knowledge from data
Big data (Gandomi and Haider, 2015)	Largely unstructured data existing in such formats as text, audio, imagery, and video that can be collectively characterized by such attributes as *volume, variety, velocity, veracity, variability* (and *complexity*), and *value*
AI ("artificial intelligence," 2020)	The theory and development of computer systems able to perform tasks normally requiring human intelligence, such as visual perception, speech recognition, decisionmaking, and translation between languages
ML ("machine learning," 2020)	The capacity of a computer to learn from experience (i.e., to modify its processing on the basis of newly acquired information)

text. These techniques require a significant amount of data (and the ability to collect, store, process, and prepare those data for analysis), as well as human input to define the problem and integrate the results into a decisionmaking framework. People who are skilled in coding and data analysis are also needed to develop, train, and provide assurance that analyses and automated processes are working correctly. As a result, these techniques should be thought of as tools that perform a narrow set of tasks to inform decisionmakers or execute predefined priorities, not as a substitute for human input into the decisionmaking process.

Data Science and the U.S. Coast Guard

The field of data science is broad and provides many opportunities—and challenges—for the Coast Guard to streamline manual systems, track patterns across the organization, and better plan for the future by using data-driven analysis. Maximizing the benefits of data science will require three main steps, described in the rest of this section.

Relationships Between Key Data Science Concepts

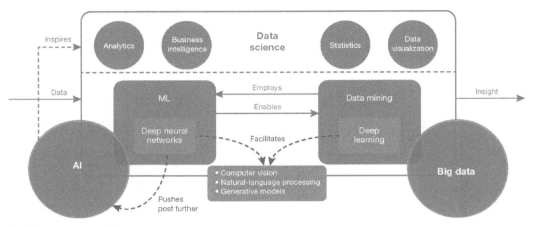

SOURCE: Adapted from Mayo, 2016.

Decide How the Coast Guard Should Use Data Science

Data science systems are most useful when they have been thoughtfully designed to support an organization's needs and long-term goals. Data science is not a silver bullet, but it can be a powerful tool for supporting decisionmakers. Before investing heavily, the Coast Guard should define its long-term vision and goals for using data science in the context of its responsibilities and long-term strategies. Some considerations that the Coast Guard should assess when designing a data science strategy include the desired level and requirements for data gathering and storage, the trade-offs that come with using increasingly complex data-driven analytic tools, the development of in-house data science managers, and the ways in which data science can complement and support policy- and decisionmaking.

To integrate data science into long-term plans and daily operations, the Coast Guard needs to gain an appreciation for how data science can and should be best used within the organization and its potential implications on future operations. Important considerations in Coast Guard plan development include

- *strategy:* establishing a strategic agenda for data science and analytic development, aligned to Coast Guard strategy and goals. This agenda should be incorporated into the funding process by prioritizing projects that speak to those goals.
- *technology:* making decisions related to information technology (IT) infrastructure and expertise based on the service's future needs. A pool of individuals with strong analytical talent or knowledge of day-to-day operations (or both) should be consulted to provide valuable, organization-specific insights while designing Coast Guard–specific systems.
- *organizational culture:* creating an organizational focus on ensuring that the data gathered and analyzed provide specific, timely answers that aid decisionmaking. Leaders should use analytics in decisionmaking to promote a fact-based culture.

Determine the Data Needed and How to Manage Them

The Coast Guard has several needs to consider in expanding its use of data science for any purpose.

Managing Data

Data management is the baseline requirement for all data science systems. To implement any sort of data science system, data are needed. This may seem obvious, but developing useful and effective systematic processes for collecting, storing, protecting, and cleaning data can be complex and resource-intensive. A new data-gathering initiative often requires time for training across multiple groups to ensure that consistent and high-quality data are gathered.

The challenges are not insurmountable; indeed, the capacity to gather data is likely critically required for the future. Developing these systems requires leadership vision and enabling mechanisms to set the tone for investment in capturing data and doing so in ways that align with the Coast Guard's long-term strategies. Understanding how the data will be used is critical to ensuring the right balance of factors to get "quality data," as illustrated in Figure 3. It is important to note that data-management tasks are not discrete stovepipes; instead, there are feedback loops between them and within the policy and decisionmaking structures. It is critical to approach data management not as a stagnant or permanent state but as an iterative development process based on new information and dynamic input from leadership on priorities and goals.

Setting up a system for data gathering should be considered a significant up-front investment in both time and resources. But if planned for and aligned to strategic plans and resources, the data-gathering step could no longer be a challenge once effective systems and processes are in place, and the benefits of analysis should build over time to support decisionmaking and planning.

Defining and Collecting Data

Defining which set of attributes and metrics to record is critical for data to be useful for decisionmakers. The task begins with an inventory of the decisionmaking process as

FIGURE 3
Factors in Collecting Quality Data

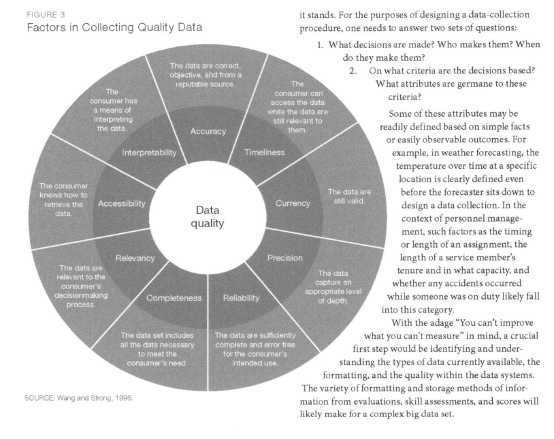

The data are correct, objective, and from a reputable source.

The consumer has a means of interpreting the data.

The consumer can access the data while the data are still relevant to them.

The consumer knows how to retrieve the data.

The data are still valid.

The data are relevant to the consumer's decisionmaking process.

The data capture an appropriate level of depth.

The data set includes all the data necessary to meet the consumer's need.

The data are sufficiently complete and error free for the consumer's intended use.

Accuracy · Interpretability · Timeliness · Accessibility · Currency · Relevancy · Precision · Completeness · Reliability · Data quality

SOURCE: Wang and Strong, 1996.

it stands. For the purposes of designing a data-collection procedure, one needs to answer two sets of questions:

1. What decisions are made? Who makes them? When do they make them?
2. On what criteria are the decisions based? What attributes are germane to these criteria?

Some of these attributes may be readily defined based on simple facts or easily observable outcomes. For example, in weather forecasting, the temperature over time at a specific location is clearly defined even before the forecaster sits down to design a data collection. In the context of personnel management, such factors as the timing or length of an assignment, the length of a service member's tenure and in what capacity, and whether any accidents occurred while someone was on duty likely fall into this category.

With the adage "You can't improve what you can't measure" in mind, a crucial first step would be identifying and understanding the types of data currently available, the formatting, and the quality within the data systems. The variety of formatting and storage methods of information from evaluations, skill assessments, and scores will likely make for a complex big data set.

The set of attributes and metrics to collect defines the scope of the questions that can be addressed with the data set. At the same time, practical and legal restrictions might limit that scope. Collection of personnel information is especially likely to be subject to legal restrictions, and the design of the data-collection process will likely need to be undertaken in concert with legal counsel.

Storing and Presenting Data

Considerable investment is necessary to safely store and agilely present the data that have been collected. Though many of the most dramatic uses of data come from analysis, simply having the data available to relevant stakeholders in a digestible form when needed can provide vital situational awareness for decisionmaking.

Protecting the data and the authorities to access those data can present challenges for integration and use. Classified, law enforcement sensitive, and personally identifiable information are just three types of access control that need to be identified and planned for in the management and analysis process. For example, personnel data can be particularly sensitive and represent an especially attractive target for malicious actors as a result. The 2015 cyberintrusion into the Office of Personnel Management (Zengerle and Cassella, 2015) is a dramatic demonstration of the value of U.S. government personnel data to well-resourced, sophisticated malicious actors. Regardless of how the data are stored, it will take effort, resources, policies, and practices to protect against intrusion and unauthorized access.

Designing the process and infrastructure that present the data to decisionmakers begins with answering the first set of questions above. Successful utilization of the data will require investments in infrastructure to deliver the data, training to ensure that the data are understood, and policies to prevent abuse of the data.

Develop Data Analysis Systems with Several Considerations in Mind

Although popular articles promote the seemingly boundless benefits of data science (especially ML and AI), there are many issues to take into account while developing a data science–based strategy for analysis.

In-House Talent

A consideration for developing a robust data analysis system is having the data science talent in-house. A cohort of individuals who understand and can facilitate machine-aided decisionmaking is needed to ensure that the algorithms are working correctly and the results are correctly interpreted. The algorithms' design can be outsourced, but internal capabilities in coding and math can be useful in designing the actual tools and applications that end users need. While each federal agency stands up an office of the chief data officer and determines the office's roles and responsibilities, this timely concern can be factored into that planning process.

Transparency and Explainability

More-complex ML techniques can be risky in several ways that could compete or conflict with some ideals, such as transparency. ML algorithms are developed by the machine itself and can be a "black box," obscuring from the user a full understanding of what algorithms are being used and why. The answers derived often cannot be clearly traced to the algorithmic decisionmaking process, which reduces transparency. Because ML relies on existing data for predictive actions, it may unearth and propagate unconscious bias originating in the provided data sets. This poses significant risks when applied to certain actions, such as hiring and promotions (Zengerle and Cassella, 2015; DeBrusk, 2018). Risk increases with anything linked to networked computers; the trade-off between having a computer-assisted broad view of data also means that decisions guided by machines are vulnerable to cyberintrusions, such as denial of service or insertion of deceptive information. The issues are not insurmountable but require forethought, study, and planning.

A related issue in data analysis is how well the result of a particular algorithm can be explained to a decisionmaker. In applications that do not directly interact with humans, such as predictive load balancing in computer network routing, explainability might not be very important to the user. However, explainability is important when using data analysis algorithms to support decisionmakers, particularly when the decisions directly affect other people. If decisionmakers cannot offer any rationale for the algorithm-driven parts of the decision beyond broad confidence in the algorithm or an explanation of how the algorithm works in general, it may impede buy-in to the decision itself and the decisionmaking structure more broadly.

For decision tasks in general, it is exceedingly unlikely that a computer can automatically analyze every consideration going into the decision. It will eventually fall to a person to integrate information that may span qualitative information that cannot be digested by a computer,

computer-optimized solutions, and computer-generated predictions in order to arrive at a final decision. To weigh these different types of information against one another, a decisionmaker must be able to understand what information the computer used and how it arrived at its prediction or solution, as well as the inherent computation limitations.

Culture

Decisions aided by machines are still subject to the policies that ultimately shape the decision landscape. Although data-driven decisionmaking can help an organization better adhere to these policies—or highlight their positive and negative impacts—the algorithms themselves cannot mitigate misaligned policies. Having a culture that values the results and insights suggested by data-driven decisionmaking and is prepared to consider them is key to reaping the benefits of data science. Often, policy change lags behind technological change, and those lagging policies will need to be identified early to pave the way for future development. Thus, it is important to cultivate a culture in which people are willing to consider technology-driven change and evolve policies accordingly.

Parallel Processes

To implement the expanded use of data science, the Coast Guard will first need to consider the long-term strategic goals for how it wants to use data and identify the gaps and hurdles that will be budget and policy drivers, especially with regard to its overarching data-collection and management structure. Long-term changes are not made in a vacuum, so even incremental advancements and changes must support current needs and workflows in the interim while any prototype or new applications designed to improve workflow or decisionmaking are being developed and implemented. Understanding this parallel development process will be beneficial for smoothing the proverbial bumps in the road that come with significant process and system changes. Additionally, the Coast Guard will need to review policies to inform the scope of change possible using data science techniques. The Coast Guard should consider how to adapt such functions as acquisition, protection, and sustainment to meet needs in the digital environment as it increases its leverage of data science.

A Deeper Dive: Types and Examples of Data Analysis

A variety of analytical techniques fall under the "data analytics" heading. The methodology used to perform data analysis depends on the question being asked, the types and amounts of data available, computing and network capacity, and the desired level of accuracy. The list of techniques and examples in this section is not exhaustive but provides a sense of the breadth of the field and some idea of the process of deploying these techniques.

Supervised ML is a technique likely to be deployed to support day-to-day personnel decisionmaking. The term refers to a set of techniques that searches for a good approximation of the statistical relationship between inputs and outputs. Supervised ML is well adapted to certain tasks, such as predicting the future price of an asset based on historical price data, identifying the presence or absence of elements in an image, or predicting the next word in

a sentence based on the preceding words. Abstractly, the steps to perform this technique are

1. *Select a model.* A model is a tunable representation of the relationship between inputs and outputs. When a model is selected, some parameters can be adjusted to the choice that best represents the data. Generally speaking, selecting a model is based on some partial knowledge about likely relationships in the data.
2. *Train.* A subset of the data, called training data, is used to tune the parameters of the model. The exact details of this process vary from model to model and can be adjusted to the particular case at hand, but, broadly speaking, the model is tuned with training data so that it produces an output as close as possible to the true (known) output.
3. *Validate.* The remaining data are then used to test the accuracy of the machine-learned map from inputs to outputs. This step is necessary because the model is likely to be more accurate on the training data than on the rest of the data.
4. *Deploy.* The model is used to predict likely outputs on real-world inputs.
5. *Monitor and update.* The model is updated as additional data are gathered.

In the real world, work does not proceed uniformly along these steps. Steps 3 and 4 frequently produce evidence that requires returning to step 1 to reengineer the model or returning to step 2 with more training data. Similarly, the simple descriptions of steps 1 and 2 elide the engineering effort or level of domain-specific expertise that may be necessary to select an appropriate model and identify the amounts of data that might be necessary to train it. In general, the more complex the inputs, outputs, and their relationship, the more data and time will be necessary to successfully deploy a working model.

The classes of models available vary significantly. The framework outlined here focuses primarily on tunability, but other models may have more functionality (e.g., statistical measures of a prediction's uncertainty or tests for overall model quality). Additional functionality can offer decisionmakers more information, but the need for these functions should be weighed against predictive power.

Use Cases for Machine Learning

The following use cases attempt to illustrate some predictive ML applications and capabilities. Although this set of examples is not exhaustive, it gives a sense of the degree to which solutions based on supervised ML must be engineered to the specific problem they are attempting to address. Both the amount of data required and the design details of the state-of-the-art models vary from application to application.

Example 1: Image Classification

In some use cases, a large volume of digital image data needs to be analyzed. For example, the maker of an autonomous vehicle may need an analysis to help the vehicle's optical sensors automatically recognize a stop sign in its video feed, so that the vehicle comes to a halt. Or a smartphone company might want to use the front-facing camera to automatically unlock the phone when the user's face is detected. In these cases, the typical approach is to use supervised ML to automatically build a function that

assigns the presence or absence of the target feature in the image.

As another example, image classification was one of the tasks in the ImageNet challenge (Russakovsky et al., 2015), a competition for image-labeling algorithms that ran from 2010 through 2017. The task required teams to build a model that predicts which of 1,000 possible objects are present in an image. To do this, the teams were presented with a training set of 1.2 million hand-labeled images. The winner of the competition achieved an accuracy rate of 97.7 percent (ImageNet, 2017).

As detailed by the challenge organizers (Russakovsky et al., 2015), assembling such a massive data set of manually labeled images was a significant feat in itself. Such a large data set was necessary because the task required of the final algorithm was so complex. A modern smartphone camera produces images bigger than 10 megapixels. This means that on the order of 33,554,432 variables characterize a full-color digital image. Combined with the subtlety and general nature of the task, the sheer size of the space of possible images means that a significant amount of data is required to reach these levels of accuracy. These considerations also drive the typical choice of model type and neural networks, which can automatically learn important predictors in large, complicated inputs. Even within this class of model, however, some designs of neural networks are more successful than others at making use of image data in particular. Careful engineering and computer vision–specific expertise are required to build a state-of-the-art model.

A possible Coast Guard application of this type of modeling is the 2017 "N+1 fish, N+2 fish" challenge (DrivenData, undated), offered by DrivenData and hosted by the Gulf of Maine Research Institute and the Nature Conservancy to automate fishery observation data. For this challenge, video cameras were placed on board participating commercial fishing vessels, and algorithms were developed to automatically analyze the video images for the sequence of fish, fish species, counts, and measurements (DrivenData, undated).

Example 2: Time-Series Prediction

Time-series prediction is a commonly used supervised ML model that utilizes past data to predict future performance. Weather, stock market performance, and even traffic patterns are based on time-series prediction models. Most people use one or more time-series prediction models in their daily lives, and the concept of employing historical data to predict future outcomes is fairly straightforward.

Time-series data typically consist of only a handful of quantities tracked over time that have a relatively simple relationship with the output for which a predictor is desired. Consequently, one can frequently turn to older statistical models that are easier to understand and explain. These models also typically have better-developed tools for quantifying the uncertainty in their predictions. Similarly, the amount of data needed for good predictions is usually more modest. This is not universally true, however: Some data may have a complicated or obscure enough relationship between input and output to demand a more modern, opaque model or a larger amount of data.

A Coast Guard application of time-series prediction modeling is being developed by the Homeland Security Operational Analysis Center (HSOAC) to estimate future resourcing needs for SAR cases based on past SAR person-hour and equipment requirements. This and other data science efforts currently being pursued by the Coast Guard are indicative of interest and creativity in determining its usefulness for the service.

Example 3: Natural-Language Processing

Natural-language processing, defined broadly as the task of teaching computers to identify the meaning of speech or text, is a large and vibrant field. This is perhaps unsurprising, given the obvious utility of a computer that can interact productively with the way humans natively represent information. Natural-language processing has already produced a variety of compelling products, including speech-to-text, translation, and next-word prediction algorithms.

Text is a challenging input for ML algorithms, so a great deal of data is typically required. Although labeled data sets might not be large enough to accomplish the desired task, a wealth of unlabeled data is available as text-based content on the internet and in books. Consequently, many state-of-the-art methods for natural-language tasks use a methodology known as *transfer learning*. In transfer learning, a model is first trained on a task for which ample data are available, and then pieces of the trained model are used as building blocks for a model to be trained on a related task for which much less data are available.

A Coast Guard application of natural-language processing models could be developing a tool that automatically and systemically combs social media channels to confirm that a person reported missing is, in fact, missing and not currently posting on social media.

Although supervised ML is a natural fit for day-to-day decisionmaking, related techniques, such as unsupervised ML or reinforcement learning, could conceivably play a role in longer-time horizon analyses. Briefly, *unsupervised*

ML refers to a set of techniques designed to find compact representations of the data (or, equivalently, patterns in the data) rather than predicting likely values of a particular output. Unsupervised ML techniques can be useful for exploring a data set for unanticipated phenomena. *Reinforcement learning* refers to techniques that enable a virtual agent to optimally control its environment by learning only from data in its past interactions. Reinforcement learning is perhaps most famous for its use in designing AI that can outperform humans at competitive games, such as DeepMind's AlphaGo for the game of Go (Silver and Hassabis, 2017).

The preceding excursion into supervised ML and three examples expounding on methods within this field provide some insights and ideas on how this technique has been and could be applied.

Conclusion

Data science has the potential to provide valuable insight and capability to the U.S. Coast Guard, if the systems are carefully designed and managed. Applications can help decisionmakers make data-informed choices and improve the overall effectiveness of the service. Data science is also resource-intensive, requiring a significant number of inputs, including proper data-management systems and appropriately trained staffing to ensure that models are designed, explained, and applied appropriately. Data science should be used as a tool to support decisionmakers rather than considered a "catch-all" solution to managing the Coast Guard. That tool, being akin to a Swiss Army knife of options, has a wide variety of topic and mission areas of potential applications in the Coast Guard, from

human resource (HR) management (HRM) to fishery management and enforcement processes.

Some potential next steps to evaluate the utility of data science applications for the Coast Guard include

- *Perform benchmarking.* Researching best practices and success stories of other governmental and private organizations that promoted data cultures can reveal concrete steps that the Coast Guard can take to strengthen its data management and analysis.
- *Support leaders looking for ways to make data-informed decisions.* Coast Guard decisionmakers can use advanced data analysis to promote a culture of data-driven choices. Data-based knowledge can be considered a resource that supports the organization as a whole.
- *Make the invisible visible.* Data analysis can answer questions and provide insight into patterns that individuals cannot detect without computer-supported data analysis. Predictive tools could help project future needs and implications of decisions and policies, all of which could serve to better inform leadership decisionmaking processes.

Understanding and planning for the investments required in such areas as IT infrastructure and talent needs and how each area are affected by long-term strategic plans and goals is critical to starting down the most efficient and effective path to harnessing the potential of data science. As William Cameron said, "Not everything that counts can be counted, and not everything that can be counted counts" (Cameron, 1963, p. 13). *The most important factor in implementing data science in an organization is clearly defining the organization's strategy and goals for using and promoting data science.*

Appendix A. Evergreen V Pinecone Results

To support executive service leaders in their roles as the Coast Guard's key strategic decisionmakers, Evergreen V is conducting several foresight engagements, called Pinecones, on key topics over a two-year period. After each Pinecone, the Evergreen team produces reports and other focal material to identify service implications and strategic choices for the 27th Commandant of the Coast Guard's leadership team. The first Pinecone was in September 2019, with the topic "Workforce 2040." The second Pinecone was part of the Maritime Risk Symposium, held in November 2019. The topic of the second Pinecone was "Future Risks to the Marine Transportation System." In both workshops, themes related to data science technology emerged as areas that warranted further analysis; this appendix is a discussion of the implications and applications of big data in these two topic areas.

Workforce 2040

Like most employers, the U.S. Coast Guard will face challenges recruiting qualified candidates because of emerging technologies and the gig economy's influence on employment trends. Participants in the Coast Guard's Workforce 2040 workshop determined several ways in which technology could also help the Coast Guard recruit and maintain its future workforce if the technology is used efficiently and systems are designed thoughtfully.

Participants explored future recruiting challenges and discussed ways to mitigate employment trends that adversely affect the Coast Guard, including better information-sharing practices and applying new technology in workforce management decisions. Data science techniques—from ML and predictive analytics to data conditioning and basic task automation—were recognized as having great potential impact on the Coast Guard and its personnel management systems. During the workshop, participants identified the importance of making investments today to establish and enable a data culture. Key points include (Office of Emerging Policy, 2019)

- making the invisible visible by using data to gain insight
- supporting leaders looking for ways to leverage data analytics and ML to make data-informed decisions
- creating and empowering a data workforce to gain a competitive advantage.

Applying Data Science to Coast Guard Human Resource Management

For several decades, data science has been effectively used in personnel and talent management (see, e.g., Fitz-enz, 1984), suggesting that the Coast Guard could expand its use of broadly defined data science techniques for HRM functions without pushing accepted boundaries or navigating uncharted waters. The growth of data availability and the advancements in data science technology have transformed business strategies and enabled organizations to bring together data from a variety of disparate sources. They can now go beyond standard administrative insights about their employees, applying ML techniques to foster the development of necessary skills and talents organizationwide (Chui et al., 2018). The Coast Guard can

TABLE A.1

Some Data Science Techniques and Applications That the Coast Guard Could Use for Human Resource Management

Example HRM Activity	Data Management	Data Analysis	
		Less Complex	More Complex
Developing strategic plans	Training future scenarios with data	Projecting force structure based on assumptions	Predicting future shortfalls in key personnel
Creating and filling positions	Compiling billet type, filled status, and location	Tracking billets and flagging unfilled billets	Reporting fleetwide trends in unfilled billets over time and connecting to future personnel planning
Recruiting candidates	Digitizing data collected by recruiters	Mapping the most-fruitful recruiting locations	Developing a recruitment portfolio
Managing compensation and benefits	Tracking organizational compensation and benefit costs	Projecting future compensation and benefit costs given force structure planning	Predicting future compensation and benefit costs based on external and internal market factors
Managing payroll and time	Recording hours worked and associated payroll requirements	Analyzing trends in overtime hours	Optimizing staffing size based on overtime projections
Enabling training and development	Documenting workflows	Analyzing feedback from training programs	Tracking training types to operational and career (promotion, tenure in service) outcomes
Managing talent, performance, and succession	Leveraging more-detailed experience identifiers in electronic personnel files	Determining how frequently personnel use special experience in future assignments	Optimizing personnel matches based on experience
Engaging employees	Developing and administering surveys	Analyzing survey trends and takeaways	Triggering adaptive plans
Retaining specific employees	Tabulating reasons for personnel departures	Associating departure reasons and timing with career fields	Calculating retention incentives needed to retain personnel

SOURCES: Labelle and Dyer, 1992; UK Civil Service Human Resources, 2018; U.S. Coast Guard, 2019.

16

investigate data science applications to improve decision-making with respect to such issues as

- determining workforce requirements through work measurement (see, e.g., Chen, 2019)
- recruiting, including how and from where to attract talent
- making assignments that better optimize individual skills, experience, and preferences with operational needs
- improving retention, such as predicting the effects of new policies or highlighting cohorts that might be at risk for separation, health, or other issues.

Many data science techniques and applications could be leveraged (further) for Coast Guard personnel management. Table A.1 outlines some example applications. The first column gives examples of HRM activities compiled and adapted from academic literature and discussions at the 2019 Workforce 2040 workshop. The next three columns summarize types of data science–related applications at the levels of *data management* and *less-complex and more-complex data analysis*. At its most fundamental structure, higher levels of data analysis must be built on a foundation of data management (see, e.g., Frické, 2009). We use these levels to demonstrate the varying levels of complexity to which data science can be applied.

Broadly, *data management*–related applications enable data to be collected and prepared for analysis. Fundamentally, these applications include data collection and conditioning techniques that prepare data for analysis. The applications categorized under *less-complex data analysis* prepare data for consideration by a decisionmaker or automate (entirely or parts of) basic HR

tasks.[A] These amount to basic data analysis and coding. Finally, *more-complex data analysis* applications support decisionmaking by teaming with or replacing humans in the most-complex cognitive processes. These applications leverage advanced big data analytics and AI.

As discussed in the main body of this document, the Coast Guard must make some large-scale decisions about its plan for and use of data science before these applications can be realized. Nevertheless, there are significant opportunities for the Coast Guard to apply data science techniques to its HRM systems.

Autonomous Systems and the Maritime Transportation System

The Coast Guard faces key opportunities and challenges with the advance of autonomous systems in the maritime domain. Several recurring themes emerged from the 2019 Maritime Risk Symposium workshop—with implications for the future of the Marine Transportation System (MTS)—that are directly related to autonomous systems (Savitz, Davenport, and Ziegler, 2020):

- *differential paces of technological adoption:* Advances in autonomous systems that operate in the maritime domain can put less advanced response and regulatory agencies at a disadvantage in the timely completion of planning, regulatory, legal, and operational response to this technology.
- *workforce competency:* A major concern is that personnel must be capable of handling both advanced

---

[A] This can include such tasks as filling out forms, transferring data, and disseminating information to constituents.

and legacy technologies, in addition to partially autonomous systems. This affects the ability to recruit and retain personnel with those technological skill sets that are in increasingly high demand.

- *uncertainty about capacity demands throughout the MTS:* It is unknown how the industry will adapt and whether government agencies will be able to keep pace with the speed of technology as cargo ships, work boats, and port facilities become more automated.
- *governance challenges for governmental agencies:* As nations aim to address technological, economic, and environmental changes, they need to do so without imposing conflicting policies that either hinder MTS activities or pose new unintended and unanticipated risks. Developing new marine industry regulations and standards requires a deeper technical and operational understanding of the implications of an MTS that operates with greater autonomy.
- *increased Arctic activity:* As the Arctic becomes more accessible, increased maritime activity there could present daunting challenges and opportunities for the Coast Guard, even as land infrastructure becomes harder to build and maintain because of climate effects, such as thawing permafrost and coastal erosion. Commercial and tourism use of Arctic shipping routes could increase the need for rescue capabilities, and autonomous system technology might provide both a safer and more persistent capability in harsh, remote environments.
- *Coast Guard operations doctrine:* The operations doctrine will need revisions. Techniques, tactics,

and procedures will need to be adapted to a different MTS operating environment, as will internal policy implications for responding to autonomous system failure and resulting collisions, allisions, groundings, spills and other safety-of-navigation incidents, security events, and human-caused and natural disasters.

How an Autonomous Maritime Transportation System Might Use Data Science

The broad field of data science has many applications for autonomous maritime transportation systems (AMTSs), such as the vessel shown in Figure A.1. An individual system can use AI and ML in many functions and subsystems:

- *perception:* A key task of many AMTSs is to understand the environment around the system and to recognize objects and activities (e.g., recognizing humans in a SAR context or recognizing threatening activity in port, waterway, and coastal security applications). ML is central to developing and improving object and activity recognition functions of the AMTS.
- *sensor fusion:* A single AMTS can have multiple sensors to gather data about and make sense of the environment. These can include multiple cameras, sonar, the Global Positioning System (GPS), inertial navigation systems, and depth sensors. There are also many proprioceptive sensors to measure the internal state of the system. These systems can produce enormous amounts of data per second that must be fused to produce a coherent state of

the system's external and internal world. Thus, sensor fusion requires big data and AI applications simultaneously.

- *simultaneous localization and mapping (SLAM):* Many AMTSs may operate in areas that are unknown or for which high-fidelity maps are unavailable—for example, in underwater applications or remote areas. In these environments, AMTSs may perform SLAM, in which the system simultaneously creates a map of the world while identifying its location within that mapped world. SLAM is a classic application of AI and ML.

- *path planning:* AMTSs by definition are mobile, so they usually require some sort of path planning (i.e., the ability to develop a plan for how to navigate from point A to point B). Like SLAM, path planning

FIGURE A.1

An Autonomous Vessel Prototype: *Sea Hunter*, U.S. Navy, Office of Naval Research

SOURCE: U.S. Coast Guard Innovation Program, 2017, p. 4.

19

is a fundamental AI application that builds on perception and sensor fusion to navigate around obstacles in the environment, reach intended destinations, and respond to changes.

- *task prioritization and allocation:* Many uses of AMTSs require performing tasks (e.g., retrieving objects A, B, and C and delivering them to locations X, Y, and Z). This higher-order functioning of organizing and prioritizing tasks is another classic AI/ML application. The system identifies the tasks it must complete, calculates the efficiency or value of performing tasks in a particular order or with particular resources, and chooses or prioritizes tasks that maximize some goal typically defined by the operator.

Data science is also important for the Coast Guard to manage future fleets of AMTSs in at least two ways:

- *operations management:* A set of AMTSs must be managed to ensure that tasks and activities are completed, resources are allocated, and the AMTSs are maintained. As with many kinds of assets, data analytics and AI are important for managing AMTS fleet operations.

- *fleet learning:* The observations and activities of a set of AMTSs may be greater than the sum of the observations of a single system. For example, imagery simultaneously gathered and integrated from several systems might be needed to effectively identify, monitor, and assess maritime environmental damage and recovery. Big data applications and ML may be critical for integrating data from across the fleet and identifying patterns in those data (e.g., assessing the spread and containment of oil after a spill from the operations of multiple AMTSs).

When interacting with an external market that, like the MTS, might embrace autonomous systems at a rapid pace, the Coast Guard should preemptively examine its related goals, capabilities, and responsibilities well in advance of any broad-scale adaptation and proliferation.

References

"artificial intelligence, n.," *OED Online*, Oxford University Press, March 2020. As of April 20, 2020:
http://www.oed.com/view/Entry/271625

Balboni, Fred, Glenn Finch, Cathy Rodenbeck Reese, and Rebecca Shockley, *Analytics: A Blueprint for Value—Executive Summary*, IBM Institute for Business Value, October 2013. As of April 27, 2020:
https://www.ibm.com/downloads/cas/4WBWGBJL

Boyer, Sebastien, Ben U. Gelman, Benjamin Schreck, and Kalyan Veeramachaneni, "Data Science Foundry for MOOCs," paper presented at the 2015 Institute of Electrical and Electronics Engineers International Conference on Data Science and Advanced Analytics, Paris, 2015, pp. 1–10.

Cameron, William Bruce, *Informal Sociology: A Casual Introduction to Sociological Thinking*, New York: Random House, 1963.

Chen, Te-Ping, "Three Hours of Work a Day? You're Not Fooling Anyone," *Wall Street Journal*, July 19, 2019.

Chui, Michael, James Manyika, Mehdi Miremadi, Nicolaus Henke, Rita Chung, Pieter Nel, and Sankalp Malhotra, *Notes from the AI Frontier: Applications and Value of Deep Learning*, discussion paper, McKinsey Global Institute, April 2018. As of April 20, 2020:
https://www.mckinsey.com/featured-insights/artificial-intelligence/notes-from-the-ai-frontier-applications-and-value-of-deep-learning

"Data Analysis," *Responsible Conduct of Research*, Faculty Development and Instructional Design Center, Northern Illinois University, undated. As of November 5, 2019:
https://ori.hhs.gov/education/products/n_illinois_u/datamanagement/datopic.html

DeBrusk, Chris, "The Risk of Machine-Learning Bias (and How to Prevent It)," *MIT Sloan Management Review*, March 26, 2018.

DrivenData, "N+1 Fish, N+2 Fish: About the Project," undated. As of April 20, 2020:
https://www.drivendata.org/competitions/48/identify-fish-challenge/page/91/

Fitz-enz, Jac, *How to Measure Human Resources Management*, New York: McGraw-Hill, 1984.

Frické, Martin, "The Knowledge Pyramid: A Critique of the DIKW Hierarchy," *Journal of Information Science*, Vol. 35, No. 2, 2009, pp. 131–142.

Gandomi, Amir, and Murtaza Haider, "Beyond the Hype: Big Data Concepts, Methods, and Analytics," *International Journal of Information Management*, Vol. 35, No. 2, April 2015, pp. 137–144.

ImageNet, "Large Scale Visual Recognition Challenge 2017 (ILSVRC2017)," c. 2017. As of October 2019:
http://image-net.org/challenges/LSVRC/2017/results

Labelle, Christiane M., and Lee Dyer, *A Role-Based Taxonomy of Human Resource Organizations*, Ithaca, N.Y.: Cornell University, School of Industrial and Labor Relations, Center for Advanced Human Resource Studies, Working Paper 92-35, July 1992. As of April 20, 2020:
https://digitalcommons.ilr.cornell.edu/cahrswp/322/

"machine learning, n.," *OED Online*, Oxford University Press, March 2020. As of April 20, 2020:
http://www.oed.com/view/Entry/111850

Mayo, Matthew, "Deep Learning Key Terms, Explained," *KDnuggets*, October 2016. As of April 27, 2020:
https://www.kdnuggets.com/2016/10/deep-learning-key-terms-explained.html

Office of Emerging Policy, U.S. Coast Guard, *Workforce 2040: Executive Summary*, October 2019.

Provost, Foster, and Tom Fawcett, "Data Science and Its Relationship to Big Data and Data-Driven Decision Making," *Big Data*, Vol. 1, No. 1, March 2013, pp. 51–59.

Russakovsky, Olga, Jia Deng, Hao Su, Jonathan Krause, Sanjeev Satheesh, Sean Ma, Zhiheng Huang,, Andrej Karpathy, Aditja Khosla, Michael Bernstein, Alexander C. Berg, and Li Fei-Fei, "ImageNet Large Scale Visual Recognition Challenge," *International Journal of Computer Vision*, Vol. 115, No. 3, December 2015, pp. 211–252.

Savitz, Scott, Aaron C. Davenport, and Michelle D. Ziegler, *The Marine Transportation System, Autonomous Technology, and Implications for the U.S. Coast Guard*, Homeland Security Operational Analysis Center operated by the RAND Corporation, PE-359-DHS, 2020. As of May 4, 2020:
https://www.rand.org/pubs/perspectives/PE359.html

Silver, David, and Demis Hassabis, "AlphaGo Zero: Starting from Scratch," DeepMind blog post, October 18, 2017. As of April 20, 2020:
https://deepmind.com/blog/article/alphago-zero-starting-scratch

UK Civil Service Human Resources, *Global HR Design Principles and Process Taxonomy*, briefing, March 2018. As of April 20, 2020:
https://www.gov.uk/government/publications/global-hr-design

U.S. Coast Guard, "Workforce 2040," Evergreen workshop discussions, September 2019.

U.S. Coast Guard Innovation Program, *Autonomous Systems Challenge*, July 2017. As of April 20, 2020:
https://www.uscg.mil/Portals/0/Strategy/
Autonomous%20Systems%20Challenge%20Report%202017.pdf

Wang, Richard Y., and Diane M. Strong, "Beyond Accuracy: What Data Quality Means to Data Consumers," *Journal of Management Information Systems*, Vol. 12, No. 4, Spring 1996, pp. 5–33.

Zengerle, Patricia, and Megan Cassella, "Millions More Americans Hit by Government Personnel Data Hack," Reuters, July 9, 2015. As of April 20, 2020:
https://www.reuters.com/article/us-cybersecurity-usa/millions-more-americans-hit-by-government-personnel-data-hack-idUSKCN0PJ2M420150709

About the Authors

Aaron C. Davenport is a senior policy researcher at the RAND Corporation. His research focuses include border and maritime security, emergency preparedness and response, occupational health and safety, and national security strategy. He is a graduate of the U.S. Coast Guard Academy and a retired Coast Guard senior officer with security assistance, search-and-rescue, and law-enforcement experience. He has an M.S. in environmental sciences, with a certificate in industrial hygiene and a minor in hazardous materials.

Michelle D. Ziegler is a technical analyst at the RAND Corporation. Her research focuses include U.S. Army logistics, disaster recovery, U.S. Coast Guard capability and capacity analysis, and cooperation and domain awareness in the Arctic. She has an M.S. in astronomy.

Abbie Tingstad is a senior physical scientist and associate director of the Engineering and Applied Sciences Department at the RAND Corporation. Her research focuses on issues related to strategy and planning in defense and homeland security, and for the environment. Much of her work explores the intersections between organizations, processes, technologies, and people. She has a Ph.D. in geography.

Katherine Anania is a technical analyst at RAND and has multidisciplinary experience with the U.S. Department of Defense, the U.S. Department of Homeland Security, and in the environmental field. She has an M.E.S.M. in environmental science and management and an M.A. in economics.

Daniel Ish is an associate physical scientist at RAND, focusing on technical and quantitative analyses. He has done work involving cybersecurity, logistics, supply chain risk management, supervised machine learning and bibliometric analyses of scientific abstracts. He has a Ph.D. in physics.

Nidhi Kalra is a senior information scientist at the RAND Corporation. Her research focuses on autonomous vehicle policy, climate change adaptation, and tools and methods that help people and organizations make better decisions amid deep uncertainty. She spearheads RAND's autonomous vehicle policy work. She has a Ph.D. in robotics.

Scott Savitz is a senior engineer at the RAND Corporation. Much of his research focuses on how to improve the effectiveness and resilience of operational forces, as well as the impact of reallocating resources among those forces. He has a Ph.D. in chemical engineering.

Rachel Liang is the Nuclear Section chief for the Cybersecurity and Infrastructure Security Agency. She was a Department of Homeland Security fellow with the RAND Homeland Security Research Division in 2019–2020. She has a master's degree in weapons of mass destruction security policy from George Washington University's Elliott School of International Affairs.

Melissa Bauman is a communications analyst who helps researchers make their complex findings accessible to a sophisticated audience of lawmakers, journalists, and practitioners. She has a B.A. from the University of Kansas William Allen White School of Journalism and Mass Communications.

About This Perspective

This Perspective documents support by the Homeland Security Operational Analysis Center (HSOAC) to the U.S. Coast Guard's Evergreen project. Founded in 1996, Evergreen is the Coast Guard's strategic foresight initiative, which has historically run in four-year cycles and uses scenario-based planning to identify strategic needs for the incoming service chief. In 2019, Evergreen was restructured to best support executive leaders in their roles as the Coast Guard's decision engines. The project objective is to help posture the Coast Guard to better bridge the gap between future challenges and near-term plans, which typically focus on the urgent needs of the present. HSOAC analysts reviewed Evergreen activities, examined Coast Guard strategy-making and planning processes, adapted an approach for developing scenarios, and narrated a set of exemplar global planning scenarios. The individual Perspectives that resulted from this project reflect themes and specific subjects that have emerged from a series of workshops that were conducted with subject-matter experts and were identified as areas of particular interest for senior leadership strategic-planning activities and emerging policy development.

This research was sponsored by the U.S. Coast Guard Office of Emerging Policy and conducted within the Strategy, Policy, and Operations Program of the HSOAC federally funded research and development center (FFRDC).

The RAND Corporation operates HSOAC under contract to the U.S. Department of Homeland Security (DHS). RAND is a research organization that develops solutions to public policy challenges to help make communities throughout the world safer and more secure, healthier and more prosperous. RAND is nonprofit, nonpartisan, and committed to the public interest. For more information, visit www.rand.org/hsrd/hsoac.

HOMELAND SECURITY
OPERATIONAL ANALYSIS CENTER

An FFRDC operated by the
RAND Corporation under
contract with DHS

PE-A150-1

OCTOBER 2021

Shaping Coast Guard Culture to Enhance the Future Workforce

MICHELLE D. ZIEGLER, AARON C. DAVENPORT, SUSAN A. RESETAR, SCOTT SAVITZ, KATHERINE ANANIA, MELISSA BAUMAN, KARISHMA PATEL

Perspective
EXPERT INSIGHTS ON A TIMELY POLICY ISSUE

HSOAC | HOMELAND SECURITY OPERATIONAL ANALYSIS CENTER

About this Perspective

This Perspective documents support by the Homeland Security Operational Analysis Center (HSOAC) to the U.S. Coast Guard's Evergreen project. Founded in 1996, Evergreen is the Coast Guard's strategic foresight initiative, which has historically run in four-year cycles and uses scenario-based planning to identify strategic needs for the incoming service chief. In 2019, Evergreen was restructured to best support executive leaders in their role as the Coast Guard's decision engines. The project objective is to help posture the Coast Guard to better bridge the gap between future challenges and near-term plans, which typically focus on the urgent needs of the present. HSOAC analysts reviewed Evergreen's activities, examined Coast Guard strategy-making and planning processes, adapted an approach for developing scenarios, and narrated a set of exemplar global planning scenarios. The individual Perspectives that resulted from this project reflect themes and specific subjects that have emerged from a series of workshops that were conducted with subject-matter experts and were identified as areas of particular interest for senior leadership strategic-planning activities and emerging policy development.

This research was sponsored by the U.S. Coast Guard Office of Emerging Policy and conducted within the Strategy, Policy, and Operations Program of the HSOAC federally funded research and development center (FFRDC).

The RAND Corporation operates HSOAC under contract with the U.S. Department of Homeland Security (DHS). RAND is a research organization that develops solutions to public policy challenges to help make communities throughout the world safer and more secure, healthier, and more prosperous. RAND is nonprofit, nonpartisan, and committed to the public interest. For more information, visit www.rand.org/hsrd/hsoac.

About the Homeland Security Operational Analysis Center

The Homeland Security Act of 2002 (Section 305 of Public Law 107-296, as codified at 6 U.S.C. § 185) authorizes the Secretary of Homeland Security, acting through the Under Secretary for Science and Technology, to establish one or more FFRDCs to provide independent analysis of homeland security issues. The RAND Corporation operates HSOAC as an FFRDC for the DHS under contract HSHQDC-16-D-00007.

The HSOAC FFRDC provides the government with independent and objective analyses and advice in core areas important to the department in support of policy development, decisionmaking, alternative approaches, and new ideas on issues of significance. The HSOAC FFRDC also works with and supports other federal, state, local, tribal, and public- and private-sector organizations that make up the homeland security enterprise. The HSOAC FFRDC's research is undertaken by mutual consent with DHS and is organized as a set of discrete tasks.

2

154

This report presents the results of research and analysis conducted under task order 70Z02318FM7P03200, Evergreen V.

The results presented in this report do not necessarily reflect official DHS opinion or policy. For more information on HSOAC, see www.rand.org/hsoac.

Introduction

To cultivate an effective future workforce, the Coast Guard is purposefully considering ways to address culture change and reshaping its organizational culture. The service wants its 2030 workforce to have greater technological fluency, human-centric skills, and the ability to develop new skills and capabilities within the force.[1] The Coast Guard's organizational culture—the behavioral norms and shared values consistently exhibited by its personnel—will play a critical role in creating an environment where the workforce can put those skills into action. However, the Service is increasingly concerned that the current policies for managing personnel, its homogenous workforce, and the way it prioritizes specific skills may over time become barriers to fostering the workplace culture required to meet future challenges. Changing parts of the culture of a large, complex organization is difficult, as it requires the Service to address recruiting, training, retaining, and empowering the future workforce.

To realize its workforce objectives, the Coast Guard will need to identify the aspects of its current organizational culture that it wants to retain, recognize which aspects that require change, and make a plan to overcome any cultural barriers to achieving the desired change. The purpose of this Perspective is to inform the effort for culture change through three main objectives: to stimulate an exploration of how the Coast Guard can adapt its culture to cultivate a more agile, adaptable, and diverse future workforce; to demonstrate how other organizations with similar traits to the Coast Guard have deliberately leveraged organizational culture to affect outcomes; and to highlight necessary elements of the change-management process to maximize the potential of recruitment, retention, and career development, and modernization practices.

Throughout this Perspective, we highlight brief representative cases that illustrate how other large organizations have purposefully utilized organizational culture to achieve specific

> **PROJECT EVERGREEN V**
>
> The topic of this Perspective is the result of a series of Project Evergreen strategic foresight subject-matter expert workshops (called Pinecones) that were conducted by the U.S. Coast Guard Office of Emerging Policy (DCO-X), from 2018 to 2021. Like previous Perspectives, this document is intended to provide an overview and potential suggestions based on the expertise of the participants and the authors. It is not intended to be an exhaustive, authoritative document, but to spurn thoughtful discussion, ideas, and suggest where the Services' senior leadership might effect change for the future of the force.
>
> Each Pinecone workshop involved between 20 and 70 participants from the Coast Guard, academia, government agencies, or the maritime industry. The "Workforce 2030", "Semper Adaptus", and "Flash to Bang" Pinecones all included organizational culture and its relationship to cultivating the desired workforce of the future, and enabling them to harness and employ the technologies aboard assets being developed and fielded now, as well as utilize developments in the coming decades.
>
> Project Evergreen employs scenario-based planning to identify strategic needs for incoming service chiefs, with the goal of supporting executive leaders in their roles as the Coast Guard's strategic decisionmakers.

---

[1] According to the participants in multiple Project Evergreen Pinecones in the 2019-2021 timeframe.

outcomes or cultural change related to what Coast Guard members have identified as needed for the future of the force. We also discuss later in this document how a framework of attributes could be used to determine how applicable the experiences of other organizations could be to the Coast Guard.

What Is Organizational "Culture" and Why Does It Matter?

> "Culture is what keeps the heart beating. Organizational culture is your company's DNA, a sequence of millions and millions of data points that in its entirety makes a living, breathing corporate organism. It is the intangible sum of an organization's history, principles, traditions, actions, language, perks, policies, accomplishments, failures, procedures, ambitions, fears, expectations, values, benefits, and leadership, among other things. Organizational culture, if done well, guides your team towards the right decisions in the absence of direction. If done poorly, culture becomes a cancer that drains morale and drives up risk."[2]

There are many definitions of and nuances surrounding organizational culture, but they generally relate to the behavioral customs and common values regularly demonstrated by an organization's personnel. These behavioral norms and shared values are established consciously and unconsciously through common experiences and interactions over time, such as through leadership, communication and language, expectations, values, customs, and practices. An organization's culture is not homogeneous—large organizations may have many subcultures— nor is it necessarily static over time.[3] There are some key aspects of culture that should be highlighted. First, even though a group's culture evolves over time, culture provides a level of stability to the organization. Second, the more deeply that culture is ingrained in a group, often in ways that are not necessarily visible, the more stable it likely is. Furthermore, culture is comprehensive: it is present in all functions of a group or organization and furnishes an overarching frame for engaging and operating within the overall environment, which provides consistency and predictability to individuals.[4]

An organization should care about its culture because it determines how individuals apply or operationalize policies and procedures to pursue the mission, and how they respond to change. In effect, culture serves as a control mechanism that encourages individuals to act in ways that will achieve the organization's mission objectives and contribute to its survival, as well as thwart

---

[2] Jake Wood, "Why Organizational Culture is Important," webpage, December 18, 2017.

[3] John Kotter, *Leading Change*, Harvard Business School Press, Boston, MA, 1996; Michael D. Watkins, "What Is Organizational Culture? And Why Should We Care?" *Harvard Business Review*, May 15, 2013.

[4] Edgar Schein H., *Organizational Culture and Leadership*, Vol. 4, Jossey-Bass, San Francisco, CA, 2010. Schein is considered to be one of the seminal researchers on organizational culture and leadership and is widely cited.

those who would not effectively contribute or thrive from joining. It follows that a successful organization aligns its culture with its strategy and structure.[5]

> "Regardless of level or location, culture is important because it can powerfully influence human behavior, because it can be difficult to change, and because its near invisibility makes it hard to address directly. Generally, shared values, which are less apparent but more deeply ingrained in the culture, are more difficult to change than norms of behavior."[6]

Decentralized Decisionmaking Can Provide Agility in Conflict

British Royal Navy Captains Lost Autonomy—and Battles—After Technical Advancements Enabled Centralized Control

Not all organizational culture aspects should be changed! In one historical counterexample, unwelcome culture change brought on in part by technological shifts had disastrous consequences for the British Royal Navy. In the 18th and 19th centuries, Royal Navy fleets fought with little centralized direction, and captains had great autonomy. In key struggles such as the Battle of the Nile (1798) and the Battle of Trafalgar (1804), fleets relied minimally on signal flags to coordinate their actions, recognizing that they could not depend on them in battle: the flags could be obscured by smoke and the masts from which they flew could be knocked down. Moreover, winds and enemy action inevitably disrupted initial battle plans. However, captains knew the Royal Navy's doctrine, they knew the overall battle plan, and they knew each other. This shared understanding allowed them to continually and dynamically respond to the situation as it evolved, by adhering to their collective doctrine and their knowledge of what the plan was meant to achieve.

In the 20th century, wireless telecommunications technology enabled a far greater degree of centralized control than could possibly have been exerted using signal flags. The Royal Navy command culture and doctrine adapted to use these communications channels extensively, so that captains were expected to act in response to direction from above. Instead of responding to the situation as they perceived it, they increasingly had to wait for direction from levels of command that had less immediate awareness than they did, and who could only coordinate actions with a substantial delay. This cultural evolution, influenced by technology, contributed to the tied outcome of the Battle of Jutland in 1916, as described in historian Andrew Gordon's book, *The Rules of the Game*. Captains were reliant on communications channels, many of which were damaged by the battle, and they did not have the degree of autonomy needed to respond rapidly and effectively to a dynamic situation.

The Coast Guard's existing culture delegates considerable autonomy to personnel at various levels of command. A key risk in the next several decades is that as communications technology becomes even more ubiquitous, high-bandwidth, and reliable, the Coast Guard will shift to relying on communications and centralized control at the expense of command autonomy. Cultural choices, continual awareness, and vigilance can help to prevent this and ensure that commands have the devolved authority to make decisions.

For sources and more information, see the British Royal Navy section of the references.

---

[5] Kotter, 1996; Watkins, 2013. The Society for Human Resource Management has a useful toolkit for identifying and managing organizational culture that can be found here: https://www.shrm.org/resourcesandtools/tools-and-samples/toolkits/pages/understandinganddevelopingorganizationalculture.aspx

[6] John Kotter, *Leading Change, With a New Preface by the Author*, Harvard Business School Press, Boston, MA, 2012, p. 156.

Evergreen Strategic Foresight Workshops Described Cultural Barriers to Attracting and Adapting to the Workforce Needed for the Future

Project Evergreen is the Coast Guard's program for exploring potential scenarios that may occur decades in the future and analyzing how the Coast Guard can prepare for those scenarios to reduce future risks. In 2018–2021, Project Evergreen's "Pinecone" workshops revealed that the future Coast Guard workforce and culture are central to meeting a wide array of anticipated challenges. This Perspective builds on several of the common themes that connect to organizational culture, as identified in multiple workshops. Participants specified several examples in which the service needs to evaluate and address aspects of the organizational culture by 2030, and how that culture could support or hinder the identified goals and changes.

- **Technological fluency.** As information technology and data science become more pervasive, the USCG as an organization will need to cultivate its culture to embrace and enable a workforce that can more effectively work with both, even as technology obviates the need for people to perform some routine tasks. The result is that individuals at all levels of the organization will need to exceed a "high floor" for technical skills in diverse fields to be able to leverage these technologies and to contribute effectively, and that the culture needs to empower the Service to regularly adopt and adapt to the changing availability of various technologies and data analytics.[7]
- **Human-centric skills.** Even as technology eliminates some roles, the need will only increase for personnel who are not only trained, but also encouraged and empowered to can do what technology cannot, such as building partnerships, creatively solving problems, applying judgment, and cultivating leadership.

---

[7] Aaron C. Davenport, Michelle D. Ziegler, Abbie Tingstad, Katherine Anania, Daniel Ish, Nidhi Kalra, Scott Savitz, Rachel Liang, and Melissa Bauman, *Decoding Data Science: The U.S. Coast Guard's Evolving Needs and Their Implications*, Homeland Security Operational Analysis Center operated by the RAND Corporation, PE-A150-1, 2020.

10

159

- **Adaptive and evolving skill sets.** The pace of change in the technological and operational environments will require fostering a climate that embraces continuous learning and personnel who can build multiple skill sets over the course of their careers, both through formal training and informal experience and mentoring.

Culture Can Help Expedite Innovations

A 'Warrior Spirit' Helps Southwest Airlines Adapt and Innovate Rapidly

As Executive Vice President and CFO Tammy Romo told Forbes, "Teamwork, collaboration, and having a warrior spirit reign king at Southwest Airlines." Romo considers culture and the sense of ownership and pride it infuses to be critical to the airline's success.

She attributes the airline's ability to rapidly adapt to unforeseen, externally driven changes to employees' "warrior spirit." That spirit is composed of 3 key tenants: Strive to be the best, display a sense of urgency, and never give up. The company's culture is credited with enabling and encouraging innovation, especially in adapting new technology and creating efficiencies. Wary of consistency potentially leading to complacency or "group think", Southwest actively encourages its employees to innovate, including by building a new innovation center where employees design and test out new ideas.

This type of "focus on the force and embrace change to enable adaptability" has regularly been echoed in Coast Guard workforce-focused discussions and Evergreen Pinecones.

For sources and more information, see the Southwest Airlines section of the references.

Workshop participants enumerated several cultural barriers to achieving these skillsets and the organization to employ them. The usual assumption is that Coast Guard culture is most closely tied to recruiting, training, and retaining, but culture also reflects the organization itself: how it embraces or resists change, how it empowers innovation or adheres to history, and how the priorities of the service align with the priorities of the people.[8] Workshop participants listed three key cultural barriers:

- **Valuing generalists over specialists.** Some point out that the service has focused historically on creating and valuing generalists versus specialists as manifested in the assignment and promotion processes. The rigid processes for entry and departure provide few opportunities to bring in mid-career talent or to allow personnel to leave the service and then return. Providing more flexibility and choice in Coast Guard career paths can help the service retain members with technical savvy, experience, and good judgment. The service can also do more to reward the skills that it wants to retain and to offer more diverse career progressions that enable personnel to take risks. In several Pinecones, "stitched careers" were identified as a way to retain certain skills and demographics, as well as allow people to leave, gain new training and experience, and then bring that experience back to the service. However, these ideas are often in conflict with the "up or out" culture and policies, where time away from active duty would result in a delay of advancement and no longer being eligible for the billet due to rank gap, despite potentially having exceptional skills in a particular area of focus. Placing greater value on

---

[8] Note: For additional insights on the connections between the identified culture related topics and the proposed needs for the Coast Guard in the future, please see Appendix A for a concise table formatted example.

11

knowledge, skill, and experience, rather than on titles alone in assigning roles can also help to ensure that the strengths of the workforce are being effectively leveraged. In the words of Rear Admiral Grace Hopper: "The most dangerous phrase in the language is, 'We've always done it this way.'"[9]

- **A culture that has not successfully enabled diversity and inclusion.**
  Despite a desire to further diversify the Coast Guard, the proportion of underrepresented minorities at each rank declines as rank increases, ultimately resulting in a less diverse senior leadership.[10] The Coast Guard's Diversity and Inclusion Action Plan states "To ensure we remain Ready, Relevant, and Responsive, we must continue to recruit and retain a highly skilled total workforce that reflects the people we serve. Diverse representation alone will not increase our readiness if we do not retain our diverse total workforce. Inclusion in the workplace drives employee engagement and is paramount for attracting and retaining employees."[11] The Military Leadership Diversity Commission final report recommended making diversity a critical part of the service's organizational culture and fostering a culture in which a leader who is "faced with a choice between two very different individuals of equal qualifications, he or she must be ready to choose the person who best enhances the effectiveness of the work unit, knowing that diversity has the potential to improve the work of that unit. This 'difference' could relate to race/ethnicity, gender, or religion, but it could also relate to educational background, specialty, or international experience."[12] While the Coast Guard has made strides in identifying and addressing diversity and inclusion challenges, the current demographics limit the Coast Guard's ability to attract the largest pool of qualified candidates and harness diverse perspectives to effectively shape relationships and solve problems[13]. This representation problem is not only critical but also potentially growing, given that half the Coast Guard's future recruiting pool (Americans younger than 15) are racial or ethnic minorities. If the service cannot adjust to this apparent demographic shift, it will continue to lose opportunities to access the talents and capabilities of the majority of the population. Participants see this as a barrier to developing human-centric and "soft" skills, especially those that will be critical in the increasing number of interactions personnel will have with cultures around the world. As Commandant Admiral Shultz announced in the Diversity and Inclusion Plan in 2018,

  > "The Coast Guard's ability to respond to emerging threats in a fast-paced, ever changing world requires that we maximize the full potential of our diverse workforce. It is our duty to ensure that all members belong and are valued in solving the complex problems that the Coast Guard faces. This is paramount to improving productivity, performance, innovation, job satisfaction, and achieving mission excellence. Diverse representation without inclusion degrades our readiness. Barriers to inclusion are the

---

[9] Esther Surden, "Privacy Laws May Usher In 'Defensive DP'," *Computerworld*, Vol. 10, No. 4, Newton, Massachusetts, January 26, 1976, Page 9, Column 3.

[10] CNA, "Population Representation in the Military Services," webpage, undated.

[11] U.S. Coast Guard, "Diversity & Inclusion: Action Plan 2019 – 2023," May 2020.

[12] Military Leadership Diversity Commission, *From Representation to Inclusion: Diversity Leadership in the 21st-Century Military, Final Report,* March 2011.

[13] U.S. Coast Guard, "Diversity & Inclusion: Action Plan 2019 – 2023," May 2020.

12

unconscious biases we carry without our awareness. As individuals, we will identify and mitigate our biases and work to build bridges that connect us to one another. As an organization, we will identify bias and barriers within the system, policies, and procedures and take action to mitigate them. Achieving and maintaining a culture of respect begins with understanding and exhibiting inclusive behaviors that are fair, open, cooperative, supportive, and empowering. Diversity and inclusion are cornerstones of high organizational performance and mission effectiveness. A diverse workforce stimulates innovation, new approaches, and fresh perspectives to solve complex organizational challenges."[14]

- **Unclear cultural priorities.** Clarity in human resource management policy regarding what new skills and traits are explicitly valued, promoted, and communicated to the various stakeholders is an important consideration[15]. The perception among workshop participants was that the service defaults to a set of cultural norms (that appear to value mainly afloat and aviation leadership and skills over cyber, intel, language, and foreign policy proficiencies, etc.) that need to be reevaluated and updated to reflect the future workforce demographics and the future needs of the service—moving away from the more rigid paradigm for acquiring and developing talent and towards a more agile and nimble paradigm that enables the recruiting and retraining of personnel in new or differing areas as the need arises. Additionally, the Pinecone participants enumerated that without prioritizing culture that embraces innovation, technology adoption, and data utilization[16], the service will continue to struggle to recruit, utilize, and retain those with the necessary skill sets to keep pace with the future technological developments and assets. During a 2019 trip to the lower Mississippi River, Admiral Shultz acknowledged that while progress has been made, there are still challenges yet to be addressed in these areas. He remarked that the U.S. Coast Guard Academy is finally providing cyber as a major with the first class to graduate in 2022, but also caveated concerns about retaining that talent after their 5-year commitment has been fulfilled. "We have to generate and re-generate expertise, we have to make people feel valued and want to stay as part of the brand," Schultz said. "Technically smart people are central."[17]

How the Coast Guard Can Assess New Approaches to Reach the Right Outcomes

There are many external examples of purposeful organizational culture development or change that could yield ideas and lessons learned or suggest focus areas for the Coast Guard.

---

[14] Karl L. Schultz, "Diversity and Inclusion Policy Statement," The Commandment of the United States Coast Guard, June 1, 2018.

[15] Susan A. Resetar, Michelle D. Ziegler, Aaron C. Davenport, and Melissa Bauman, *U.S. Coast Guard Workforce 2040: Better Management Through Transparency*, Homeland Security Operational Analysis Center operated by the RAND Corporation, PE-358-DHS, 2020.

[16] Davenport et al., 2020.

[17] Greg Trauthwein, "Admiral Schultz Emphasizes Maritime as a Driver of U.S. Commerce," *Maritime Logistics Professional*, July 9, 2019.

13

However, no single organization likely shares all the attributes of the Coast Guard. Therefore, the service will need to examine multiple examples that address different shared attributes or combinations of them. Additionally, focusing on organizations that proactively sought change (either before a crisis or in a forced reaction to a challenge) and that share some of the same characteristics as the Coast Guard could potentially help the Coast Guard sort out good ideas that are likely applicable to the service from good ideas that would likely not have the same positive results in the Coast Guard. The USCG could identify potential approaches to changing desired aspects of its organizational culture by using this type of multiple case study analysis, which analyzes multiple cases as part of an overall research design to discover case-based themes and generate insights from observations within and between cases.[18]

We designated several attributes as fundamental to the Coast Guard's case; when selecting external examples of options to pursue, the Coast Guard should look for organizations with the following similar attributes that may have cultural features worth studying (examples in this section are illustrative only):

- Asymmetric risks of success and failure: Public organizations, particularly those with a regulatory function, are especially prone to asymmetric risks—that is, an aversion to change because the risks may outweigh the rewards. The Coast Guard has both regulatory and safety functions, which create strong incentives to operate with care, first and foremost. As a result, the consequences of failure may exceed the uncertain rewards resulting from change. Stability, certainty, and "good enough" performance are highly valued by the public and the regulated community. Private sector examples that are comparable to the Coast Guard would be firms that require high consumer confidence (e.g., pharmaceuticals); high reliability or performance with severe consequences of failure (e.g., aircraft manufacturing, electricity generation/transmission); or an exemplary public image (e.g., family entertainment).
- High organizational complexity: Organizations with several distinct functions (law enforcement, search and rescue, environmental protection) that are performed at many levels (headquarters, regions, districts, and sectors) and that have distributed operational elements would have similarities to the Coast Guard. For example, other federal agencies, such as the Department of Agriculture or the Environmental Protection Agency, perform functions ranging from scientific research to regulatory enforcement, have a wide geographic distribution, and may have some cultural features that could provide insights for the Coast Guard.
- Geographically distributed functions: Organizations whose functions and command levels are distributed across a wide variety of locations around the world, and that include required foreign policy and language variables would share attributes with the service. International shipping, airlines, and chemical companies are examples of organizations in this category.
- Varied partner and stakeholder engagement: The Coast Guard works closely with a range of industries; other federal, state, and local law enforcement; homeland and national

[18] C. Grima-Farrell, *The Collective Case Study Design: Comparing Six Research to Practice Case Studies. In: What Matters in a Research to Practice Cycle?*, Springer, Singapore, 2017.

14

security; natural resource management; and international partners. The EPA is very similar in this regard.

- Hierarchical decisionmaking but some localized authority: Organizations that are rules-based but give operational elements some localized decision authority would have similarities to the Coast Guard. Large public-school systems or franchising organizations may fall in this category.
- Planned, periodic change in senior leadership: Organizations that create and sustain long-term visions amid purposeful leadership changes at all levels (especially in the senior ranks) would share attributes with the Coast Guard. For example, federal agencies experience periodic leadership change.

In addition to the examples throughout this document highlighting various aspects of the Pinecone-identified challenges, the Coast Guard can also draw from institution-specific studies on managing change to construct a plan that is more tailored to its organization. For example, a 2017 RAND study identified promising approaches to institutional change in the Army,[19] which has many institutional similarities to the Coast Guard. In addition to the basic steps discussed in the next section, it noted that a holistic approach that focuses on cultural drivers in a coordinated way is necessary to effect long-term change. This approach differs from a "crisis-response" approach that treats a persistent cultural problem as a transient issue; once the immediate crisis passes, the problem is likely to reappear because no true institutional change has occurred. While the Army is a hierarchical organization in which direction flows from the top, it is also an organization in which leadership responsibility exists at virtually every level. Consequently, leaders at all levels in the organization need to be engaged in the change process to ensure that it is executed throughout the entire organization.[20] The Coast Guard has institutional similarities to the Army, and therefore could take advantage of this research.

---

[19] Lisa S. Meredith, Carra S. Sims, Benjamin Saul Batorsky, Adeyemi Theophilus Okunogbe, Brittany L. Bannon, and Craig A. Myatt, *Identifying Promising Approaches to U.S. Army Institutional Change: A Review of the Literature on Organizational Culture and Climate*, Santa Monica, Calif.: RAND Corporation, RR-1588-A, 2017.

[20] Meredith et al., 2017.

15

**Space Force Builds a New Culture from the Ground Up to Avoid
Inheriting One that Doesn't Align with its Mission**

The U.S. Space Force (USSF) is poised to inherit a culture from the Air Force, but as a new service, its ultimate culture is still emerging and highly malleable. To establish the right culture from the start, the USSF is proactively trying to identify the type of culture it will require and the likely challenges in cultivating it.

One challenge is that the USSF will be bringing together units and personnel from multiple services, each with its own culture. As Peter Garrison summarized it in an article in *War on the Rocks*, personnel involved in missile operations work in a "compliance driven culture" because even a small deviation or error can have massively negative consequences, and that many space officers began their careers in ICBM culture, and that while they shifted out of the missile field and in to Air Force space focused missions, the culture from their early experiences stays with them. He also points out that Air Force Space Command was under the purview of US Strategic Command, which has the nuclear mission as a key tenant and thus also has need for a compliance driven culture. So it is of no surprise, that the compliance culture would be where USSF starts. Meanwhile, special forces operate with a significant level of autonomy in decisionmaking and have a "can do" culture. The article posits that because of the rapidly changing technology, footprint of the force, and even goals and missions, a "can do" culture needs to be at the heart of the USSF, but establishing that culture is a substantial challenge because it is inheriting a compliance driven culture ingrained in a deliberate, but slow to innovate, capabilities-and-requirements-based system (as opposed to threat-based).

Without waiting for a negative event to drive the change, USSF is trying to determine how to recruit the right people to cultivate the right culture. One senior official said, "We want people to be recruited into the Space Force as similar to the way the Marine Corps recruits Marines. We don't recruit Marines into the Navy—they go after a specific kind of people with a vision that is necessary to build that culture."

Similarly, the Coast Guard might find significant variances in the cultures of its different communities because the needs and underlying drivers for a fixed-wing pilot differ from those of a port security unit. Looking forward to how the Coast Guard will operate in the future, the culture required for those

What the Coast Guard Can Learn from Research About Effecting Change

Changing culture is difficult but not impossible. Understanding how to adapt an organization's culture to a changing environment is a fundamental leadership challenge. The specific problems a changing environment creates for the organization provide the motivation for change, for which culture is likely one aspect.[21] Once the Coast Guard identifies what aspects of its culture to preserve, what aspects to change, and what the barriers are to implementing those changes, it must proceed with a plan.[22] To maximize the chance of success, the Coast Guard could leverage lessons learned from research. Research prescribes three distinct steps for successfully pursuing and managing change: prepare, execute, and support.[23]

---

[21] Schein, 2010.

[22] Schein proposes a formal cultural self-assessment process as part of a managed change process in his book.

[23] Nancy Young Moore, Laura H. Baldwin, Frank Camm, and Cynthia R. Cook, *Implementing Best Purchasing and Supply Management Practices: Lessons from Innovative Commercial Firms*, Santa Monica, Calif.: RAND

16

Preparing for change refers to the necessary activities that create the foundation for change to occur. These involve communicating why change is necessary, developing a vision and direction for the future, establishing senior leadership support[24], and developing an action plan for moving toward the envisioned future. Leaders should link the necessary culture change to the identified reasons for why change is necessary. In other words, leaders must understand where the existing culture aligns and where it conflicts with evolving external conditions and trends specific to the service's operating environment. [25] For example, a previous RAND analysis of public sector organizations revealed that the case for change was built from evidence that existing practices were out of step with the times, that survival of the organization necessitated change, and that there was a sense of urgency so that employees understand the importance of adapting the culture and are motivated to change their behaviors in the necessary ways.[26]

A clearly articulated vision for the future motivates and guides change and ideally should be explainable in five minutes or less to improve the likelihood that it will be understood and internalized.[27] Another approach requires developing a short, reasoned, compelling statement that clearly states the aspirations for the organization (the "big opportunity"), preparing a vision for how changes will allow the organization to seize on this opportunity, and developing activities that will move the organization forward.[28] Preparing for cultural change also specifically includes developing formal training opportunities, allowing flexibilities for individuals to control their own informal learning process, and providing opportunities for group learning. Having general support structures, role models, and feedback mechanisms (in both directions) are also essential. While providing a motivation catalyzes change, these activities help facilitate change by providing support and reducing the barriers to change. They will require resources and time to help individuals learn new ways of doing things and to ensure that organizational practices are consistent with the vision of the future.[29]

Corporation, DB-334-AF, 2002; Debra Knopman, Susan A. Resetar, Parry Norling, and Irene T. Brahmakulam, *Systems of Innovation Within Public and Private Organizations: Case Studies and Options for the EPA*, Santa Monica, Calif.: RAND Corporation, DB-393-EPA, 2003.

[24] David Stauffer, "How to Win the Buy-In: Setting the Stage for Change," *Harvard Business Review*, February 26, 2008.

[25] B. Groysberg, J. Lee, J. Price, and J. Cheng, "The leader's guide to corporate culture," *Harvard Business Review*, Vol. 96, No. 1, 2018, pp.44-52.

[26] Knopman et al., 2003.

[27] Paul Charles Light, *The Four Pillars of High Performance: How Robust Organizations Achieve Extraordinary Results: Lessons from the RAND Corporation*, McGraw Hill, 2005, p. 229; Susan Resetar, et al., "Guidebook for Multi-Agency Collaboration for Sustainability and Resilience," American Association of State Highway and Transportation Officials, 2020; and Susan Resetar, Frank Camm, and Jeffrey Drezner, *Environmental Management in Design Lessons from Volvo and Hewlett-Packard for the Department of Defense*, RAND, Santa Monica, CA, 1998.

[28] John P. Kotter, "Forget the Strategy PowerPoint," *Harvard Business Review*, April 22, 2014, pp. 2-4.

[29] Schein, 2010, pp. 299-310.

17

Change is not possible without senior leadership support, and other organizations have focused on selecting a cadre of leaders—either internal or external—who support the strategy and vision for the future, can provide incentives for change, and can reduce barriers to change, such as organizational stovepipes, personnel management practices, etc. For example, when the Army introduced a new logistics management approach (Velocity Management), it created a rotation of general officers to oversee this change. The coalition of officers provided consistent leadership support that transcended the usual turnover driven by the military assignment process.[30] The action plan should identify the measures of success, responsible parties for overcoming barriers to change, and how to track progress and ensure accountability for success.

Culture Can Affect Objectives and Outcomes by Empowering People

VA Bases Culture Change on Principles
Rather Than Rules in Order to Better Serve Veterans

In 2014, new Secretary of Veteran Affairs Robert McDonald set out to substantially redesign the VA, relying heavily on guidelines for effective organizational change developed by John Kotter (Harvard professor, and an authoritative voice on organizational culture and change). A key tenet for McDonald was that the organization should be based on principles, not rules. He described the VA's culture before he arrived as "risk averse", "rules based", "a culture of learned helplessness." Employees could stand by every step they did or did not take through to the General Counsel's office, but they lacked the support and freedom to act and make decisions that would actually benefit the patients or improve the organization.

McDonald stated that "building a principle-based organization is about creating a culture in which everyone knows that if they act in accordance with the VA's principles, the leadership team would support them." Part of that culture and employee empowerment is also aimed at generating a flow of information about problems and gaps from the front-line efforts, all the way up to the Secretary, who can work with Congress to ensure that the VA is properly resourced to close those gaps. Additionally, to support the right types of changes and efforts, they needed to adjust what they were measuring. While the metrics had been hyper focused on wait times, the VA realized that patients prioritized streamlined systems and feeling valued. As the Kotter steps indicate, the VA found it to be true that "there's no hope of effective transformation when leaders' sights are set on the wrong objectives."

Through these efforts, the VA has effectively transformed, with markedly higher satisfaction with the care received, more timely care, and greater employee satisfaction. While the missions differ, many of the VA's underlying principles and challenges are similar to those faced by the Coast Guard.

For sources and more information, see the VA section of the references.

Executing. Change often requires a formal process for piloting new ideas, evaluating the results, monitoring progress, and adapting as necessary to be successful. Moreover, change, especially cultural change, is a long process and requires sustained attention. To sustain organizational change, it is essential to align cultural norms and shared values with the desired change. Typically, culture evolves with the early and intermediate successes of organizational change; as employees see that change produces positive results, they begin to value the cultural

---

[30] John Dumond, Marygail K. Brauner, Rick Eden, John R. Folkeson, Kenneth J. Girardini, Donna J. Keyser, Eric Peltz, Ellen M. Pint, and Mark Y.D. Wang, *Velocity Management: The Business Paradigm That Has Transformed U.S. Army Logistics*, Santa Monica, Calif.: RAND Corporation, MR-1108-A, 2001.

18

elements that support the new way of operating.[31] Ensuring that the desired behaviors and norms are in place to develop future leaders and that the current leaders model them is critical. Fostering transparency, being open to feedback, using implementation teams, and creating explicit milestones can facilitate the implementation process.[32] In short, success breeds success. One potential lever for this is to employ organizational design to pursue the desired change. Senior leadership should look for opportunities to align organizational policies, structures, processes, and practices with the vision for the organization and its culture. [33] Examples in literature, echoed in Pinecones, include promotion practices, performance management, and training programs.

Supporting change includes engaging in resonating and reinforced communications throughout the organizational levels, providing training and skills development opportunities, creating incentives for individuals to implement the change, and ensuring that necessary funding and resources are available. Routine, multilateral communication is necessary for a variety of reasons. While leadership is directing the ship by making the case for change and articulating the vision of the future, individuals within the organization are responsible for operationalizing this direction. If frontline workers do not understand the vision and motivations for change, the old culture and way of doing things will prevail and any momentum will be lost. Moreover, individuals may operationalize change in ways that don't quite line up with the vision (similar to a game of "Telephone" in which the original message morphs with each retelling). In other words, multi-lateral and frequent communication is necessary to keep change moving in the desired direction and to prevent misinterpretations or alterations that hamper or redirect progress.[34] Some organizations identify champions to help lead and sustain momentum for cultural change by communicating to frontline personnel the motivation and sense of urgency while exemplifying the desired change. Essentially, the communication lever should engage the workforce in all practicable venues, from social media, to leadership seminars, to informal and formal training forums. This approach to communications is especially important for cultural change since culture can affect behavior in imperceptible ways.

To expand the depth and breadth of communications, many organizations seeking change create a coalition of change agents or key stakeholders to oversee change, communicate the desired change, and maintain accountability for achieving it. Other ways of encouraging change are through performance reviews, promotions, and training. In an interview with Harvard Business Review, IBM CEO Samuel Palmisano spoke about the strategic importance of values at

---

[31] Kotter, 1996.
[32] Stauffer, 2008.
[33] Stauffer, 2008.
[34] Light, 2005; Kotter, 1996.

19

IBM and how he purposefully changed the culture amid thriving business and rapidly evolving operations:

> "I'm talking about decisions that support and give life to IBM's strategy and brand, decisions that shape a culture. That's why values, for us, aren't soft. They're the basis of what we do, our mission as a company. They're a touchstone for decentralized decision-making. It used to be a rule of thumb that 'people don't do what you expect; they do what you inspect.' My point is that it's just not possible to inspect everyone anymore. But you also can't just let go of the reins and let people do what they want without guidance or context. You've got to create a management system that empowers people and provides a basis for decision-making that is consistent with who we are at IBM."[35]

Regular Communication from Leadership Can Connect Culture to Current Plans and Choices

At Team Rubicon, Culture Communication from Leadership Drives Decisionmaking on All Levels

At Team Rubicon, a veteran-based disaster relief organization with more than 100,000 volunteers, its service principles—tenacity, impartiality, accountability, collaboration, and innovation—guide the planning and direction of the organization, and its cultural values drive almost everything else. Codified in 2015, the cultural values are painted on the walls at headquarters, are taught during the onboarding process, and are at the heart of the leadership and action cycles.

Outside of the organization, the values might not make much sense. But every employee and volunteer in the organization knows and understands them. They are applied to nearly every decision, action, and communication within the organization. From reminding each other to take a break when needed, to pivoting from natural disaster response to pandemic response operations that were unlike anything the organization had ever done before, the culture drives those choices. In addition, CEO and cofounder Jake Wood gives a new presentation on culture every year at Team Rubicon's Leadership Conference that encourages, supports, and reinforces various efforts and the direction of the organization. Team Rubicon focuses on having a culture that is consistent across the organization, regardless of level or location, and strong enough for the organization to not require a policy for everything, as it is the culture that is driving decisions and actions.

Being able to clearly communicate how seemingly disconnected efforts are inherently tied to the culture, and regularly reiterating how culture should be driving decisions and actions can help the Coast Guard understand the intent of senior leadership and ensure that even in a somewhat decentralized organizational design, the choices and actions of its personnel can be in step with the vision, principles, and values of the force.

For sources and more information, see the Team Rubicon section of the references.

Summary

Traditional organizational cultures are being challenged as occupations become more technical, specialized, and complex; organizations become more global and interconnected; and information technologies proliferate. These trends suggest that any individual organization may

---

[35] Paul Hemp and Thomas A. Stewart, "Leading Change When Business Is Good," *Harvard Business Review*, December 2004.

20

have many subcultures internally and be influenced by a wider range of national or ethnic macrocultures. These changing dynamics necessitate cultural change, but will also complicate leadership toward it.[36] Similarly, in multiple Pinecone workshops, it was suggested that organizational culture is at the heart of addressing issues that will shape the Coast Guard's future, such as workforce enhancement, technology implementation, information sharing, and training needs. Some aspects of current culture will need to be preserved and enhanced, while others may serve as barriers to change, and still others are not well defined and are opportunities to lean in and shape the force.

Externally, there are countless examples of organizations purposefully changing their cultures with specific goals in mind. The Coast Guard's missions and service type, the complexity of its structure, and its long history make the service unique in such a way that no single example organization can serve as a "how-to" guide. However, there are many lessons learned and partially applicable examples that can help guide the way to purposefully pursuing and supporting change.

Looking forward, the Coast Guard can go beyond the examples identified here. The service can help shape its future by not only identifying goals, but also creating a thorough understanding of the current culture, identifying which aspects should continue to be embraced and which ones should be reformed, and then planning for and effecting the changes deemed necessary. To pursue change, the Coast Guard will need a comprehensive process for managing the transition from the present state to the future vision, or organizational inertia created by existing policies, practices, and culture will slow or ultimately prevent progress. Lessons from previous research are that organizational change will take years and requires perseverance.[37] Leadership and support at all levels, with initiative from the highest ranks, transparency about aspirations and plans, and follow-through with the vision can help the Coast Guard maximize the beneficial aspects of its current culture, and identify and effect change where needed to achieve the workforce the service needs to meet the demands of the future Coast Guard.

> "Culture is like the wind. It is invisible, yet its effect can be seen and felt. When it is blowing in your direction, it makes for smooth sailing. When it is blowing against you, everything is more difficult."[38]

---

[36] Schein, 2010.

[37] Light, 2005.

[38] Bryan Walker, and Sarah A. Soule, "Changing Company Culture Requires a Movement, Not a Mandate," *Harvard Business Review*, June 20, 2017.

21

Appendix A

How do you connect cultural values to reasonings and outcomes for innovation?

Participants in the Pinecones recommend that the Coast Guard pursue the strategy of innovation as an organizational competency to stay ahead of a changing environment. Along with norms and artifacts, Schein's model includes values as one critical aspect of organizational culture. This Appendix presents a concise look at the values typically observed in innovative organizations. Table 1 (below) from "Organizational culture, innovation, and performance" in the *Journal of Business Research*[39] presents a list of common values found in innovative organizations and presents the rationales provided in the research literature for how these values support innovation. Innovation-oriented cultures typically value: success, openness and flexibility, internal communication, competence and professionalism, inter-functional cooperation, responsibility of employees, appreciation of employees, and risk-taking. In Schein's model, used for this analysis, values are one aspect of organizational culture, and norms and artifacts are the others. The authors assessed the presence of these values, their associated norms, and existing artifacts (e.g., stories of innovators, physical arrangements that provide opportunities to discuss new ideas, etc.) to model firm performance.[40]

Table 1. Common value dimensions and rationales for cultural change for encouraging innovation

Value dimension	Definition	Rationale
Success	The degree to which an organization values success, strives for the highest standards of performance, & values giving staff challenging goals & encouragement to excel	* Raises performance expectations of employees; * Creates psychological ownership of organizational goals; * Enhances intrinsic motivation & feelings of self-efficacy; * Increases employees' motivations to find novel solutions to organizational problems; * Improves innovative performance
Openness & flexibility	The degree to which an organization values openness & responsiveness to new ideas, & a flexible approach to solving problems	* Facilitates creativity, empowerment, & change that are essential for the exploration that drives innovation; * Encourages intrinsic interest in, & appreciation of novelty, variety seeking, receptiveness to new ideas, & tolerance for ambiguity associated with creativity and innovation; * Facilitates idea generation and divergent thinking that enable problem identification & implementation of creative solutions
Internal communication	The degree to which an organization values open communication that facilitates internal flows of information	* Social development theory and situational learning theory emphasize cognitive growth through social interaction & communication of information;

---

[39] Suellen Hogan, and Leonard Coote, "Organizational culture, innovation, and performance: A test of Schein's model," *Journal of Business Research*, Vol. 67, No. 8, August 2014, pp. 1609-1621.

[40] Hogan and Coote, 2014.

22

Value dimension	Definition	Rationale
		* Provides access to and availability of diverse knowledge, cross-fertilization of ideas, improved quality of decision-making, & consideration of novel alternative solutions that yield innovation
Competence & professionalism	The degree to which an organization values knowledge & skills, & upholds the ideals & beliefs associated with a profession	* Professional knowledge, expertise & technical skills (i.e., domain-relevant knowledge) constitute the raw material for innovation; * Increased professional knowledge & expertise lead to increased problem analysis & solution provision, increased initiation of and adoption of technical innovations, increased total, technical & administrative innovation adoption, increased innovative human resource practices & increased radical innovation capability
Inter-functional cooperation	The degree to which an organization values coordination & teamwork	* Resource dependence theory suggests that when working on highly innovative projects, members from different functional areas consider their tasks to be more heavily reliant on the expertise, information, & resources of other functional specialists to achieve buy-in & successful & innovative outcomes; * High levels of integration & sharing among teams is facilitated through complex coordination, communication, information-sharing, cooperation & conflict resolution processes, which in turn influences innovation success
Responsibility	The degree to which an organization values employees' proactiveness, initiative, autonomy & responsibility for their work	* A relatively high degree of responsibility, autonomy & encouragement of initiative fosters innovation; * When employees perceive responsibility for achieving the overall goals of a project & have discretion in how goals are accomplished, they develop a sense of ownership & control over their own work & ideas, overcome potential problems with persistence & determination, & produce more creative & innovative outcomes
Appreciation	The degree to which an organization values, rewards & recognizes employees' accomplishments	* As a directive mechanism, output expectations are more successful when accompanied by rewards & feedback, & the provision of rewards & recognition of innovative accomplishments positively influences innovation; * The synergistic effects of extrinsic motivation (e.g. recognition) & intrinsic motivation (e.g. commitment to work & exploratory learning) influence innovation; * performance–reward dependency & risk-taking are positively related to all stages in the development of new technological innovations
Risk-taking	The degree to which an organization values experimentation with new ideas & challenging the status quo	* Valuing risk-taking (encouraging taking meaningful & calculated risks within the scope of one's job, & encouraging challenging the status quo in an effort to produce positive job-related outcomes) is related to the psychological safety construct where employees feel able to experiment with new ideas & do things differently without the fear of negative consequences to self-image, status or career; * Encouraging risk-taking strengthens superordinate identity & when combined with supervisory support & encouragement positively influences product innovativeness

Source: Suellen Hogan, and Leonard Coote, "Organizational culture, innovation, and performance: A test of Schein's model," *Journal of Business Research*, Vol. 67, No. 8, August 2014, pp. 1609-1621.

23

References and Recommended Reading

Abbey, A., and J.W. Dickson, "R&D work climate and innovation in semi-conductors," *Academy of Management Journal*, Vol. 26, No. 2, 1983, pp. 362-368.

Amabile, T.M., "A model of creativity and innovation in organizations," *Research in Organizational Behavior*, Vol. 10, JAI Press, Greenwich, 1988, pp. 123-167.

Amabile, T.M., R. Conti, H. Coon, J. Lazenby, and M. Herron, "Assessing the work environment for creativity," *Academy of Management Journal*, Vol. 39, No. 5, 1996, pp. 1154-1185.

Baker, N.R., and J.R. Freeland, "Structuring information flow to enhance innovation," *Management Science*, Vol. 19, No. 1, 1972, pp. 105-116.

Battisto, Dina, Deborah Franqui, *A Standardized Case Study Framework and Methodology to Identify Best Practices, The Visibility of Research Sustainability: Visualization Sustainability and Performance*, Clemson University, ARCC 2013.

Binnewies, C., S. Ohly, and S. Sonnentag, "Taking personal initiative and communicating about ideas: What is important for the creative process and for idea creativity?," *European Journal of Work and Organizational Psychology*, Vol. 16, No. 4, 2007, pp. 432-455.

Caldwell, D.F., and C.A. O'Reilly III, "The determinants of team-based innovation in organizations: The role of social influence," *Small Group Research*, Vol. 34, 2003, pp. 497-517.

CNA, "Population Representation in the Military Services," webpage, undated. As of June 11, 2021: https://www.cna.org/research/pop-rep

Davenport, Aaron C., Michelle D. Ziegler, Abbie Tingstad, Katherine Anania, Daniel Ish, Nidhi Kalra, Scott Savitz, Rachel Liang, and Melissa Bauman, *Decoding Data Science: The U.S. Coast Guard's Evolving Needs and Their Implications*, Homeland Security Operational Analysis Center operated by the RAND Corporation, PE-A150-1, 2020. As of April 28, 2021: https://www.rand.org/pubs/perspectives/PEA150-1.html

De Clercq, D., B. Menguc, and S. Auh, "Unpacking the relationship between an innovation strategy and firm performance: the role of task conflict and political activity," *Journal of Business Research*, Vol. 62, 2009, pp. 1046-1053.

Defense Advisory Committee on Women in the Services, "DACOWITS Reports and Meeting Documents," webpage, undated. As of June 7, 2021: https://dacowits.defense.gov/Reports-Meetings/

Dewett, T., "Creativity and strategic management: Individual and group considerations concerning decision alternatives in the top management teams," *Journal of Managerial Psychology*, Vol. 19, No. 2, 2004, pp. 156-169.

24

Dumond, John, Marygail K. Brauner, Rick Eden, John R. Folkeson, Kenneth J. Girardini, Donna J. Keyser, Eric Peltz, Ellen M. Pint, and Mark Y.D. Wang, *Velocity Management: The Business Paradigm That Has Transformed U.S. Army Logistics*, Santa Monica, Calif.: RAND Corporation, MR-1108-A, 2001. As of April 06, 2021: https://www.rand.org/pubs/monograph_reports/MR1108.html

Dwertmann DJG, Nishii LH, van Knippenberg D. "Disentangling the Fairness & Discrimination and Synergy Perspectives on Diversity Climate: Moving the Field Forward." *Journal of Management.* 2016;42(5):1136-1168. doi:10.1177/0149206316630380

Garcia-Morales, V.J., F. Matías-Reche, and A.J. Verdu-Jover, "Influence of internal communication on technological proactivity, organizational learning, and organizational innovation in the pharmaceutical sector," *Journal of Communication*, Vol. 61, 2011, pp. 150-177.

Grima-Farrell, C, *The Collective Case Study Design: Comparing Six Research to Practice Case Studies. In: What Matters in a Research to Practice Cycle?*, Springer, Singapore, 2017. https://doi.org/10.1007/978-981-10-2087-2_3

Groysberg, B., J. Lee, J. Price, and J. Cheng, "The leader's guide to corporate culture," *Harvard Business Review*, Vol. 96, No. 1, 2018, pp.44-52.

Gumusluoglu, L., and A. Ilsev, "Transformational leadership, creativity, and organizational innovation," *Journal of Business Research*, Vol. 62, 2009, pp. 461-473.

Hemp, Paul, and Thomas A. Stewart, "Leading Change When Business Is Good," *Harvard Business Review*, December 2004. As of April 15, 2021: https://hbr.org/2004/12/leading-change-when-business-is-good

Hogan, Suellen, and Leonard Coote, "Organizational culture, innovation, and performance: A test of Schein's model," *Journal of Business Research*, Vol. 67, No. 8, August 2014, pp. 1609-1621.

Howell, J.M., and K. Boies, "Champions of technological innovation: The influence of contextual knowledge, role orientation, idea generation, and idea promotion on champion emergence," *The Leadership Quarterly*, Vol. 15, No. 1, 2004, pp. 123-143.

Khazanchi, S., M.W. Lewis, and K.K. Boyer, "Innovation-supportive culture: The impact of organizational values on process innovation," *Journal of Operations Management*, Vol. 25, 2007, pp. 871-884.

Knopman, Debra, Susan A. Resetar, Parry Norling, and Irene T. Brahmakulam, *Systems of Innovation Within Public and Private Organizations: Case Studies and Options for the EPA*, Santa Monica, Calif.: RAND Corporation, DB-393-EPA, 2003.

Kotter, John P., *Leading Change*, Harvard Business School Press, Boston, MA, 1996.

25

174

Kotter, John P., "Forget the Strategy PowerPoint," *Harvard Business Review*, April 22, 2014, pp. 2-4.

Kotter, John P., *Leading Change, With a New Preface by the Author*, Harvard Business School Press, Boston, MA, 2012.

Light, Paul Charles, *The Four Pillars of High Performance: How Robust Organizations Achieve Extraordinary Results: Lessons from the RAND Corporation*, McGraw Hill, 2005.

Lim, Nelson, Abigail Haddad, and Lindsay Daughtery, *Implementation of the DoD Diversity and Inclusion Strategic Plan: A Framework for Change Through Accountability*, Santa Monica, Calif.: RAND Corporation, RR333, 2013. As of April 28, 2021: https://www.rand.org/pubs/research_reports/RR333.html

McKinsey & Company, "Understanding organizational barriers to a more inclusive workplace," webpage, Survey, June 23, 2020. As of April 15, 2021: https://www.mckinsey.com/business-functions/organization/our-insights/understanding-organizational-barriers-to-a-more-inclusive-workplace#

Meredith, Lisa S., Carra S. Sims, Benjamin Saul Batorsky, Adeyemi Theophilus Okunogbe, Brittany L. Bannon, and Craig A. Myatt, *Identifying Promising Approaches to U.S. Army Institutional Change: A Review of the Literature on Organizational Culture and Climate*, Santa Monica, Calif.: RAND Corporation, RR-1588-A, 2017.

Military Leadership Diversity Commission, *From Representation to Inclusion: Diversity Leadership in the 21st-Century Military, Final Report*, March 2011. As of April 29, 2021: https://diversity.defense.gov/Portals/51/Documents/Special%20Feature/MLDC_Final_Report.pdf

Moore, Nancy Young, Laura H. Baldwin, Frank Camm, and Cynthia R. Cook, *Implementing Best Purchasing and Supply Management Practices: Lessons from Innovative Commercial Firms*, Santa Monica, Calif.: RAND Corporation, DB-334-AF, 2002.

Moorman, C., and A.S. Miner, "The impact of organizational memory on new product performance and creativity," *Journal of Marketing Research*, Vol. 34, 1, 1997, pp. 91-106.

Mumford, M.D., G.M. Scott, B. Gaddis, and J.M. Strange, "Leading creative people: Orchestrating expertise and relationships," *Leadership Quarterly*, Vol. 13, No. 6, 2002, pp. 705-750.

O'Reilly, C., "Corporations, culture, and commitment: motivation and social control in organizations," *California Management Review*, Vol. 31, No. 4, 1989, pp. 9-25.

Open Universities Australia, "3 reasons you'll need human-centric skills for the future," webpage, September 25, 2019. As of April 15, 2021:

26

https://www.open.edu.au/advice/insights/3-reasons-youll-need-human-centric-skills-for-the-future

Redmond, M.R., M.D. Mumford, and R. Teach, "Putting creativity to work: Effects of leader behavior on subordinate creativity," *Organizational Behavior and Human Decision Processes*, Vol. 55, No. 1, 1993, pp. 120-151.

Resetar, Susan, Frank Camm, and Jeffrey Drezner, *Environmental Management in Design Lessons from Volvo and Hewlett-Packard for the Department of Defense*, RAND, Santa Monica, CA, 1998.

Resetar, Susan, et al., "Guidebook for Multi-Agency Collaboration for Sustainability and Resilience," American Association of State Highway and Transportation Officials, 2020.

Resetar, Susan A., Michelle D. Ziegler, Aaron C. Davenport, and Melissa Bauman, *U.S. Coast Guard Workforce 2040: Better Management Through Transparency*, Homeland Security Operational Analysis Center operated by the RAND Corporation, PE-358-DHS, 2020. As of April 28, 2021: https://www.rand.org/pubs/perspectives/PE358.html

Schein, Edgar H., *Organizational Culture and Leadership*, Vol. 4, Jossey-Bass, San Francisco, CA, 2010.

Schultz, Karl L., "Diversity and Inclusion Policy Statement," The Commandment of the United States Coast Guard, June 1, 2018. As of May 4, 2021: https://media.defense.gov/2018/Jun/01/2001925986/-1/-1/0/DIVERSITY-30MAY18_SIGNED.PDF

Sethi, R., D.C. Smith, and C.W. Park, "Cross-functional product development teams, creativity, and the innovativeness of new consumer products," *Journal of Marketing Research*, Vol. 38, No. 1, 2001, pp. 73-85.

Song, M., and M. Swink, "Marketing–manufacturing integration across stages of new product development: Effects on the success of high- and low-innovativeness products," *IEEE Transactions on Engineering Management*, Vol. 56, No. 1, 2009, pp. 31-44.

Sonnentag, S., and J. Volmer, "Individual-level predictors of task-related teamwork processes: The role of expertise and self-efficacy in team meetings," *Group & Organization Management*, Vol. 34, No. 1, 2009, pp. 37-66.

South, Todd, "Diversity of 'races, religions, backgrounds and genders' essential to warfighting in the information age, 3-star says," *Marine Corps Times*, September 30, 2019. As of April 15, 2021: https://www.marinecorpstimes.com/news/your-marine-corps/2019/09/30/diversity-of-races-religions-backgrounds-and-genders-essential-to-warfighting-in-the-information-age-3-star-says/

27

Stauffer, David, "How to Win the Buy-In: Setting the Stage for Change," *Harvard Business Review*, February 26, 2008. As of April 12, 2021: https://hbr.org/2008/02/how-to-win-the-buyin-setting-t-1

Subramaniam, M., and M.A. Youndt, "The influence of intellectual capital on the types of innovative capabilities," *Academy of Management Journal*, Vol. 48, No. 3, 2005, pp. 450-463.

Surden, Esther, "Privacy Laws May Usher In 'Defensive DP'," *Computerworld*, Vol. 10, No. 4, Newton, Massachusetts, January 26, 1976, Quote Page 9, Column 3.

Tellis, G.J., J.C. Prabhu, and R.K. Chandy, "Radical innovation across nations: The preeminence of corporate culture," *Journal of Marketing*, Vol. 73, 1, 2009, pp. 3-23.

Trauthwein, Greg, "Admiral Schultz Emphasizes Maritime as a Driver of U.S. Commerce," *Maritime Logistics Professional*, July 9, 2019. As of May 4, 2021: https://www.maritimeprofessional.com/news/admiral-schultz-emphasizes-maritime-driver-348129

U.S. Coast Guard, "Diversity & Inclusion: Action Plan 2019 – 2023," May 2020. As of June 11, 2021: https://www.dcms.uscg.mil/Portals/10/CG-1/diversity/DIAP/Diversity-and-Inclusion-Action-Plan.pdf?ver=2020-06-25-153724-670

Walker, Bryan, and Sarah A. Soule, "Changing Company Culture Requires a Movement, Not a Mandate," *Harvard Business Review*, June 20, 2017. As of April 12, 2021: https://hbr.org/2017/06/changing-company-culture-requires-a-movement-not-a-mandate

Watkins, Michael D., "What Is Organizational Culture? And Why Should We Care?" *Harvard Business Review*, May 15, 2013.

West, M.A., "Sparkling fountains or stagnant ponds: an integrative model of creativity and innovation implementation in work groups," *Applied Psychology: An International Review*, Vol. 51, No. 3, 2002, pp. 355-424.

Wood, Jake, "Why Organizational Culture is Important," webpage, December 18, 2017. As of April 12, 2021: https://teamrubiconusa.org/blog/why-organizational-culture-is-important/

Team Rubicon References

For more specifics on the Team Rubicon cultural values and how they applied to the 2020 pandemic: https://teamrubiconusa.org/blog/coronavirus-disaster-relief-leadership/

Wood, Jake, Creating Culture that Counts, LinkedIn, December 2017, As of April 15, 2021: https://www.linkedin.com/pulse/creating-culture-counts-jake-wood/

Wood, Jake, TR Culture, Team Rubicon Leadership Conference: Fire Superiority, Houston TX, June 2018.

28

Wood, Jake, the peTRi dish, Team Rubicon Leadership Conference: Retreat? Hell We Just Got Here!, Estes Park, CO, August 2019.

Wood, Jake, Keynote Address, Team Rubicon Leadership Conference: Dig In, Virtual, August 2020.

Southwest Airlines References

Thomson, Jeff, "Company Culture Soars At Southwest Airlines," *Forbes*, December 18, 2018. As of April 12, 2021: https://www.forbes.com/sites/jeffthomson/2018/12/18/company-culture-soars-at-southwest-airlines/?sh=71f59637615f

Razetti, Gustavo, "Mapping Southwest's Fun Loving Culture," *Fearless Culture*, January 12, 2020. As of April 15, 2021: https://www.fearlessculture.design/blog-posts/southwest-airlines-culture-design-canvas

Barbour, Hilton, "The Beating Heart of Southwest Airlines' Culture", *The Digital Transformation People*, November 4, 2019. As of April 15, 2021: https://www.thedigitaltransformationpeople.com/channels/people-and-change/the-beating-heart-of-southwest-airlines-culture/

Arnold, Kyle, "Southwest Airlines is building an innovation lab at Dallas Love Field," *Dallas News*, January 2020. As of April 15, 2021: https://www.dallasnews.com/business/airlines/2020/01/20/southwest-airlines-is-building-an-innovation-lab-at-dallas-love-field/

Space Force References

Galer, John, "Op-ed | Only a separate service can create a space culture," *SpaceNews*, June 9, 2019. As of April 12, 2021: https://spacenews.com/op-ed-only-a-separate-service-can-create-a-space-culture/

Garretson, Peter, "Space Force's Jupiter-Sized Culture Problem," *War on the Rocks*, July 11, 2019. As of April 12, 2021: https://warontherocks.com/2019/07/space-forces-jupiter-sized-culture-problem/

Garamone, Jim, "Officials Explain U.S. Space Force Need, Culture," Department of Defense, March 1, 2019. As of April 12, 2021: https://www.defense.gov/Explore/News/Article/Article/1772212/officials-explain-us-space-force-need-culture/

Veteran Affairs References

Buell, Ryan W., "A Transformation Is Under Way at U.S. Veterans Affairs. We Got an Inside Look," *Harvard Business Review*, December 22, 2016. As of April 12, 2021: https://hbr.org/2016/12/a-transformation-is-underway-at-u-s-veterans-affairs-we-got-an-inside-look

29

British Royal Navy References

The Rules of the Game, by Andrew Gordon, provides a book-length study of the comparison between the Royal Navy cultures of command in the early nineteenth and early twentieth centuries. See Gordon, Andrew, *The Rules of the Game: Jutland and British Naval Command*, London: John Murray Publishers, Ltd., 1996. An article that adapts Gordon's argument for the present-day U.S. Navy is Roberts, Lieutenant Commander Colin, "The Long Calm Lee of Midway," Proceedings of the U.S. Naval Institute, January 2018, Vol. 144/1/1,379. As of March 9, 2021: https://www.usni.org/magazines/proceedings/2018/january/long-calm-lee-midway.

Another good source is Hughes, Wayne P., *Fleet Tactics and Coastal Combat, 2nd edition*, Naval Institute Press, Annapolis, MD, 1999, which discusses how captains adapted during the Battle of the Nile in 1798.

Appendix D. HSOAC Quick Looks

This appendix contains the Quick Looks that the HSOAC team developed to summarize the findings, insights, and key takeaways from each of the workshops.

Contents

PROJECT EVERGREEN V
THE COAST GUARD'S STRATEGIC FORESIGHT INITIATIVE

Workforce Futures Workshop
September 10-12 at Coast Guard Training Center Yorktown

The Evergreen Workforce Futures 2040 Workshop was held from 10-12 September at Coast Guard Training Center Yorktown. After plenary sessions to explain the workshop and its context, the participants were divided into four groups, each of which contained 8-9 individuals with diverse backgrounds within the Coast Guard, as well as 1-2 Coast Guard facilitators and an HSOAC contributor. During the workshop, each group was given a distinct scenario characterizing the future world within which the Coast Guard is operating, as well as "shocks" that imposed stress on the Coast Guard within a limited timeframe. Using their assigned future scenarios and shocks participants engaged in a series of facilitated activities to:

Individually generate a series of potential advantages, challenges, and opportunities (see "How the workshop was conducted on Page 2).

- Collectively identify several key strategic needs—i.e., enduring problems that need to
- be addressed.
- Enter potential solutions to strategic needs into a matrix. One axis of the matrix consisted of the strategic needs, while the other listed five categories of actions, namely authorities, policy, tools, culture, and other items.
- Extract the solutions which they perceived as best, then characterize those solutions
- in terms of relative importance and difficulty of implementation. This resulted in four categories: "strategic" (important and hard), "best return on investment" (important and easier), "low-hanging fruit" (less important and easier), and "luxury" (less important and hard).
- Integrate their assessments into a single poster that summarized key elements of pursuing these strategic needs to include a clearly defined problem statement, strategy statement, stakeholders, potential barriers, and measures of progress.

Groups also analyzed how future contexts would lead them to allocate funding across the eleven statutory missions, and how their choices would change if overall funding levels were halved. They also were asked individually to rate the factors that would most affect the workforce of the future before the brainstorming activities and after the posters were completed.

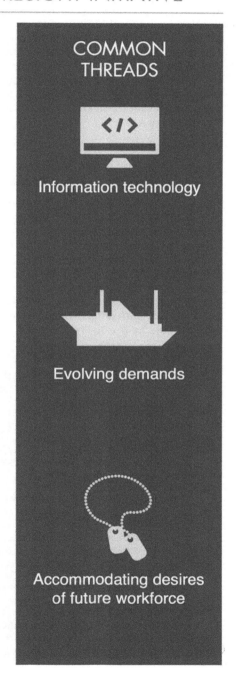

COMMON THREADS

Information technology

Evolving demands

Accommodating desires of future workforce

1

PROJECT EVERGREEN 2040

Workforce Futures Workshop

A number of key themes emerged from the workshop, which we describe in the next several pages. This document represents a quick-response, initial overview of the workshop, and it will be followed by more in-depth analysis and documentation at a later date. Note also that the following is not informed by interviews or document reviews, but solely by the results of the workshop itself.

Strategic Needs

Most of the strategic needs that the four groups identified belonged to one of three categories:

Information technology. This included recruiting and retaining personnel with IT (and especially cyber) expertise, as well as investment in improving IT infrastructure. The Coast Guard's perceived shortcomings in terms of IT infrastructure and expertise make it more difficult to recruit and retain IT experts, or those with IT career aspirations. Even if the Coast Guard contracts out much of its IT expertise needs, it still requires personnel who know about IT to oversee

those contractors. High-quality IT systems are needed to provide the data and information required to improve workforce planning and personnel management. More analysis is needed of the types and numbers of cyber-experts that will be needed. Additionally, several of the groups enumerated HR challenges, indicating that the system was insufficiently flexible and responsive to meet all the current needs of the workforce.

Evolving demands. The demand on the Coast Guard to perform different missions will likely vary over time. For example, growing and aging coastal populations and more severe storms may increase demand for SAR, overexploitation of other nations' fisheries and changing environments may increase demand for the OLE mission, and offshore wind farms may create new PWCS or SAR demands, or obstruct access in ways that increase the resources needed to perform other missions.

Managing talent and accommodating the future workforce. The Coast Guard has traditionally had a single approach to talent

HOW THE WORKSHOP WAS CONDUCTED

1. Plenary sessions explained the workshop and its context to Coast Guard participants

2. Four groups were formed, each with 8-9 individuals with diverse CG backgrounds, 1-2 CG facilitators and an HSOAC contributor.

3. Each group received a distinct scenario characterizing the future world within which the Coast Guard is operating, as well as more time-specific "shocks" that imposed stress on the Coast Guard.

4. Individuals identified potential advantages, challenges, and opportunities, and then as a group identified several key strategic needs.

5. They developed a matrix to structure the development of ideas to address these strategic needs. One axis contained the strategic needs themselves, while the other listed five categories, namely authorities, policy, tools, culture, and other items.

6. Participants filled the matrix with ideas, extracted those which they perceived as best, and then prioritized these ideas based on importance and difficulty of implementation.

7. They integrated their assessments into a single poster that summarized key take-aways. Groups also analyzed how future contexts would lead them to allocate funding across the 11 statutory missions, and how their choices would change if overall funding levels were halved.

2

management, with individuals joining the service at a young age and then being promoted or exiting the service over time. However, this may not be ideal for recruiting and retaining specialized technical personnel in key fields, such as IT. Moreover, millennials and "Generation Z" increasingly want more flexible career options, and many seek geographic or job stability, or a work-life balance that differs from current Coast Guard expectations. Also, future workforce demands may shift the desirable balance between uniformed and civilian personnel: civilian specialists may be needed for a number of roles that do not require the broader capabilities of a uniformed individual, or require the strict military standards currently imposed on the entire uniformed workforce, regardless of duties assigned.

Other strategic needs included better shaping public perceptions of the Coast Guard to improve recruitment, assessing and enhancing partnerships to complement Coast Guard capabilities, and addressing other emerging technologies, such as unmanned vehicles, by recruiting and retaining the right expertise.

Other Key Issues

Participants also identified a number of other issues for consideration:

Compensation factors that influence recruitment and retention.
- Why join or stay in the Coast Guard if the private sector offers greater compensation?
- How would single-payer healthcare, a universal basic income, changing retirement plans, or other wide-scale policy changes affect the Coast Guard workforce?

The pros and cons of the emergence of a "gig economy" for the Coast Guard.
- The Coast Guard may struggle to recruit people who are conditioned to short- term employment, or it may attract people who are looking for long-term careers that are hard to find in the wider labor market.

- Also, the Coast Guard may be able to hire expertise on demand for short contracts, though that also requires more contracting personnel, potentially with new skills.
- There also may be cultural clashes between gig workers for the Coast Guard and uniformed, civilian, or long-term contractor personnel, particularly if the last three groups perceive their work as undervalued.

Tensions between homeland-centric and global missions.
- Global demand for the Coast Guard may affect the types of skills that are needed, such as linguistic and cultural skills, as well as strategic thinking.
- Some individuals may be more attracted to the service by increasing opportunities to travel internationally, while others may be reluctant to serve extensively overseas.
- Global demand may also impose more stress on personnel and families, particularly if OPTEMPO increases to cover both homeland and global missions and personnel are required to serve in unaccompanied duty assignments.
- If overseas operations included large-scale participation in maritime wars, this could strain Coast Guard capacity more than the wars of the last two decades have. The impact on recruitment and retention would be unclear: surges of patriotism might also be balanced by fear of personal risk.

Increasing demand for Arctic and Antarctic activity by the Coast Guard
- This can similarly create interesting opportunities that attract individuals, but negative perceptions of operating in these areas may diminish recruitment or retention.
- Increasing overall demand for the Coast Guard, together with increasing frequency and intensity of natural disasters, may strain Coast Guard capacity to deal with multiple simultaneous events.

There is a need for more expertise in a range of technical areas beyond IT, such as unmanned

3

systems with varying degrees of autonomy, medical and epidemiological issues, biological and other WMD threats, and environmental characterization.
- This may require more flexible arrangements to bring in expertise at various levels of the organization.

The need for both policy and cultural changes to address talent management.
- Policy changes can take months to years, but cultural changes can take decades or longer.
- There is an inherent conservative bias regarding talent management, because the people currently shaping the organization emerged from its prior approaches to talent management.

Some missions (e.g., ATON, icebreaking) could potentially be privatized or passed on to other agencies, though there are strong political and cultural headwinds opposing this.

The Coast Guard's roles in space and cyberspace, together with the accompanying technical requirements, are unclear. Other agencies (such as CISA) could potentially manage cybersecurity for all entities other than the Coast Guard itself and DoD.

The meaning of supply and demand for Coast Guard presence, including in cyberspace, and the extent to which this shapes demand for personnel with specific skill sets, still needs to be better defined.

The Coast Guard faces unknown infrastructure liabilities and needs in the face of imprecisely known rates of climate change. This can help to shape what types of expertise are needed to oversee the building and maintenance of future infrastructure.

Policy changes can take months to years, but cultural changes can take decades or longer. There is an inherent conservative bias regarding talent management, because the people currently shaping the organization emerged from its prior approaches to talent management.

Approaches to Addressing Needs and Issues

Individuals and groups also offered a number of ideas regarding how to contribute to the future Coast Guard workforce in the coming decades.

Accommodate changing workforce desires by making policies and cultures more flexible
- Provide various levels of on-boarding and off-boarding ramps, including the option of accelerated return to the service
- Provide personnel with more individual choices and control of their careers. o Provide more HR and other support to individuals, particularly those with in-demand specializations and/or may be most prone to leave due to family circumstances
- This includes, but is not limited to, better career counseling and offering greater individual participation in and transparency of the HR management system.
- Overall, make HR more responsive to individuals' needs and better-integrated into the overall organization. Some groups called for a radical overhaul of HR and OPM
- Recognize that there will be tensions between the needs of individuals and those of the service Provision time for self-directed development and training

4

PROJECT EVERGREEN 2040

Workforce Futures Workshop

- Encourage something like Master Resiliency Training (includes mental, physical, lifestyle health)

- Anticipate that decriminalization of some drugs and changing patterns of use may constrain recruiting if use is wholly forbidden, so policy changes specific to individual drugs may be in order—e.g., treating marijuana more like alcohol

Promote geographic stability and the ability to work remotely

- Encourage individuals to perform more rotations in a single geographic area

- Have longer rotations in a given position

- Expand remote-working options, improve IT to enable remote working, and foster a corresponding culture

Increase and retain specialized knowledge

- Enable personnel who have left the Coast Guard, or who were never part of it, to more readily enter or return it at various stages of their careers

- Expand direct-commission and direct-enlistment programs, including for more limited timespans than are currently available

- Create additional financial and promotional incentives for specialists to join and stay in the Coast Guard, or to return to it

- Create incentives for personnel departing active duty, particularly those with specialized knowledge, to remain in the reserves

    o Encourage "stitched careers" in which people can move back and forth between active duty and the reserves

- Target tuition-assistance programs for high-demand areas

- Develop and expand exchange programs with other agencies and the private sector

- Permit line officers and foster the promotion of specialists, even (or especially) if they have not "checked all the boxes" from a traditional career

- Partner more with specific universities on recruitment

- Better track and analyze the supply and demand for particular specialized skills within the Coast Guard

- While facilitating entry into and exit from the organization, strive to avoid loss of organizational culture by creating opportunities for assimilation

- Emphasize skill sets, not rank and rate, when selecting individuals for positions

Improve and expand IT infrastructure to better retain cutting-edge IT-savvy personnel, as well as to make all personnel more efficient and effective

- Create an "Office of Emerging Technology" akin to DoD's Strategic Capabilities Office (SCO), accelerating the acquisition and deployment of new COTS, near-COTS, and GOTS technologies

    - Achieving higher levels of technological sophistication can help to recruit and retain technically skilled individuals, creating a virtuous cycle

    - Technologies can also increase capacity, increase capabilities, or reduce workforce requirements

HSOAC
HOMELAND SECURITY
OPERATIONAL ANALYSIS CENTER
An FFRDC operated by the RAND Corporation under contract with DHS

Project Evergreen (EVG) employs Strategic Foresight to support executive leaders in their role as the Coast Guard's decision engines. This product is a first look into the results of Workforce 2040, one of eight "pinecones" on the Evergreen tree. In summer 2021, Team EVG will begin a meta-analysis of the Pinecones to identify strategic choices for the 27th Commandant of the Coast Guard's leadership team.

PROJECT EVERGREEN V

WORKSHOP QUICK LOOK

Future Maritime Risk Workshop
November 14-15, 2019 | Maritime College,
State University of New York

This short document represents a rapidly written initial overview of key themes from the workshop "Future Threats to the Maritime Transportation System (MTS)." The workshop immediately followed the annual Maritime Risk Symposium, held in the same venue. The workshop's two half-day sessions involved about 70 participants from the Coast Guard, research institutions, maritime industry stakeholders, and interagency partners.

Objectives
The workshop's objective was to engage the maritime transportation community in a discussion of underappreciated future risks to the MTS. Participants addressed three questions:

- What are the most significant potential future risks or threats for the MTS and how will they manifest themselves?

- What are the implications of the risks or threats?

- How are they different from what we face today?

Throughout the workshop, participants also considered actions to mitigate the risk and the respective roles of community members. Outputs of the workshop will inform USCG strategic decision-making.

Key Findings
Climate change may modify infrastructure and interfere with vessel navigation. The MTS will likely face profound impacts as disasters grow more intense and frequent, along with chronic sea-level rise, periodic drought, and other conditions. Damaged infrastructure will need to be repaired or reconstructed; some infrastructure will need to be relocated or modified to account for sea-level rise. Recurring cycles of damage and rebuilding of infrastructure may strain budgets. Efforts to mitigate the effects of climate change may also negatively affect the MTS; for example, land reclamation or physical barriers to limit flooding may interfere with vessel navigation. Participants unanimously cited addressing resiliency throughout the MTS as imperative to mitigate the effects of climate change.

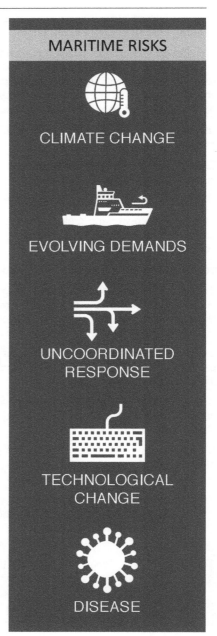

MARITIME RISKS

CLIMATE CHANGE

EVOLVING DEMANDS

UNCOORDINATED RESPONSE

TECHNOLOGICAL CHANGE

DISEASE

1

PROJECT EVERGREEN V

WORKSHOP QUICK LOOK: Future Maritime Risk

Demands on MTS capacity may shift in unpredictable ways. Domestic and international demand for goods may shift over time. For example, rising demand for protein in emerging parts of Asia could increase demand for U.S. protein products or grain for animal feed, while Americans may decrease their meat consumption as plant-based products become more popular. Over time, some goods— particularly agricultural and energy products— may originate in different locations than they do now due to climate change and evolving patterns of extraction. These uncertainties make decisions about where and how to invest in infrastructure capacity for the long term more difficult. Already, greater reliance on the MTS to keep pace with increasing maritime supply chain demand has created congestion and competition for waterway access and port services, and has strained shoreside infrastructure and transportation systems. This trend will continue to stress the capacity of all MTS users and increase risk across the enterprise.

HOW THE WORKSHOP WAS CONDUCTED

1 Evergreen leadership briefly described Evergreen and the workshop itself.

2 Participants were split into four groups, each with a Coast Guard facilitator, a senior mentor to help shape the discussion, and a synthesizer to capture key themes and discussion.

3 Each group was assigned a different scenario describing a plausible state of the world in 2030. Group members individually noted what they considered the key implications of that scenario.

4 Participants grouped the ideas into common risk themes affecting the MTS, then voted for the general themes and more specific "ideas" they considered most important.

5 They arranged sticky notes listing the risks on a graph to indicate the group's assessment of each risk's the relative importance or impact for the MTS (on the horizontal axis) and the level of difficulty or cost associated with addressing that risk (on the vertical axis). The graph was then split into four quadrants, and risks were broadly characterized by which quadrant they were in.

6 The group selected a risk that was important and difficult, and composed a slide describing the risk, how it might emerge, and implications.

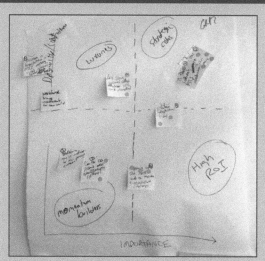

One group's four quadrants.

7 Each group briefed the other participants on their findings. They summarized their scenario, explained key risks and how they had ranked them, and discussed how the risk they had selected might emerge over time and what its implications might be.

2

187

PROJECT EVERGREEN V

WORKSHOP QUICK LOOK: Future Maritime Risk

WHAT PARTICIPANTS WERE SAYING

"More disruptions from environmental change, shifting demographics, and changing alliances create greater uncertainty and will increase the demand for determining how to prioritize investments in the MTS."

"Demand on the maritime supply chain is increasing —stressing the capacity of shoreside infrastructure and transportation networks."

"The average vessel draft, size, and capacity, as well as the overall number of vessel arrivals within the US MTS are on the rise."

The MTS's broad response to risks is piecemeal and uncoordinated. Successfully adapting to rapid technological and environmental change will require action by multiple actors both internationally and domestically. Yet there is no single governance structure that strategically guides the maritime community's response. Domestically, response is complicated by the multiple levels of government that affect the MTS but act autonomously. Internationally, the changing distribution of geo-political power suggests that previous approaches to ensure economic and national security interests may no longer be effective. Coordination of MTS governance is needed to provide strategic guidance to effectively respond to these challenges while maintaining U.S. economic and national security interests. Two key factors affect global governance: the degree of international cooperation overall, and the relative strength of the U.S. and like-minded states compared with other powers in shaping that system. If cooperation has been degraded through an overall climate of distrust and hostility, or if the U.S. and its allies wield little ability to influence global governance, regulations and their enforcement are less likely to be consistent or aligned with U.S. interests. Rising near-peer powers or regional hegemons in specific locations could attenuate U.S. power through a combination of economic, political, and military gains. The U.S. may also find that frayed relationships with longstanding allies diminish its ability to shape maritime governance. Conversely, there may be some opportunities for the U.S. to enhance its strengths by building new relationships (for example, with India).

The MTS workforce will handle new technologies and old ones simultaneously. The future MTS workforce will need the ability to handle a set of emerging technologies. These include operating and maintaining increasingly automated vehicles and vessels, many of which will be electrically powered, as well as using 3-D printing, managing vast information flows, and defending against sophisticated cyber-threats and unmanned aerial systems, among others. However, they will also continue to handle a range of current and former technologies for two reasons. First, many current technologies—such as manned vessels powered by fossil fuels—will coexist with emerging ones for decades and will need to be supported. Second, advanced technologies will be susceptible to varied types of attacks or unexpected failures:

3

PROJECT EVERGREEN V

WORKSHOP QUICK LOOK: Future Maritime Risk

if GPS is unavailable, or the computers coordinating port operations suddenly go black, the workforce will need to be able to use less technologically sophisticated systems. The number of people who will be needed with which skill sets is uncertain, and the necessary skill sets will likely evolve over time, reflecting technological changes. The result is that individuals supporting the MTS will need continual training over the course of their working lives to sustain required competencies. New approaches for training and developing the necessary certifications will also evolve, as will methods for assessing and maintaining infrequently applied competencies. Moreover, aging populations, more widespread drug abuse, use of alternative work arrangements, and other societal changes will also necessitate giving greater attention to recruitment and retention of available personnel who are capable of fulfilling key roles supporting the MTS.

The MTS may lag behind private and illicit actors in adopting technologies. Private-sector companies and illicit actors may adopt novel technologies more rapidly than government agencies due to more ample funding and greater organizational agility. The result is that the Coast Guard and other government agencies involved in the MTS may struggle to keep up with the technology being used by those whom they seek to regulate or to counter.

Potential for epidemics increases risks to the workforce. Several factors will likely contribute to increased epidemic risks in the next decade and beyond. These include higher population densities and increasing mobility around the world, more livestock, overuse of some prescription drugs in ways that foster resistance, and diminished levels of international cooperation on a range of issues, including disease control. These risks can impinge on the MTS by necessitating more frequent quarantines (including of mass populations, such as cruise ship passengers), by inhibiting some commercial interactions for fear of exposure during epidemics, and by incapacitating parts of the MTS workforce during those epidemics (due to illness, fear of illness, or the need to care for family members).

A rapidly changing Arctic will affect shipping, infrastructure, and operations. The risks cited above are not regionally specific, though they may affect some regions more than others. The Arctic stands out as a region that is undergoing unusually rapid change, with roughly twice the rate of warming as the planet as a whole. This creates risks for the MTS in that region that need to be addressed. Decreasing ice cover contributes to increased shipping through and within the region, along with increasing interest in resource extraction. At the same time, thawing permafrost, rising sea levels, and other environmental changes are degrading existing infrastructure in this harsh, remote region, making it harder to maintain, replace, or expand that infrastructure. The harsh operational environment also requires specialized afloat assets, equipment, and personnel skills not used in other regions. Greater activity in the Arctic, along with the associated risks from pollution and accidents, will increase demand for these capabilities in the MTS.

This Quick Look was produced by the Homeland Security Operational Analysis Center (HSOAC). HSOAC is an FFRDC operated by the RAND Corporation under contract with the Department of Homeland Security.

PROJECT EVERGREEN V

WORKSHOP QUICK LOOK

Emerging Technology and the Brown-Water Marine Transportation Industry

June 10-11, 2020

This short document represents a rapidly written initial overview of key themes from a virtual workshop about how the Marine Transportation System (MTS) can safely adopt emerging technologies. Participants were maritime industry representatives based in the lower Mississippi River, and discussions focused on inland waterways and rivers. The workshop was organized by the Coast Guard's Office of Emerging Policy, DCO-X, with support from HSOAC (a federally funded research and development center, run by the RAND Corporation).

The workshop's objective was to elicit insights and ideas from members of the maritime industry for best practices and standards that could help the MTS safely adopt emerging technologies, adapt them to increase efficiency and promote innovation, and do so voluntarily. This workshop also initiated a dialogue with MTS stakeholders regarding alternative approaches that could potentially improve regulation obsolescence, relevance, interpretation, and enforcement. Participants were asked to address three broad questions:

- How can MTS governance become more adaptable and responsive to emerging technology and changing safety and security imperatives, operating environment, and marine transport operations?
- What alternative governance structures and models for establishing and enforcing standards can be employed?
- How can the Coast Guard support the maritime industry in safely adopting technology and adapting to its increasing usage?

Key Findings

Brown-water vs. blue-water maritime transportation. The operating environment in inland waterways and offshore differ, so using the same governance and regulatory approach may not be the most efficient and effective path. Participants noted that, compared to blue-water operations, the brown-water industry operates in more confined spaces, maneuvers through higher density traffic in a more dynamic physical environment, and involves less international focus. Tugs and barges are the workhorses of the brown-water environment.

ISSUES

BROWN WATER VS. BLUE WATER

Perception that Coast Guard is too blue-water focused

COAST GUARD RELATIONS

Industry seeks partners, not adversaries

Tensions between CG's many roles

RIGIDITY OF REGULATION

Regulations do not consider relative risks or allow for local conditions

1

PROJECT EVERGREEN V

WORKSHOP QUICKLOOK: Emerging Technology and the MTS

Key Findings (cont'd)

The competitiveness of the brown-water maritime industry is sensitive to the availability of waterway infrastructure, waterway traffic management practices, environmental factors, and the global economy. The U.S. Army Corps of Engineers' (USACE) management and infrastructure investments have direct effects on the brown-water industry's ability to compete with rail. Environmental considerations—notably reduced demand for coal due to low-cost natural gas and renewables—also heavily influence the industry. Similarly, global economics, especially related to energy and agriculture, drive the demand for brown-water transport, affecting companies' ability to adopt and adapt to new technology.

Coast Guard-industry relations are more adversarial than desired, and industry is keenly interested in cooperation. Some participants said the industry perceived an increasingly adversarial relationship over the last 20 years, stemming in part from the enhanced homeland security posture and approach of the Coast Guard after 9/11. They also took issue with the perceived blue-water focus of the Coast Guard, to the exclusion of regulating appropriately for or even having awareness of brown-water considerations (e.g., navigation is fundamentally different in the open ocean than between river banks). On the other hand, they affirmed the critical need for the Coast Guard to regulate the industry, and they would sorely miss the Coast Guard playing this role. Ideas included creating a "brown-water Coast Guard" or reforming the existing Coast Guard to make it more attuned to brown-water needs. The participants wanted changes to the regulatory process and increased communication, but they were emphatic about the need for the Coast Guard for regulation, inspections, and enforcement. In some cases, such as traffic control, they would welcome more Coast Guard activity. Participants had a sense that there are tensions among the Coast Guard's various roles as a regulator, enforcement agency, and rescuer.

HOW THE WORKSHOP WAS CONDUCTED

1. COVID-19 triggered the first virtual Evergreen workshop. It started with introductions and a series of briefings about discussion topics.

2. Participants split into two groups with a facilitator. They discussed stakeholders, timelines, and challenges to technology adoption, then organized topics by importance and difficulty.

3. Participants discussed potential solutions to specific challenges and addressed key questions about the roles of multiple stakeholders.

4. The workshop ended with a plenary discussion of key themes and closing remarks.

2

PROJECT EVERGREEN V
WORKSHOP QUICKLOOK: Emerging Technology and the MTS

Key Findings (cont'd)

Participants discussed the extent to which even minor regulatory items need to be approved at high levels, and the rigidity with which some Coast Guard personnel adhere to the rules when a more lenient interpretation could be appropriate. They noted that regulatory enforcement is subject to the relative individual risk tolerance, competency, and experience of each Coast Guard captain of the port, investigator, or inspector, and it is not uncommon for enforcement to be personality-driven and dynamic due to the frequent CG personnel changes. The private sector could also benefit from additional cooperation and coordination of information.

There is a tension among three central regulatory desires: consultation, responsiveness, and consistency. Consultation takes time, which limits responsiveness, and both consultation and responsiveness can lead to changes that diminish consistency.

Small regulatory changes can have disproportionate effects. For example, limited changes in draft requirements and controlling depths can affect industry competitiveness with rail and the competitiveness of U.S. bulk agricultural products with those from Brazil or Argentina, since imposing even small costs can inhibit exports. The effects are hard to anticipate because they are complicated by external factors, such as trade wars, changing global demands, and productivity in alternative supply countries.

Technology adoption depends on many factors that affect individual owner-operators differently. Technology adoption depends on socio-political factors, regulations, and complementary technological developments (e.g., blockchain will not be widely used until banks and financial regulatory agencies accept electronic documents). Some technology diffusion is driven by customer demands; smaller owner-operators are disadvantaged when technology is really new but sometimes can leverage their relationship with larger customers. Adoption of new technology can also be driven by owner-operator needs and regulatory requirements for suppliers. For example, the oil industry has high standards and expectations and also is concerned with cyber issues. Yet, in some past instances, the industry and the Coast Guard have independently generated technical guidelines without communicating and coordinating, thus creating redundancies, conflicting requirements, or regulations with a lower standard than the industry generated and supports. Customers also are driving requirements without consulting others. Differences in owner-operators' ability to access technology may change the structure of the industry by giving advantages to larger companies that can cover the overhead costs of new technologies.

Information technology is the primary focus in the industry, recognizing the rapid pace of cybersecurity threats, while expectations for autonomous vehicles are mixed. Information technology is driving the industry, and it is changing relationships with customers and other stakeholders as demands for near real-time data, system status, and transparency occur. IT allows operational control and management to take place from a distance. But the volume of information and frequent alarms and notifications can distract workers from more important signals. In addition, coupling technologies can create efficiencies but also increase overall systemic risk if the technologies are web-based. The speed at which threats evolve also makes it very hard for firms to keep up with cybersecurity.

3

192

PROJECT EVERGREEN V

WORKSHOP QUICKLOOK: Emerging Technology and the MTS

WHAT PARTICIPANTS WERE SAYING

"You can't treat brown-water environments the same as blue-water ones."

"We would really miss the Coast Guard if it ceased to exist."

"Underinvestment in infrastructure is the top threat (channel maintenance, lock repair). High water is making the system less reliable than it used to be. All the autonomous, ninja barges in the world will not help if the infrastructure falls apart."

Key Findings (cont'd)

There was some debate about whether autonomous systems will ever operate in inland waterways and rivers, but participants quickly recognized that unmanned aircraft already are. In fact, the inland waters of the Coast Guard's Eighth District (including the Mississippi and its tributaries) pioneered a 24-hour notice protocol for unmanned aircraft that is now applied nationwide. Cranes can now operate automatically, except for operations that are restricted due to facility labor policies. There may also be partly autonomous systems in the water in the not-too-distant future, like unmanned barges that follow manned counterparts (often referred to as "leader-follower"). One discussion invoked the potential for autonomous survey vessels, and the need to communicate with them to get out of the way. In fact, virtually every rig in the Gulf can now be operated remotely (albeit not autonomously), which is an indicator of increased confidence in unmanned technology and may contribute to future comfort with autonomous systems.

Participants also mentioned the challenges of adapting to a hybrid human/automated environment in terms of workforce training and human interfaces. Before autonomous vessels are deployed, a number of issues need to be addressed, such as navigation, communications, risk-management, and training issues. Thorough planning is required to ensure that these vessels can operate in limited-broadband environments, that emergency procedures are in place, and that there is enough redundancy to ensure resilience. Participants also struggled with how to balance technology advances that may trade a known risk, such as human error, with less clearly identified risks that may involve different liability considerations. In general, they struggle to adopt new technologies quickly enough to meet current MTS needs, let alone future ones.

Current regulations do not appear to consider relative risks and all available expertise, nor are there mechanisms for readily adapting rules to local conditions or changing conditions. Regulations are often focused on process and paperwork, and sometimes miss the ultimate objective of achieving a given level of performance in terms of security, safety, and other considerations. Some threats are much bigger than others; for example, losing a

4

PROJECT EVERGREEN V

WORKSHOP QUICKLOOK: Emerging Technology and the MTS

Key Findings (cont'd)

barge-load or two is a lot less consequential than a collision that damages an 80-year-old lock and closes the waterway for an extended time. Communication among stakeholders—essential for exchanging priorities, understanding localized needs, and leveraging expertise—is limited, patchy, and imposes resource and time costs. For example, FACA committees, a primary mechanism for incorporating industry perspectives and expertise into decisions about regulation, have languished. Appeals processes can take six months to a year to pursue. Nor is the intent of the regulation always communicated effectively to stakeholders.

Finally, participants recognized that, on one hand, regulation needs to be responsive to changing conditions, but on the other, changing regulations imposes costs. Firms need consistency if they are to make investments. Several factors that the participants viewed as diminishing regulatory consistency included perceived judicial overreach, political forces, and vocal public opinion (which has become more extreme and amplified due to social media), but the bigger issue is the need to base policy and regulations on rigorous analysis, and then ensure that priorities are communicated and consistently upheld.

Waterways are congested and inefficient. Authorities on the waterways are siloed among geographic areas and state and federal agencies, which creates inefficiencies that affect throughput volume. Throughput volume is sensitive to operating conditions, accidents, and infrastructure maintenance or failure. Participants advocated state-of-the-art systems to generate telemetry data to better plan and manage throughput based on the operating conditions.

It is important to view the entire waterway as an integrated system. The waterway is only as efficient as its most constrained part, so there is a need for the Coast Guard to help address potential or actual bottlenecks. These can be due to infrastructure shortfalls (which the USACE should help to address, particularly aging, decrepit infrastructure), environmental conditions (e.g., water levels), congestion, state regulations, and many other factors.

Coordination is key. Governmental stakeholders often act in isolation from one another and from the private sector. One participant noted that the industry is heavily engaged with both DHS (USCG, TSA, and others) and DoD (the USACE), which necessitates substantial cooperation if industry is to avoid conflicting regulatory demands. The Coast Guard also needs to engage with state authorities to ensure that regulations are consistent along the entire waterway and to protect industry from state impediments to interstate commerce—a central federal role embodied in the Constitution.

Suggested Paths Forward

Workshop participants expressed the desire for a maritime governance system that is more explicitly based on documented risks and more effectively meets the needs of the inland maritime transportation community. The desired governance system should be a partnership between industry and regulating agencies that also engages other stakeholders. The system should employ substantial data analytics and shared information to more strategically and holistically make waterways more effective and efficient. To achieve this goal, participants suggested a series of actions and priorities:

5

PROJECT EVERGREEN V

WORKSHOP QUICKLOOK: Emerging Technology and the MTS

Suggested Paths Forward (cont'd)

Let data drive regulatory decisions. The participants wanted regulation to be increasingly driven by knowledge and data, rather than guesswork and reliance on past protocols. They know that data sets are often incomplete or incompletely accurate, but improvements in data quality and comprehensiveness are needed for exactly this reason.

Move to risk-based regulations. Expand existing data systems (such as the Coast Guard's MISLE database) and perform data analytics to determine the risks of maritime transport and infrastructure maintenance and design. Use this information to inform regulations development, enforcement activities, infrastructure development and maintenance, and priorities for federal funding. These data sets can be used to show problematic areas and to understand the choke points in the system, to guide advocacy and infrastructure funding, or to develop a better relationship with the USACE comparable to the CG. Brown- and blue-water maritime industry sectors have different risk profiles, and relying on incident data will help to reduce inefficiencies.

Increase communication between industry and regulating agencies to ensure industry understands the rationale and evidence driving safety standards and regulations (which ideally should be based on data-driven risk assessments), and have state and federal agencies learn from industry about feasibility, technical constraints, and cost-benefit trade-off options. Rules should communicate the intent or rationale and risk, so as to move the discussion away from scrutinizing the language of the law and toward achieving the desired outcomes. Interagency coordination at both the state and federal levels is needed to coordinate and harmonize activities, investments, regulatory standards, and roles to support an efficient marine transportation systems across agency silos and geographic areas. Two specific activities that could be pursued are 1) reinvigorating industry-government FACA groups and ensuring agencies use them to leverage industry's expertise, needs, capabilities, and constraints, and 2) expanding industry-government cross-training (ride along).

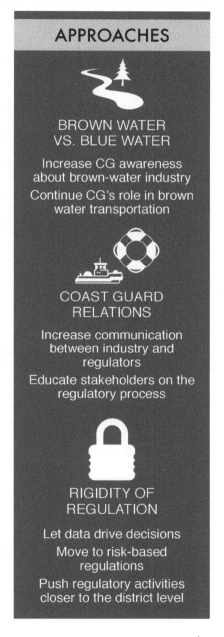

APPROACHES

BROWN WATER VS. BLUE WATER

Increase CG awareness about brown-water industry

Continue CG's role in brown water transportation

COAST GUARD RELATIONS

Increase communication between industry and regulators

Educate stakeholders on the regulatory process

RIGIDITY OF REGULATION

Let data drive decisions

Move to risk-based regulations

Push regulatory activities closer to the district level

6

PROJECT EVERGREEN V

Suggested Paths Forward (cont'd)

Industry would like to see the Coast Guard continue to play a key role in inland maritime transportation. While self-governance works in niche areas—tanker and towing self-inspection, Responsible Carrier System, and self-help cooperation, providing greater operational flexibility and routine assessments as opposed to just a snapshot—broader industry self-regulation may not be universally accepted. Industry needs a controlling organization like the Coast Guard to gather and synthesize information on relative risk and safety needs, negotiate and communicate with other agencies and stakeholders, and maintain incident data (MISLE). Without Coast Guard control, an industry sector would not have enough data and visibility to fully understand and manage risk (Balkanization of risk), nor would there be the proper incentives to balance all stakeholder risk within a public/transparent process that has some recourse for appeal.

Consider organizational changes that expand organizational awareness and knowledge about the brown-water maritime industry. In addition to having more Coast Guard personnel ride industry vessels, those personnel could serve longer rotations in relevant districts to develop the knowledge base and relationships necessary to effectively ensure waterway safety and efficient operation. Longer rotations have the added benefit of improving continuity and consistency in applying policy and enforcing regulations. Participants also suggested relying more on civilian personnel in technical areas for inspections and regulatory functions while leveraging Coast Guard personnel for law enforcement. The benefit is shifting away from a rigid, punitive approach and moving toward problem-solving and common-sense solutions outside of the often-contentious regulatory process that can stifle open communication and transparency.

Push regulatory activities closer to the district or regional level. Currently some regulations and standards are driven by international standards that may not always be helpful for safe brown-water operations in a specific locale. Industry needs opportunities to provide input, and regulations should be made regionally so that policymaking is more agile and regulations can be locally tailored to achieve safety levels in ways that can be consistently enforced and do not harm the industry's competitiveness. The Coast Guard would still be needed to provide data and normalize rules across jurisdictions to increase movement/efficiency on a given waterway. The districts should be empowered to execute the regulatory process and create an open process for allowing variances to the Code of Federal Regulations when local conditions and the data indicate it is warranted, with industry input from FACA groups.

Educate the stakeholder community on the regulatory process and the tension between regulatory speed on the one hand, and thorough consultation with stakeholders and data collection/analysis on the other.

Project Evergreen (EVG) employs Strategic Foresight to support executive leaders in their role as the Coast Guard's decision engines. This product is a first look into the results of Emerging Technology and the MTS, one of eight "pinecones" on the Evergreen tree. In summer 2021, Team EVG will begin a meta-analysis of the Pinecones to identify strategic choices for the 27th Commandant of the Coast Guard's leadership team.

HSOAC
HOMELAND SECURITY
OPERATIONAL ANALYSIS CENTER
An FFRDC operated by
the RAND Corporation
under contract with DHS

7

PROJECT EVERGREEN V

PINECONE WORKSHOP QUICK LOOK

Total Workforce 2030

September 10-11, 2020 | Coast Guard Headquarters

This document represents an initial overview of key themes and concepts that emerged from the "*Total Workforce 2030*" workshop. The workshop expanded on the results of a previous pinecone. Workshop participants were Coast Guard HR professionals and program SMEs. It was organized by the Coast Guard's Office of Emerging Policy, DCO-X, with support from HSOAC, a federally funded research and development center, operated by the RAND Corporation.

The Coast Guard must create a transparent talent management system that gives members greater control over their lives and meets the needs of operational field commanders. The types of changes and the need for an agile talent management system will mean identifying and overcoming significant cultural, technological, and data-based barriers.

To identify barriers and promising solutions for furthering the ideas that were generated during a workshop in fall 2019, participants in the Workforce 2030 sessions were asked to consider:

- What will be the workforce implications in the year 2030 of major drivers of change?

- What are the challenges and opportunities created by these implications in getting to the needed workforce?

- How might the Coast Guard overcome barriers to achieve the workforce that it needs to successfully accomplish its missions in the future?

Key Demands on the 2030 Workforce

Workshop participants identified several ways in which the Coast Guard would be affected by potential futures, characterized in three scenarios and associated vignettes. They emphasized that future change will occur more rapidly than in the past, spurring a need to incorporate agility and recurring updates not currently found in Coast Guard culture.

Increasing demand for cutters, inspectors, shallow-water boat operations, and international operations will boost demand for a workforce comfortable with more expeditionary, at sea, and global operations. Workers who are multi-lingual or who can work effectively with partner nations or in inter-agency contexts will be in demand.

ISSUES

INCREASING DEMAND

Increasing demand for cutters, inspectors, shallow-water boat operations, and international operations will boost demand for a workforce comfortable with more expeditionary, at sea, and global operations

TECH ADVANCES

Technological advancements will drive future workforce needs

WORKPLACE TRENDS

Changing demographics, social norms, family structures, and workplace practices will affect the relative attractiveness of the Coast Guard as an employer of choice

1

PROJECT EVERGREEN V
WORKSHOP QUICKLOOK: Total Workforce 2030

HOW THE WORKSHOP WAS CONDUCTED

1 The Evergreen workshop, held at Headquarters, started with introductions and a series of briefings about discussion topics.

2 Participants split into three groups of 6 people and met separately over the next two days with a facilitator from DCO-X.

3 Each group explored the implications of their future scenario, the challenges and opportunities created by these implications, and solutions to specific challenges.

4 Each team briefed their strategic solutions to the 2030 Workforce challenge, followed by a group discussion with leadership from CG-1, FORCECOM, and Personnel Readiness; ending with closing remarks

Key Demands on the 2030 Workforce (cont'd)

A rapidly changing climate will have substantial effects on Coast Guard missions and infrastructure. More frequent and higher-intensity storms, fire events, and flooding events will elevate the disaster response missions, including increasing the demand for inland response capability. Also, as fisheries adapt and competition for protein sources increases, greater demand for enforcement will elevate the fisheries enforcement mission.

Coast Guard infrastructure and locations will also be vulnerable to climate change-induced damage, which could displace personnel and their families, disrupt response operations, and put additional strain on the workforce.

These potential futures will drive the need for an agile workforce that has an expanded surge capability. The increased OPTEMPO may create more stress on the force, especially if other missions are sustained at a baseline level.

Technological advancements were another frequently cited factor driving future workforce needs. In particular, the proliferation of information technology, sensors, and data analytics capabilities is creating new tools for both performing the mission and managing the workforce. Keeping pace with the private sector will be necessary to ensure the Coast Guard is attractive to prospective recruits. These advancements will continue to exert pressure on the Coast Guard to modernize its information infrastructure and to have a workforce capable of exploiting, maintaining, and securing it from cyber-attacks. Increasing levels of automation will also reshape jobs and alter skills needed to perform missions.

Changing demographics, social norms, family structures, and workplace practices will affect the relative attractiveness of the Coast Guard as an employer of choice. As the United States becomes more diverse, the Coast Guard has an opportunity to harness that culture and mindset. Ensuring that personnel management policies and practices align more closely with overall workplace trends will be essential to recruiting and retaining people with

2

PROJECT EVERGREEN V
WORKSHOP QUICKLOOK: Total Workforce 2030

WHAT PARTICIPANTS WERE SAYING

"Prospective members need to trust that they are joining a quality organization."

[Given the] rapidly changing workforce, we could fall behind in mission execution if we cannot meet changing demands. [The Coast Guard] needs to be flexible and adaptable in culture to meet the demands."

"We need better messaging about what made someone the leader they are today."

"Culture is hard to change."

Key Demands on the 2030 Workforce (cont'd)

the needed skills and proficiencies. For example, we heard from Samuel Brannen of CSIS that workers will have nearly 10 different jobs as they enter mid-career, suggesting that society will increasingly value career flexibility, opportunities for skills development, and varied career pathways. Family structures are more varied, so individuals may be single parents or caretakers to elderly relatives, for example, and need added flexibility. In addition, a 2017 National Academies report noted that "*nontraditional types of employment—other than the 40-hour-per-week job at a single company offering health and retirement benefits— appear to be increasing*" and that "*IT advances now make it easier to access such employment opportunities, and in some cases to perform work remotely over the Internet.*"[3] Given these trends, Coast Guard personnel management practices, built off a more rigid military model, are at risk of being out of step with societal and workplace trends.

Strategic Solutions for Future Needs

Participants generated many overarching strategies and opportunities for recruiting and managing a future workforce that meets the mission demands of the Coast Guard. These strategies validated the ideas developed in a previous workshop in many ways and added more detail to what is required to accomplish these goals.

One overarching strategy proposed is to develop greater visibility into enterprise-wide workforce demand and supply and to establish more responsive approaches for aligning them. Participants would like to see the Coast Guard establish a more dynamic, responsive, and comprehensive personnel management system that can better align evolving mission needs with workforce capabilities across the active duty, reserve, and civilian workforces. To implement this strategy, it will be necessary to determine mission workforce requirements that are essential for success; discern what skills and capabilities exist within the workforce; and apply available talent management tools to ensure that the workforce is willing and capable of meeting changing mission demands. Since mission demands are constantly evolving and at a more rapid pace than in the past, an agile system and a cultural shift will need to ensure that billets are distributed in a more

3 National Academies of Sciences, Engineering, and Medicine, Information Technology and the U.S. Workforce: Where Are We and Where Do We Go from Here? Washington, DC: The National Academies Press, 2017.

3

Strategic Solutions for Future Needs (cont'd)

fluid and less permanent manner to reduce tendencies to hoard them. The personnel management system should also account for surge staffing needs, especially since participants expect these events to increase in the future. Expanding information on individuals' capabilities was also recommended, such as primary and secondary skills (e.g., language skills, IT, plumbing) in a centralized and accessible database to inform talent management across the Coast Guard workforce as well as the assignment process.

To be truly dynamic and responsive, the system will need to incorporate feedback on mission performance, workload, or ideally both. Investment in a state-of-the-art information management system and data analytics will be crucial, but the intentional leadership focused on identifying and overcoming cultural barriers and changes will be critical to lasting change.

Develop a broader range of workforce management tools to enable it to more quickly meet mission demands. By allowing greater flexibility in filling some billets with either active duty, reservists, civilians, or auxiliarists, the Coast Guard could eliminate some workforce inefficiencies, while at the same time offering expanded opportunities to a broader number of individuals. Providing incentives such as rest and recuperation (R&R) after deployments, the option to remain at home for twice the period spent deployed, additional childcare assistance during deployments, civilian recognition programs, or financial rewards for those who deploy or assume extra responsibilities due to surges in work can help fill challenging billets. These incentives have the added benefit of demonstrating to members that the Coast Guard values the sacrifices they and their families make for such missions, such as lengthy afloat tours, high OPTEMPO, and demand surges.

Seek policy, practices, and culture change to provide greater choice. To ensure that the Coast Guard can attract and retain top talent, it will need to align its personnel management more closely with overall workplace trends and appeal to a more varied and heterogenous workforce. One way to do this is to provide more flexibility and choice in career pathways. Another is to offer alternative work arrangements when feasible. Both options require enhanced IT systems and knowledgeable staff—as well as leadership commitment and culture change.

By introducing varied career pathways, the Coast Guard recognizes that different talents are needed to execute the mission—from the technical to the generalist—and that by offering alternatives, the Coast Guard can access essential talent and boost career satisfaction and engagement. However, this solution will require substantial culture change. Ideas for career flexibilities include developing different structured tracks for technical specialists and generalists; establishing opportunities to enter, re-enter, and exit the Coast Guard or move laterally without penalty; or offering career opportunities that allow more geographic stability to those who want it. Participants noted that geographic stability can be especially advantageous for certain locations that some may see as undesirable, but others are fans who wish to stay or are in positions that engage partner organizations. Geographic stability is also valued by those with families.

Finding the right balance across the workforce of those with broad geographic knowledge and experiences and those with deeper knowledge of a more limited geography will be necessary Moreover, to implement this strategy, boards and panels may have to be established to develop distinct evaluation criteria for those who seek to remain specialists versus those who

4

Strategic Solutions for Future Needs (cont'd)

wish to become generalists. Efforts will have to be made to ensure that the evaluation and assignment processes are aligned with communicated organizational values and that they generate results that are aligned with workforce management goals and objectives. A 360-degree evaluation would be useful for personal development purposes (and not necessarily performance evaluation) and can be a way to reinforce the need for greater cultural awareness and sensitivity. More progressive organizations employ 360-degree evaluation systems to improve communication, foster personal development, and encourage leadership accountability, which improves individual and organizational performance. And managing for high retention across all Coast Guard career fields may no longer be achievable, nor desirable.

Create opportunities for continuous learning and leadership experiences to ensure the workforce retains knowledge, skills, and abilities essential for the mission. It is recommended that additional resources for leadership, technical training and certifications, specialized skills development, or higher education be requested. There may be novel ways to tap into civilian epicenters of STEM, IT, or specialized skills talent either through partnerships or internships with industry to recognize skills or training that the Coast Guard did not provide. Having a tech-savvy workforce will increase productivity and contribute to high-quality work environment, which will also improve recruiting and retention.

Participants also recommended that where feasible the Coast Guard provide greater flexibility and support for alternative work arrangements that cover the location or timing that work is performed. To implement more remote work, greater IT infrastructure and support for the required equipment will be necessary. The Society for Human Resource Management developed a rubric of the types of flexibilities that could be offered (below).

Types of Workplace Flexibility	Type of Policy/Practice
Work schedule	• Flex time • Compressed workweek • Flex-shift work/workday schedule • Self-scheduled breaks • Part-year/seasonal work • Weekend/evening/night work
Location	• Telework, home-based work • Remove work • Hoteling
Amount of work	• Job sharing • Reduced load or customized work/part-time work
Continuity of work	• Long-term breaks/sabbaticals, career flexibility • Family and Medical Leave Act (FMLA) • Compensatory time off

SOURCE: Ellen Ernst Kossek, Leslie B. Hammer, Rebecca J. Thompson, and Lisa Buxbaum Burke, Leveraging Workplace Flexibility for Engagement and Productivity, Society for Human Resource Management Foundation, 2014.

5

PROJECT EVERGREEN V

WORKSHOP QUICKLOOK: Total Workforce 2030

Strategic Solutions for Future Needs (cont'd)

Managing an agile and responsive personnel management system with all of the flexibilities and choice described earlier, while ensuring the Coast Guard's core values are sustained, is more complex to execute than the current system, and will require leadership, attention to circumstances that create cultural friction, and additional investment in the people and authoritative data required for effective personnel management.

Participants also discussed ways to respond to changing demographic trends that portend a more diverse and aging workforce. Societal changes in the structure of family units is one trend. Consequently, a one-size-fits all WWII-era benefits package may no longer appeal to a broad swath of the working population, putting the Coast Guard at a competitive disadvantage for recruitment and retention. Offering choice within a portfolio of benefit options creates an opportunity to more closely tailor the value proposition of the Coast Guard over an individual's career life-cycle and allows them to better meet the specific needs of their families. Examples of benefits that are likely to appeal to a subset of the workforce at different phases in their careers are student loan assistance, childcare, reproductive support, sabbaticals, and eldercare. Changing policies to be more inclusive, such as the marriage requirement for BAH is a way of adapting to changing family structures that may include unmarried cohabitants with dependents, single parents, or those who are caring for older relatives.

Diverse backgrounds (in every sense) are needed to draw on the entire talent pool and to leverage specialized skill sets that are relevant for a more expeditionary, more internationally centered Coast Guard. For example, individuals with international experience will increase proficiency abroad, but cultural sensitivity will be required to counter biases and tensions that emerge. Recruiting and retaining a more diverse workforce increases cognitive diversity valuable for problem solving and critical thinking essential for effective leadership, mission execution, and technical superiority.

Expand outreach and recruitment. Recruitment is the first step toward creating a robust candidate pool. In addition to its general outreach, the Coast Guard should consider more targeted outreach to youth or underrepresented demographic groups to broaden the awareness of opportunities the service

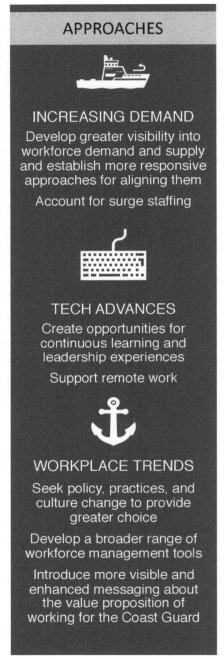

APPROACHES

INCREASING DEMAND
Develop greater visibility into workforce demand and supply and establish more responsive approaches for aligning them

Account for surge staffing

TECH ADVANCES
Create opportunities for continuous learning and leadership experiences

Support remote work

WORKPLACE TRENDS
Seek policy, practices, and culture change to provide greater choice

Develop a broader range of workforce management tools

Introduce more visible and enhanced messaging about the value proposition of working for the Coast Guard

6

PROJECT EVERGREEN V

WORKSHOP QUICKLOOK: Total Workforce 2030

Strategic Solutions for Future Needs (cont'd)

provides. Programs for youth before they enter college could be established, either as a stand-alone auxiliary cadet program or in collaboration with scouting-type programs. A task group at the Coast Guard Recruiting Command could create an outreach strategy for historically black colleges and universities, for example, or universities with strong technical programs. Outreach could include fellowships at these institutions. The Coast Guard could offer a variety of incentive and benefit options for select positions and skills, ensuring that new recruits are properly integrated into a career path that leverages the longevity of the career through talent optimization and retention. Concomitant with increased member diversity is the need for leadership and awareness training to identify and eliminate cultural barriers.

Introduce more visible and enhanced messaging about the value proposition of working for the Coast Guard and implement strategies for recruiting and retaining talent. This could be done by leveraging mission success and workforce trust to be the employer of choice for active duty, reservists, and civilians. For example, the Coast Guard could leverage public-facing missions such as disaster response to increase awareness of the service, the "greater good" aspects of its mission, and the plethora of "*jobs that matter.*"

Consider investing in wide-reaching platforms such as TV, movies, NASCAR or similar events, or emphasize the unique experiences the only the Coast Guard can offer to tap into young people's interest in travel and having experiences overseas. Other ideas are to feature the Coast Guard career of esteemed public figures to demonstrate the value of such experiences in building one's career and network. Surveying the workforce on what members value about working for the Coast Guard would be as helpful as exit surveys.

Many of the solutions are consistent with recommendations contained in a recent National Academy report that suggests employers focus on the needs of individuals and their career development, while monitoring the changing workplace to routinely evaluate their work environment, job requirements, and personnel policies and practices.

In closing, any change will require sustained leadership to communicate why the change is necessary, signal the direction of the change, and hold people accountable. It will require assessing and reassessing the core values and culture of the Coast Guard, and deemphasizing those that are barriers to greater inclusion and flexibility. Several of these initiatives may require legislative and policy change. Others will require seeking additional resources. However, in the longer run these investments will pay dividends to the missions and will yield a high-quality workforce as the Coast Guard seeks to be the employer of choice.

In closing, any change will require sustained leadership to communicate why the change is necessary, signal the direction of the change, and hold people accountable. It will require assessing and reassessing the core values and culture of the Coast Guard, and deemphasizing those that are barriers to greater inclusion and flexibility. Several of these initiatives may require legislative and policy change. Others will require seeking additional resources. However, in the longer run these investments will pay dividends to the missions and will yield a high-quality workforce as the Coast Guard seeks to be the employer of choice.

PROJECT EVERGREEN V

PINECONE WORKSHOP QUICK LOOK

"Semper Adaptus" workshop

December 2–3, 2020 | US Coast Guard Headquarters

This document presents the key themes and concepts that emerged from the "Semper Adaptus" workshop, organized by the Coast Guard's Office of Emerging Policy, DCO-X, with support from HSOAC, a federally funded research and development center operated by the RAND Corporation.

"Semper Adaptus," is the first of three planned workshops in which the Evergreen core team will explore the implications of future scenarios. The goal of the exercise is to generate ideas on how demand for Coast Guard missions in the future might change, and what capabilities and cultural shifts would be needed across the enterprise. The focus was identifying promising strategies for ensuring that the USCG is well-positioned to quickly adapt to change that is reshaping the operational environment—rapid technological shifts, increasing globalization, evolving transnational crime, and climate change. More than 20 members of the DCO-X Evergreen core team took part in the exercise.

During the workshop, participants were asked to consider:

- What future drivers are likely to affect the USCG and how might they change mission demand and delivery?
  - What are the implications for how the Coast Guard assesses risks and threats?
  - What are the potential implications of these questions for Coast Guard culture?
  - What are the implications for mission support?
- Will the Coast Guard have the right capabilities, and which strategic choices does it need to make now to be ready?
- What investments should the Coast Guard make to thrive in the future, assuming that talent management and technological capabilities are updated?

Upcoming workshops are "Flash to Bang" (expediting the implementation of new concepts) and "CONCEPTS 2040" (new operational concepts to meet emerging demands). The ideas generated in these workshops will be rigorously stress-tested and examined using gaming methods in year four. In late FY2021, a report will synthesize the results from all the workshops and provide strategic context and potential implications regarding critical planning decisions that the incoming commandant and senior leadership may consider.

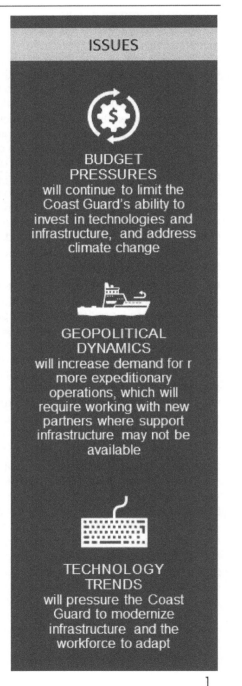

ISSUES

BUDGET PRESSURES will continue to limit the Coast Guard's ability to invest in technologies and infrastructure, and address climate change

GEOPOLITICAL DYNAMICS will increase demand for r more expeditionary operations, which will require working with new partners where support infrastructure may not be available

TECHNOLOGY TRENDS will pressure the Coast Guard to modernize infrastructure and the workforce to adapt

1

PROJECT EVERGREEN V

WORKSHOP QUICKLOOK: "Semper Adaptus"

HOW THE WORKSHOP WAS CONDUCTED

1 The workshop started with introductions and discussion of how foresight analysis is done, and how the workshop would be conducted.

2 Participants split into four groups of 5-6 people and met separately over the next two days with a facilitator from DCO-X.

3 Each group explored the implications of their future scenario, the challenges and opportunities created by these implications, and solutions to specific challenges. The participants will continue to "live" in their scenario for the remaining two workshops.

4 The workshop ended with a plenary session where each group presented its most salient initiative for the future to RDML John Mauger, Assistant Commandant for Capability.

Key Demands on the Future Coast Guard

Workshop participants identified several ways in which the Coast Guard would be affected in four future scenarios that differ in how they portray geopolitical dynamics, the U.S. economy, climate change effects, and the pace of technological advancement.

For one, the increasing potential for a global presence driven by changing geopolitical dynamics and climate change suggests that the Coast Guard will be called upon to perform more expeditionary missions with new global partners, or in new regions, where support infrastructure like that in the United States may not be available. Even as sensors and remote operations capability expand, a physical presence in the area of responsibility will likely be required to gather additional intelligence and better interpret information from other sources. While the scenarios' regions and missions may differ, all require the Coast Guard's workforce to be comfortable engaging in the Arctic, South China Sea, Central and South America, and Middle East. Perhaps Coast Guard doctrine will

also need to more explicitly delineate CONUS and OCONUS roles, since "doctrine influences the way policy and plans are developed, forces are organized, trained and employed, and equipment is procured and maintained. It promotes unity of purpose, guides professional judgment, and enables Coast Guard active duty, reserve, civilian, and auxiliary men and women to best fulfill their responsibilities."[1]

Furthermore, a changing climate will have substantial effects on where the USCG operates and how it supports its missions. As sea level rises, storms affect aging infrastructure, and mission demands shift locations, the Coast Guard may need to operate in CONUS areas that lack infrastructure or sufficient capacity. Instead of making infrastructure more resilient to climate change, the Coast Guard may consider moving it to less vulnerable locations (perhaps temporarily with the seasons, or on a more expeditionary basis). Also, as fisheries adapt and competition for protein sources grows, increased demand for enforcement will likely

---

[1] http://wow.uscgaux.info/content.php?unit=AUX80&category=publication-1-pub1-1

2

PROJECT EVERGREEN V

WORKSHOP QUICKLOOK: "Semper Adaptus"

Key Demands on the Future Coast Guard (cont'd)

elevate the importance of fishery-enforcement missions, domestically and abroad. All these shifts could put additional pressure on budgets. The solutions described next do not isolate a set of solutions for climate change effects, but rather see them as going hand-in-hand with the other concepts.

Technological advancement—especially the proliferation of information technology, sensors, data analytics, and artificial intelligence capability—is creating new opportunities for more efficient, flexible, and responsive operations. These advances, and their adoption by partner agencies and stakeholders, will continue to exert pressure on the Coast Guard to modernize its information infrastructure and ensure the workforce is capable of exploiting, maintaining, and securing this infrastructure from cyber-attacks. Technologies are opening potential USCG missions in intelligence, space, and cyber operations. Related advances such as increasing levels of automation will also provide more operational flexibility, and potentially free up financial and personnel resources from administrative functions that can be refocused toward frontline or customer-facing duties. Unmanned systems may offer new capabilities

and efficiencies, but the Coast Guard is lagging in adopting them.[2] New technologies in the hands of transnational crime organizations or U.S. adversaries will also pressure the Coast Guard to achieve technological parity or superiority. These shifts may require cultural adjustment from engaging in predominantly manual activities (such as flying and maintenance) to more analysis and interpersonal-oriented activities (such as cyber threat assessment or managing friction with forces of competing nations).

Finally, general budget pressures will continue to limit USCG's ability to invest in technologies and infrastructure that could help it adapt. These constraints will also put pressure on balancing mission performance as needs and priorities change. Historical Coast Guard budgets will not support sustained increases in mission demand nor rapid technology adoption. And while budget pressures can stimulate organizational and policy change that allow the Coast Guard to find cost savings and redistribute its budget among the 11 statutory missions, those changes may not be enough to meet new priorities and demand at the desired performance levels.

Strategic Solutions for Future Needs

The strategic solutions generated by the groups leveraged the Coast Guard's strengths in conducting diverse maritime safety and security missions, including those in the gray zone. For example, the multi-mission Coast Guard is lean, customer-focused, and can operate globally, which suggests that members have basic collaborative or stakeholder-engagement skills, and sensitivity to a variety of stakeholder perspectives. These skills are essential for sustaining domestic and foreign partnerships,

as well as for dealing with potential adversaries. Participants noted that the Coast Guard can help enhance collaboration and cooperation between the DHS and DoD, since Title 10 and Title 14 authorities allow the service to pivot as needed to meet the challenges of DHS- and DoD-mission operations. Moreover, Coast Guard members typically engage with a variety of customers— the public, the maritime industry, foreign countries, scientific research organizations,

2 National Academy of Sciences, Engineering and Medicine. 2020. "Leveraging Unmanned Systems for Coast Guard Missions," National Academies Press, Washington, DC, p. 101.

PROJECT EVERGREEN V

WORKSHOP QUICKLOOK: "Semper Adaptus"

WHAT PARTICIPANTS WERE SAYING

"Acquisition is [focused on] getting a technology to the field vs adoption, which is having the organizational structure to leverage and exploit technology."

"I think what we need is to export what we are already doing to a greater extent. Our sister services often categorize threats as targets, and that's not how we see things. We don't often speak in terms of threats; we speak in measures of success. The cultural issues are becoming more important."

"Climate change mitigation, sometimes CG is a leader and sometimes not; there is a need to codify our role if [we are] going to have influence the future course and engagements with Russia/China in the Arctic."

Strategic Solutions for Future Needs (cont'd)

and the defense agencies. The Coast Guard also enjoys a positive national and international reputation as a fair and neutral global actor.

Workforce issues and talent management were discussed in all groups, but the discussion is not detailed in this summary because it appears the Coast Guard has already committed to adapting and reshaping the way in which it manages talent. However, the continued focus on the workforce speaks to the importance of people to making the USCG more agile.

Participants in the four groups generated many overarching strategies and opportunities for meeting the Coast Guard's future mission demands. Key themes included the following:

1. Increase visibility of the Coast Guard and its resource needs.
2. Deepen and expand relationships with other countries.
3. Collaborate more closely with other U.S. government partners.
4. Ensure that the Coast Guard can leverage technological advancements in a timely manner by pursuing policy and process change.
5. Aggressively pursue technological investments and organizational changes to improve data acquisition, analysis, dissemination, and application.

We describe these below.

1. Increase the visibility of the Coast Guard with Congress and other external stakeholders and be prepared to articulate what resources are needed to meet evolving mission demands and priorities. Because the CG is viewed differently by many stakeholders depending on their engagement (e.g., armed force, first responder, search and rescue, law enforcement, regulator, inspector), participants suggested that the Coast Guard do more to highlight its contributions to maritime safety and security. The capabilities the Coast Guard brings to search and rescue (SAR), its role in disaster response, and its ability to build international relationships through collaboration with partners on law enforcement and scientific research were specifically mentioned. Participants noted that the Coast Guard could participate more in public events such as sporting events or generate more media and social media engagement. More

4

PROJECT EVERGREEN V

WORKSHOP QUICKLOOK: "Semper Adaptus"

Strategic Solutions for Future Needs (cont'd)

interaction with legislators was also mentioned—for example, more actively engaging with appropriations committees that focus on national security and looking for opportunities to align funding with the Coast Guard's Navy counterparts. Additionally, the Coast Guard should seek to ensure that it is included in developing and executing U.S. security strategies, particularly its capabilities to engage with potential adversaries in ways other than armed conflict. As such, and with the platforms and capabilities coming online, the Coast Guard can bridge the gap between DHS and DoD. By increasing visibility and relevance with stakeholders, the Coast Guard will be in a better position to compete for resources.

Having a permanent, physically present representative at the International Maritime Organization (IMO) who could help shape climate and international policy would also enhance the visibility of the Coast Guard domestically and internationally. Finally, some participants stated that it was important to demonstrate to external stakeholders what missions, and at what performance level, the USCG could execute with available funding levels. This would require developing data and planning tools that demonstrate the mission trade-offs for these funding levels, mission performance objectives, and mission priorities.

2. Leverage and expand existing operations across the globe to deepen relationships with other countries or establish new ones for both national security and economic security objectives. For example, participants suggested that the Coast Guard continue to apply its expertise in fisheries enforcement, marine safety, etc., to enhance regional stability by increasing partner countries' capabilities and diminishing the potential for conflict, especially in hotspots. Participants also were interested in expanding the range of

activities conducted by the successful Patrol Forces Southwest Asia (PATFORSWA) and the Africa Maritime Law Enforcement Partnership (AMLEP) programs, which could be scaled up from training engagements to joint operations, mission support, and intelligence functions. Participants recommended that these forces should not be limited to patrol boats but should also include aviation elements or deployable specialized forces (MSST, MSRT), which would give the Coast Guard more capabilities to operate in the gray zone and more easily integrate operations with DoD. Additional foreign partnerships and engagements will also provide the Coast Guard with more diverse points of view that can help it better understand and anticipate the full range of threats and risks. These operations must be sustainable, and assets and mission support systems must be strengthened globally and made adaptable to enable the Coast Guard to quickly move to emerging hotspots. Finally, increasing the cadre of Coast Guard liaisons and attachés in potentially adversarial countries could be valuable for maintaining relationships on issues of common concern (SAR, migration, fisheries), especially in areas where gray-zone operations are key. The Coast Guard might consider establishing diplomacy as a skillset, increasing incentives and opportunities for developing language competencies, and strengthening collaboration with Department of State entities.

3. Collaborate more closely with other government partners on complementary missions to enhance performance and leverage efficiencies. Coast Guard authorities are broad enough that the service has substantial flexibility to pursue missions that will likely be needed, but there may be resource savings if, in addition to integrating information in real-time and leveraging mutually

5

PROJECT EVERGREEN V

WORKSHOP QUICKLOOK: "Semper Adaptus"

Figure 1. Maritime security activities performed by USCG and USN

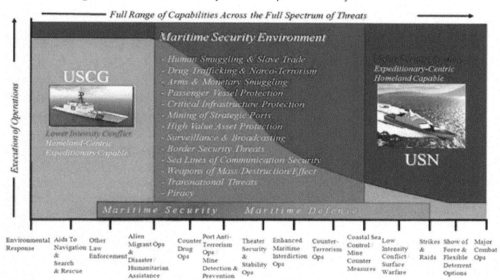

Source: USCG, Proceedings magazine, Spring 2020, p. 13.

Strategic Solutions for Future Needs (cont'd)

beneficial technology development, the Coast Guard found opportunities to share mission-support functions and infrastructure or align operations with other federal agencies. Looking at complementary and overlapping roles among agencies could uncover ways to achieve greater efficiencies and greater responsiveness, leading to improved mission performance within the limits of available resources. Government partners such as CISA, CBP, NOAA, USACE, MARAD, and DoD/USN are potential candidates, although the Coast Guard might need additional authorities to work in some of those domains. Given the Coast Guard's perhaps unique position for operations in the gray zone, it could develop a "Maritime Gray Zone Center of Excellence" to experiment with operations at the tactical, operational, and strategic levels. The spectrum of maritime security activities that could guide these discussions are identified in Figure 1.

In addition, the Coast Guard might look for innovative ways to obtain support at lower cost by transferring some functions to the private sector (e.g., warehousing or maintaining aids to navigation). One group suggested devolving the Maritime Safety and Security teams to redistribute these resources to increase surge capacity.

4. Ensure that the Coast Guard can leverage technological advancements in a timely manner by pursuing policy and process change that enables the Coast Guard to access and more rapidly adopt new technology. Many Coast Guard assets are long-lived investments that have lengthy development and acquisition cycles, yet technological improvements are occurring at a rapid pace. To remedy this misalignment, participants suggested that the Coast Guard seek policy and organizational changes to upgrade systems with new technology

6

PROJECT EVERGREEN V

WORKSHOP QUICKLOOK: "Semper Adaptus"

Strategic Solutions for Future Needs (cont'd)

continuously throughout the development and acquisition process, emphasizing the quality of Coast Guard platforms, as well as their quantity. They also suggested changes to shorten the time-frame from when a requirement is identified to when the capability is fielded, including the testing and evaluation phase. To more effectively utilize scarce resources and more quickly access new technologies, the Coast Guard could also find ways to more systematically leverage the development, testing, and evaluation work of other federal agencies as much as possible and deploy technologies that can rapidly integrate with the Joint Force or international partners such as NATO. Providing more training or assignments with the tech industry or research and development organizations such as DARPA or the Defense Innovation Unit was also mentioned.

5. Aggressively pursue technological investments and organizational changes to expand and enhance the Coast Guard's ability to acquire and exploit information through improved data acquisition, analysis, dissemination, and application. The proliferation of sensors and expansion of data-science capabilities creates opportunities for mission effectiveness and efficiencies (and threats in the hands of criminals and adversaries) for the Coast Guard. These technologies become even more essential as the Coast Guard increasingly operates in global environments or as climate change collides with constrained budget resources in the maritime domain. Participants would like to see the Coast Guard use data analytics and artificial intelligence to communicate requirements more holistically, facilitate policy change, and speed decision-making. Greater use of data analytics and artificial intelligence technology could improve mission performance and operations by better focusing resources to where they are needed, allowing the Coast Guard to more effectively and efficiently cover a geographic area for search and rescue, law enforcement, or fisheries management, for example. Greater data collection and analytics support risk-based decision-making, an approach that is desired by stakeholders in the marine transportation industry. Not only can data analytics provide mission benefits, but greater data collection and analysis can also be used to improve mission-support functions such as inventory management of supplies.

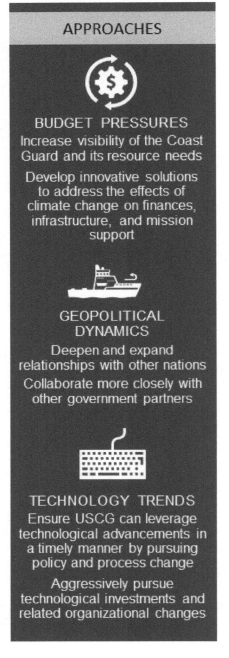

APPROACHES

BUDGET PRESSURES
Increase visibility of the Coast Guard and its resource needs

Develop innovative solutions to address the effects of climate change on finances, infrastructure, and mission support

GEOPOLITICAL DYNAMICS
Deepen and expand relationships with other nations

Collaborate more closely with other government partners

TECHNOLOGY TRENDS
Ensure USCG can leverage technological advancements in a timely manner by pursuing policy and process change

Aggressively pursue technological investments and related organizational changes

7

PROJECT EVERGREEN V

WORKSHOP QUICKLOOK: "Semper Adaptus"

Strategic Solutions for Future Needs (cont'd)

In summary, many participants would like to see greater sharing of both information-technology infrastructure and data with other intelligence and law enforcement agencies such as CBP and DoD. They envisioned a seamless system where law enforcement and intelligence communities work more closely to facilitate nearer-to-real-time decision-making regarding national and economic security interests threatened by transnational criminal or terrorist organizations. Furthermore, exchanging information with international partners could not only strengthen these relationships but also give the Coast Guard greater situational awareness and remove blind spots in certain operating environments. Debated for years, this suggestion will require legislation that mandates the development of an interagency law enforcement-intelligence sharing database that may only occur if there is strong leadership and a clearly articulated need.

However, the Coast Guard will have to invest in data gathering, improve tech equities, and change its culture to incentivize knowledge management while overcoming organizational stovepipes. It should establish data science as a distinct function, as opposed to collateral duty within the service, either with its own command structure or a competency in ways that develop expertise. Participants cautioned that there may be cultural resistance to change and data science from those concerned about existing mission sets being pared down or the organization shifting away from traditional structures.

Specific Questions from Semper Adaptus Workshop Sponsor

In addition to the workshop questions identified earlier, participants were asked to consider additional questions posed by the workshop's sponsor, CG-7, Assistant Commandant for Capability.

Q. Technology makes it increasingly easy to conduct work from multiple locations. What capabilities do we need to have forward positioned (why and where?) and what capabilities can we centralize or operate remotely? Do these changes affect how we C2 our forces/operations?

A larger globalized force posture in the future necessitates that the Coast Guard deploy more personnel to critical areas of operation abroad, while seeking savings from divesting under-utilized resources and infrastructure and leveraging autonomous capabilities where prudent. Fundamentally, some level of forward presence will always be necessary, either to supplement and contextualize sensor data, engage partners during operations, or provide mission support; however, command and control can be more centralized if organizational layers are streamlined. Command-and-control functions will also likely trend to centralization into C2 centers as the Coast Guard more closely coordinates operations with the Navy and Marine Corps. Greater integration of intelligence and law-enforcement information gathered by various federal agencies could also catalyze greater centralization. While the distribution of mission activities will shift away from manned to unmanned systems, providing improved mission performance and cost benefits, the value of organizational engagements and partnering will continue to require some level of forward presence.

8

211

PROJECT EVERGREEN V

WORKSHOP QUICKLOOK: "Semper Adaptus"

Specific Questions from Project Evergreen's Sponsor (cont'd)

Q. What skills/capabilities will our regulators need in this technologically driven world? What capabilities will investigators/inspectors need?

Regulators, investigators, and inspectors will need new legal authorities, advanced technological tools, and expertise in cyber and data science. Several participants argued that Congress and the DOJ will need to create a new legal regime to regulate how surveillance is conducted, how information is shared among government agencies, and how offenders are prosecuted when identified by technology such as automated surveillance. To inform risk-based regulations and enforcement paradigms, the Coast Guard will need to ensure it is gathering the necessary complete and high-quality incident data. Additionally, the Coast Guard needs to invest in recruiting, training, and retaining personnel with cyber, technological, and data-science skills at all ranks and in all areas of operation. The service could do this by better managing and leveraging existing knowledge, and by building new knowledge through educational opportunities and incentives. Lastly, the Coast Guard could improve retention of critical skills and personnel by allowing for more rapid promotions for individuals with critically needed skillsets.

Q. In a hyper-connected world, what will the public's expectation for Coast Guard services be? What capabilities will we need to manage those expectations/ perceptions?

Participants anticipated that a hyper-connected world would increase both domestic and international demand for Coast Guard services and more expansive Coast Guard missions. As reasons, they cited the likely effects of climate change, including more frequent natural disasters, new opportunities in the Arctic due to melting ice, and competition for natural resources. The Coast Guard has an opportunity to raise its international profile and authority by participating in the IMO full-time and in-person in part to demonstrate leadership in pursuing long-term solutions to global warming, protecting natural resources, leading disaster-relief efforts, and coordinating diplomacy with foreign states in the Arctic. The Coast Guard will need to expand its partnerships with foreign actors, especially given its unique reputation as an international diplomatic force. Providing incentives to personnel to hone foreign language and diplomacy skills and expanding liaison opportunities with international organizations could help develop a workforce that can successfully engage globally. The Coast Guard should also seek partnerships with other USG agencies and private industry, so that it can leverage existing knowledge and infrastructure, especially regarding technology and mission support.

Q. How will reduced emissions/carbon neutral footprint affect Coast Guard capabilities and missions?

Reducing emissions could potentially drive the shift toward consolidation of physical units and increased reliance on advanced technology. It could also provide an additional incentive for the Coast Guard to divest unnecessary property, especially platforms approaching obsolescence.

Q. Capability that used to be only in the hands of the wealthiest states can now be acquired as a service or developed through collection and analysis of information. How will the reduced barriers to gaining insights into the maritime domain reshape Coast Guard capabilities/missions?

9

212

PROJECT EVERGREEN V

WORKSHOP QUICKLOOK: "Semper Adaptus"

Specific Questions from Project Evergreen's Sponsor (cont'd)

This trend may lead to an increased demand for Coast Guard capabilities in the deep Pacific to counter Chinese expansion and collection. The Service will also have to invest more in defensive security measures to protect its port systems. Lastly, Congress will have to articulate the Coast Guard's role as a regulator and protocols for how to respond to nefarious actors' use of these technologies.

Q. The Coast Guard operates its assets for many decades. Many of the capabilities that we're operating or acquiring now will continue to operate in 2040. Will they still be relevant? If not, can they be modified to be relevant? Are there capability design/ deployment models that we should consider to ensure relevance?

Participants repeatedly emphasized that the Coast Guard should shift from investing in physical assets toward investing in advanced technologies. This means cutting stations and retiring vessels, replacing personnel with automation and unmanned vehicles, investing in cutting-edge technologies or leveraging other agencies' technological capabilities, and fostering a more skilled and specialized workforce. The Coast Guard can also modify its assets for future challenges. For example, participants anticipated needing fully automated boats, aircraft and ice-capable cutters in the future. They said small-boat stations should become more weather hardened and better equipped to survive harsh climate conditions caused by climate change. Lastly, participants suggested that the Coast Guard may lose rescue assets and other physical resources as the use of AI and automation becomes more common.

Q. In a rapidly changing world, what capabilities will the Coast Guard need to own versus what will they contract out?

The Coast Guard's increasing role in the U.S. competition with China does not necessarily mean the USCG will need to invest in new assets and infrastructure. For example, the Service could leverage the substantial existing DoD infrastructure in Indo-PACOM, including maritime patrols, C2 centers, Naval ships, bases, technology, and intelligence services. Where possible, Coast Guard personnel could use existing host-nation or other USG infrastructure when deploying abroad. However, frontiers such as the Arctic may require building infrastructure from scratch. Participants also suggested that the Coast Guard look for ways to partner with private companies like Amazon to contract out warehousing and other logistics needs or the commercial sector in general to provide maintenance to aids to navigation. Alternatively, there may be opportunities to expand the Coast Guard's authority to reorient its missions where the Service has complementary or overlapping interests with other federal agencies, such as MARAD, NOAA, USACE, or CBP. The Coast Guard should focus its own investments on increasing the skills and knowledge of its workforce, building an autonomous and weather-resistant SAR capability, and ice-capable cutters, and developing the requirements for more forward deployments.

Project Evergreen employs Strategic Foresight to support executive leaders in their role as the Coast Guard's decision engines. This product is a first look into the results of "Semper Adaptus", one of many "pinecones" on the Evergreen tree. A summary to be produced in fall 2021 will provide pinecone highlights and identify strategic implications for the 27th Commandant's leadership team. The Evergreen core team is comprised of active duty and civilian subject matter experts with diverse backgrounds from various program offices, field commands, and special assignments that range in rank from Chief Petty Officer to Captain and have committed to participating on a recurring basis in Evergreen workshops and gaming exercises. Their continued participation will enable more in-depth, consistent analysis and richer material for alternative futures.

HSOAC
HOMELAND SECURITY
OPERATIONAL ANALYSIS CENTER
An FFRDC operated by
the RAND Corporation
under contract with DHS

PROJECT EVERGREEN V
PINECONE WORKSHOP QUICK LOOK

Flash to Bang Virtual Pinecone
February 23–25, 2021 | Coast Guard Headquarters

This document provides an overview of the key themes that emerged from the "Flash to Bang" workshop. The workshop was part of the Coast Guard's Project Evergreen, which aims to anticipate long-term challenges for the Service and provide insights for how to address them; this workshop and similar events have been termed "pinecones." It was sponsored by RADM Kevin Lunday, Deputy for Material Readiness, and organized by the Coast Guard's Office of Emerging Policy, DCO-X, with support from HSOAC, a federally funded research and development center operated by the RAND Corporation.

"Flash to Bang" is the second of three workshops in which approximately 20 members of the Evergreen CORE team explore how the Coast Guard should prepare for future challenges and opportunities. The first workshop, "Semper Adaptus," focused on examining how the Coast Guard could strategically position itself in the future. "Flash to Bang"—meaning the time between the inception of an innovative idea and its implementation—explored what the Coast Guard needed to do and acquire in order to meet its anticipated future positioning. The final workshop, "Concepts 2040," will help shape new potential concepts of operations (CONOPs) for the Coast Guard to meet future demands. The resulting CONOPs will be tested in a series of serious games in 2021 and 2022. The results of these games and previous Evergreen pinecones will be synthesized in the comprehensive report at the end of the fiscal year 2021 to inform the commandant's strategic planning.

Purpose and Structure of the Workshop

The speed of change in the Services' operational environment is accelerating. The concern is that the Service is consistently "behind the curve". How can it harness creativity from leadership to the deck-plate level to drive faster adaptation to everything from increasingly automated vessel systems to the nefarious and creative activities of bad actors?

The workshop's objective was to answer the question: How can the Service better capitalize on innovation and adapt more quickly? Participants were organized into the same four groups with the same future scenarios as in the prior workshop. (See "How the Workshop Was Conducted" on p. 2.)

ISSUES

RE-POSITIONING
to quickly access and exploit the latest technology

BETTER METHODS
to allocate and manage assets and mission support

CULTURAL SHIFTS
to expedite organizational and technological innovation

BUDGET AND RESOURCES
to keep up with the pace of innovation and change

WORKFORCE AND TALENT MANAGEMENT
to shape the future CG

1

PROJECT EVERGREEN V
PINECONE WORKSHOP QUICK LOOK

Day 1

Participants were organized into the same four groups with the same future scenarios as in the previous workshop, and accomplished the following:

Identified the major imperatives for change in each future scenario.

Categorized the imperatives according to which Coast Guard mechanisms need to be activated to effect change

Voted on 3–5 mechanisms the USCG should prioritize

Discussed the implications of chosen priorities would have on USCG culture, mission support, and mission delivery

Day 2

Teams created a "causal layered analysis" of their ideas—juxtaposing the "way things are" now to the "way things might be" in the future

Explored specific ways that the Service could make this transition.

Voted on the most important things the Coast Guard should work on.

Considered the various barriers and opportunities implicated in their recommended priorities

Day 3

Each team crafted and honed its ideas and then briefed their findings to other workshop participants.

Key Demands for the Future Coast Guard

The teams predicted several common future demands despite each group being assigned a distinct scenario representing divergent trends of key economic, geopolitical, technical, and environmental drivers. According to participants, the future demands are the following:

The Coast Guard of the future must be better positioned to quickly access and exploit the latest technology for mission success. The Coast Guard is operating in an increasingly technologically complex world. Rapid technological change could shape the future in ways that are difficult to anticipate. And the proliferation of information technology is driving faster decisionmaking and increasing the disruptive potential of misinformation. To keep pace, the Coast Guard needs to reconsider its paradigm for owning and operating systems and exploiting the capabilities of these systems. The Coast Guard's current capabilities primarily derive from large assets such as cutters, boats,

and aircraft; as a result, the Service's organization, culture, and investments are largely asset-centric. However, in an increasingly networked, information-centric world with distributed, low-cost sensors and more capable autonomous unmanned vehicles, the Coast Guard will need to shift its emphasis. More of the Coast Guard's capabilities will involve information technology, including defenses against cyber and electronic attacks, the automated integration and analysis of data from disparate sources into actionable information, and coordination of unmanned systems. All of this will require greater investments in skilled information technology (IT) personnel and equipment, as well as corresponding cultural and organizational shifts. While the Coast Guard will continue to have large, manned assets that perform most of its missions, its focus on these other areas will need to expand.

2

PROJECT EVERGREEN V
PINECONE WORKSHOP QUICK LOOK

Key Demands for the Future Coast Guard (cont'd)

In addition to the assets and capabilities themselves, the current requirements, acquisition, and deployment processes are out of sync with the pace of technological advancement. The Coast Guard needs to reimagine the processes used to acquire and sustain its systems. Furthermore, because of global access to new technologies, the Coast Guard will need better approaches for understanding the consequences of new technologies so that it can proactively engage international organizations. For example, helping to develop regulations for cyber or autonomous systems will be important.

In summary, new technology developments will affect policy, manning, resourcing, port and other security postures, international engagements, and operations in general.

Cultural shifts are necessary to pursue more rapid organizational and technological innovation. The Coast Guard will need to become less hierarchical, rules-based, and risk-adverse. It will need to evolve to become more tech-savvy, incentivize outside-the-box problem solving, and promote more rapid technological and operational innovation for improved performance and services.

Better methods are needed for more rapidly and effectively allocating, deploying, and performing command and control of operational assets across missions and districts in order to adapt and respond to changing mission drivers and priorities. The future Coast Guard needs new operational concepts to enable operators to respond quickly and effectively to changing conditions. As assets become more capable, there must be corresponding changes to CONOPS; tactics, techniques, and procedures; assets numbers and mixes; and support infrastructure that reflect these improved capabilities. The Coast Guard also needs better, more responsive systems for providing mission support in novel ways.

The Coast Guard does not currently have the budget and other resources to keep up with the pace of technology innovation and diffusion and changing mission priorities and demands. For example, a greater global presence, and the effects of climate change may require the Coast Guard to become more involved in protecting Western Hemisphere fish; visiting the ports of U.S. allies; or operating in the Arctic, Africa, the South China Sea, and space.

Many future demands on the Coast Guard will require upfront investment either in technology or infrastructure that cannot be sourced completely by finding new efficiencies in existing operations. The Service may need to expend some of its political capital and must continue to articulate and communicate its role and value to stakeholders, acknowledging that economic conditions and competition with other agencies for federal funding will ultimately determine available resources.

Workforce and talent management must be part of any initiative to shape the future Coast Guard. While not the focus of this workshop, the workforce continues to be identified as an important contributor to the future success of the Coast Guard. Participants suggested that the Coast Guard must manage the workforce in ways that align with societal norms and the expectations regarding work arrangements, benefits, and work-life balance. They also identified the necessity of a diverse, tech-savvy workforce that has multiple pathways for developing skills and capabilities needed by the Coast Guard. Finally, participants noted that mission priorities and technological changes will require holistically reconsidering the roles of active-duty officers, active duty enlisted, civilians, and reservists, and the training opportunities available to them.

3

PROJECT EVERGREEN V
PINECONE WORKSHOP QUICK LOOK

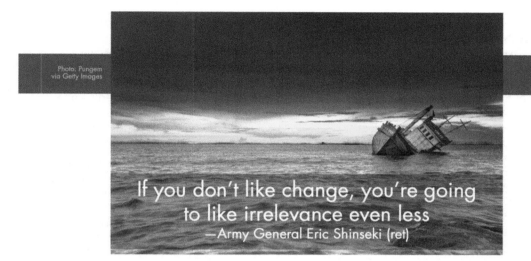

Photo: Pungem via Getty Images

If you don't like change, you're going to like irrelevance even less
—Army General Eric Shinseki (ret)

Initiatives to Enable the Service to More Rapidly Adapt to Change

To enable a more rapid "flash to bang" (movement of ideas from inception to implementation), three of the four teams focused on increasing access to the latest technology to enable innovation. The fourth concentrated on new operational concepts. The four initiatives developed by the teams are the following:

1 Develop a Commandant's Innovation Strategy, create an Innovation Center of Excellence, and build a culture to implement both by creating an executive champion for innovation, including innovation as a criterion in decisionmaking, identifying innovation as a competency, and rewarding efforts to innovate.

2 Pursue a culture and acquisition process that maximizes asset flexibility by employing modular solutions, where the Service views major assets as a platform or container for new technology.

3 Integrate and prioritize baseline technical proficiency into Coast Guard culture, beginning at enlisted and officer accession sources.

4 Develop nimble adaptive force packages that can be employed at home or abroad, and use data and technologies to help inform rapid decisionmaking during contingency responses.

4

PROJECT EVERGREEN V

PINECONE WORKSHOP QUICK LOOK

Initiatives to Enable the Service to More Rapidly Adapt to Change (cont'd)

Commandant's Innovation Strategy and an Innovation Center of Excellence: Coast Guard cutters or aircraft start becoming outdated almost as soon as they leave their first hangar or shipyard. To enable a greater speed of "flash to bang", workshop participants focused on increasing access to the latest technology through new organizational constructs and workforce development activities. They also presented ideas for adapting the acquisition process to incorporate technology updates more readily through incremental system changes. For example, participants suggested that establishing new offices or arrangements such as a Center for Innovation[1] or developing formal public-private partnerships with industry could lower the barriers to working with the private sector and provide greater access to novel technologies. An Innovation Center of Excellence could tap into cutting-edge ideas and technologies emerging in academia, the National Laboratories, and industry forums. Public-private partnerships are a means of building relationships with industry to access the latest technologies more quickly, although it was noted that the Coast Guard may need new authorities to engage in such partnerships. Before establishing partnerships, the Coast Guard would have to determine how to entice industry to participate, be clear what each partner has to contribute to the partnership and seek to build relationships and trust.

A culture and acquisition process that maximizes asset flexibility: Similarly, participants wanted to see changes to the acquisition process and, where necessary, to the federal acquisition regulation to shorten the time to get new technology into operational systems. This could include establishing a rapid procurement authorization for mission-critical technology or adapting the Navy development squadron concept. It could involve changing policy and practices to allow new technologies to be incorporated as new systems are developed, rather than locking into tech solutions during the development phase.

One team suggested using modular design concepts so that equipment and subsystems could be upgraded as soon as more advanced technology becomes available. Modularity ensures that from the time an operational asset comes off the line, it is subject to an ongoing process of modernization that moves in real-time with technology, treating deployable assets as containers for technologies. Participants envisioned a "plug-and-play" model in which self-contained modules can simplify both upgrades and repairs across a wide range of different classes and platforms. This would require a change in mindset from necessarily long-lived systems to those that could be readily replaced as the technology becomes obsolete. One successful example of the Coast Guard's success with disposable assets is the employment of cube-satellites that can be deployed for relatively low cost, provide service during their useful life or technological relevance, then be disposed of and replaced with new state of the art technology. Incorporating excess defense article transfers and foreign military sales into acquisition lifecycle planning could also help.

They noted that maintaining the interoperability of systems could be a challenge, and that the logistics and maintenance processes must be adapted so that these updates could be installed throughout the fleet systematically. Practices that ensure new assets or systems

---

1 While not specifically discussed this center could build off and expand the activities of the existing Coast Guard Innovation Program, established in 2000, that seeks to develop and implement innovation strategies enterprise-wide and foster a culture of continuous learning and innovation. The program implements the crowdsourcing, CG_Ideas@Work. See: https://www.dcms.uscg.mil/Our-Organization/Assistant-Commandant-for-Acquisitions-CG-9/Innovation/Innovation-Program-Overview/

5

PROJECT EVERGREEN V
PINECONE WORKSHOP QUICK LOOK

WHAT PARTICIPANTS WERE SAYING

In a world of increasing disorder, innovation at the speed of relevance requires foresight and agency to execute.

We're in an information age, but we're still thinking/structured in an industrial or pre-industrial way.

How do we design change management leadership training to be peppered throughout a career so that an O-6 isn't learning how to lead change management as you are doing it?

But what we really want to do is not do away with capital assets, but when it comes to operationally flexible assets, we need to not only adjust how we acquire them but also how we repurpose them.

Initiatives to Enable Rapid Change (cont'd)

are interoperable with joint forces and international partners will be important.

Adopting more commercially available technology in the areas of computing and automation versus relying on C5ISC could be another opportunity. Finally, R&D and budget priorities will also need to change to reflect greater reliance on technology. Recognizing that budget constraints are likely to continue and that the Service lacks the DoD's buying power, participants also recommended organizational and acquisition process changes to leverage other government research and development and procurement investments for greater efficiencies and faster development times. Greater engagement of joint requirements with the DoD and Intelligence Community may also help. However, other participants suggested that the Coast Guard's R&D budget should be increased to be proportionately comparable to DoD's and that more risk should be taken.

More generally, participants suggested the Commandant's Innovation Strategy combined with an executive champion for innovation could create momentum and cultural change necessary to implement the strategy and elevate, catalyze, and implement innovative thinking and technological investments enterprise-wide. Including innovation as a criterion in decisionmaking, identifying innovation as a competency, and rewarding efforts to innovate either through meritorious advancement or cash rewards were other suggestions. To more proactively manage the potential consequences that new technologies may have on missions, the Service should increase its physical presence and engagement at the International Maritime Organization and other United Nations bodies, perhaps in coordination with the Department of State. In particular, it should seek additional legal authority to better regulate cyber-security in the marine transportation system.

Integrate and prioritize baseline technical proficiency into Coast Guard culture. Cultural change at both the organizational and individual levels is also crucial to achieving flash to bang. The culture must question the status quo and promote out-of-the-box thinking, instead of relying exclusively on HQ-driven innovation and rules-based thinking

6

PROJECT EVERGREEN V
PINECONE WORKSHOP QUICK LOOK

Strategic Solutions for Future Needs (cont'd)

to improve mission performance or efficiencies. Another desirable culture change is to accept "failure" as both an opportunity to learn and as a cost of doing business when building and fielding new technologies or innovative ways of performing a task. Creating this culture will require incentives for "healthy" or "calculated" risk-taking and out-of-the box problem solving, and recognition or rewards for leaders who are innovative and forward-thinking. Hand in hand with these new cultural norms, the Service will need to become better at identifying and diffusing good ideas throughout the organization. This could be facilitated by ensuring there is a baseline technical proficiency throughout the Service for enlisted personnel and officers, beginning with accessions but also integrating IT skills development into basic training, including technology qualifications in promotion decisions, increasing promotions of cyber offices, and encouraging direct commission engineers to cross-train and serve in operational roles. Organizationally, the Service could move away from concentrating technical expertise in the Deputy Commandant for Mission Support toward distributing expertise throughout the enterprise. For greater risk-tolerance, cultural change is needed at both the individual and organizational or systems levels for faster innovation and responsiveness.

Develop nimble adaptive force packages, and use data and technologies to help inform rapid decisionmaking during contingency responses. Another initiative presented focused on generating innovative operational models through a combination of rethinking organizational structures and authorities, with sustained investment in world-class IT. The idea involves developing data-driven operational force packages for domestic and international missions, and new concepts

of operations that enable responsive command and control decisionmaking away from headquarters and at lower echelons that are closer to the operational environment. Because of investments in IT, these performance-based operational planning concepts could be developed using an expanded array of data and automated analysis methods such as artificial intelligence. Resources and assets could then be more readily shared across sectors and districts and deployed to where the need is greatest. If IT can help eliminate redundant organizational layers, these resources could be reprogrammed for expanding or priority missions across geographical "boundaries." To complement a more nimble model and decision process for assets, there needs to be a complementary IT and technological model for logistics functions to ensure they are adapted to the new operational model and resilient to climate change effects. A data-driven, performance-focused decision process might also reveal less productive assets or infrastructure that could be divested and the cost savings applied to other priority needs.

Budget constraints and changing mission priorities will force the Coast Guard to think more strategically about its 11 statutory missions, develop new relationships with industry and other government entities, and invest in novel forms and locations of infrastructure. It will be even more critical to focus on messaging the Coast Guard's "brand" and relevance. Developing a more programmatic and standard approach for involving the government affairs officer with unit commanders or integrating the Coast Guard with state offices of emergency management could generate greater political capital. It is critical that the Service develop the ability to either seek additional funds, especially for R&D, or reprogram budgets as the Service

7

PROJECT EVERGREEN V

PINECONE WORKSHOP QUICK LOOK

Strategic Solutions for Future Needs (cont'd)

shifts away from assets to other capabilities. Managing the effects and associated costs of climate change could include building primary infrastructure inland and using a forward basing concept on the coast.

Finally, all teams discussed ideas for **increasing the technical proficiency of the workforce as a priority.** They ultimately recommended that the Service continue to prioritize flexible, innovative workforce programs and initiatives, especially those that increase liaison and training positions with industry, academia, and other government agencies such as DoD. These programs can help bring new ideas into the Coast Guard while building the technical skills of the individuals. Another recommendation was to treat cyber security as an operational-centric skill, instead of a mission support function with no career pathway, to be more competitive in recruiting candidates with these skills and to align with DoD, DHS, and IC partners. The Coast Guard could also partner with CISA or DISA or DoD to gain technical parity; mimic the DoD, which is finding ways establish the mission of this career field as being on the cutting edge of national security; and encourage greater permeability with the outside world.

APPROACHES

Develop an innovation strategy, a Center of Excellence, and an executive champion

Use modular solutions for acquisitions that maximize asset flexibility

Integrate and prioritize baseline technical proficiency into CG culture

Think more strategically about statutory missions, engage with industry and other government entities, and invest in infrastructure

Increase the technical proficiency of the workforce

HSOAC
HOMELAND SECURITY
OPERATIONAL ANALYSIS CENTER
An FFRDC operated by
the RAND Corporation
under contract with DHS

Project Evergreen (EVG) employs Strategic Foresight to support executive leaders in their role as the Coast Guard's decision engines. This product is a first look into the results of Flas to Band, one of eight "pinecones" on the Evergreen tree. In summer 2021, Team EVG will begin a meta-analysis of the Pinecones to identify strategic choices for the 27th Commandant of the Coast Guard's leadership team.

8

PROJECT EVERGREEN V

PINECONE WORKSHOP QUICK LOOK

CONCEPT 2040 virtual workshop

June 1–3, 2021

This document provides an overview of the key themes that emerged from CONCEPT 2040, a "pinecone" workshop, organized by the Coast Guard's Office of Emerging Policy and HSOAC, a federally funded research and development center operated by the RAND Corporation. Approximately 15 members of the Evergreen core team attended.

CONCEPT 2040 is part of the Coast Guard's Project Evergreen, intended to anticipate long-term challenges for the Coast Guard and provide insights for how to address them. Sponsored by Rear Admiral Pat DeQuattro, Deputy Commandant for Operations Policy and Capabilities, CONCEPT 2040 is the last in a series of 2019-2021 pinecones to explore how the Coast Guard should prepare for future challenges and opportunities. Recent pinecones in this series focused on how the Coast Guard could strategically position itself to meet future challenges (Semper Adaptus) and accelerate the time between the inception of an innovative idea and its implementation (Flash to Bang). The discussions and material developed in CONCEPT 2040 will help shape new strategic concepts of operations (CONOPS) for the Coast Guard to meet potential future threats. The material will be used to develop a series of serious games in 2021 and 2022 conducted with a range of Coast Guard personnel and senior leadership that will stress-test illustrative/notional strategic CONOPS. In fall 2021, the results and materials from the pinecones will be compiled into a report noting key takeaways and common themes. In 2022, a second report will document the results and analysis from the series of games. Both are intended to inform the Commandant's strategic planning activities.

Purpose and Structure of the Workshop

The goal of the CONCEPT 2040 pinecone was for each team to design and develop strategic CONOPS that confronts the challenges of their assigned scenario. The CONOPS included developing a set of goals and priorities to meet each individual future scenario differently from the Coast Guard of today. Resource, posture, and policy trades were also explicitly articulated in each CONOPS.

Participants were organized into the same four groups and assessed the implications of the same future scenarios as in the previous pinecones, and then developed a CONOPS that

CATEGORIES OF DOMINANT THEMES

NEW TECHNOLOGY will allow new operational paradigms for managing human capital and assets, and require a workforce with basic "cyber hygiene" skills

GREATER ENGAGEMENT with other U.S. agencies and foreign governments will be needed to support foreign policy, security, and maritime law enforcement missions

INDO-PACIFIC AND ARCTIC OPERATIONS will demand more of the Coast Guard's attention

RESOURCE CONSTRAINTS will cause priorities to shift and the Coast Guard to make its case to Congress

1

PROJECT EVERGREEN V

WORKSHOP QUICK LOOK: CONCEPT 2040

Purpose and Structure of the Workshop (cont'd)

met the demands of the scenario. This 2.5-day workshop was structured differently from its predecessors, which were focused on ideation and encouraging participants to step outside the norms of today. On day one, each team engaged in a series of guided activities to build their respective strategic CONOPS. These activities centered on a series of questions:

1. What is an overall strategic vision and associated priorities for the USCG to meet the prioritized future threats?

    a. What are the most pressing threats to USCG missions under the scenario and how do they compare to today?

    b. What roughly equivalent set of today's priorities must be given up to meet future demands?

2. What resources are important to the proposed strategic vision, and how must missions and geographic presence be realigned to support it?

3. What institutional, organizational, and cultural shifts are necessary to meet this strategic vision?

4. What are the most pressing drivers of institutional, operational, and other risks to mission accomplishment, given the allocation of priorities and resources?

5. How should the Coast Guard collaborate with DoD, other DHS components, U.S. government, private, and foreign actors?

A key feature of the strategic CONOPS was that they had to be resource neutral, so participants were asked to identify priorities and make difficult choices throughout the exercise.

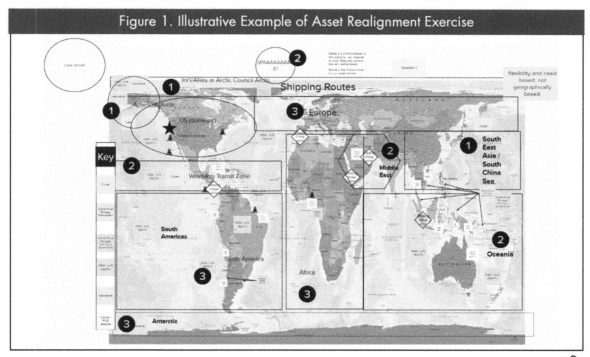

Figure 1. Illustrative Example of Asset Realignment Exercise

PROJECT EVERGREEN V
WORKSHOP QUICK LOOK: CONCEPT 2040

Purpose and Structure of the Workshop (cont'd)

Facilitators guided participants through each session's activities using visuals (for example, Figure 1) and detailed questions designed to break down the thought process, understand critical aspects of the response, and force the groups to make the difficult choices necessary to respond to the series of questions. Input from the virtual working sessions was collected using Mural, a virtual collaborative platform that supports structured brainstorming and discussion. Because the "why" is as important as the "what and the how" for game development, the specific discussions, arguments, and nuances around each topic were captured by note-takers.

The second day was devoted to writing and refining each team's strategic CONOPS using a common template that contained the following elements:

- **Strategic Vision** that contains goals and objectives, operating environment, and indicators of success
- **Key assumptions** about the overall environment and resource availability
- **Key threats**, drivers of change, and areas of operations
- **Method of execution** that includes critical tasks, missions, or responsibilities
- **Resource application** that addresses the placement of assets, key capabilities the USCG must acquire, key changes in the capacity of specific capabilities, and substantive investments and trades
- **Major risks and mitigation strategies**
- **Support concept**
- **Responsibilities and authorities**
- **Necessary institutional changes**

Teams met individually to review the maps and material generated during day one and to draft a CONOPS. In the afternoon all teams came together and presented their CONOPS to the group for discussion and feedback. Teams then met individually to revise their CONOPS based on this feedback and exposure to other CONOPS. On day three, Rear Admiral DeQuattro, Deputy for Operations, Policy and Capabilities, provided remarks, and (due to time constraints) one CONOPS was presented for discussion with the Rear Admiral and workshop participants. All strategic CONOPS will be presented to Rear Admiral Pat DeQuattro at a later date.

As mentioned earlier, the deliberations and the results of this pinecone will inform a series of games that will involve implementing a global USCG operating concept and associated force design at the strategic level given an uncertain future. During the game, participants will have to balance competing priorities, address multiple challenges across operating areas, examine wider service implications, determine acceptable levels of risk, and allocate limited service capabilities and resources.

3

PROJECT EVERGREEN V
WORKSHOP QUICK LOOK: CONCEPT 2040

Summary of the Four Strategic CONOPS

Four separate strategic CONOPS were developed, each addressing the demands of their scenario. Scenarios were constructed from the intersection of multiple trends that include climate change, shifting geopolitical patterns, evolving global economy, advancing technologies, and varying demographic patterns. The decision context for the scenarios was framed around how the Coast Guard should be realigned, given its evolving mission sets. The descriptions below are simplified summaries that admittedly sound quite similar at this level, but there are substantial divergences in the specifics. The full, more detailed CONOPS will be available in a later publication, and the scenarios can be found in the HSOAC report *Developing New Future Scenarios for the U.S. Coast Guard's Evergreen Strategic Foresight Program* (www.rand.org/t/RR3147, starting on page 67).

Scenario: Beyond the Horizon

Operating Environment: China is increasing its global presence while Japan-South Korea tensions are rising. The available labor pool is expanding, and maritime trade and port security entities are incorporating automation for efficiencies. There are also increasing effects from climate change. Overseas deployments/Coast Guard operational tempo remain high, contributing to some force stress.

Strategic Vision: The Coast Guard evolves to better advance dynamic U.S. maritime interests by being globally dispersed and nimbly responsive. The Coast Guard will prioritize defense readiness and DoD interoperability, while becoming more central to the national security discussion, to remain relevant in the era of strategic competition (and competitive budgets). Through decentralization, and increased integration with DoD, the USCG increases agility and gives the nation a decisive advantage in global strategic competition. Tradeoffs to achieve this include being more of a services provider (fines and fees), shifting from conducting all operations to overseeing them, and repurposing assets or replacing them with technology advancements and partnerships.

Scenario: Steady Growth

Operating Environment: The threats of 2021 have grown in scope and complexity by 2040 in terms of climate change effects, smuggling, and counterdrug missions. USCG has an icebreaker capability, uses space-based navigation technology, and engages in expanded global partnerships. The world economy is prosperous, and extended family support systems and geographic stability are the norm.

Strategic Vision: The Coast Guard of 2040 meets traditional threats that have steadily grown in scope and complexity by being globally dispersed and nimbly responsive, with widespread connectivity and maritime domain awareness (MDA) enabled by whole-of-government and international relationships, cyber capabilities, space infrastructure, and data/AI capabilities. The presence of our physical assets is based on operational need, not geographic basing. This is a shift in our concept of operations—not necessarily a complete reorganization. We pay for this with offsets, operational prioritization, risk management, and tech-based efficiencies.

4

PROJECT EVERGREEN V
WORKSHOP QUICK LOOK: CONCEPT 2040

Summary of the Four Strategic CONOPS (con't)

Scenario: Divergent Paths

Operating Environment: China is engaging international organizations and is active in the Arctic, while the United States and Russia have turned to internal issues. California has bi-lateral agreements with China and is engaging in diplomatic efforts. The economy is strong and the debt is down. The workforce has flexibility, given a minimum income and universal health insurance. Western ports have minimal manning, with untested centralized control and security management. Climate criminals are capitalizing on extreme events. Domestic and global fisheries are moving northward and are nearing collapse, while migrants are bypassing the United States. All areas of the country are experiencing extreme weather.

Strategic Vision:
The Coast Guard is a source of exportable expertise of high value to foreign partners, and leverages partnerships, foreign and domestic to ensure the US remains the partner of choice in a competitive strategic environment. Due to the nature of this scenario, deprioritizing or reallocating responsibility of some missions are required to bring adaptive and scalable solutions to emergency events at home and abroad. This is achieved with technology that enhances MDA, a centralized robust cyber workforce providing remote and fly away support, and an increased number of geographic locations of deployments and the associated robust supply chain and logistics.

Scenario: Increasing Disorder

Operating Environment: American society has become more risk tolerant and less reliant on employers for institutional support. Rising sea levels and intensifying storms are occurring year-round. Russia has established dominance in the Arctic through infrastructure investments and increased MDA technologies. China has increased trade and infrastructure investments in Mexico. There has been wide adaptation of electric propulsion systems in air, land, and sea vehicles.

Strategic Vision: The Coast Guard meets the challenges of an increasingly disordered world by allocating people and capital to the missions that demand them (asserting U.S. sovereignty in the maritime domain and building partner maritime governance capacity). Operational effectiveness is increased by leveraging technology and data fluency to inform organizational decisionmaking and by transformational changes in how the Coast Guard conducts legacy missions and delegates responsibilities to external organizations. Investments in unmanned systems and other technologies allow humans to be placed in roles where they are required, rather than acting as a sensor.

5

PROJECT EVERGREEN V
WORKSHOP QUICK LOOK: CONCEPT 2040

Dominant Themes

All the teams acknowledged that the USCG is uniquely positioned to address the diverse needs and threats in the maritime domain. They recognized the USCG's strengths, such as its broad (and deep) legal authority to act, diverse missions and capabilities, strong international and domestic partnerships, and versatility. Each of the notional CONOPS leveraged and maintained these capabilities to meet future mission needs and threats, while releasing some activities that were either not inherently governmental or did not make use of essential capabilities for meeting priority threats. While each concept has details, prioritization decisions, and trade-off choices unique to its future and the way the service would operate in that future, several dominant themes emerged across all four notional strategic CONOPS.

The USCG should use different operational paradigms enabled by new technologies to deploy human capital and assets to priority threats as they emerge both domestically and globally. Teams used the terms "surge," "intermittent," or "seasonal" to characterize the more fluid approach for primarily deploying resources to meet dynamic threats in lieu of today's predominately geographically-focused placement. Furthermore, a more fluid or strategic application of resources would free up resources assigned to today's homeland missions to provide sustained support to enduring foreign policy efforts, and to security and international law or treaty enforcement missions in the future. A consequence of this approach is that more units will deploy globally, and these deployments will be longer in duration. This approach is enabled by greater use of automation and unmanned systems, improved sensors, and other ISR capabilities to increase MDA and engagement zones, in addition to IT systems that facilitate greater use

of data analytics and communication. The extent of USCG engagement internationally may depend on the acceptable levels of loss to domestic mission readiness.

The USCG should pursue greater coordination and resource sharing with other U.S. agencies and foreign governments, particularly for improving MDA, interoperability and communications, and robust logistics support for overseas deployments (for example with other DHS, DoD, and DNI agencies). Some teams mentioned using contracted services for logistics support. Leveraging other government facilities and systems or contracted services could avoid having to make the investments and institutional changes required to scale organic logistic capabilities globally and help remain resource neutral.

Greater international engagement will support foreign policy, security, and international maritime law enforcement missions. The Coast Guard will become a valued instrument of national power while continuing to lead international maritime governance—from setting regulations for autonomous shipping at the IMO to helping Pacific Island nations assert their sovereignty through maritime patrols, natural resource patrols, and bi-lateral engagement. Effective maritime governance requires years or decades of sustained engagement with partners to develop and maintain long-term relationships. As a result, the USCG will need to build a culturally fluent, substantially sized corps of officers and enlisted members to act as attachés (CGATTs) and liaisons (CGLOs), and a trained cadre of foreign affairs officers to engage and work with partners around the world, including those with which the United States has a significant maritime interest.

6

PROJECT EVERGREEN V
WORKSHOP QUICK LOOK: CONCEPT 2040

Dominant Themes (con't)

Coast Guard operations in the Indo-Pacific and the Arctic will grow in importance and frequency. Differences in geographic placement of assets emerged among the teams as priorities were driven by scenarios that differed in fisheries enforcement and interdiction demands. However, two regions, the Indo-Pacific (to counter China) and the Arctic (to counter China and Russia) were important to the foreign policy and security support mission for all teams.

The need for a technology-savvy workforce that has basic "cyber hygiene" skills, and the organizational culture to embrace and utilize the expertise was universally acknowledged. Some also included establishing flexible career pathways to enable accessing needed talent and help with retention. (See previous previous Quicklooks from Workforce pinecones and the HSOAC publications "Decoding Data Science" and "U.S. Coast Guard Workforce 2040" for more details.)

Resource constraints will catalyze the Coast Guard and Congress to reconsider some of today's activities that may not be central to future Coast Guard mission requirements. There was agreement that the ATON maintenance does not need to be a Coast Guard mission for the Coast Guard to maintain its waterways management responsibilities, although teams differed in whether to completely divest this mission, either to the USACE or private sector, or to continue in an oversight capacity. Counterterrorism, counter-drug activities, traditional ice patrol, and marine safety were other mission areas that teams prioritized lower by either accepting greater mission risk or determining they could be performed by others. These were tied to the threat level of each future scenario. Furthermore, the Coast Guard must articulate to Congress its vision for the future to meet a changing threat, and in turn Congress will need to support shifts in resource streams and the adoption of authorities to provide the Coast Guard with greater operational agility and flexibility in operations and basing locations.

The USCG must position itself to acquire the budget needed to successfully perform its future missions, and use political capital to ensure that necessary changes to asset laydown, resourcing and deployments, authorities, etc. are communicated widely and are well understood both internally and externally. While changing deployment paradigms and exploiting new technologies may provide some efficiencies, investment is needed to establish and acquire them, which will put additional pressure on near-term budgets. The USCG can no longer agree to "do more with less" and must position itself to push for additional budget.

Project Evergreen (EVG) employs Strategic Foresight to support executive leaders in their role as the Coast Guard's decision engines. This product is a first look into the results of CONCEPTS 2040, one of the "pinecones" on the Evergreen tree. In summer 2021, Team EVG will begin a thematic analysis of the pinecones to identify strategic choices for the 27th Commandant of the Coast Guard's leadership team.

HSOAC
HOMELAND SECURITY
OPERATIONAL ANALYSIS CENTER

An FFRDC operated by
the RAND Corporation
under contract with DHS

7

PROJECT EVERGREEN V

STRATEGIC GAME QUICK LOOK

Paratus Futurum: Ready for the Future
January 11–12, 2022 | Virtual Pinecone workshop

What might the future hold and how might the Coast Guard prepare to adapt and excel? To explore these questions, Evergreen and the Homeland Security Operational Analysis Center (HSOAC) team developed a serious game to examine how plausible scenarios in 2040 may require the Coast Guard to adjust strategic-level roles and missions today.

Conducted January 11-12, 2022, with almost 30 Coast Guard personnel, the game Paratus Futurum ("Ready for the Future") forces players to make distinct choices about mission priority and investments to prepare for an uncertain future in which climate change, technological advancements, the U.S. economy, and the global competition for power all shape the demand for USCG missions. Participants probe the trade-offs that must occur to meet USCG priorities and to enable Coast Guard leadership to articulate a vision to Congress, the Executive Branch, the Department of Homeland Security, and the Coast Guard workforce.

The following sections will describe overviews of:

- How the game is played
- The results of each team's game play
- Overarching observations
- The Delphi method that was used to evaluate strategic options
- Benefits of gaming for USCG personnel who are the service's future leaders

OBSERVATIONS FROM THE GAME
(explored in more detail starting on page 4)

To allocate resources, teams relied heavily on:
- the assigned scenario and strategic vision
- their understanding of the USCG's role and mission in a region

Investment strategies for new capabilities were largely motivated by the efficiencies they generate

Homeland missions are enduring

A strong focus on the demand signals tied to a scenario's strategic vision can override the perception of "untouchable" missions

Service culture is a concern as the Coast Guard's focus and talent needs evolve

What is good for the play of the game is good for Coast Guard planning and investment processes

1

PROJECT EVERGREEN V

GAME QUICKLOOK: Paratus Futurum

Game Play Overview

At the beginning of the game each team was given a unique scenario and corresponding strategic vision that was developed in the prior Evergreen CONCEPT 2040 Pinecone workshop. During game play, teams have a fixed number of resources that they can allocate to select missions in regions across the globe or invest in longer-term capabilities to meet the demands and priorities of their unique scenario (Figure 1 is an example).

After these resources are allocated, facilitators introduce a series of events representing shifting global trends into the scenario. HSOAC

researchers evaluate the success of the Coast Guard response to each event using a combination of available investments in the region, the allocation of resources given to each region-mission pair, and an element of chance. "Success" is scored along the dimensions of public opinion, Congressional opinion, and Executive Branch opinion. The resulting scores, domestic changes, and Coast Guard culture determine the available resources for the next turn and any potential constraints on resource allocation choices. The game begins in 2025, and each turn represents a four-year period. Teams play 3-5 rounds, progressing to 2040 and beyond.

Figure 1. Example Game Board Depicting Key Operational Regions and Mission Areas

2

PROJECT EVERGREEN V
GAME QUICKLOOK: Paratus Futurum

How the Game Works

In the first round, players begin by discussing the scenario, strategic vision, and corresponding intelligence briefs to determine which critical Coast Guard missions to prioritize and invest in across a selection of missions in the seven operational regions, based on their strategic goals and anticipated trends. If teams decide to deviate from the strategic vision at any point in the game, they must articulate a reason. The subsequent turns begin with an intelligence brief of the Coast Guard's best available intelligence aligned with the team's assigned scenario. Players then choose how to allocate available resources across missions and investment areas given the new information. All missions are performed by the Coast Guard, but players allocate their budgeted resource tokens to prioritize selected missions within geographic areas to ensure they have a higher rate of success. Resource tokens represent the level of effort devoted to a mission.

The probability of success is scored at three levels of effort, beginning with "risk," progressing to "focus," and finally advancing to "priority." They also may choose to make limited investments to reduce costs or improve performance in future turns. Some capabilities investments decrease the score for Coast Guard culture to underscore

the need for institutional adaptation. Teams can mitigate negative institutional consequences from adopting new capabilities by investing directly in culture. Once the resources are allocated, the global event cards (e.g., trends such as climate change or aggressive behavior by adversaries) are presented and adjudicated.

The round is "scored" based on a combination of chance (represented by a roll of the die) and how well resources and investments within a given region are positioned to respond to the presented events. Scores represent stakeholders' opinion of the Coast Guard mission's success. After the event cards are played, societal changes throughout the United States are introduced using end-of-turn event cards that may also alter Coast Guard resources. Changes to Coast Guard culture, created by changes in Coast Guard investments, may also make operating more difficult (or easier) in future turns.

The game was played virtually using an electronic game board that was accessible to all players. Each team spent roughly a day completing between three and five turns of the game.

The following sections present each team's game results, as organized in Figure 2.

Figure 2. How the Team Insights/Results Are Organized

The following sections present the results of the game for each of the four team scenarios:

| Beyond the Horizon | Steady Growth | Diverging Paths | Increasing Disorder |

Each section has three elements:

| 1 | 2 | 3 |
| Assigned scenario | Strategic vision | Team investment decisions and trade-offs |

PROJECT EVERGREEN V
GAME QUICKLOOK: Paratus Futurum

Scenario: Beyond the Horizon

1 In "Beyond the Horizon," the team faced a declining U.S. economy, growing Chinese aggression, climate change effects, technological advances in automation, and a growing population.

2 The team's strategic vision prioritized DoD interoperability, CONUS/Indo-Pacific/Latin America missions, and the use of technology to advance efficiency.

3 Team 1 focused on buying investments and resourcing its strategic vision in the early turns of the game, allocating resource chips across the Indo-Pacific, CONUS, and Latin America mission sets. In later turns, the team felt that the events that transpired forced them to become more global. The players attempted to mitigate risk in the Arctic and other regions by leveraging investments made in earlier turns and allocating additional resources, but they continued to bolster the regions listed in their strategic vision. In later turns, the team decided to deviate slightly from the strategic vision by moving resources from Latin America to the Arctic to respond to a growing Chinese threat.

Scenario: Steady Growth

1 In "Steady Growth," the team faced growing Chinese aggression and technology advancements that led to automation and the digitization of the shipping industry.

2 The team's strategic vision stated that deployable teams would support OCONUS missions except in the Arctic, where a continuous presence was expected. As a result, the Coast Guard would likely shift to an "away focus" culture that draws resources from CONUS and emphasizes international relationship building and fisheries enforcement.

3 Players focused on investments in future capabilities (rather than using resources for elevating mission priorities) at the start of the game and distributed their remaining resource tokens across the missions prioritized in their strategic vision. They retained a heavy focus on Arctic missions and gave additional resources to Latin America drug interdiction and CONUS PAC missions. In later turns, players poured resources into keeping their culture score positive. As their investments came to fruition, players focused on filling out missions in the Indo-Pacific, CONUS, and Latin America. In the final turn, the team made no additional investments and applied resources to bolster the Arctic and begin resource allocation in Africa.

4

PROJECT EVERGREEN V

GAME QUICKLOOK: Paratus Futurum

Scenario: Diverging Paths

1 In "Diverging Paths," the team faced U.S. economic decline and an increasingly aggressive China.

2 The strategic vision was to devote resources to the Indo-Pacific and Africa, draw down the ATON and Ice Operations missions, and reduce the "search" aspect of SAR. The vision also emphasized the PWCS mission, growing cyber capabilities, and enabling commerce and disaster response through adaptive solutions.

3 The team used 11 of its 25 resource tokens to buy investments in the first turn, fewer than teams 1 and 2. The team did not invest in Latin America, Europe, or the Arctic in early turns; instead, it invested across CONUS, Africa, and the Indo-Pacific. The team applied investments to reduce costs of operations in CONUS. Continued investments required purchasing culture to keep the score above the minimum. The team did not resource Europe throughout the game but otherwise spread its investments and focus across regions and its mission sets. The team brought all its missions except Marine Safety and SAR in CONUS to a focus level. It also deployed unmanned systems to LANT, PAC, Africa, and Latin America to reduce risk in these regions.

Scenario: Increasing Disorder

1 The team faced increasing impacts of climate change, Russian influence in the Arctic, maturing electric car and vessel technology, and a weakening U.S. economy.

2 The team's strategic vision was to integrate with DoD, leverage technology, use a heavy presence in Europe and the Arctic to combat Russian influence, and shift to an oversight role for missions such as ATON and disaster response.

3 The team spent 11 resource tokens on investments in the first turn. Throughout the game, the team had to invest in culture to keep its score above the minimum. The team first focused on CONUS missions, then gave the remaining resources to 1-2 mission areas in Europe, the Indo-Pacific, and the Arctic. In later turns, it began to prioritize Arctic, Indo-Pacific, and Latin America missions. In response to new trends, the team deviated from its strategic vision and later shifted investments from Europe and Latin America to CONUS and the Arctic. After a Europe-focused event in turn three, the team realigned the vision to invest in Europe but responded to new trends by investing in Latin America drug interdiction and marine safety in CONUS.

5

PROJECT EVERGREEN V

GAME QUICKLOOK: Paratus Futurum

Overarching Observations

Teams relied heavily on their given scenario and strategic vision to guide resource allocation. Player decision making hinged on the scenario, their operationalization of the strategic vision, and additional information provided in the intelligence briefs. These guidance documents provided the mission demand signals that were used to prioritize resource allocation. This was somewhat easier to do at the start of play, and most teams immediately began making investments that would contribute to longer-term objectives. Most teams began with a discussion of which modernization investments would allow them to effectively meet the needs of their given future scenario (one team did not focus as much on the scenario-driven capability needs and concentrated on investments that provided efficiencies or greater flexibility). They then discussed what was essential for the strategy or scenario, followed by a discussion of how to allocate any remaining resources, often focused on enduring CONUS missions.

At times intelligence briefs led to lively discussion and debates regarding how to balance more immediate needs while ensuring longer-term objectives. As game play progressed players often had to revisit the scenario and strategic vision to take stock of where resources were allocated, to remind themselves of these longer-term objectives, and to ensure that recent trends would not necessarily disrupt progress toward these objectives. Teams frequently examined where the most recent intelligence conflicted with the goals of the strategic vision. However, no team decided to update its strategic vision after discussing the intelligence briefs.

Delphi Analysis Helped Participants Rethink the Strategic Objectives Generated by Evergreen V Workshops

One of the Coast Guard's stated objectives for the game was to see if it changed participants' minds about which strategic objectives were most important for the Commandant to consider.

To answer this question, we used a modified Delphi exercise, which is a structured elicitation process designed to help groups reach a consensus. The exercise asked participants to rate the strategic objectives (synthesized from previous Pinecone workshops in Evergreen V) along two dimensions—anticipated level of impact and implementation difficulty.

In a modified Delphi exercise, subject matter experts are asked to provide inputs (or assessment of the strategic objectives, in this case). In this case the process was conducted in three steps: 1) a survey that asked participants to rate strategic objectives issued before game play, 2) discussion of the results during game play, and the play of the game itself and 3) a repeat survey after game play.

Prior to the game the most impactful strategic objectives revolved around technology such as IT infrastructure upgrades, data integration, and unmanned systems. The participants also rated creating a flexible talent management system, taking a deliberate role in the modernization of the Maritime Transportation System, and committing resources overseas while accepting risk for CONUS missions as the most difficult options to implement based on institutional and cultural costs.

Participants remarked that "seeing the whole board" through the events of the game made them think about some of the strategic objectives differently. Completed analysis of the results will be in the final report.

6

PROJECT EVERGREEN V

Overarching Observations (con't)

A strong focus on the demand signals associated with a scenario's strategic vision can override the focus on "untouchable" missions such as search and rescue and the need to continue to prioritize them. Discussions about facilities investments were sometimes catalyzed by an intelligence brief, such as increasing vulnerabilities to storms or improving quality of life to help recruiting and retention, but most often investments were made because a player felt investment was overdue or was a priority for Congress. At the end of the game, some players recognized that decision trade-offs would have been a lot more challenging if they had not made early investments.

Understanding the Coast Guard's role for a given mission in a region and the advantages the service provides were also inputs into resource allocation. Because missions can be performed in many ways, there often was debate on exactly how missions might be operationalized to meet demand signals, and what would constitute acceptable mission performance. Discussions also centered on allocating resources in ways that take advantage of the service's leadership, law enforcement, assets, or technical capabilities, while also leveraging the capabilities of partners and allies (for example, suggesting the Navy had more capacity for HADR or that Arctic SAR could be done by partners with Coast Guard support) to efficiently use resources to meet the mission needs.

Understanding or articulating the marginal improvement in mission was also debated. For example, there were discussions about how the Coast Guard might increase its involvement in defense operations to either supplement or complement the DoD mission or whether maritime transportation security was best served by ports, waterways, and coastal security or by marine safety missions. What might be the Coast Guard's specific level of involvement or engagement in the mission and how is this contribution measured or assessed? Another example centered on how to measure the contribution of increased Coast Guard resources allocated to counter-terrorism or marine-safety missions. Players recognized that "stretching the rubber band" or expanding Coast Guard roles across missions and regions has both short- and long-term costs.

In a practical sense for game play this sometimes made it more difficult to determine the value of adding resources to a mission in a region or whether investing resources in longer-term capabilities or efficiencies would be of greater benefit. From a learning perspective, the discussions demonstrated that gaming creates an environment for substantive discussions about the Coast Guard, its institutional strategy, and the kinds of strategic trades that it must evaluate.

Homeland missions are enduring. All teams acknowledged that failure to execute homeland missions would have deep political consequences to stakeholder opinions regardless of scenario. In contrast, overseas missions have additional resource costs, including culture and risk to stakeholder opinions, for priorities that may wax and wane with geopolitical events and Executive Branch priorities. Early in the game teams were willing to take on some calculated risk for CONUS missions despite their importance, but as intelligence brief trends affected the MTS, PWCS became a concern, or as climate-related issues increased during the game, more resources came back to CONUS. At the end of turn four, each team had allocated significant resources to CONUS.

7

PROJECT EVERGREEN V

GAME QUICKLOOK: Paratus Futurum

Overarching Observations (con't)

Investment strategies for new capabilities were largely motivated by the efficiencies they generate, allowing the Coast Guard to resource additional missions at a higher priority in the future. They were also motivated to satisfy the perceived needs of key stakeholders such as Congress and the Executive Branch (both of which must support new technology and facilities or administration strategy), although the emphasis teams placed on stakeholder interests varied. While not central to the game, teams only minimally discussed how new capabilities might be used creatively to increase mission performance; instead they focused on how these capabilities could be leveraged to free up resources for other priorities. For example, investing in UAS and C5ISR was motived by the desire to either free up traditional assets that are difficult to sustain in remote locations or leverage the capabilities they provide to gain efficiencies that free up traditional resources for other priorities. Similarly, discussions about investing in expeditionary logistics often focused on keeping resources available in the next round, rather than on performance gains from enabling more independent or longer-duration operations. There was a reluctance to "fully commit" limited resources by investing in facilities or prioritizing missions to a high level without strong, enduring signals that these investments would result in efficiencies or technologies that reduce mission risk. In the final turn, teams' investment strategies were mixed. Teams either focused on near-term mission priorities and maximizing their stakeholder opinion score to "win" the game, or they invested in long-term capabilities to set the service up for future success.

Cultural considerations are a concern as the Coast Guard's focus and talent needs evolve. Throughout the game participants expressed concern about Coast Guard culture as they made investments in technology or international capabilities that prioritized the "away game." These investments will influence the culture, or behavioral norms and values that are common throughout the Coast Guard. Some teams actively monitored the culture's status and bought down risk. Investments in culture use resources to support leadership, training, and other activities that sustain an effective or supportive culture. For others, this was an important but secondary consideration. There was also some discussion about redefining what it means to be a Coast Guardsman in the future, as demand for traditional skills wanes and new skills become more prominent. Players were concerned with anticipating how these changes may influence the organization's identity and culture.

What is good for the game is good for Coast Guard planning and investment processes. Two key points emerged during game play. One is that revisiting the scenario and vision is essential for determining resource trades for near-term demands and longer-term objectives (i.e., ensuring the Coast Guard has the future capabilities it needs while moderating cultural churn). Occasionally it was also necessary to assess whether current events may have shifted long-term objectives and develop a narrative about why this may or may not be true. The second key point is that taking calculated risks is acceptable in some mission areas to free up resources for investment or shift the culture to achieve long-term objectives. The game's structure allowed teams to explore and understand where calculated risk is acceptable. The events introduced in each turn stimulated discussion of strategy and missions from the scenario, but teams did not focus on the ultimate outcome; in several instances players acknowledged being happy with the risk they took, even with a bad outcome.

8

PROJECT EVERGREEN V

GAME QUICKLOOK: Paratus Futurum

Game Value to Participants

Paratus Futurum participants successfully immersed themselves in their assigned scenario and strategic vision, actively participated in discussion, and made resource allocation decisions aligned with these priorities. Participants noted that the game revealed the importance of sticking to strategy—and "perhaps militant adherence" to strategy—even when other events occur. This takeaway suggests that a robust strategic vision that is communicated and understood broadly can be a powerful means to guide investment.

Participants also discovered that some level of risk is acceptable, and that random events will happen but may not necessarily have significant, negative consequences. Players felt that including culture considerations in the game design made the decision trades more realistic and that the game helped them better understand the potential second-, third-, and fourth-order effects of geopolitical trends, which may not be initially apparent. These insights could be especially helpful for senior leadership.

> Participants noted that the game revealed the importance of sticking to strategy—and "perhaps militant adherence" to strategy—even when other events occur. This takeaway suggests that a robust strategic vision that is communicated and understood broadly can be a powerful means to guide investment.

Finally, and perhaps most often mentioned, the game gave participants a greater appreciation for the strategic risks and budget constraints across the entire Coast Guard mission set. Participants could probe the implications of various futures in a collaborative setting. It allowed participants to get out of their individual mission focuses or siloes by immersing them

into decisions that require trading off strategic risks among the mission areas amid resource constraints. Participants also repeatedly mentioned that exposure to this type of thinking and gaming should start much earlier in the career progression, as often those who are making trade-off decisions are confronting that sort of strategic thinking for the first time.

Project Evergreen (EVG) employs Strategic Foresight to support senior leaders in their role as the Coast Guard's decision engines. This product is a first look into the results of game 1 of Paratus Futurum, a game of strategic choices made for the Coast Guard, allowing participants to experience the effects of trade space between mission priorities and investment options across a variety of potential future scenarios

HS AC
HOMELAND SECURITY
OPERATIONAL ANALYSIS CENTER
An FFRDC operated by
the RAND Corporation
under contract with DHS

9

PROJECT EVERGREEN V

STRATEGIC GAME QUICK LOOK

Paratus Futurum: Ready for the Future

March 30-April 1 | Game 2

What might the future hold and how might the Coast Guard need prepare to adapt and excel? To explore these questions, Evergreen and the Homeland Security Operational Analysis Center (HSOAC) team developed a serious game to examine how plausible scenarios in 2030-2040 may require the Coast Guard to adjust strategic-level objectives and missions today.

Conducted March 30 and April 1, 2022, the game drew over 25 senior Coast Guard leaders—who VADM Paul Thomas called the "All Star List.... Some of our best and brightest and boldest thinkers"—to RAND's offices in Arlington, Va. Paratus Futurum ("Ready for the Future") forced players to make distinct choices about mission priorities and investments to prepare for an uncertain future in which climate change,

technological advancements, the U.S. economy, and the global power competition shape the demand for USCG missions. Participants probed the trade-offs that must occur to meet national and USCG priorities and to enable Coast Guard leadership to articulate a vision to the public, Congress, the Executive Branch, the Department of Homeland Security, and the Coast Guard workforce. After a welcome by RDML Joseph Buzzella, event champion VADM Thomas urged participants to be bold as they help shape the thinking of the next leadership council and prepare today's Coast Guard for tomorrow.

The following sections will give overviews of:

- How the game is played
- Each team's strategic game play
- Overarching observations

> "This is a low-risk environment, with the potential for high gains. So be bold." —Vice Admiral Paul Thomas

DCO-X
Office of Emerging Policy and Strategic Foresight, U.S. Coast Guard

HSOAC
A federally funded research and development center operated by the RAND Corporation

PROJECT EVERGREEN V
STRATEGIC GAME QUICK LOOK

How to play

1 Teams are assigned a unique scenario and corresponding strategic vision developed in a prior workshop. The game is intended to demonstrate how efforts to achieve this vision may be challenged by the need to make tradeoffs among competing priorities.

2 The game begins in 2025. Each turn represents a four-year period. Teams play 3-5 rounds, progressing to 2040 and beyond.

3 At the start of each round, each team receives an intelligence brief on key trends for the next four years and a fixed number of "resource tokens" that they can use to prioritize missions or invest in longer-term capabilities for use in future turns or investing in support through Operations and Maintenance or Facilities and Infrastructure.

4 As in real life, investing in some capabilities requires culture change—investment in institutional adaptation, new kinds of training, changes in personnel management priorities and desired recruit attributes, as well as new types of equipment, organization, and their integration costs. Teams can invest in culture to aid the adoption of new capabilities and the expansion of career fields.

5 At the end of each round, events that create challenges for the Coast Guard are introduced. Mission success depends on the effort allocated—that is, how well resources and investments are positioned in each region —and an element of chance (a roll of the die).

6 The score reflects how stakeholders—the public, Congress, and the Executive Branch— perceived success. These scores and additional domestic events determine the resource constraints for the next round.

Image 1. A view of the layout of the board, set to begin the game.

2

PROJECT EVERGREEN V
STRATEGIC GAME QUICK LOOK

Scenario
Beyond the Horizon

- Large U.S. debt
- Growing Chinese aggression
- Record hurricane damage
- Advances in automation
- Growing population

Team Vision
Prioritize DoD interoperability, CONUS/Indo-Pacific/Latin America missions, and the use of technology to advance efficiency.

Summary

Players believed that acquiring and sharing data was of the highest importance for the CG moving forward. Players believed that in addition to the strategic vision handed down, stakeholders would require the CG to continue to emphasize its traditional domestic missions. There was therefore a constant tradeoff between what they had been directed to achieve and where they expected stakeholders to devote the greatest attention. Players focused on the aspects of international missions where the CG was better positioned than DoD to form a complementary force rather than a mini-Navy. Significant investments in technology (C5ISR, unmanned systems) allowed players to generate efficiencies in later turns that helped them cover international missions to a greater extent.

Scenario
Steady Growth

- U.S. economic boom
- Stable storm intensity
- Increased U.S. partnerships abroad
- Digitized shipping industry targeted by cyber effects

Team Vision
Deployable teams would support OCONUS missions (except in the Arctic, due to the need for a continuous presence). As a result, the Coast Guard would likely shift to an "away focus" that emphasizes international relationship building and fisheries enforcement.

Summary

At the outset, players invested more heavily in future capabilities than in mission priorities. The team took near-term risk in domestic missions and culture to cover their investments, planning to return them to home turf after investments were realized. Because investing in future capabilities often requires culture change, the team poured resources into culture to try to keep the culture score positive. As investments came on-line, the players shifted mission resources back to the Western Hemisphere and used their investments to mitigate risk in Asia and the Arctic.

Players balanced investments between hardware solutions (C5ISR, unmanned systems) and organizational/training ones (FAOs, LEDets, expeditionary logistics, adaptive force packages)

Scenario
Diverging Paths

- China takes a larger global role
- Gig economy on the rise
- Migration flows increase
- Extreme weather damages across the U.S.

Team Vision
Devote resources to the Indo-Pacific and Africa, draw down the ATON and Ice Operations missions, and reduce the "search" aspect of SAR. Emphasize the PWCS mission, growing cyber capabilities, and enabling commerce and disaster response through adaptive solutions.

Summary

Players decided to be bold by investing heavily in future capabilities at the outset, taking some risk in domestic missions and culture. As new capabilities were deployed, resource allocation focused on prioritizing enduring missions and enabling those driven by geopolitics in other regions in ways that were adaptable or efficient. After several turns had passed and investments realized, resource allocation shifted from capability investments to culture, facilities, and maintenance and operationally to domestic missions. Players described this as a "SOF-like" service without substantial enduring presence, but with the capability and agility to respond quickly to a range of events domestically and abroad. Players also noted that any time the "big picture" of the service footprint and priorities changes, additional investment in culture will be needed to address the "old guard" mentality.

3

PROJECT EVERGREEN V
STRATEGIC GAME QUICK LOOK

Scenario

Increasing Disorder

• Intense, frequent storms
• Russian influence in the Artic
• Electric vessels and vehicles mature
• Weaker U.S. economy

Team Vision

Integrate with DoD, leverage technology, use a heavy presence in Europe and the Arctic to combat Russian influence, and shift to an oversight role for missions such as ATON and disaster response.

Summary

The team focused on how to best deal with constrained resources and emphasized building partnerships with DoD, USG entities, and allies and partners. Initial investments focused on capabilities that allowed the CG to maintain presence overseas but involved huge declines in CG culture that were not responded to for several turns.

While CONUS missions were performed at a risk level initially, over time priorities shifted to domestic missions while using a much more targeted presence overseas, and employing flexible operational approaches rather than a commitment of significant resources. This led to the team taking risks in regions abroad that did not always pay off, but ultimately the team believed they took the right risks. Being bold meant relying on these international investments to enable a greater focus on the CG core missions.

Overarching observations

In response to VADM Thomas' charge to "be bold", several teams relied on the current, positive progress of the service to sustain operations, and their dominant strategy for the first round of game play was to invest in new capabilities. Notably, C5ISR capabilities was uniformly identified as the priority investment (consistent with the results of a parallel survey of strategic objectives), despite the resources and lead-time required to realize the capability. Early investments were seen as enabling the Coast Guard to remain successful despite uncertain futures and to gain efficiencies that could be reinvested in future rounds. Some teams invested in desired capabilities without necessarily considering where they may be deployed, while others invested to cover specific regions and mission needs identified in the scenario and intelligence brief. In all cases, careful consideration and prioritization were given to investing in capabilities that efficiently extended the Coast Guard's presence while maintaining flexibility to adapt to changing conditions.

The teams' early investment strategies nearly universally accepted some level of short-term risk in traditional missions and often in culture to pay for future capabilities—but pivoted back to domestic missions as game play progressed. Teams sought to meet future mission demand through investments in efficient or flexible assets such as expeditionary logistics, adaptive force packages, and unmanned systems. The specific focus of these investments varied by scenario and team. While all teams acknowledged the cultural costs of these investments, not all devoted resources to mitigate them.

Before investments or resources were committed to a region, partner and ally capabilities were considered. Furthermore, teams were generally reluctant to commit to fixed assets such as a permanent forward operating base despite a long-term presence in a region after several rounds of game play.

Each team acknowledged the importance of investing in operations, maintenance, and facilities, and were unwilling to take risk over several consecutive rounds of play. Yet these investments were not always made in the first round and frequently took a "back seat" to capabilities investments. Often the catalyst for these investments was an intelligence brief that specified domestic workforce trends that would make it harder for the Coast Guard to recruit and retain members if the quality of life was poor, or that identified threats to facilities due to storms and other natural hazards.

4

PROJECT EVERGREEN V
STRATEGIC GAME QUICK LOOK

The concept of an adaptive force package emerged as a key approach for covering a broad range of missions. The concept shifts the focus from platforms and their activity level to mission performance by bringing together capabilities and assets in a flexible manner for operations ranging from emergency management to international engagements. Adaptive force packages were used by all teams as "insurance" against unpredictable or varied mission needs and were deployed both domestically and abroad. Participants repeatedly offered the multi-mission role of Coast Guard organizations and platforms as a risk mitigation strategy and, perhaps not surprisingly, gravitated toward investments that enabled multi-mission response (such as adaptive force packages and unmanned systems) over the more targeted investments of foreign area officers and law enforcement detachments. Multiple players said that this shifted their thinking from assets and days to capabilities and goals.

Ensuring mission success in the future while leveraging the 4th industrial revolution and attracting and retaining a highly capable workforce will require investment in culture. In the game, cultural investments explicitly recognize that to accommodate new technologies and ways of performing missions the Coast Guard leadership must commit resources and attention to adjusting training curriculums and requirements, promotion and career pathways, deployment practices, and other organizational processes. Players expressed general awareness of the importance of balancing investments in new capabilities with culture. Some teams were very concerned about over-extending culture and recognized that while the workforce often embraces change, the rate of change needs to be actively managed. Teams varied in their tolerance of cultural risk with mixed results during game play, but all acknowledged that change takes substantial time and resources and cannot be avoided for too long.

Teams generally spread resources to cover mission demand signals contained in the intelligence briefs and relied on surge capability as insurance against plausible surprises. Only one team moved a mission to the highest priority level (the Atlantic emergency management/disaster response mission). The search and rescue mission was most often the "bill-payer" for elevating the priority of other missions. However, participants had lively discussions about the SAR mission's importance to the Coast Guard identity; to public awareness and opinion of the service; its role as an enabler for the capabilities and capacities needed for contingencies such as hurricane response; and its influence over training, aircraft configuration, and stationing. When confronted with a challenge, teams generally weighed the likelihood of mission success with the consequence of inadequate response. Deploying an adaptive force package was the preferred surge method because it avoided tapping into future resources (although players noted the service's natural inclination is to surge regardless of resource trades). However, on several occasions, teams considered using surge options to gain favor with stakeholders in the hopes this would improve resourcing in the future.

Domestic missions are enduring and fundamental to the Coast Guard, and this was reflected in resourcing decisions. Participants expressed that the Coast Guard's purpose is saving lives, helping people, and facilitating safe and prosperous maritime trade in support of the economy. They noted that these missions are what distinguishes the Coast Guard and allows it to satisfy the expectations of stakeholders such as the executive branch, Congress, and the public. This branding defines and drives recruiting and retention, and capabilities development. As a result, resource allocation considered the asymmetric risks of performing poorly in these missions. Demand for capabilities overseas wax and wane with geopolitical developments and changing national priorities, necessitating an adaptable force when resources are limited. Participants also sought to prioritize missions that used the service's specialized capabilities abroad for roles that added value to DoD or complemented the perceived capabilities of partners or allies. After several rounds of game play teams tended to shift resources back to domestic missions regardless of scenario, relying on their agile investments to respond abroad as needed.

Participants noted that while the principal Coast Guard mission set may not change, the way in which they are performed or accomplished may be different. For example, new opportunities to leverage new technologies such as UASs or service providers from the private sector may change the service's activities. Furthermore, while USCG operations facilitate trade while maintaining safety, other mechanisms historically have been used for these purposes, such as funding grants or developing industry standards.

5

Appendix E. Game Method and Rulebook

The design for USCG Evergreen gaming is divided into the following three stages:

1. A one-day game for each of the four DCO-X core teams from the previous Pinecones to gain a better understanding of gaming attributes, and examine the game system and their respective concepts,
2. A two- to- three-day game for senior leaders of the incoming commandant's transition team to examine force design and global operating concepts,
3. An educational game based on the previous gaming efforts aimed at district-level training.

The game involves participants implementing a global USCG operating concept and associated force design at the strategic level. Participants have to balance competing priorities, address multiple challenges across operating areas, examine wider service implications, and allocate limited service capabilities and resources. In terms of execution, each turn is comprised of two components: a planning stage and a facilitated discussion. During the planning stage, participants complete a strategic planning template, which outlines their courses of action. The White Cell, or design team, introduces multiple scenarios that pose significant dilemmas across theaters each turn. In the following discussion stage, a facilitator from the White Cell leads the participants in examining the wider doctrine, organization, training, materiel, leadership, personnel, facilities plus regulations, grants, and standards (DOTMLPF+R/G/S) implications of their course of action. This can range from support considerations to personnel and training requirements.

Overall, the game has a total of three turns and a facilitated after-action discussion. Each of the four Pinecone teams is asked to implement the concept of operation and force design from the CONCEPT 2040 workshop. It is important to note that although the Pinecone endeavors to produce CONOPS for a specific theater or mission, the overarching scenario of the game is global, with a wide range of challenges. After the conclusion of all the Core Team games, the design team continues to refine the game design, which will be used for the incoming commandant's transition team and subsequent district staff focused game.

Fundamental Gaming Questions:

- What does the Coast Guard of the future look like in terms of capabilities, personnel, and operations?
- What are the central tenets underlying the proposed Coast Guard force design?
- What missions or tasks is the proposed Coast Guard concept optimized for? And why?
- How will the Coast Guard operate in a future time frame? Be specific in details and provide examples.

- What are the key differences between the proposed Coast Guard and the current force?
- What changes in policy, resources, or capabilities are required for the proposed construct?
- What are the service mission support challenges to achieving the goals and objectives?

Strategic Concept of Operations Template

Strategic USCG Vision: This section should address the overarching strategic vision for the service, outlining its goals and objectives. It should also discuss its role in wider U.S. foreign and military policy and its role within the Joint Force (2–4 paragraphs).

Key Threats and Challenges: This section should highlight the central problems that USCG is focusing on in the future. It should elaborate on enemy threats, capabilities, key drivers of change, and areas of operations that inform this strategic USCG vision (2–4 paragraphs).

Global Concept of Operations: This section should highlight critical tasks that USCG must be equipped to address, whether they are specific missions or responsibilities. Moreover, this section should highlight the concept of global operations for how USCG will execute and achieve its desired objectives. The section must identify actions and capabilities and their corresponding effects and missions (6–8 paragraphs).

Force Posture by District: This section should provide a detailed breakdown of USCG units by district. The force posture should highlight key capabilities and capacities within each specific district and its role within the wider USCG (graphics with accompanying text of 4–6 paragraphs).

Strategic Risk Assessment: This section should identify key areas of risk for USCG as it pursues its new strategic CONOPS. This can include risks related to institutional culture, operational tempo, emerging technologies, acquisitions, budget, or any other areas of risk that threaten to undermine the new USCG strategic vision and force structure (3–5 paragraphs).

Force Design Proposal Template

Key Capabilities: This section should highlight key capabilities that USCG is building, acquiring, or reforming in order to pursue its strategic CONOPS. For instance, if USCG is planning to incorporate unmanned cutters into the force, this section should highlight how that capability will be used and how it will be supported. Each major capability should have at least one paragraph describing its utility and function.

Key Capacity: This section should highlight key changes in the capacity of specific capabilities or units within USCG. For instance, is there an increase in USCG personnel allocated to cyber operations? Each major capacity alteration should be accompanied by a paragraph justifying the change and rationale.

Key Acquisition Priorities: This section should highlight key areas of acquisition priorities for USCG. Each acquisition should be ranked in priority (1 being the highest) and be accompanied by a paragraph describing the justification for its priority level.

Personnel Reform: This section should highlight key personnel changes or reforms for USCG. Each major personnel alteration should be accompanied by a paragraph justifying the change and rationale.

Required Policy: This section should identify any key areas of policy that need to be altered or changed for USCG's new force structure and CONOPS to be effective. Each major policy alteration should be accompanied by a paragraph justifying the change and rationale.

Budget and Trade Space: All services are limited by finite resources. Thus, this section should identify how the service will resource the aforementioned changes in capabilities, capacity, acquisition, and personnel. This can involve a budgetary increase or trading a legacy capability for another. However, the service should not expect more than a 10-percent increase of the current budget.

Appendix F. U.S. Coast Guard Office of Emerging Policy Reports

This appendix lists several documents that were produced by the USCG DCO-X in support of the Evergreen Program. Evergreen V represents a service shift from providing a single major report for the incoming commandant to instead delivering a series of more targeted reports based on scenario-based workshops with flag sponsors representing various directorates within the Deputy Commandant for Operations and Deputy Commandant for Mission Support enterprise. Over the course of the four-year Evergreen V effort, DCO-X staff produced several internal reports, program white papers, and correspondence for senior service leadership based in part upon HSOAC-supported workshop activities and analytical and research support from the HSOAC project team through regular collaborative and iterative interactions.

Contents

F1. Coast Guard Summary of Project Evergreen

STRATEGIC FORESIGHT (Project Evergreen)
Preparing the Coast Guard to Thrive in an Unpredictable Future
CG-DCO-X

WHAT IS STRATEGIC FORESIGHT?

It is a decades-old strategic discipline that creates functional views of the future as a foundation for strategic decision making. These well-informed future glimpses allow us to test current strategy, reveal hidden obstacles and opportunities on the horizon, and create transformative change.

1. *Foresight* **is not** *forecasting*, which sets our course for a single future that no one can truly know.
2. **Ready for the** *futures.* Instead, we use researched methods to discover plausible *futures*.
3. **Set the course.** Strategic foresight is a methodology – a critical piece of strategic decision making. Project Evergreen uses Strategic Foresight to equip senior leaders with a menu of robust strategic choices.
4. **Prepare future leaders.** Our methods provide deliverables like reports that shed light on "now" problems for flag sponsors, but the real value lies in **creating a culture of adept practitioners who can think ahead and plan strategically.**

A BRIEF HISTORY OF THE FUTURE

Strategic Foresight and its most common tool, scenario planning, have been used successfully at the corporate planning level for decades; the most famous use case is petrochemical giant Royal Dutch Shell. During the oil crisis of the late 1960s, Shell altered its strategy and successfully propelled itself to the top of the industry, a move accredited to the use of scenario planning. Today, organizations like Intel, Ford, and Disney – and federal partners like CIA, Special Operations Command, and GAO – have joined Shell in employing futurists to leverage foresight tools for organization-wide strategy development and innovation.

READY, RELEVANT, RESPONSIVE

Project Evergreen is the best known and longest running strategic foresight initiative in the Coast Guard. At the launch of Project Evergreen V in the fall of 2018, the Evergreen team conducted an "**Evergreen@20**" audit. The audit found that Evergreen was widely viewed as the "gold standard" for scenario planning in the interagency, but had become less relevant to Coast Guard leaders over the past decade. After engaging with a wide variety of foresight experts from industry, government, and academia, **DCO-X re-launched Project Evergreen as a component of a broader strategic foresight program.**

AN OPPORTUNITY

Strategic Foresight offers a simple yet powerful tool to our senior leaders: an opportunity to rise above the urgency of the immediate to gain new perspectives and deliver **robust strategic choices.**

USCG STRATEGIC FORESIGHT INCLUDES:

Project Evergreen

Disruption & Disorder Series

Convenings

Think-pieces & White Papers

GOALS

- Prepare the Coast Guard for an uncertain future by identifying and exploring the implications of trends and "distant signals."
- Provide senior leaders with a menu of robust strategic challenges and choices.
- Create a corps and culture of strategic foresight practitioners.
- Find institutional integration points into Service strategy writing and resource planning.

Written and compiled by DCO-X (CDR Kate Higgins-Bloom and LCDR Ryan Hawn) Strategy@uscg.mil)

WORKFORCE 2030

U.S. Coast Guard

Project Evergreen

PROJECT EVERGREEN

Contents

PROJECT EVERGREEN

3

WORKFORCE 2030 - EXECUTIVE SUMMARY

The resilience and flexibility of the force is at the heart of what has made the Coast Guard successful for well over 200 years. An adaptive force continues to be our greatest strength. However, the environment the Coast Guard must navigate to build its force has changed dramatically since 2000. The rate of change will only accelerate. The "Fourth Industrial Revolution" is well underway, with deep implications for Service missions, capabilities, and challenges. Persistent demographic and social trends will fundamentally alter the American population from which the Service recruits and serves. **What has worked in the past will not work in the future.**

The Coast Guard will be trying to retain its top talent in an increasingly competitive environment. Specialists, such as cyber space operators, will be in high demand. New needs may emerge to make a different set of skills the "new cyber." Rather than predicting how many of which specialty we will need, **Workforce 2030 focuses on creating a system with the ability to generate the force we need, when we need it.**

The Coast Guard must create a **transparent talent management system that gives members greater control over their lives and meets the needs of unit commanders.** Ensuring that the "talent" in the talent management system has the right skills will require a change in the way the Service thinks about training. We should prepare our Service for a future of **continuous learning.** The success of these endeavors rests on the establishment of a **data culture**, enabled by robust, flexible, and interconnected IT and data management systems. Moreover, these initiatives must be more than aspirational; **they must be actionable** and begun in the near future.

METHODOLOGY
Scenario-Based Planning | Multiple Futures | Rapid Iteration
On September 10-12, 2019, the Project Evergreen team hosted a "Workforce 2030" workshop. A cohort of 38 Coast Guard members ranking from E3 to GS12 to O6 formed four teams and explored divergent futures. **While each team worked with a unique future scenario, the recommendations were consistent.**

WHAT FORCE WILL WE NEED IN 2030?
Tech Fluent. Whether it is a detailer using Artificial Intelligence (AI) to develop candidate lists or a BM2 setting electronic buoys, the entire workforce must have a higher "floor" for technical fluency.

Human Focused. The need for STEM skills will continue to grow, yet all trends indicate that many of today's technical roles will eventually be taken by AI and autonomous systems. Human-centered skills, such as partnership building, creativity, and judgment, will become increasingly valuable.

Skill Stacking. Members should expect to learn many different sets of skills over the course of their careers.

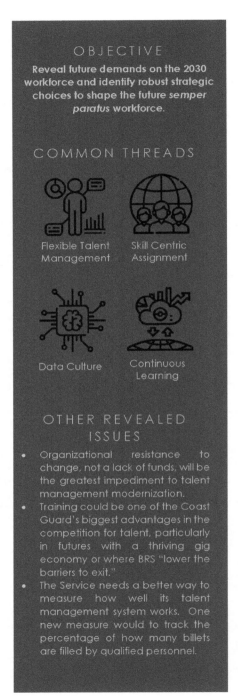

OBJECTIVE
Reveal future demands on the 2030 workforce and identify robust strategic choices to shape the future *semper paratus* workforce.

COMMON THREADS

Flexible Talent Management

Skill Centric Assignment

Data Culture

Continuous Learning

OTHER REVEALED ISSUES

- Organizational resistance to change, not a lack of funds, will be the greatest impediment to talent management modernization.
- Training could be one of the Coast Guard's biggest advantages in the competition for talent, particularly in futures with a thriving gig economy or where BRS "lower the barriers to exit."
- The Service needs a better way to measure how well its talent management system works. One new measure would to track the percentage of how many billets are filled by qualified personnel.

WHAT INVESTMENTS DO WE NEED TO MAKE NOW TO MEET THE NEEDS?

Revolutionize Talent Management

Flexibility and Choice. Changes in the demographics and social norms of the American population will make flexibility for the Service and the member an important factor in retaining top talent. In the future, particularly one filled with increasingly unpredictable crises and other challenges, members should be able to easily use a wide range of "*on-ramps, off-ramps, and merge lanes*" to create successful "*stitched careers.*" "Pacing" will be just as critical as the ability to transition in and out of service.

Skills vs. Titles. The Coast Guard should leverage its relatively small size to find creative ways to assign, retain, and recognize members based on their skills – it should reward those skills it wants to retain. The promotion process should allow for risk taking in emerging fields or specialization in critical skill sets without resorting to a rigid staff/line officer system. The Service must determine how to reward the less tangible leadership traits that will be at a premium in the future, such as anticipating change and valuing diversity.

Commit to Transparency. Whether it is defined as fairness to the member or the ability to measure the system's effectiveness, transparency is key to a successful revolution in talent management.

Prepare for Continuous Learning

In Situ C Schools. Coast Guard should plan on all members, even the most senior, spending more time on learning than they do now, largely through engaging and focused on-line training modules.

NextGen Schoolhouses. The future is more than on-line classes. NextGen Schoolhouses customize learning to the member and the Service. We must also prepare to help the Service build new skills, such as data analytics, that are not explicitly included in the current training regime.

Reskilling. Most groups agreed that members joining the Coast Guard today should plan on "reskilling" over the course of a career; this presents deep implications for the USCG training enterprise.

Continuous Learning Requires Continuous Connectivity. Presently, IT infrastructure and policies do not support state-of-the-market tools to make affordable, timely, and effective training possible. We must transition to a system of continuous learning based on continuous connectivity to meet the specific needs of each member.

Establish and Enable a Data Culture

Make the Invisible Visible. Enable a flexible talent management system with rich data, robust analytical tools, and skilled analysts who turn data into insight, and insight into action.

Support Leaders Looking for Ways to Make Data Informed Decisions. Intentionally seek out and support homegrown efforts to leverage data analytics and machine learning as the bases for wise decisions.

Create and Empower a Data Workforce. Emulate the best practices of successful data cultures to gain a competitive advantage for the Coast Guard and to become a leader in the interagency data enterprise.

STRATEGIC CHOICES AND FIRST STEPS

This report concludes with some recommendations based on Team Evergreen's assessment of the results of WORKFORCE 2030. In short, Coast Guard leadership must take action to start an **iterative revolution** in talent management and training. This revolution must be enabled by **deliberate culture change** and **urgent action on IT infrastructure and data culture.** The report also includes some "first steps." These consist of more specific ideas on how to begin implementing these management approaches in the near term.

ABOUT PROJECT EVERGREEN AND WORKFORCE 2030

Project Evergreen employs Strategic Foresight to support executive leaders in their role as the Coast Guard's decision-making engines. Workforce 2030 is one of eight "Pinecones" on the Evergreen tree. In the summer of 2021, Team Evergreen will begin a meta-analysis of each of the Pinecones to identify strategic choices for the 27th Commandant of the Coast Guard's leadership team. To join the conversation, contact the Project Evergreen Team in the Coast Guard's Office of Emerging Policy (CG-DCO-X) at strategy@uscg.mil.

5

INTRODUCTION

PROJECT EVERGREEN

Project Evergreen is the Coast Guard's Strategic Foresight Initiative. Founded in 1996 as Project Longview, Project Evergreen has historically run in 4-year cycles; using scenario-based planning to identify strategic needs for incoming Commandants. In 2019, Evergreen restructured in order to best support executive leaders in their role as the Coast Guard's decision-making engines. Team Evergreen plans to conduct up to eight foresight engagements, "Pinecones," focusing on key topics over the next 2 years. After considering each Pinecone, Team Evergreen will produce a report within 60 days. In the summer of 2021, Team Evergreen will begin a meta-analysis of the Pinecones to identify strategic choices for the 27th Commandant of the Coast Guard's leadership team. Workforce 2030 is the first of eight "pinecones" on the Project Evergreen tree.

WORKFORCE 2030

Why WORKFORCE 2030? As Project Evergreen V kicked off, DCO-X engaged hundreds of Coast Guard personnel and experts as part of a rigorous process to identify the biggest drivers of change for the Service in the coming years. Then we led a workshop to identify the "most wicked" challenges those drivers might create. Whether we presented teams with global war or autonomous cargo barges, the need to focus on the future workforce dominated the conversation. As result, the first of eight planned Project Evergreen chapters is WORKFORCE 2030.

CULTURE

This report mentions the concept of "culture" a great deal in its pages. The concept is the topic of conversation at leadership lunches and in senior staff e-mails. In our work to date, "culture" has also been identified as our greatest strength and as the greatest barrier to modernizing our talent-management system. Some of the recommendations in this report call for large scale culture change–stepping away from doing things the way they have generally been done for over half a century. But none of them call for us to give up the parts of our culture that make the Coast Guard a success. In particular, this means our core values, or the flexibility, creativity, and initiative that have always enabled our people to thrive and carry out the many missions of the Service in a range of challenging and ambiguous environments.

URGENCY

Most of the ideas in this report are NOW ideas. In some cases, they are YESTERDAY ideas. Project Evergreen is charged with looking over the horizon. This distant focus was an important part of the process, but the road to that future is paved with the years that lie directly in front of us. The actions we take NOW will determine if the Coast Guard continues to matter a great deal to the Nation in the years ahead.

To join the conversation, contact the Project Evergreen Team or reach out to the Office of Emerging Policy (CG-DCO-X) at strategy@uscg.mil.

SEMPER PARATUS

PROJECT EVERGREEN

6

254

METHODOLOGY
Scenario-Based Planning | Multiple Futures | Rapid Iteration

On September 10-12, 2019, the Project Evergreen team hosted a "Workforce 2030" workshop at Training Center Yorktown with FORCEOM Commander as the sponsor. A diverse cohort of 38 Coast Guard members ranking from E3 to GS12 to O6 formed four teams and explored divergent futures.

Team Evergreen grounded all its activities in scenario-based planning. This is a classic strategic foresight practice applied by organizations ranging from the CIA to Disney. These scenarios included narratives around the four divergent, but plausible, futures. The team applied the "design double diamond" in structuring this workshop and employed Human Centered Design-trained facilitators to drive curated ideation exercises and down-selection or prioritization techniques to the scenarios. The team overlaid these group outputs to find common themes and decisions that were the most robust in many scenarios.

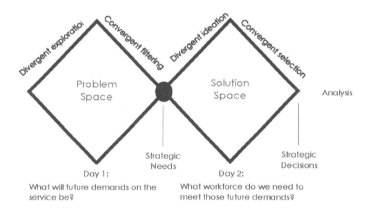

By the end of Day 1, each team had identified critical strategic needs for the future force. They then spent Day 2 addressing how the Coast Guard might meet those needs. The final half day was spent sharing ideas across all four groups. **While each team dealt with a unique future, their recommendations were consistent.**

Over the course of the engagement, participants generated hundreds of very specific ideas and proposals. They created concept posters and shared feedback on the future of Coast Guard missions. This report contains a synthesis of their ideas, with additional research and consultation with experts, and makes high-level recommendations on where the Service should invest.

Results Overview

THE FORCE WE NEED

Analysis of Workforce 2030 indicates the Coast Guard will need a workforce who are universally **tech fluent**, exhibit **human-focused** judgment and leadership skills despite a greater reliance on machine-enabled decisions, and are **skill-stackers** who can quickly master new specialties as the Service requires.

WHAT INVESTMENTS DO WE NEED TO MAKE NOW TO MEET THAT NEED?

These common threads represent areas where leaders have the opportunity to make robust strategic decisions.

Revolutionize Talent Management

 Create Flexibility and Choice for the Member and the Service. Changes in the demographics and social norms of the American population will make flexibility an important factor in retaining top talent. That same flexibility and choice will be critical to the Coast Guard as it adapts its force to shifting missions and increasingly unpredictable contingencies and crises.

 Assign for Skills, not Titles. The rapidly evolving operating environment make it likely that the Coast Guard will need skills that don't always line up with our existing functional titles.

 Reward What You Want to Retain. The promotion process should allow for and reward risk taking in emerging fields or specialization in critical skill sets.

 Commit to Transparency. Whether it is defined as fairness to individual members or the ability to measure the system's effectiveness, transparency is key to a successful revolution in talent management.

Prepare for Continuous Learning

 In Situ C Schools. The Coast Guard should plan on all members, even the most senior, spending more time on learning than they do now, though largely through focused and effective on-line modules.

 NextGen Schoolhouses. The future is more than on-line classes. NextGen Schoolhouses customize learning to the member and the Service. We must also prepare to help the Service build new skills, such as data analytics, that are not explicitly included in the current training regime.

 Reskilling. Most groups agreed that members joining the Coast Guard today should plan on "reskilling" at least once over the course of a career; this raises deep implications for the Service's training enterprise.

 Continuous Learning Requires Continuous Connectivity. Our current IT infrastructure and policies do not support state-of-the-market tools that make affordable, timely, and effective training possible.

Establish and Enable a Data Culture

 Make the Invisible Visible. Enable a flexible talent management system with rich data, robust analytical tools, and skilled analysts who turn data into insight.

 Support Leaders Looking for Ways to Make Data-Informed Decisions. Intentionally seek out and support homegrown efforts to leverage and make use of data analytics and machine learning effectively.

 Create and Empower a Data Workforce. Emulate the best practices of successful data cultures to gain a competitive advantage for the Coast Guard and to become a leader in the interagency data enterprise.

STRATEGIC CHOICES AND FIRST STEPS

This report concludes with some recommendations based on Team Evergreen's assessment of the results of WORKFORCE 2030. In short, Coast Guard leadership must **take action to start an iterative revolution** in talent management and training. This revolution must be enabled by **deliberate culture change** and **urgent action on IT infrastructure and data culture.** The report also includes some "first steps," which are specific ideations to begin implementing these choices in the near term

8

The Force We Need

As the WORKFORCE 2030 teams examined four plausible but divergent futures, they quickly realized there was more than one right answer. At the same time, the realized that there were lots of wrong ones. Technical specialists, such as cyberspace operators, will be in high demand in almost any future, but there may be new needs that emerge which make an entirely different set of skills the "new cyber." Rather than predicting how many of which specialty the Coast Guard will need, Workforce 2030 participants focused on creating a system that could generate the force we need, when we need it.

The teams operated under two key assumptions. First, the future Coast Guard will recruit and retain a diverse pool of top tier talent in an increasingly competitive environment. Second, the Coast Guard will continue to holds its core values of Honor, Respect, and Devotion to Duty.

 Tech Fluent. The entire Coast Guard workforce–officer, enlisted, civilian, reserve, and auxiliary-will be defined by technical acumen. Leaders ranging from CDOs to CFOs will apply analytics, visualization, AI, and decision science to make timely and prudent decisions based on vast amounts of data. Enlisted rates typically seen as "hands on" will see increasing automation and digitization. Whether it is a detailer using AI to develop candidate lists or a BM2 setting electronic buoys, the entire workforce will possess a higher "floor" of technical fluency.

 Human Focused. The need for talented personnel with STEM skills will continue to grow. However, all trends indicate that AI and autonomous systems will eventually take over many of today's technical roles, Human-centered skills, such as partnership building, creativity, and ethical judgment will become increasingly valuable.[1] The Coast Guard is already in a strong position in this regard with a set of missions and an operational culture that require daily collaboration with the American public, interagency partners, and the international maritime community. Retaining this key advantage will take continued leadership and focus as the rush for the best tech talent continues.

 Skill-Stacking. The old saying about "being a lifelong learner" will become a daily reality. The pace of technological and organizational change we expect to see in the future means that members joining the Coast Guard today should plan on reskilling over the course of a career. While every team recommended some version of lateral entry to fill critical skill gaps, there was also a consensus that reskilling existing members would be part of any sustainable solution.

In some groups reskilling meant enlisted members changing rates multiple times in a career to meet emerging needs. In others, it meant that specialists should expect the nature of their work to change dramatically. While a marine inspector's overarching mission is to ensure vessels do not pose undue risk to MTS and the maritime

What is Decision Science?

Decision Science is an interdisciplinary practice that leverages theories and methods drawn from psychology, economics, philosophy, statistics, and management science to support "decision making under conditions of uncertainly."[1]

---

[1] For more, see the Millennium Foundation's longitudinal "meta" study of future workforce projects. http://www.millennium- project.org/projects/workshops-on-future-of-work-technology-2050-scenarios/

9

community, the way in which she does it in 2030 would be almost unrecognizable to her Steamboat Inspection Service predecessors of the late 1800's.

The need for continuous skill building is not limited to coding or robotics repair; it also includes deliberate investments in critical thinking and crisis-management skills. At the same time, the Coast Guard must be mindful of the special challenges posed by growing competition with near peers, increasingly severe natural disasters, and the rise of the "super empowered" individual or organization. The United States can no longer rely on full dominance of the spectrum. As new skills replace old ones, the Service must

still retain some capacity to operate in a degraded environment, without normal connectivity, during periods of crisis.

The attributes described here are often in tension with each other. Growing demand for technical experts sits alongside an enduring need for "human centered" generalists. We call for skill swapping personnel who can transition from an obsolete specialty to a new one, even as we warn about the need to retain the ability to operate in a degraded, low-tech environment. Workforce 2030 identified three areas of strategic investment that leaders must take on today if the Coast Guard plans to balance these tensions in the future.

10

What Investments Do We Need to Make Now to Meet That Need?

REVOLUTIONIZE TALENT MANAGEMENT

The Workforce 2030 participants were immersed in four divergent futures, yet they came away with one single "must-do" recommendation. Regardless of the challenges the Coast Guard faces in 10, 20, or 50 years, it must rapidly modernize the talent management system if it hopes to remain relevant. Calls for an overhaul of the military personnel system are not new, but the urgency of the work is.[2] While the Coast Guard has undergone some gradual, almost generational, changes, it is not enough to keep pace with impacts of rapid (and accelerating) technological, economic, demographic, and cultural shifts.

Create a System that Provides Flexibility to the Member and the Service. A more flexible talent-management system not only serves as an important retention tool for talented members. It also gives the Service the ability to manage its force to meet emerging missions or to respond to increasingly unpredictable and extreme crises.

A consistent theme across all four futures–whether the United States is wracked with frequent disasters, or the economy is so strong that people join the Coast Guard as a form of "community service"–was some version of **"stitched careers."** Teams proposed a wide range of "on-ramps, off-ramps, and merge lanes" that could be used to create careers that leverage outside experience with active duty and civilian members and provide members with opportunities to meet their work-life commitments. One participant observed "**it sounds like you want a lot more super-reservists.**" This observation deserves

some serious consideration, particularly as the long-term implementation of the **Blended Retirement System** (BRS) may present an opportunity to sunset certain policies and regulations, such as the dated "sanctuary" rule, which limit the flexible use of reservists.

The long-term impact of BRS is unknown. In most potential futures where the barriers to exit are lower, it is reasonable to expect to see a more linear and steady departure of talent between the 13 and 25 year points, while members are at their peak level of marketable qualifications. The flexible "stitched" model could give the Service a chance to more easily reacquire qualified members who leave the Service but then wish to return on a full- or part-time basis.

The desire for flexibility was not limited to shifting between civilian and reserve and active duty status. The second important element of flexibility was the "pacing." For example, many participants raised the potential for a "no-penalty opt out" for consideration by a promotion board for any members in the process of changing specialties or addressing work-life issues.

One of the "on ramps" the group discussed was more regular use of lateral entry to bring in key skills. The discussion of lateral entry raised a second question about pacing; if it is possible for the Service to lateral someone into a position up to O-6 with no military experience, why can't high performing officers compete for faster promotions based on their skills and performance? Participants cited other allied military services, including those in Canada and Australia, with policies that enable

---

[2] Many readers will remembers books like "Bleeding Talent" from 2012 or the 2015 Pentagon "Force of the Future" initiative. In some ways, these were the break out moments for this conversation. It is also worth noting that the scope of change required is also much greater. All but one of the previous Evergreen's alluded to the need for a "dynamic, needs based HR system" – but it was clear that the assumption was that the system would remain largely unchanged, and that the service would need to use existing tools to recruit its way out of the problem. Diversity and inclusion were never mentioned.

members who take on particularly demanding assignments or pursue additional education to promote faster than their peers. Conversely, officers who are transitioning to new specialties or balancing a work-life need could slow their advancement pace without being forced out.

Assign for Skills, not Titles. The rapidly evolving operating environment make it likely that the Coast Guard will need skills that don't always line up with our existing titles. In some cases, it might be better to create "bracketed" billets to allow multiple ranks or rates–or a blend of civilians and military members–to apply, and for the most competent individual to be assigned. Examples included Sector Command Center Watchstanders or staff tours requiring specific data-science or strategic-thinking proficiency. As some billets become even more specialized, it may also become necessary to fill some enlisted billets based on required skills, rather than a simple rate and rank match. Currently the Service makes only a few enlisted assignments, notably OIC, XPO, and Senior Enlisted Advisors, that way.

In addition to bracketed billets, the idea of creating "communities" instead of rates for emerging fields was discussed as a lower risk option than creating new, often very small, rates. This also has the benefit of giving members a "try out" period in the Service to ensure they have not only the technical aptitude, but the core values and leadership traits needed for challenging and often interagency assignments. In short, teams envisioned the cyber operators being organized in a way that mirrors the special operations community, such as the SEALs, where Navy members compete to get in once they have demonstrated their core values and where rating is only secondary.

Reward What You Want to Retain. Once the Coast Guard has identified the skills or attributes it wants to retain (a major challenge in its own right!), it needs a

How might flexibility and transparency changes things?

The interplay between evaluations, assignments, and promotions is important but sometimes appears haphazard and rigid. It resembles three separate gears that seem to be operated by different people who do not speak to each other. When they connect properly, they propel the machine forward. If there is any slippage, however, there does not appear to be a mechanic that can step in and make a repair in real time.[1]

Transparency would allow leaders and member to better "see" the gears and their interactions – making adjustments if they want to see different results from the system. Flexibility, either for talent managers or members, would allow them to make individual adjustments in closer to real time to accommodate near term goals.

(The ideal system would be more like a multi-geared, super-smooth racing bike rather than a slot machine which is designed to produce random results.)

12

more coordinated and responsive mechanism for retaining that talent.

While Service leaders have held up intel-cued operations, unmanned systems, cyber operations, and big-data analytics as an important part of the Coast Guard's future, there was a great deal of anecdotal evidence that the promotions process is "not kind" to people in these fields. In short, there was a sense our Service culture does not value emerging career paths. Conversely, the current system often penalizes people who specialize in critical skills (e.g., marine inspection, data analytics) in ways that do not map cleanly to the "ideal" career path.

Given the Coast Guard's small size, it should be nimble enough to create opportunities for members to specialize in critical skills or blaze new trails while remaining competitive for promotion. The staff corps model of the other armed services was seen as too cumbersome. However, "LDO" or "SDO" type programs where members apply for designation later in their career were seen as sources of inspiration. It is important to note that this is likely to be a minority of officers. Based on our enduring need for human centered leadership, technically competent but adaptive generalists will still make up a significant portion of the officer corps.

The idea of rewarding what you want to retain does have some implication for the quality and usefulness of our evaluations. Some members expressed concern that the current evaluations tend to reward individual achievement and short-term results at the expense of more collaborative leadership practices and long-term impacts. Participants expressed keen interest in the ongoing OER review project, and were hopeful that there would be meaningful and positive changes.

Commit to Increased Transparency. It is likely that adding flexibility to the Service will introduce some uncertainty, at least in the short term. A thoughtful transparency effort is vital to building and maintaining trust within the force as the Coast Guard transforms its talent management system.

The concept of "transparency" came up multiple times during the engagement. While it can mean different things to different stakeholders, the definitions tended to fall into two complementary categories.

How do I know the system supports readiness or mission effectiveness? From the perspective of an enterprise, transparency means the talent management measures the system uses to ensure it is working are readily accessible and understandable. Historic metrics, such as retention figures or the percentage of members getting their first choice, will be less meaningful in a future of stitched careers. Aggregate data, such as the number of billets filled or vacant, often lack context. As the Service moves forward with a modernized talent management system, it must be supported by meaningful measures that illustrate how the system is impacting readiness on a unit-by-unit basis.

How do I know the system fair to me? The participants generally saw the "boards and panels" process as fair and transparent. However, the inputs to those processes, evaluations and assignments, were seen as much less transparent. Assignments in particular were seen as the least transparent–and potentially the least fair–part of the process. Many of the participants saw assignments below the O6 level as relying on a rotating, unpublished, and often arbitrary set of unpublished "business rules" that assignment officers applied in their work

These impressions were formed in a relative vacuum of information, and they may not be completely valid. However, it is important to note that the participants shared them to a lesser or greater extent.

13

There was also an acknowledgement that assignment officers are working under a tight set of constraints as they attempt to fill any given assignment year's most critical gaps. Additional research also confirms the sense that talent-management personnel are not supported with state-of-the-market data management or forecasting tools, and must invest significant amounts of time entering, extracting, checking, sorting, and analyzing basic data. This is important time that could be better spent matching the right person to the right job. Assuming that there were not be an influx of personnel anytime soon, the Service must leverage technology to solve this problem.

Any successful revolution in talent management will require a robust investment in data quality, sophisticated analytics, and other decision-support tools. Employing these tools will require a major change in culture as well as policy as members compete for assignment and promotions in the out years. Everyone wants those systems both to be fair and to appear to be fair.

14

PREPARE FOR CONTINUOUS LEARNING

Rapid changes in technology, mission-related challenges, and society will require even the most experienced operators to get frequent skill upgrades. The Coast Guard should plan on all its members, even the most senior, spending more time on learning essential skills than they do now. This can best be accomplished through on-line or virtual-reality modules tailored to each member's specific needs. This has deep implications for a training system that is already running at full capacity and in a challenging budget environment.

The other key factors will include fully capturing the acquired skills and looking over the horizon to predict which skills the force will require in the future.

Some skills will be "lateraled" into the Service. This would be similar to DOD's current practice of bringing successful, service-minded Silicon Valley entrepreneurs to lead development of the JAIC. But demand for skills that are not widely found outside the Coast Guard (e.g., marine inspectors) or where there is fierce market competition means the Service will have to continue to grow much of its own talent.

Training could be one of the Coast Guard's biggest advantages in the competition for talent, particularly in futures with a thriving gig economy or where Blended Retirement and near universal health care "lower the barriers to exit."

In-Situ C Schools. Post-graduate schools are renowned for the practice of blending a mostly on-line, at-home learning environment with a cohort of paced fellow learners. Industry has begun to explore the use of virtual reality to deliver technical training to employees across the globe. As the cost of connected communications technology diminishes, learning outside the physical classroom will become commonplace.

Coast Guard-sponsored C-schools and other advanced training opportunities will similarly leverage in-situ learning frameworks, providing immersive, effective educational experiences, all without incurring the travel and time costs required to physically bring members from far away to a central location. The In-situ approach is an important component of a truly tailored learning experience. Why should a member spend 4 weeks in Yorktown at the SAR Planner course, or at the 2-week refresher, when all that member needs is a 2-day upgrade on the wind and current models?

Rather than going on a temporary duty trip to Yorktown, Petaluma, or Mobile, members may be assigned to a week of online, module-based C-school or recurrent training. They could work from home, a library, or even a leased space (WeWork or a base "Learning Lab."). The course could exist on a spectrum from completely self-paced to fully interactive with a cohort of students who are connected via a virtual experience (AR, VR, or other online classroom method). Of course, successful implementation of any such plans will require a culture shift. All members must view their on-line training time as sacred. Moreover, their home unit must trust members to focus on successfully completing their module(s) and avoid interrupting their studies.

NextGen Schoolhouses. Not only will the Coast Guard need to reconsider where it teaches members new skills, but also what it teaches and how it evaluates the results.

Competency-based schooling is at the leading edge of "NextGen" educational projects with personalized implementations.[3] The Service must embrace a schoolhouse model that prioritizes and balances the skills the Service must obtain and the technology involved to blend in-classroom opportunities with in-situ training upgrades. These schoolhouses will also acknowledge, credit, and certify Coast Guard and external experiences that contribute to a member's competency. Ideally, the NextGen schoolhouse will translate Coast Guard experience and training into externally recognized qualifications.

---

[3] Study.com - they have been embraced by public, private, primary, secondary, and graduate education centers and show the most promising, scalable results

The NextGen schoolhouse will also enable the force to rapidly adopt new tactics, tools, and policies as it makes training and upgrades available directly to the field in real-time, not just when a unit can get a coveted seat in Yorktown.

Reskilling. Most groups agreed that members joining the Coast Guard today should plan on "reskilling" over the course of a career. In some groups this meant enlisted members routinely reskilling and changing rates to meet the Service's emerging needs. In others, it meant assigning personnel based on all of their skills rather than their rate/specialty or even their billet history. In either case, this has deep implications for the Coast Guard training enterprise.

The pace of change and emerging needs cannot be managed solely by individual rating forces. Rather, it requires a system that can anticipate and prepare for the inevitable changes in the needs of the Service. A Chief Reskilling Officer could oversee this process and form a nexus between FORCECOM, PSC, the rating forces, and the programs. Rather than attrite individuals, or allow a rate to languish until disestablishment, this role should be given authorities for proactively reskilling the workforce.

The case for reskilling has been embraced by the private sector. The service can create "re-launchers"[4] who already understand the organization's values and merely need an updated skillset, particularly when combined with the "stitched career" model.

Continuous Learning Requires Continuous Connectivity. Our current IT infrastructure and policies are not capable of supporting state-of-the-market tools that are essential to making affordable, timely, and effective training possible.

The success of the future workforce depends our ability to rapidly upgradable skillsets. To get there will require a human-centered design perspective that views investment in these tools as a leadership imperative. Investment in personnel training are invaluable, and the emerging future of skills acquisition and capabilities points towards state-of-the-art software as an essential purchase and service.[5]

Reskilling In Practice

Innovative private sector leaders are taking the Fourth Industrial Revolution and its potential impacts very seriously. As an example, Amazon recently announced a plan to reskill roughly a third of its U.S.-based workforce by 2025, some 100,000 employees, as automation eliminates many of its warehouse jobs. In the near term, Amazon is hoping to fill the 20,000 worker gap in its coding staff. But the other employees are being trained in new skills, such as nursing, to prepare for a strategic expansion into healthcare. Amazon, a company famous for its cost-cutting zeal, is not embarking on this effort purely out of loyalty to its employees. It has identified that applying foresight and retraining an existing team member is often a better long-term investment than simply hiring and firing based on the skill needs of the moment.

---

[4] "How Carefully Managed Career Restarts Can Benefit Individuals and Employers.", Harvard Business School, Managing the Future of Work, September 11, 2019.

[5] https://innovation.defense.gov/software/

16

ESTABLISH AND ENABLE A DATA CULTURE

Most leaders intuitively understand that data-informed decisions are the most prudent in adding value to an organization. By 2030, mid to senior leadership will be steeped in tools and metrics to inform their judgment and decision spaces. The Coast Guard must create a data culture with purpose. This is a double imperative. First, the success of a flexible but cost-effective talent management system rests on it. Second, the workforce will demand it to support their daily operations, as well to undergird long-term strategic planning.

Make the Invisible Visible. The Coast Guard is sitting on a vast collection of data about its workforce. Some of it, like the data in MISLE, is generally accessible, but, in technical terms, "it lacks goodness." Other data, such as much of the information contained in OERs, EERs, and other personnel related records. is rich in context and well curated, but is in silos or confederated in pockets across the Service, making it very difficult to collect and analyze. For example, creating a roster of current female cuttermen requires OPM to cull data from multiple systems and then "ask around" to validate the information. The current roster lives as a spreadsheet in a shared folder, disconnected from the rest of the personnel system.

Data analytics and visualization could transform this data into knowledge and actionable insights. It could shine a light on patterns and trends, supporting the design of impactful initiatives designed to improve diversity and inclusion. It could support complex talent-management decisions, adding transparency and building trust within the force. It could provide near-real-time indicators of the "health of the force," rather than the lagging indicators that make it hard to manage critical skills and make accurate workforce predictions.

Investing in the quality and use of data will make the invisible visible and usable.

Support leaders looking for ways to make data-informed decisions.
Forward-thinking Coast Guard leaders are already surmounting siloed data and pushing AI-enabled analytics into their decision spaces. For example, OPM-2 is exploring AI techniques to develop candidate lists and provide career counseling. This effort has already made connections with the Harvard Kennedy School's leading machine-learning expert to gain insights and tools for workforce management.[7] Leaders at that program and field level across the Service are already leveraging data analytics and AI-enabled tools to convert messes of un-curated or confederated data to impact operations positively.

> How do you know you have a "data culture?"
>
> Your total workforce understands:
> data as an asset is curated to produce
> information as currency which is interpreted, creating
> knowledge as a resource for the purpose of
> wisdom in decision making[6].

These homegrown ML and AI practices are heralds of an emerging specialty the Service must intentionally nurture, leverage, and scale up if its senior leaders are to have the data transparency they need to make the best possible data-driven decisions.

---

[6] Coral, Lilian. Notes from "Open Cities" speech given at Harvard Kennedy School on 4/8/2019. [Is this speech available on-line? If so, where?)]

[7] The US Navy's "Navy Algorithms" project has developed a tool that uses predictive ML techniques to outperform human detailers in successfully matching members' dream sheets with assignments. This "stable marriage" algorithm can include the desires of the Service Chiefs in matching skills to best fit service needs.

17

Create and Empower A Data Workforce. Benchmarking against other successful data cultures reveals common elements of successful data cultures; this is just the culture the Coast Guard should emulate following the steps below.

First, the Coast Guard must appoint a Chief Data Officer with a high level of expertise and direct access to the executive or deputy leaders of the organization.[8] Working with senior leaders, this person must build a curious, engaging team of problem solvers, not regulators.[9] The team element is important; data engineers are generally more effective working in teams, rather than in solo positions.

For the Coast Guard, this could mean a Chief Data Officer, with a background in data analytic teams, could be "lateralled" in to build a mix of active-duty, reserve, and civilian data analysts to whom the directorates report. They would assist offices with building up their data measures and form the "top" of the data-specialty's leadership.

Second, the organization must invest in establishing a common language and narrative to understand the means and ends of data-informed decision making. This is reinforced by a disciplined approach to creating and curating data such that it is fully useful for current and future analysts.

Third, the organization must store information and leverage the tools that exist in "the cloud." Organizations shift from legacy individual computing networks to empower a distributed workforce with both data and tools. The Coast Guard workstation of 2030 will not be a desktop; it will be an app that provides secure access to specific tools and data the user requires on a variety of connected devices including wearables, multi-function phones and tablets, and traditional laptops.

[8] "How New York City Used Analytics to Solve Urban Challenges. 15NOV17, https://govinsider.asia/smart-gov/new-york-city-urban-analytics-amen-mashariki/
[9] Goldsmith, Stephen and Neil Kleiman. "Chapter Three: UX: Placing Citizens and

Those Who Serve Them at the Center." A New City O/S: The Power of Open, Collaborative, and Distributed Governance. Washington, D.C.: Brookings Institution Press, 2017. 49-74

18

STRATEGIC CHOICES

The Revolution Will Be Iterative

As a 229 year old military organization, the Coast Guard will only be willing to enable so much "grass roots" change to its talent management and training systems at one time. However, these proposed changes must be more than aspirational; they must be actionable. Senior leaders must prioritize, resource, support, and model the changes they want to see, and they need to start now.

We call for a revolution, but we do not want to fall into the age-old trap of designing the "ideal" system, investing significant resources, and then watching as it is consumed by unintended consequences or overtaken by events. Project Evergreen advocates for forward leaning but small-scale pilots, as well as investments in modeling or gaming to predict potential outcomes. **This incremental approach, however, should not obscure the need to act toward the goal of creating a new model that works for our future. We cannot merely optimize our current model to make it moderately better and sustainable.**

Lead Deliberate Culture Change

Some of the concerns and frustrations that participants voiced with our talent-management system were actually culture issues. Our norms on what "command presence" looks like, which skills are important, **what kinds of change are even possible,** and/or our expectations for what constitutes a "good Coast Guard career" all transcend policy. Changing the structures will force a partial culture change, but it will take leadership to ensure the culture changes that do take place are the ones we want. As leaders at all levels engage in an ongoing dialogue on our Service culture, there are some elements that Project Evergreen assesses as critical in creating and retaining the successful workforce of the future.

Change, or a culture of change, will be an element of its own. Leaders must prepare for things to be different, different career goals, and different ways of getting there, than they were in the past.

Trust will be critical as well. As operators, we tend to have deep trust in our people. We place our lives and the lives of others in their hands. Building a data culture and leading the talent and training revolution at the speed of need will require a different kind of trust. Leaders must manage risks in the policy space as opposed to on the flight deck. Letting a BM2 take an online class at home, without a supervisor, requires trust of a different kind.

Transparency will be vital as members take on far more responsibility for their own career progression. Ready access to credible and authoritative career information, coupled with faith in the fairness of the system, will be more important than ever.

Transparency will also allow us to measure the effectiveness of this "revolution." The Service must refine its measures for how the force-development and talent-management systems are positively impacting readiness.

Take urgent action on IT and data analytics as an operational necessity, a talent management tool, and a training enabler. This is not a new idea or revolutionary recommendation. However, it is becoming increasingly urgent every day. The fact that this point surfaced repeatedly in a session designed to focus on our workforce is indicative of its importance. In the context of training and talent management, the Service requires a more nuanced and forward-leaning system for documenting required skills and assessing the skills of our members in near real time. Talent-management professionals require powerful decision-support tools. Students will need connectivity to leverage a rich library of potential learning experiences. None of this can happen with our existing IT infrastructure, data architecture, and data workforce.

19

267

FIRST STEPS

It will take years, or even decades, for some the strategic choices made today to bear full fruit. Workforce 2030 did identify some first steps, which can be executed in the near term. Some are harder than others to execute, but are urgently needed to tackle today's most pressing issues.

- Make personnel and training data—largely contained within Direct Access, but also TMT, ALMIS, and other data bases—available for a pilot cloud-based data lake and apply robust data analytics to generate insight on the force. Make the results widely available, and use it to inform future policy development choices.

- For AY20, produce a "skill match" score for operational units that reflects each unit's total "skill match" level before and after the assignment season. This is a starting point for more meaningful and transparent metrics.

- Refresh guidance to boards and panels. Encourage the use of existing tools to reward good performance and "career" risk taking. Guidance should instruct board members not to penalize members for actually using newly introduced flexibility tools.

- Engage current and recently selected Senior Education and Fellowship officers, graduate students, and undergraduates to engage in research on talent management, AI, training- decision science, and the potential impacts of the Fourth Industrial Revolution. Provide forums for them to share the practical implications of their work with decision makers.

- Benchmark and collaborate, where possible, with other companies and agencies undergoing their own "talent revolutions." This includes potential partnerships with DOD and other military leaders, as the other Armed Services launch parallel talent management revolutions.

- Seize the opportunity to take on a leadership role in the Department of Homeland Security's data enterprise. DHS has directed each component to designate a Chief Data Officer. Rather than mere compliance, the Coast Guard should aim for leadership. Instead of double hatting an existing Assistant Commandant, hire a Chief Data Officer from outside the Service with proven leadership experience in building a data culture in medium to large organizations and position him or her "above the line" or as close to above the line as possible. The new Chief Data Officer could then build a team of data engineers to support the entire enterprise. In doing so, he or she would follow best industry practices.

- Every day that passes, more uncurated and siloed workforce data is being created. The profusion of such data makes the transition to a data culture that much more difficult. Leverage existing pools of homegrown talent (e.g., ORDOG, as well as other grass roots efforts) to begin to build the business rules[10] and structure.[11] Recommend following the IC and CYBER community paradigms for meta tagging and labeling such data to support future integration.

- Start a candid conversation across the service about transparency in talent management

---

[10] https://channels.theinnovationenterprise.com/articles/say-goodbye-to-your-data-lake-in-2017

[11] https://www.forbes.com/sites/danwoods/2018/01/10/can-failed-data-lakes-succeed-as-data-marketplaces/#4366be902454

20

268

CONCLUSION

WORKFORCE 2030 is the first of eight planned Project Evergreen Pinecones. The choice to focus on the workforce was a deliberate one. Previous Evergreen cycles aspired to identify the key strategic choices that senior leadership needed to make in the years to come. **Within months of starting our 4-year project, it was clear that the future of the Coast Guard and the future of the Total Workforce were one and the same.** While future Pinecones will be dedicated to questions ranging from geostrategic competition to driving innovation into practice, the future of our people will continue to loom large in all such discussions and initiatives.

As the first Pinecone, WORFORCE 2030 is a bit of an experiment. The immediate goal was to illuminate strategic choices the Coast Guard must make to be ready for 2030. In the long run, it will become part of the larger Project Evergreen report, which will include a cross-cutting analysis of all eight Pinecones. There were many creative ideas and proposals shared during this 2-1/2-day event. While the specifics of most of them did not make it into this report, they are archived on the Project Evergreen portal page and are available for future consideration and use.

Thank you to the many members of the Total Workforce, along with partners from the interagency, academia, and industry, who have contributed their valuable time and ideas to Project Evergreen. Thank you as well to the commands who shared their talented people with us so that they could gain exposure to different parts of the Coast Guard enterprise and contribute directly to its future.

PROJECT EVERGREEN

21

FLAG SPONSOR
Rear Admiral Brian Penoyer, Forcecom

TEAM EVERGREEN
CDR Kate Higgins-Bloom
LCDR Ryan Hawn

FACILITATORS
CDR Benjamin Perman, CG-DCO-X
(Facilitator)
LCDR Ryan Hawn, CG-DCO-X (Facilitator)
LCDR Robert Whiteside, CG-DCO-81
(Facilitator)
LCDR Celina Ladyga, CG-DCO-81
(Facilitator)
LCDR Timothy McNamara, CG-DCO-81
(Facilitator)
LCDR Christopher Kimrey, CG-DCO-81
(Facilitator)

PARTICPANTS
CAPT Tim Haws, FORCECOM
CAPT Richter Tipton, FORCECOM
CDR James Bendle, CG-PSC-OPM4
CDR Richard Knight, CG-R57
CDR Angie Hidalgo, CG Cyber
LCDR Rhianna Macon, CG-PSC-OPM2
LCDR Victor Galgano, FORCECOM
LCDR Krysia Pohl, PAC11
LCDR Rachel Stutt, FORCECOM
LCDR Kenneth Sauerbrunn, Training Center
Yorktown
GS13 Gina Corbit-Rice, FORCECOM
GS13 Jeffery Thomas, USCGA LDC
GS13 Brenda Nickel, FORCECOM
LT Matthew Delahunty, Air Station Elizabeth
City
LT Joe Bannon, Training Center Yorktown
LT David Bourbeau, USCGA Company Officer

LT Shaun Grant, Training Center Yorktown
GS12 George Brooks, FORCECOM
GS12 Adam Butner, FORCECOM
LTJG Thomas VandeZande, Training Center
Petaluma
OSCM Andrew Swett, Training Center
Petaluma
BM1 Wil Wiggins, CGC BLUEFIN
AMT1 Kyle Stalter, Air Station Elizabeth City
OS1 Lecia Mauge-Chan, Sector Hampton
Roads
MST1 Steven Andrzejewski, Sector Hampton
Roads
OS1 Danielle Deaver, Sector Hampton Roads
ME2 James Demetrius, Sector Hampton
Roads
ET3 Nathan Raney, CGC FORWARD
SN Nathan Barkley, CGC Forward

22

F3. "Workforce 2030 Executive Sneak Peek

COAST GUARD WORKFORCE 2030

The resilience and flexibility of the force is at the heart of what made the Coast Guard successful for over 200 years. An adaptive force will continue to be our greatest strength, but the environment the Coast Guard must navigate to build its force has changed dramatically since 2000. The rate of change will only accelerate. The 4th industrial revolution is well underway, with deep implications for Service missions and capabilities. Persistent demographic and social trends will fundamentally change the American population the Service recruits from and serves. **What worked in the past will not work in the future**.

The future Coast Guard will almost certainly be trying to retain its top talent in an increasingly competitive environment. Technical specialists like cyberspace operators will be in high demand, but there may be new needs that emerge which make an entirely different set of skills the "new cyber." Rather than predicting how many of which specialty the Coast Guard will need, **Workforce 2030 focused on creating a system that could generate the force we need, when we need it.**

The Coast Guard must create a **transparent talent management system that gives members greater control over their lives and meets the needs of unit commanders.** Ensuring that the "talent" in the talent management system has the right skills will require a change in the way the Service thinks about training. We should prepare our Service for a future of **continuous learning.** The success of these endeavors rests on the establishment of a **data culture**, enabled by robust, flexible, and interconnected IT and data management systems.

METHODOLOGY

Scenario-Based Planning | Multiple Futures | Rapid Iteration
On September 10-12, 2019, the Project Evergreen team hosted a "Workforce 2030" workshop. A cohort of 38 Coast Guard members ranking from E3 to GS12 to O6 formed four teams and explored divergent futures. **While each team had a unique future, the recommendations were consistent.**

WHAT FORCE WILL WE NEED IN 2030?

- **Tech Fluent**. Whether it is a detailer using AI to develop candidate lists or a BM2 setting electronic buoys – the entire workforce will have a higher "floor" for technical fluency.
- **Human Focused.** The need for STEM skills will continue to grow, yet all trends indicate that many of today's technical roles will eventually be taken by AI and autonomous systems. Human-centered skills like partnership building, creativity, and judgment will become increasingly valuable.
- **Skill Centric**. Members should expect to learn many different sets of skills over the course of their career.

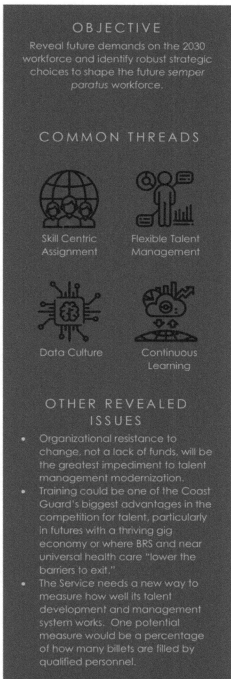

OBJECTIVE

Reveal future demands on the 2030 workforce and identify robust strategic choices to shape the future *semper paratus* workforce.

COMMON THREADS

Skill Centric Assignment

Flexible Talent Management

Data Culture

Continuous Learning

OTHER REVEALED ISSUES

- Organizational resistance to change, not a lack of funds, will be the greatest impediment to talent management modernization.
- Training could be one of the Coast Guard's biggest advantages in the competition for talent, particularly in futures with a thriving gig economy or where BRS and near universal health care "lower the barriers to exit."
- The Service needs a new way to measure how well its talent development and management system works. One potential measure would be a percentage of how many billets are filled by qualified personnel.

WHAT INVESTMENTS DO WE NEED TO MAKE NOW TO MEET THAT NEED?

Revolutionize Talent Management

Flexibility & Choice Changes in the demographics and social norms of the American population will make flexibility for the Service and the member an important factor in retaining top talent. In the future, particularly one filled with increasingly unpredictable crises, members should be able to easily use a wide range of "**on-ramps, off-ramps, and merge lanes**" to create successful "**stitched careers.**" "Pacing" was just as critical as the ability to transition in and out of service. Faster promotions based on performance or skill is an important retention tool for top talent, particularly if lateral entry is available to others. Conversely, members changing specialties or managing work-life concerns desire the ability to opt out of a screening without penalty.

Skills vs Titles The Coast Guard should leverage its relatively small size to find creative ways to assign and retain members based on their skills.

The Service should **reward what it wants to retain.** The promotion process should allow for risk taking in emerging fields or specialization in critical skill sets without resorting to a rigid staff/line officer system. There are implications here for how we value the less tangible leadership traits that will be at a premium in the future.

Transparency There was consensus that the current talent management system is not transparent enough and lacked genuinely meaningful measures of success. There was, however, very little agreement on how to address the challenge. DCO-X will expand on this topic in its final report.

Prepare for Continuous Learning

In Situ C Schools Rapid changes in technology, politics, and economics will require even the most experienced operators to get frequent skill upgrades. The Coast Guard should plan on senior members spending more time on learning than they do now, though largely through on-line modules.

NextGen Schoolhouses Some skills may be lateraled into the Service but demand for skills that are not widely found outside the Coast Guard (i.e. marine inspectors) or where there is fierce market competition mean we will continue to grow much of our own talent. If those talents include data analytics, critical thinking skills, and other competencies that are not explicitly included in the current training system, we must develop a strategy for building those skills through experience, external education, or developing a Coast Guard alternative.

Reskilling Most groups agreed that members joining the Coast Guard today should plan on "reskilling" over the course of a career. In some groups this meant enlisted members routinely reskilling and changing rates to meet emerging needs. In others, it meant assigning personnel based on all of their skills rather than their rate/specialty or even billet history. In either case, this has deep implications for USCG training.

Establish and Enable a Data Culture

You can't manage what you can't see. A flexible talent management system must be supported by rich data, robust analytical tools, and skilled analysts

Leaders will continue to look for ways to make data informed decisions. This requires a talent pool, competent in AI, machine learning (ML), and data analytics, the Coast Guard does not currently have.

Continuous learning requires continuous connectivity. Our IT infrastructure and policies are not capable of supporting state-of-the-market, much less state-of-art, tools that make affordable and timely training possible

ABOUT PROJECT EVERGREEN & WORKFORCE 2030

Project Evergreen (EVG) employs Strategic Foresight to support executive leaders in their role as the Coast Guard's decision engines. Workforce 2030 is one of eight "Pinecones" on the Evergreen tree. In summer 2021, Team EVG will begin a meta-analysis of the Pinecones to identify strategic choices for the 27th Commandant of the Coast Guard's leadership team. To join the conversation, contact the Project Evergreen Team in the Office of Emerging Policy (CG-DCO-X) at foresight@uscg.mil.

STRATEGIC THREATS TO THE FUTURE MARINE TRANSPORTATION SYSTEM

U.S. Coast Guard
Project Evergreen

PROJECT EVERGREEN

Contents

PROJECT EVERGREEN

PROJECT EVERGREEN

EXECUTIVE SUMMARY

The Marine Transportation System (MTS) is the backbone of the global economy[1]. The U.S. Marine Transportation System (MTS) is an integrated network of 25,000 miles of coastal and inland waters and rivers serving 361 ports. It supports over $5 trillion of economic activity each year and accounts for the employment of more than 23 million Americans. **For the purposes of this workshop, the MTS was considered in its broadest possible sense**, and includes the companies, communities, and individuals who interact with that system, as well as the greater international maritime community.

The MTS of the future will be characterized by increased **complexity**, driven by rapid technological change, with significant implications for the workforce and domestic governance. A broad community of stakeholders must proactively manage this uncertainty to avert its many potential downsides while seizing the opportunities. Almost every group identified **failure to adapt the MTS for a changing physical environment** as the most significant long term risk. Lastly, the **erosion of the rules based order and inadequate governance** are a direct threat to the ability of the maritime community to take any collective action on pressing challenges in the MTS.

Methodology
Scenario-Based Planning | Multiple Futures

Over November 14-15, 2019, the EVG team hosted a six hour "Risks to the Future MTS" workshop in conjunction with the annual Maritime Risk Symposium. Sixty-eight professionals from industry, academia, national labs, and government, formed four teams and explored divergent futures. **While each team had a unique future, the findings were very consistent.** This Pinecone was compressed, so rather than identifying potential solutions this engagement identified risks that will impact the MTS writ large.

WHAT WILL DRIVE RISK IN THE MTS?

- **Workforce.** The rate of change will require the workforce, industry, and credentialing bodies to continuously adapt.
- **Fourth Industrial Revolution.** "Tech" will no longer be discreet issue that can be managed in isolation by a small division of experts. Technology will be infused across every aspect of the MTS.
- **Climate Change.** Rising sea levels and increasingly severe and unpredictable weather not only threaten MTS infrastructure, but shift the cargos and communities that depend on them.
- **Geostrategic Competition.** Competition will take many forms, ranging from trade wars to information wars. The maritime domain is inherently global, and challenges to the current rules based order will have wide ranging in effects on the MTS.

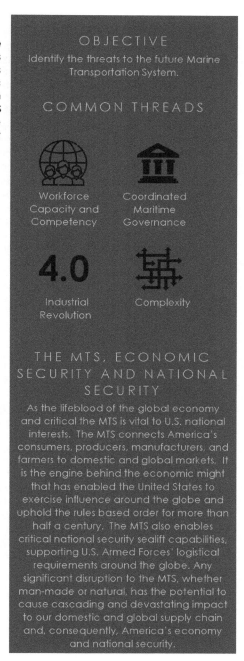

OBJECTIVE
Identify the threats to the future Marine Transportation System.

COMMON THREADS

Workforce Capacity and Competency

Coordinated Maritime Governance

4.0
Industrial Revolution

Complexity

THE MTS, ECONOMIC SECURITY AND NATIONAL SECURITY

As the lifeblood of the global economy and critical the MTS is vital to U.S. national interests. The MTS connects America's consumers, producers, manufacturers, and farmers to domestic and global markets. It is the engine behind the economic might that has enabled the United States to exercise influence around the globe and uphold the rules based order for more than half a century. The MTS also enables critical national security sealift capabilities, supporting U.S. Armed Forces' logistical requirements around the globe. Any significant disruption to the MTS, whether man-made or natural, has the potential to cause cascading and devastating impact to our domestic and global supply chain and, consequently, America's economy and national security.

1

WHAT ARE THE TOP THREE STRATEGIC THREATS TO THE MTS?

An Unmanaged Explosion of Complexity in the MTS. The fourth industrial revolution and the prevailing global economic trends will contribute to **a future MTS that is more complex than ever.** Waterways will become increasingly crowded, while changes in the economy will cause traffic to surge and shift in new ways. Simultaneously, the vessels that transit the MTS will be changing. **That change will not be uniform or linear,** creating an MTS with an unprecedented fix of technology, autonomy, and age.

The dwindling maritime workforce is unprepared for the pace of technological advance. In the coming years, the already understaffed U.S. maritime industry must recruit from an increasingly diverse talent pool in a competitive market[2]. Existing specialties will have a higher floor of "tech fluency" and the workforce must also grow to include new specialties – such as data scientists.

Governments – both as regulators and as national security providers – face a growing knowledge gap and are saddled with processes that are unable to keep pace with rate of change. Participants expressed unanimous concern about the federal, state, and local governments' ability to keep up with the changes impacting every aspect of the future MTS. These gaps have deep implications for functions ranging from rulemaking to port state. This gap is particularly critical because there was a sense that while industry had a greater ability to adapt, **government leadership will still be required** to broker solutions to the increasingly complex problems. In the national security space, the inability to keep pace will limit the USG's ability to establish persistent situational awareness. The openness and vulnerability of these new systems also have the ability to **create new threat vectors** with potentially devastating consequences.

The Failure to Prepare the MTS for a Changing Environment. Every group cited this as the most impactful long term risk to the MTS. Unpredictable and severe weather events, sea level rise, and underinvestment in **resilient infrastructure and systems** will combine to put the entire American economy at risk. The current cycle of destruction and reconstruction was seen as unsustainable. It creates a potential future where **the MTS is no longer capable of supporting America's robust economy.** This dark future was not limited to the coasts but included the network of inland rivers that are the lifeblood of the American mid-West's economy. In the maritime context, failure to take action will result in waterways that are less safe and require a more hands-on approach to managing traffic in the MTS.

The Erosion of Global Governance and Norms. Most groups agreed that the erosion of norms in the maritime domain is a strategic significant threat to the MTS of the future. This threat could manifest itself in many ways. Without unified governance, the MTS (including the internet) will become **Balkanized.** Industry will struggle to meet multiple sets of conflicting regulations, creating a drag on the industry and the global economy. Crumbling governance will also empower bad actors of all stripes. Trans-national criminal organizations will find more **gaps and seams to exploit as they engage in illicit activity.** America's competitors may also take advantage of those same gaps, potentially leveraging anonymous third parties or other "grey zone" tools, to **create confusion and gain competitive advantage**.

The gravest impact of this risk will be the **lack of collective action on important global issues.** It is likely that the future holds some nasty surprises for the maritime community. While we cannot predict what they will be, we can say that overcoming those shocks to the MTS will require transparent governance and powerful norms. On our current path, it is not certain that those will be available to future policy makers and leaders.

ABOUT PROJECT EVERGREEN

Project Evergreen employs Strategic Foresight to support executive leaders in their role as the Coast Guard's decision-making engines. This is the second of eight "Pinecones" on the Evergreen tree. In the summer of 2021, Team Evergreen will begin a meta-analysis of each of the Pinecones to identify strategic choices for the 27th Commandant of the Coast Guard's leadership team. To join the conversation, contact the Project Evergreen Team in the Coast Guard's Office of Emerging Policy (CG-DCO-X) at strategy@uscg.mil.

INTRODUCTION

PROJECT EVERGREEN

Project Evergreen is the Coast Guard's Strategic Foresight Initiative. Founded in 1996 as Project Longview, Project Evergreen has historically run in four-year cycles; using scenario-based planning to identify strategic needs for incoming Commandants. In 2019, Evergreen restructured in order to best support executive leaders in their role as the Coast Guard's "decision engines." Team Evergreen plans to conduct up to eight foresight engagements, "Pinecones," focusing on key topics over the next two years. After considering each Pinecone, Team Evergreen will produce a report within 60 days. In the summer of 2021, Team Evergreen will begin a meta-analysis of the Pinecones to identify strategic choices for the 27th Commandant of the Coast Guard's leadership team. "Strategic Threats to the Marine Transportation System" is the second of eight "pinecones" on the Project Evergreen tree.

THE FUTURE MTS

Why the Marine Transportation System (MTS)? As the economic lifeblood of a global economy and critical to U.S. national interests, the MTS connects America's consumers, producers, manufacturers, and farmers to domestic and global markets. The MTS supports over $5 trillion in commerce and more than 23 million jobs.
It is the engine behind the economic might that has enabled the United States to exercise influence around the globe and uphold the rules based order for more than half a century. In order to maintain this competitive advantage, the United States must adapt the MTS to the changes that lie ahead for our economy, environment, and society.

MARITIME RISK SYMPOSIUM

This Pinecone was done in conjunction with the 10th Annual Maritime Risk Symposium (MRS). MRS is an annual event that convenes academics, government, and commercial entities to discuss the threats, challenges, and risks associated with the MTS, both internationally, and domestically. The 2019 Maritime Risk Symposium was held by the State University of New York Maritime College, in collaboration with the National Academy of Sciences and the U.S. Coast Guard, on November 13-15, 2019.

OPPURTUNITY

This report is focused on strategic threats to the future MTS. Embedded is these threats, however, are opportunities. This "Pinecone" is unique in that it delivers only strategic challenges – without stepping into the solution space. As leaders across the maritime community take on these challenges, they will have the opportunity to innovate and transform the domestic MTS and strengthen the local rules based order.

To join the conversation, contact the Project Evergreen Team or reach out to the Office of Emerging Policy (CG-DCO-X) at strategy@uscg.mil.

SEMPER PARATUS

PROJECT EVERGREEN

3

METHODOLOGY
Scenario-Based Planning | Multiple Futures

Over November 14th and 15th, 2019, Team Evergreen hosted a six-hour "Risks to the Future MTS" workshop in conjunction with the annual Maritime Risk Symposium. A cohort of 68 professionals from industry, academia, the national labs, and government, formed four teams and explored divergent futures. The goal was to deliver insights on the gravest threats to the MTS of the future.

Team Evergreen grounds its activities in scenario-based planning. This is a classic strategic foresight practice applied by organizations ranging from the CIA to Disney. These scenarios included narratives around four divergent, but plausible, futures. Project Evergreen uses the "design double diamond" to structure workshops. These employ Human Centered Design-trained facilitators to drive curated ideation exercises and down-selection or prioritization techniques to the scenarios. The team overlays these group outputs to find common themes and decisions that are the most robust in many futures. **In this case, due to limited time, this workshop covered only the first half of the "double diamond."**

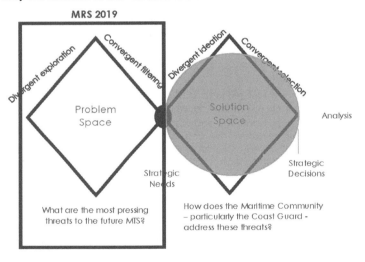

Each of the four teams started by identifying the drivers of change that were most germane to the MTS. Next, the teams articulated how those drivers might interact to threaten the MTS. Lastly, each group was asked to prioritize those threats. **While each team addressed a unique future, their recommendations were consistent.**

4

280

RESULTS OVERVIEW

WHY DOES THE MTS MATTER?

The MTS is the backbone of the economy[3]. America's MTS is an integrated network of 25,000 miles of coastal and inland waters and rivers serving 361 ports. It connects America's consumers, producers, manufacturers, and farmers to domestic and global markets. It supports over $5 trillion of economic activity each year and accounts for the employment of more than 23 million Americans. For the purposes of this workshop, the MTS was considered in its broadest possible sense, and includes the companies, communities, and individuals who interact with that system, as well as the greater international maritime community. While the emphasis of this workshop was on the U.S. MTS, participant agreed that the system so entwined with the global system that many of the issues addressed in the workshop would transcend domestic boundaries.

As the economic lifeblood of the global economy, the MTS is critical to U.S. national interests. It is the engine behind the economic might that has enabled the United States to exercise influence around the globe and uphold the rules based order for more than half a century. The MTS also enables critical national security sealift capabilities, supporting U.S. Armed Forces' logistical requirements around the globe. Any significant disruption to the MTS, whether man-made or natural, has the potential to cause cascading and devastating impact to our domestic and global supply chain and, consequently, America's economy and national security.

WHAT ARE THE BIGGEST DRIVERS OF FUTURE RISK?

Each group spent time discussing the forces that might combine to create risk or enable threats in the maritime in the coming decades. There was nearly unanimous agreement that these forces would impact the maritime transportations system in every future. Other variables, such as the state of the U.S. economy or the government's ability overcome partisan gridlock to get things done, are important and will determine how we as a nation manage those risks.

- **Workforce of the Future.** The rate of change will require the workforce, industry, and credentialing bodies to adapt continuously.
- **4th Industrial Revolution.** "Tech" will no longer be discreet issues that can be managed in isolation by a small division of experts. Technology will be infused across every aspect of the MTS.
- **Climate Change.** Rising sea levels, increasingly severe and unpredictable weather not only threaten MTS infrastructure, but shift the cargos and communities that depend on them.
- **Geostrategic Competition.** Competition will take many forms, ranging from trade wars to information wars. The maritime domain is inherently global, and challenges to the current rules based order will have wide ranging in effects on the MTS.

WHAT ARE THE GREATEST STRATEGIC THREATS TO THE FUTURE MTS?

The MTS of the future will be characterized by an **unmanaged explosion complexity**, driven by rapid technological change, with significant implications for the workforce and domestic governance. A broad community of stakeholders must proactively manage this uncertainty to avert its many potential downsides while seizing the opportunities. Almost every group identified **failure to adapt the MTS to a changing physical environment** as the most significant long term risk. Lastly, the **erosion of the rules based order** and the governance regimes that rely on it is a direct threat to the ability of the maritime community to take any collective action on pressing challenges in the MTS.

---

[3] https://business.un.org/en/entities/13 - 90% of global trade is maritime.

5

RISK DRIVERS

Each group spent time discussing the forces that might combine to create risk or enable threats in the maritime in the coming decades. There was nearly unanimous agreement that these forces would impact the maritime transportations system in every future.

- **Workforce of the Future** The workforce challenge was characterized in two distinct ways. First, the current workforce – generally, older, white, and male – is already too small to support the needs of the MTS. Based on social and demographic trends, participants expected it to be increasingly difficult to recruit new talent to the maritime industry. Second, the rapid changes to the industry itself will require mariners and other members of the maritime community to constantly adapt and develop new skills.

- **4th Industrial Revolution** "Tech" will no longer be discreet issues that can be managed in isolation by a small division of experts. They will be infused across every aspect of the MTS. Participants cited the potential for unmanned or autonomous systems, data analytics, and other emerging technology to transform the maritime industry.

- **Climate Change** Rising sea levels, increasingly severe and unpredictable weather not only threaten MTS infrastructure, but shift the cargos and communities that depend on them. Participants felt that even the most optimistic projections for sea level rise still put critical port infrastructure at risk.

- **Geostrategic Competition** Competition will take many forms, ranging from trade wars to information wars. The maritime domain is inherently global, and challenges to the current rules based order will have wide ranging in effects on the MTS. Participants were confident that competition, particularly between the United States and China, would have an enduring, if unpredictable, impact on the MTS.

Other important variables, such as the state of the U.S. economy, were considered as well. Ultimately, the teams selected these four drivers as ones that will generate risk in every future. The state of the economy or the domestic political environment will determine what resources are available to address those risks.

STRATEGIC THREATS TO THE FUTURE MTS:
The Unmanaged Explosion of Complexity in the MTS

The future MTS will be more complex than ever, with deep implications for industry, academia, and government leaders. Participants identified an **unmanaged explosion of complexity** as a serious threat to both the safety and security of the U.S. MTS. The fourth industrial revolution and the prevailing global economic trends will dramatically change the vessels and the waterways of the future. **This change will not be uniform or linear.** Some segments of the maritime industry will continue to be tech leaders, rapidly incorporating data analytics, automation, and advanced fuels into their operations. Other parts of this capital intensive industry will change much more slowly, adopting new technology only when regulations or the market make it is absolutely necessary. As a result, the MTS will contain a variety of vessels operating along the spectrum of automation and autonomy, with ships systems than run from virtually antique to simply virtual. Some will burn diesel, while others will be electric. They will all be sharing the same crowded waterway. Participants expect commercial vessels to continue to get larger, resulting in increasingly crowded waterways even if the number of transits goes down. Simultaneously, that traffic will become increasingly unpredictable as changes in the economy cause traffic to surge and shift in new ways. Port infrastructure is also likely to experience the same uneven tech revolution, with some ports or facilities leveraging emerging tech and others remaining on the far edge of the digital divide.

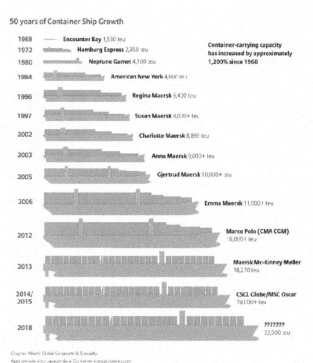

50 years of Container Ship Growth

1968	Encounter Bay 1,530 teu	
1972	Hamburg Express 2,950 teu	Container-carrying capacity has increased by approximately 1,200% since 1968
1980	Neptune Garnet 4,100 teu	
1984	American New York 4,600 teu	
1996	Regina Maersk 6,400 teu	
1997	Susan Maersk 8,000+ teu	
2002	Charlotte Maersk 8,890 teu	
2003	Anna Maersk 9,000+ teu	
2005	Gjertrud Maersk 10,000+ teu	
2006	Emma Maersk 11,000 teu	
2012	Marco Polo (CMA CGM) 16,000+ teu	
2013	Maersk Mc-Kinney Møller 18,270 teu	
2014/2015	CSCL Globe/MSC Oscar 19,000+ teu	
2018	??????? 22,000 teu	

Graphic Allianz Global Corporate & Specialty
Approximate ship capacity data: Container-transportation.com

7

Participants were not optimistic about the maritime community's ability to keep pace with the coming changes. In particular, the teams identified looming workforce challenges, capability and capacity gaps for regulators, and unmeasured security risks for the entire industry.

The dwindling maritime workforce is unprepared for the pace of technological advance. In the coming years, the already understaffed US maritime industry must recruit from an increasingly diverse talent pool in a competitive market[4]. Existing specialties will have a higher "tech fluency" floor and the workforce must also grow to include new specialties – such as data scientists.

The complex future MTS poses special challenges to the organizations and agencies which train, credential, license and hire commercial mariners. The vast spread of technology across the MTS will make determining what a mariner needs to know, and adapting curriculum and exams accordingly, will become increasingly difficult.

Regulators face a growing knowledge gap and are saddled with processes that are unable to keep pace with rate of change. Participants expressed unanimous concern about the federal, state, and local governments' ability to keep up with the changes impacting every aspect of the future MTS. These gaps have deep implications for functions ranging from rulemaking to port state control functions. Simply maintaining a workforce that is large enough to regulate and inspect such a wide variety of ships will be a challenge, even with the support of third party oversight. This gap is particularly critical because there was a sense that while industry has the ability to adapt to meet its responsibility to its **shareholders**, government leadership is required to broker solutions to increasingly complex problems with multiple **stakeholders**.

> "How do you credential an autonomous mariner? Who is at fault in a mishap – the programmer, the owner, who?"
> -Workshop Participant, Nov 2019

In the national security space, the inability to keep pace will limit the USG's ability to establish persistent situational awareness. Participants felt that the current regime, which relies on AIS and measures like Advanced Notice of Arrivals, to establish MDA was already inadequate for tracking "anyone who does not want to be seen." **This system was seen as inadequate to address emerging issues such as UAVs, unmanned submersibles, or cyber activity.** Commercial have are already outstripped most government agencies when it comes to leveraging technology to understand and even predict what is happening in the maritime domain. While some capabilities may be purchased off the shelf – the challenge of expanding the USG's limited maritime domain awareness to include subsurface, surface, air, space, and cyber space is significant and daunting.

Whether it is electronic navigation, industrial operating systems, or even social media - the openness and vulnerability of many systems **create new threat vectors** with potentially devastating consequences. In general, they have evolved faster than government's ability to regulate or guard them, and most of the private sector has been just as slow to develop and implement robust best practices. Participants felt that without significant leadership from both the public and private sectors, this trend would be amplified and expose the MTS to even more risk. Given the highly interconnected and global nature of maritime commerce, participants felt that the potential second-order impacts of a cyber-attack on the MTS, or a cyber-intrusion that is used to access other critical infrastructure, could be devastating and widespread.

9

STRATEGIC THREATS TO THE FUTURE MTS:
Failure to Prepare the MTS for a Changing Environment

Every group cited the failure to prepare the MTS for a changing environment as the most impactful, and most difficult to manage, long term risk to the MTS.

Unpredictable and severe weather events, sea level rise, and underinvestment in **resilient infrastructure and systems** will combine to put the entire American economy at risk.

America's maritime infrastructure is not simply aging, it is being placed under strains far outside its original design parameters. The majority of America's port infrastructure was built between 1930 and 1980. Since 1980, container vessels have grown from 4600 TEUs to over 20,000 TEUs. In that same interval, the frequency and severity of storms hitting our maritime infrastructure has grown dramatically. Since 1980, the United States. has sustained 258 weather and climate disasters where the overall damage costs reached or exceeded $1 billion (including adjustments based on the Consumer Price Index, as of January 2020). Sixty of them have occurred in the last four years[5] and the vast majority were storm or flood related. St Louis alone has had four "hundred year floods" in the last five years. In that same two-decade interval – most of the spending on port infrastructure has been on disaster recovery projects or investments in LNG or container facilities, with limited investment in the surrounding infrastructure.

A NOVEL NATIONAL SECURITY IMPLICATION OF RECOVERY

The rebuilding phase itself was also identified as a threat. The commercials systems and infrastructure in ports and along the entire US MTS are increasingly complex; they will more and more use constantly connected systems that collect information and use it to make decisions. This system is increasingly dual-use and will expose US infrastructure to potential monitoring by strategic competitors like China, whose state governments often own a controlling share of many of its commercial enterprises. Participants identified this as an important consideration that may become unavoidable when tight budgets and infrastructure needs drive local governments to award projects to the lowest bidder.

In the near term, failure to take action will result in waterways that are less safe. **This elevated risk will require a more active approach to managing traffic in the MTS.** The record inland floods of 2019 may serve as an example of what might happen across the MTS. Over the course of 2019, unprecedented levels of flooding on America's western rivers led to an estimated $12 billion in damages and lost economic activity. High water drove the closure of critical lengths of river for days or weeks at a time. These delays will worsen, especially in areas with infrastructure barely sufficient for this shipping. For example, there a many with bridge heights that can only clear shipping

---

[5] https://www.climate.gov/news-features/blogs/beyond-data/2010-2019-landmark-decade-us-billion-dollar-weather-and-climate

traffic by inches at a mean low tide. Even minimal sea level rise will make some river stretches impassable for some traffic without investments in bridge modifications. These closures put a heavy strain on the maritime industry and its customers[6], and was an intense resource strain on the Coast Guard commands managing the risks to the MTS from Detroit to Little Rock to New Orleans.

In the long term, the current cycle of destruction and reconstruction was seen as unsustainable. It creates a potential future where **some port communities are eventually abandoned, while the most viable ports are subsequently overwhelmed by increased traffic.** This dark future was not limited to the

> "I think most people take the river for granted – they just assume that the grain is going to get to market, the steel coils are going to show up to make the pipe, and peanuts are going to get there."
>
> -Brian Day
> Executive Director of the Little Rock Port Authority
> June 2019 Interview with the New York Times

coasts, but included the network of inland rivers that are the lifeblood of the American mid-West's economy. The impacts that this sort of future would have on the U.S. economy are dramatic and stark.

Tackling this particular threat was seen as the most difficult because it requires coordination across the broadest possible set of stakeholders, with significant tradeoffs between short and long term interests. The complex web of federal, state, local, and private interests that must be coordinated to develop and implement comprehensive strategies will complicate this necessary work, as it has for efforts to revitalize land based infrastructure.

The second element of the changing environment that the groups coalesced around was the need to "reimagine" what an MTS might look like in the Arctic. There was a sense that the United States has a fleeting opportunity to lead and innovate as it develops a new model for how to manage risk in this increasingly important part of the maritime domain. Rather than simply rebuilding what it uses in the continuous forty-eight states, with its vast network of expensive and labor-intensive physical, there is a chance to set the standard for remote, automated, virtual replacements – in navigation, monitoring, and even traffic management. These innovations could ultimately be applied across the entire MTS, resulting in greater efficiency and safety. Leading in Arctic is the opportunity to set international standards and norms and strengthen rules-based order.

---

[6] https://www.nytimes.com/2019/06/10/us/flooding-river-shipping.html

11

STRATEGIC THREATS TO THE FUTURE MTS:
Erosion of Global Governance and Norms

Most groups agreed that the **erosion of norms** in the maritime domain is a strategic threat to the MTS of the future. This threat could manifest itself in many ways. The teams discussed the different forces that are putting pressure on the currently rules based order, ranging from China's coercive diplomacy and Russian mis-information campaigns to tech savvy cartels and the rise of "super empowered" individuals and corporations. After considering these forces briefly, teams dedicated most of their time articulating how this erosion threatens the MTS.

Without unified governance and strong norms, the global maritime transport system (including the internet) will become **Balkanized**. Industry will struggle to meet multiple sets of conflicting regulations, creating a drag on the market and the economy. Many participants expressed concern that global doubts about the United States' commitment to multilateralism will weaken the U.S. ability to lead in standard setting bodies such as the IMO and allow revisionist states to reshape the status quo. If competitors set up alternate systems or regulatory regimes, as China has already demonstrated a willingness to do, participants were not confident that the American led system would remain the "default best choice" for trading partners. Ultimately, this would make the U.S. MTS less efficient and less competitive.

Crumbling governance will also empower bad actors of all stripes. Trans-national criminal organizations will find more **gaps and seams to exploit as they engage in illicit activity**. America's competitors may also take advantage of those same gaps, potentially leveraging anonymous third parties or other "grey zone" tools, to **create confusion and gain competitive advantage**.

The gravest impact of this risk will be the **lack of collective action on important global issues**. It is likely that the future holds some surprises and complex dilemmas for the maritime community. Project Evergreen cannot predict what they will be, we can say that overcoming those shocks to the MTS will require transparent governance and powerful norms. On our current path, it is not certain that those will be available to future policy makers and leaders.

> **A Collective Action Success Story**
>
> In the wake of the terrorist attacks of September 11th, 2001, the maritime community took exceptional collective action to close security gaps across the maritime transport system. The International Ship and Port Facility Security Code (ISPS) was adopted at IMO headquarters in December 2002. Passing and implementing such a comprehensive set of standards can often take years or decades, but the U.S. standing as a leader in the maritime community and the exceptional circumstances enabled ISPS to come into force in only 18 months.
>
> This effective exercise of governance across the marine transportation system has transformed maritime security around the world and fundamentally improved the security of the MTS.

CONCLUSION AND RECOMMENDATIONS

The most striking commonality among the top three threats was their truly global nature. The impact of exploding complexity, inadequate infrastructure, and crumbling global norms goes far beyond the MTS. While the threats were global, conceptualizing how they might interact with each other to impact the MTS in particular delivered new perspectives. There is also one additional "fourth threat" that also lies ahead. There is high potential for these threats to interact with each other in new and unpredictable ways. It is not hard to imagine how rapid technological change could combine with weak global governance to enable bad actors to exert malign influence or execute a crippling cyber-attack on the MTS.

In addition to the threats noted in this workshop, it is also worth noting what *did not make* the top list of threats. Terrorism or maritime piracy, for instance, did not even rank in the top ten. Public health crises and pandemics, on the other hand, were barely nudged out from the top three stand-alone threats.

This "Pinecone" is unique in that it delivers only strategic challenges – without moving into the solution space. Constrained by time, the Project Evergreen team tapped into the diverse and deep backgrounds of the participants to identify and prioritize the most pressing threats to the U.S. MTS. While the groups were not charged with developing solutions, some strategic choices began to present themselves over the course of the workshop. Managing complexity, invigorating the MTS' infrastructure, and upholding the global rules based order call for many strategic choices. Continued investment in the international bodies that uphold rules-based order and modernizing, or evening re-imaging, the governance model among the many federal, state, and local spheres were two ideas that surfaced in each group. They were big ideas that warranted more time than the teams had available. Rather than considering this a "closed chapter" for Project Evergreen, the Evergreen staff recommends continuing this conversation with a second convening focused on identifying strategic choices and potential recommendations for policy makers and senior leaders.

---

https://publications.armywarcollege.edu/pubs/3452.pdf

PROJECT EVERGREEN

13

TOTAL WORKFORCE 2030

U.S. Coast Guard
Project Evergreen

PROJECT EVERGREEN

Contents

PROJECT EVERGREEN

2

EXECUTIVE SUMMARY:
TOTAL WORKFORCE 2030

The enduring value proposition of the Coast Guard will remain anchored in its flexible, resilient workforce, regardless of how the future unfolds. The Service must intentionally design purposeful transparency, flexibility, and choice into its Talent Management system – for its members, unit commanders, and senior leadership.

The Service will be increasingly pressed to strike a balance between attracting and training specialists with developing and retaining adaptive strategic leaders. While technical skills are critical to a mission-relevant workforce and constantly changing, human-centered skills like empathy, creativity, and judgment are enduring. The Service must invest in both.

The previous Workforce 2030 pinecone described what workforce the Service will need. This Total Workforce 2030 pinecone asked, "What must the Service do to attract and manage this workforce – and what challenges and opportunities exist in getting there?"

Three themes from Workforce 2030 were validated:

What worked in the past will not work in the future.

Change must be transformative in design, iterative as a process.

Data is not a "piece" of the workforce revolution; it is the enabler.

METHODOLOGY
Scenario-Based Planning | Multiple Futures | Rapid Iteration
On September 10-11, 2020, the Project Evergreen team hosted a "Total Workforce 2030" workshop at Coast Guard Headquarters with the Deputy Commandant for Personnel Readiness as the sponsor. A diverse cohort of 22 Coast Guard members ranking from E5 to GS14 to O6 formed three teams and explored divergent futures. While each team worked with a unique future scenario, the recommendations were consistent.

HOW WILL WE GENERATE THE FORCE IN 2030?
Purposeful Transparency. Whether it is a Sector Commander looking at the list of applicants for Command Center Chief or a member looking for tailored career advice, purposeful transparency has intent: *to build trust with the workforce* while enabling transparent tools like the readiness- or flexibility-optimized billet slates.

Competing on Values and Opportunity. In all but the direst futures, Americans' expectations for meaning in their professional life are rising, and expectations about lifelong learning, flexibility, pay, and benefits are shifting. This provides opportunities for the Service to compete on its historic strengths – compelling missions and plentiful training – *if it can adapt to cultural changes fast enough.*

Accountable Autonomy. Greater autonomy is one of the most highly valued job elements for high performers. The Service must adapt to remote work, a greater range of "successful" career tracks, and more geographic and career flexibility in talent management. It must also develop effective means for more fully evaluating the performance of people and systems.

OBJECTIVE
Discover what the Service must do to succeed with its workforce in 2030.

COMMON THREADS

Talent Management by Design

Incentivize What You Want to Keep

The Data Engine for Talent Management

The Skills Library

TEAM EVERGREEN OBSERVATIONS

- Culture was not directly raised by participants as we explored barrier to achieving the workforce the Coast Guard needs. It did, however, permeate almost every conversation. Several groups down selected ideas based on their feasibility in the current culture.

"Culture eats strategy for lunch."
- Peter Drucker

- Map the work you need done: To achieve the skill-centric talent management, the Service must first measure the work it requires. As of this report, only 12% of billets had manpower requirements mapped.
- Talent Management and skill-centric assignments are the core of the Workforce Revolution; this implies significant changes for a system traditionally optimized to manage the flow of persons through the hierarchy of force structure.
- Transparent, accessible, centralized workforce data is the enabler for talent management and workforce insights at the speed of need.

3

Designed Talent Management.

Map the System We Need. To get to efficient, predictive outcomes in managing the billet slate, attrition rates, and future readiness goals, the talent management system must be designed, described, and decipherable so that leaders can apply design principles to direct shorter term efforts as part of a larger transformation. Not only do they need to know *which* policy levers to pull, but they must be able to build a *NEW* lever when needed.

More Jungle Gyms, Fewer Monkey Bars. Participants identified active duty and reserve component career progression as monkey bars which are completely linear, prevents you from going any faster than the person in front of you, and do not generally allow for team work. Additionally, if you miss one rung – you wind up "face down in the wood chips." Something closer to a jungle gym allows for multiple paths, allows you to pull folks up behind you, and enables members to move at different speeds.

Actively Discuss and Manage Our Culture. Implementing a flexible, transparent, data empowered talent management system is wholly dependent on our ability to integrate it into the Coast Guard's culture – or adapt our culture to a new system. Project Evergreen recommends leaders engage in a longer and deeper conversation on this issues, and all its implications ranging from how personnel are evaluated to how we define a "good career." It was striking to the facilitators to hear ideas dismissed during brainstorming sessions because they "would not work for us" or "there is no appetite for that much change."

Embrace the New Careers and Enable Stitched Careers.

Match Off Ramps to Onramps. Participants re-envisioned recruiting, training, retaining, and transitioning as all connected to each other - transition programs like TAPS that are not merely off ramps to civilian life, but opportunities to craft policies that link members up with future Service opportunities.

Assign for Skills, not Rank. Whether through pay-banding a billet to allow multiple ranks, or linking pay to critical skills, members emphasized the need to prioritize skill-centric assignment and careers over rank.

Leverage the Whole Skill Set. Service members have a much larger pool of talent than is currently captured by OSMS and the Personnel Development Record. The Service must embrace a method to capture and catalogue and see these skills that members acquire apart from the Service and put them *in one place*.

Empower the Data Engine to Drive Experimentation and Policy Making.

Accessible Insights for All Coasties. Build the HR Data Minimum Viable Product for talent management – where basic workforce questions can be answered without labor intensive data calls. This would dramatically reduce the number of man-hours spent on manually collecting and combining data from disparate databases, freeing up analysts to support more transformative efforts.

Accessible Data for the Analysts Powered by the cloud, Kaggle-style available data sets would simplify the workload of analysts and empower any office, shop, or motivated individual in a graduate program or Senior Executive Program to answer "wicked problems" with "wicked transparency."

Tailored Tools for the Decision Makers. Data-informed decisions start with a well-framed question and work to build the insights needed to answer that question. Building a slate that could show two perspectives – a billet slate optimized for readiness, and another optimized for member choice – would reveal how well the Service is balancing both and the tradeoffs in maximizing readiness and member choice. But to get to these kind of insights will require a streamlined minimum viable data product as well as accessible, transparent data.

ABOUT PROJECT EVERGREEN & WORKFORCE 2030

Project Evergreen (EVG) employs Strategic Foresight to support executive leaders in their role as the Coast Guard's decision engines. Workforce 2030 is one of eight "Pinecones" on the Evergreen tree. In summer 2021, Team EVG will begin a meta-analysis of the Pinecones to identify strategic choices for the 27th Commandant of the Coast Guard's leadership team. To join the conversation, contact the Project Evergreen Team in the Office of Emerging Policy (CG-DCO-X) at foresight@uscg.mil.

4

INTRODUCTION

PROJECT EVERGREEN

Project Evergreen is the Coast Guard's Strategic Foresight Initiative. Founded in 1996 as Project Longview, Project Evergreen has historically run in 4-year cycles; using scenario-based planning to identify strategic needs for incoming Commandants. In 2019, Evergreen restructured in order to best support executive leaders in their role as the Coast Guard's decision-making engines. After considering each Pinecone, Team Evergreen will produce a report within 60 days. In the summer of 2021, Team Evergreen will begin a meta-analysis of the Pinecones to identify strategic choices for the 27th Commandant of the Coast Guard's leadership team. Total Workforce 2030 is the third of eight "pinecones" on the Project Evergreen tree.

TOTAL WORKFORCE 2030

Why do another workforce report? After DCO-X published its Workforce 2030 report following its Yorktown, VA event in September 2019, the report made its way to a broad audience, including Admiral Schultz. The digest he returned to Team Evergreen concurred with the document and asked if some of its results could be pulled into the following fall. After numerous Workforce 2030 briefings, CG-1 crafted its Mission Ready Total Workforce with the Workforce 2030 report as a foundational document. While Workforce 2030 asked "what workforce will the Service need?" Total Workforce 2030 was an initiative to shed more light on critical investments the Service must make. It asked, "What must the Service do capitalize on the 2030 workforce?"

CULTURE

This report mentions the concept of "culture" in great deal in its pages. The concept is the topic of conversation at leadership lunches and in senior staff e-mails. In our work to date, "culture" has also been identified as our greatest strength and as the greatest barrier to modernizing our talent-management system. Some of the recommendations in this report call for large-scale culture change – stepping away from doing things the way they have generally been done for over half a century. But none of them call for us to give up the parts of our culture that make the Coast Guard a success. In particular, this means our core values – along with the flexibility, creativity, and initiative that have always enabled our people to thrive and carry out the many missions of the Service in a range of challenging and ambiguous environments.

URGENCY

Most of the ideas in this report are NOW ideas. In some cases, they are YESTERDAY ideas. Project Evergreen is charged with looking over the horizon. This distant focus was an important part of the process, but the road to that future is paved with the years that lie directly in front of us. The actions we take NOW will determine if the Coast Guard continues to matter a great deal to the Nation in the years ahead.

To join the conversation, contact the Project Evergreen Team or reach out to the Office of Emerging Policy (CG-DCO-X) at strategy@uscg.mil.

SEMPER PARATUS

PROJECT EVERGREEN

5

METHODOLOGY
Scenario-Based Planning | Multiple Futures | Rapid Iteration

On September 10-11, 2020, the Project Evergreen team hosted a "Total Workforce 2030" workshop at Coast Guard Headquarters with the Deputy for Personnel Readiness and the Assistant Commandant for Human Resources as sponsors. A diverse cohort of 22 Coast Guard members ranking from E5 to GS14 to O6 formed three teams and explored divergent futures.

Team Evergreen grounded all its activities in scenario-based planning. This is a classic strategic foresight practice applied by organizations ranging from the CIA to Disney. These scenarios included narratives around three divergent but plausible futures. The team applied the "design double diamond" in structuring this workshop and employed Human Centered Design-trained facilitators to drive each group through their scenario via predesigned workshop exercises. The team overlaid these group outputs to find common priorities and decisions among these teams. Those decisions that worked across multiple scenarios are robust. **Whether the Service will exist in a future with universal basic income and a gig economy or a new "war for food" and an end to the war on drugs, the choices highlighted in this document drive the Service toward success and hedge against future uncertainty.**

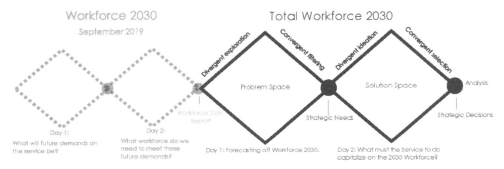

By the end of Day 1, each team had identified discrete challenges and opportunities that currently exist in getting the workforce identified in the Workforce 2030 report. On Day 2 they addressed how the Coast Guard must meet those challenges and opportunities and crafted strategic choices for addressing the gap. At the end of the design workshop, each group out briefed their findings to the D-PR, CG-1, and FORCECOM and shared ideas for implementation. **While each team dealt with a unique future, their recommendations held consistent themes.**

Over the course of the engagement, participants generated hundreds of very specific ideas and proposals. They created story boards to explain their choices and explored the intersections of future cultural boundaries, economic forces, and emerging technologies on the Coast Guard's ability to compete for future talent. This report contains a synthesis of their ideas, with additional research and consultation with experts, and makes high-level recommendations on where the Service should invest. This report is not a roadmap **– it is a call to action to choose** the most robust decisions **and to prioritize** those workforce and talent management improvements that will leverage **the Service's competitive advantages in a world of accelerating change and unpredictability.**

6

How We Will Manage the Force in 2030?

Total Workforce 2030 analysis shows that the Service will adjust to the Workforce of 2030 with policies and tools that include **purposeful transparency** to build trust with the workforce, by competing for talent by leveraging the Service's values and opportunities as an employer of choice despite the changing "why" and "how" of work in 2030, and with **accountable flexibility** that matches workforce demand for more autonomy with the Service's need for measuring and evaluating the performance of its people and systems.

Purposeful Transparency. Transparency was viewed as a necessary tool in building trust with the workforce. In fact, the sense was that **transparency is a means to get a Service whose systems interact with its members with _authenticity_**. Participants identified that such intentional transparency is a mandate both to capitalize on workforce talent and reduce organizational workforce risks. Analysis shows this would be viewed from at least three perspectives: achieving better matches for members and units, driving efficiency in the force development and employment cycle, and helping members and Service constituents understand how the Service selects talent. Groups overwhelmingly saw all three perspectives as directly contributing to the Service's ability to put the right talent on target while also producing the right tools to measure and address Service culture and workforce goals.

Competing on Values and Opportunity. All groups identified new "work values" that will impact the Coast Guard in 2030. With most futures exhibited rising standards of living for the average American and the advent of greater socials nets like universal basic income (UBI), expanded basic medical coverage, and tax-funded availability of childcare options, participants all spent time exploring the future "why" of work. They understand that while these things will not keep most people from working, they will allow enough of a safety net to more readily leave the Service, seek lower paying positions with greater type of work they enjoy, or just work fewer hours. Participants identified at least three sources of advantage for the Service to leverage: the opportunity to train and gain **mastery of useful skills**, occupations grounded in a **sense of higher purpose** and meaning, and entrance to and **participation in a community** of Coasties that is lifelong and meaningful. Leveraging these historic strengths will appeal to talent in any future – if the Service can adapt to cultural change quickly enough.

Accountable Autonomy. Autonomy is one of the most highly valued job elements for high performers. Participants expanded on the imperatives identified in Workforce 2030 for both work and career flexibility built into a talent management system. From the increasing need for specialists who can also lead with competence and empathy, to a workforce who will expect flexibility in geography, career options, and work schedule, each discussion was balanced with facilitated questions targeted at not only member desire but also Service need. It was clear that these are not "either, or" propositions. For instance – while members desire greater opportunity for remote work and telework, the Service itself becomes more resilient when members are forced to work physically distributed due to hurricanes, fires, flooding, and continued pandemic lockdowns. A coxswain may need to be physically present to run her response boat, but the operations controller could visually brief her search pattern and hazards over a secure Zoom. At the same time, discussions centered on ways that unit commanders could benefit from more flexibility in assignments. Whether solutions emphasized "flexible" billets allowing a reservist, active duty, or civilian member to fill it, or a more inclusive assignment process with measurable levers for unit commanders to more directly solicit and select talent, cultural issues inevitably rose to the surface: what might fewer "mainstream" careers mean for preparing senior leaders and the shape of the force? Does increased flexibility sacrifice _predictability_ for the member and Service? And how might the Service evaluate members in an environment where traditional paths become stitched with a single person having active duty, civilian, and reserve roles over the course of a career? **Increased flexibility and autonomy were seen going hand-in-hand with more nuanced evaluation of member performance and skills.**

Challenges and Opportunities

As the Total Workforce 2030 teams examined the futures in which the Service will be managing and leading its workforce, they quickly identified a gap between the flexible ways the Service will meet its workforce challenges in 2030 and the current system. At the same time, they realized many of the challenges add up to a larger opportunity to get more value for the Service regardless of the future that arrives.

WHAT INVESTMENTS DO WE NEED TO MAKE NOW?

The Coast Guard will be competing for outside talent while "re-competing" for its own homegrown talent throughout a single career. Total Workforce 2030 acknowledged this competition and looked for ways to leverage the values and opportunities of the Coast Guard such a sense of purpose, opportunities to acquire and master useful skills, and the community that members gain while working in teams. The groups also discovered new potential sources of competitive advance that are emerging – like increased autonomy in workplace and schedule and greater career flexibility. But ultimately, Total Workforce 2030 identified several mandates for change that must occur for the Service to meet the needs already identified.

Design for Talent Management. Participants highlighted the need to design a talent management system built for future outcomes that improves iteratively and embraces more flexible models of billets and assignments.

Map the System We Need. While participants all described specific policy outcomes, everyone struggled with describing the system as it. According to participants, the vast majority from CG-1 and FORCECOM, the current system has evolved over time without a clear system design to guide the creation of policy interventions. To get to efficient, predictive outcomes in managing the billet slate, attrition rates, and future readiness goals, the talent management system must be designed, described, and decipherable so that leaders can apply design principles to direct shorter term efforts as part of a larger transformation. Not only do they need to know _which_ policy levers to pull, they must be able to build a _NEW_ lever when needed.

More Jungle Gyms, Fewer Monkey Bars. Participants identified active duty and reserve component career progression as monkey bars which are completely linear, prevent you from going any faster than the person in front of you, and do not generally allow for team work. Additionally, if you miss one rung – you wind up "face down in the wood chips." They envisioned something closer to a jungle gym, which allows for multiple paths, allows you to pull folks up behind you, and enables members to move at different speeds. This could allow the Service to press "pause" on the member's up-or-out progress to develop and use their acquired skills in areas the Service critically needs. Whether creating a "civilian STEM corps" of cyber and data experts to allow members to build an AI-enabled SAR tool or the Service data lake solution, temporary stops on the career clock were seen as helpful for keeping talent working on wicked, technical problems vice losing it to the forced generalization of promotion or attrition.

Actively Discuss and Manage Our Culture. Implementing a flexible, transparent, data empowered talent management system is wholly dependent on our ability to integrate it into the Coast Guard's culture. Project Evergreen recommends leaders engage in a longer and deeper conversation on this issue and all its implications ranging from how personnel are evaluated to how we define a "good career." It was striking to the facilitators to hear ideas dismissed during brainstorming sessions because they "would not work for us" or "there is no appetite for that much change." The speed of the Service to adapt to the changing realities of how we work and how we reward it will directly impact who we attract and who we can retain.

> **Where Supply Meets Demand.** Participants emphasized a talent management system with an accounting for job requirements that operates more like a digital library: when unit commanders identify new skills needed for their unit, they must be able to "check back in" the volume describing an old billet and "check out" a new set of requirements. But until we measure the manpower demand of billets and give unit commanders their library card, we will struggle to supply talent at the "speed of need."

8

Embrace the New Career. The next generation's careers will have to look a lot different than they look now. The Service will not only be competing with civilian talent, but with other government organizations who are already planning for new career models. Embracing new models for a successful career was seen as essential for both remaining an employer of choice in 2030 and ensuring that the Service attracts and retains top talent.

Match Offramps to Onramps. In crafting their solutions to address talent management in 2030, participants recognized a common wicked problem of the future – the likelihood of a demographic who desires so much flexibility that a "traditional career" may not attract top talent. While groups acknowledged the role that Blended Retirement System will play, they were just as concerned about the Service's ability to retain talent it traditionally recruits. As one participant said, "we can't recruit our way out of this." Instead, **they re-envisioned recruiting, training, retaining, and transitioning as all connected to each other - transition programs like TAPS that are not merely offramps to civilian life, but opportunities to craft policies that link members up with future Service opportunities**. One group's "first steps" to that reality began small, but had large implications – adapting the Temporary Separation program to reach out to members one year out from expiring to catalogue useful skills and explore opportunities to link them back into jobs. That LT who is leaving the Service to design AI solutions for business might not need to be forever separated – through modified TEMPSEP, the Service recapture her skills later. With a Service who views her transition process as a way to tee up future recruitment, the Service could re-recruit her later and recapture that transitioning talent.

> Ethics in Talent Management: While discussing crafting talent management by design, some participants were asked what kind of expertise they might want. Several members, one a detailer, suggested their own world of work might be tweaked to eliminate perceived, if not actual, conflicts of interest.

Assign for Skills, not Just Rank. Sometimes, the best person for a job is not at the rank coded for a billet. In a future where the floor of technical fluency is constantly rising, the Service will see increasing tension between its need to fill billets with the best talent versus a system that views rank as the primary attribute. **Whether through pay-banding a billet to allow multiple ranks or linking pay to critical skills, members emphasized the need to prioritize skill-centric assignment and careers over rank.** This already occurs on a limited basis, with the Service making OIC, XPO, and Senior Enlisted Advisors that way, and it occurs in many communities like Aviation, where command of the aircraft is given to the most highly qualified, and if equal, then the most senior.

As groups wrestled with how to balance skill and rank in assignments and careers, they discussed many different cultural and practical questions: "If we divorce skills from rank, what does rank mean?" "What might determine if a billet should be filled with an active duty member, a civilian, or the best fit between the two?" They also wrestled with technical questions. With participants from CG-126 and CG-1B1 present, they emphasized that a more skill-based system would require the speed and accessibility of a streamlined HR data infrastructure.

Leverage the Whole Skill Set. Service members have a much larger pool of talent than is currently captured by OSMS and the Personnel Development Record. **The Service must embrace a method to capture, catalogue, and see these skills that members acquire apart from the Service and put them *in one place*.** ET3 may be not only be great at fixing that radar but is also a trained level two paramedic – yet without tracking these skills, the Service will not know that he would be a perfect fit for the recovery efforts following a major west coast earthquake. Members saw cataloguing this data into at least three bins: Service-trained competencies, third-party certifications, and self-reported skills. This was seen as low-hanging fruit for understanding the Coast Guard Auxiliary. While some members identified that this idea exists in theory, experts who trained in these systems demonstrated the challenge in actually using it due to the information being siloed and non-standard across platforms.

9

Empower the Data Engine to Drive Experimentation and Policy Making.

Accessible Insights for All Coasties. Don't let perfect be the enemy of good. One group asked, "What is the minimum viable product for a talent management engine to drive the insights we need and the levers we want?" Group members, from HR analytics experts to operational leaders, described a fairly concrete solution: **Coast Guard Business Analytics for HR – CGBI(HR)**, where all basic questions can be answered by members using CGBI, rather than by data calls. This would dramatically reduce the number of man-hours spent on manually collecting and combining data from disparate databases, which is the current practice in shops like CG-126. With many leaders in the Service needing transparent answers regarding basic HR questions (like, "How many minority females are currently qualified cuttermen?"), CGBI(HR) would give basic HR insights while making space for Coast Guard analytics to create more elaborate insights – ones that evaluate, forecast, and stress test workforce policies.

Accessible Data for the Analysts. Powered by the cloud, Kaggle[1]-style available data sets would simplify the workload of analysts and empower any office, shop, or motivated individuals in graduate and Senior Executive Programs to answer "wicked problems" with "wicked transparency." In each group, operational leaders and experts wrestled with both cultural and technical barriers to the workforce solutions they desired. Operational generalists tended to understand some of the insights they wanted, but they didn't understand the hurdles – such as vast amounts of uncurated, siloed data spread across multiple servers. To put that data together and understand the full history of a member, CG-126 employs one GS-13 full-time to move that data through several applications to fuse it onto unsupported "loaner" server from TISCOM. This process is time consuming, complicated, and a single point of failure for all of the Service's workforce analytics. To solve this problem, the Service *must* transition workforce data onto a single platform for both entry and storage, creating automated snapshots of the entire workforce into a single place. This data must be cleaned to account for errors and missing data, then published regularly in formats that analytics teams and empowered individuals can use to find insights from that data. Powered by the cloud, Kaggle-style available data sets would simplify the workload of analysts and empower any office, shop, and motivated individual in graduate programs and Senior Executive Programs to answer "wicked problems" with "wicked transparency."

Tailored Tools for the Decision Makers. Members asked each other what tools leaders might need to solve the most critical workforce dilemmas. While several examples emerged, *the common theme was that data-informed decisions start with a well-framed question and work to build the insights needed to answer that question.* Many of the most important questions focused on the relationship between Service readiness and member choice in building each year's billet slate. Building a slate that could show two perspectives – a billet slate optimized for readiness, and another optimized for member choice – would reveal how well the Service is balancing both, and what the tradeoffs are in maximizing readiness and member choice. To empower this type of insight, the Service **must invest in an HR Minimum Viable Product** and **create open, easily available data sets available to their analysts** as a foundation for this type of exquisite, automated, machine-learning empowered tool leaders need.

---

1 https://www.kaggle.com/datasets

CALL TO ACTION

TOTAL WORKFORCE 2030 recognized a call to action for the Service to go beyond current workforce dilemmas, and instead focus on delivering *better future dilemmas*. The tools, policies, and perspectives highlighted in this report are an attempt to kedge our Service towards the future rather than simply waiting for us to arrive. We recognize three enduring calls to action in the Workforce Revolution.

First, what worked in the past will not work in the future. Our HR system is old and designed to optimize a force construct from over a century ago. Demographics, ways of working, and the Service's national relevance have significantly changed. It is too risky *not* to change.

Second, we must design the Talent Management system we want for the outcomes we need, rather than apply short term "soft patches" and policy tweaks to the current HR system.

Third, the continuous iteration, innovation, transparency, and accountability required to evolve our HR system into a Talent Management system *require* an all-in approach to transform our data practices. And while this report limits the "data" discussion to the HR world, it is clearly a Service imperative. But unlike the many operational challenges our Service faces, which have external actors and environments outside our control, this challenge is uniquely *within our control* because we own our Talent Management data. *The problem is complex, but it is within our wheelhouse to solve, and it will enable purposeful transparency and accountable autonomy.*

The report contains many examples and anecdotes of tools, policies, and pieces of a talent management system that do not yet exist – and despite effort, very little quantitative analysis. Team Evergreen's intent is more than to get the Service to think, but to understand and "feel" the imperative for change. Thus, both Workforce 2030 reports document artifacts from futures that need the Coast Guard more than ever.

As the second workforce Pinecone, TOTAL WORKFORCE 2030 was a deliberate choice, crafted to answer the Commandant's call to further illuminate the next steps for workforce lines of effort. While it was conducted with many members of the Mission Ready Total Workforce to ground their work in the future and expose them to previous insights, one thing is enduringly clear: the Workforce Revolution *is* the Talent Management Revolution; it is anchored in transformation, but iterative in implementation.

CONCLUSION

Thank you to the many members of the Total Workforce, along with partners from the interagency, academia, and industry who have contributed their valuable time and ideas to Project Evergreen. Thank you as well to the commands who shared their talented people with us, through the challenges of COVID constraints, so they could gain exposure to different parts of the Coast Guard enterprise and directly contribute to its future.

PROJECT EVERGREEN

11

FLAG SPONSORS
Rear Admiral Paul Thomas, DCMS-DPR
Rear Admiral Joanna Nunan, CG-1

TEAM EVERGREEN
CDR Kate Higgins-Bloom
LCDR Ryan Hawn

FACILITATORS
LCDR Ryan Hawn, CG-DCO-X
CDR Aaron Delano-Johnson, CG-DCO-X
CDR Susana Lee, CG-DCO-X
CDR Dave Vicks, CG-DCO-X

PARTICPANTS

Master Chief	William Kelly	CG-00B
LCDR	Dan Sweeney	CG-R55
LCDR	Jack Smith	CG-126
CDR	Carrie Wolfe	CG-127
CDR	Tad Drozdowski	CG-ODO
LT	Taylor Peace	CG-1EA
Master Chief	Clinton Self	DCMS-D
LCDR	Pat McMahon	ODO-2
LCDR	Cecilia Williams	PSC-RPM-2
CDR	Jill Malzone	CG-1331
GS-14	Shelly Campbell	CG-122
LT	Cyrus Unvala	DCO-ES
LCDR	Keith Blevins	CG-751
CDR	Lawrence Gaillard	CG-1B1
Master Chief	Jeremiah Wolf	CG-821
GS15	Jennifter Leung	CG-122
LT	James Lord	PRTF
CDR	Zach Ford	OPM
GS-15	John Francis	CG-1B1

12

F6. "Semper Adaptus"

SEMPER ADAPTUS

U.S. Coast Guard
Project Evergreen

PROJECT EVERGREEN

Contents

PROJECT EVERGREEN

SEMPER ADAPTUS – QUICK LOOK

The Coast Guard has always operated in a dynamic environment, adapting to changing national priorities and global trends. In the coming decades, however, emerging technology and global competition will an even deeper impact on the demand for Coast Guard and how the Service does business. The Coast Guard must create absorptive capacity for new technology through concerted integration campaigns – which may ultimately call on the Service to change some of its structure and processes to reap the benefits of new systems and remain relevant as mission demands change. Preparing for shifting mission demand calls for futures-informed requirements that enable the Coast Guard to acquire adaptive capabilities to meet emerging needs and prepare for strategic surprise. Lastly – the ability to sense, collect, analyze, and share information in environments that range from permissive to austere is the most critical capability gap the Coast Guard faces. It runs through every mission and is the linchpin of success in every future.

METHODOLOGY

Scenario-Based Planning | Multiple Futures | Rapid Iteration
On December 2-3, 2020, the Project Evergreen V Core Team convened for the "Semper Adaptus" virtual workshop sponsored by the Deputy Commandant for Capability. A cohort of 25 Coast Guard members ranking from E7 to O6 explored the future of mission demand and capabilities through the lens of four different futures.

FUTURE CG CAPABILITIES

***Infor*-operable** The Naval Service's strategic approach to countering revisionist states relies heavily on giving actionable information to vulnerable partners, with Coast Guard leading the way. Sharing information with interagency, international, private, & non-profit partners is critical to every mission, including disaster response, countering IUU fishing, and securing the cyber-MTS and the Arctic. The Service has committed to a set of strategies with information at their core. Capabilities and practice must catch up.

Continuously Upgradable – Or Replaceable Leaders should expect long-lived or high cost assets – ranging from cutters to buildings to computer networks – to become obsolete earlier in their life spans than ever before. Upgradeability is a quality unto itself that should be seriously considered when acquiring assets. The Service should also explore acquiring more capabilities as a service or purchasing "disposable" assets.

Persistently Resilient The Coast Guard has demonstrated the ability to continue meeting mission through challenges as diverse as an unprecedented terrorist attack, record storms, a prolonged government shutdown, and a global pandemic. That resilience could easily be traded away in pursuit of efficiency or out of enthusiasm for new technologies. In most futures, state and non-state actors will be capable of degrading access to networks globally and holding some assets at physical risk. Additionally, the infrastructure that supports all Coast Guard operations will be subject to the stressors related to sea level rise and increasingly severe weather events. Operating through these new challenge calls for a deliberate investment in resilience.

DIVERGING DEMANDS

Semper Adaptus teams identified two divergent sets of demands on the Coast Guard across various futures scenarios. Global competition will require forces that can operate with DoD in any theater. In those same futures, increasingly severe and unpredictable storms will impact aging maritime infrastructure and densely populated communities – driving up domestic demand for response capabilities.

COMMON THREADS

Innovation + Integration

Infor-operable

Future Informed

Diverging Demands

THE BALANCING ACT

- **Deployable vs Place-Based** Some futures called for globally deployed law enforcement and training teams. Others called for more teams to surge domestically to respond to severe disasters or cyber-attacks. Some required both. Simultaneously, the Service's role as a place-based organization was a strategic advantage. The Coast Guard's de facto role as "maritime mayor" and deep local connections enable flexible problem solving as the increasing complexity the maritime domain turns almost everything into a collective action dilemma.
- **Centralized vs Distributed Decision Making** Technological advancements create opportunities to centralize to improve effectiveness or to save costs. There are also hazard associated with centralized decision-making, particularly in crisis. Distributed decision-making requires distributed support.
- **DOD vs...Everyone Else** A pillar of the Service's value proposition is its ability to bridge between lethality and diplomacy. As DOD acquires increasingly high-end tech, while international, federal, state, and local partners acquire less capable systems, the gap the Coast Guard needs to bridge is getting wider.

HOW DO WE GET THERE?

Connect Innovation with Integration

Conduct Focused Integration Campaigns. The potential value developments such as machine learning and unmanned systems is widely recognized. There was a general sense among Coast Guard participants, however, that the adoption of such technologies was "bottom up," with advocates battling a hostile bureaucracy to gain acceptance. _Evergreen recommends a senior leader directed approach, in the form of "integration campaigns" to accelerate the successful adoption of such technology,_ bringing in stakeholders from across the Coast Guard to generate holistic campaign plans and oversee their implementation.

Match Form to Function. (Or Function to Form). In Clay Christianson's seminal work, "The Innovator's Dilemma," he observes that market leaders are often the first to spot or create disruptive ideas. _They fail to reap the benefits of those disruptions because they are unwilling to alter their structures or processes._ The Coast Guard must reassess its organization and processes, and be willing to make significant change, to fully enjoy the benefits of emerging technology and concepts.

Create an Innovation "Risk" Budget. Many participants recommended an expansion of the Coast Guard's partnerships with R&D efforts at other departments and agencies, as well as increased investments in organic R&D. After examining the fate of many past Coast Guard R&D efforts, Evergreen assesses that _many ideas fall into the implementation gap, because most sponsors must take on the innovation out-of-hide_ – with no allowance for potential drops in productivity or effectiveness as they onboard a new concept or technology. Each innovation should come with an initial "risk budget" to encourage adaptation of new ideas.

Recognize Decision Making and Information Sharing as an Operational Function

Information as a Service. The public, particularly _the maritime community, views sharing timely information as a vital government service._ The Coast Guard has been filling this role for centuries. Taken to its logical end, a buoy is a way to provide mariners with information about their environment. What has changed is the volume of information that the Coast Guard could collect, and the public's expectations for how they will receive it.

Information as an Operational Resource The amount of data available to operational commanders and enterprise leaders will continue to grow as proliferating sensors provide information on everything from weather patterns and fish stocks to supply chains and drug flows. Bad actors, competitors, and adversaries will also have access to increased amount of data. _The ability to rapidly turn data from a variety of sources into knowledge is what will deliver competitive advantage,_ enable effective planning, and empower real time decision making.

Information as a Tool for Competition. Acting as an honest information broker in the maritime domain imparts the Coast Guard with the credibility _to protect rules and norms._ Information about illicit activities can be leveraged; when appropriate, to "apply sunlight" to deny malign actors the anonymity they seek.

Lead from the Middle. Or the Bottom. Building a seamless information-sharing ecosystem is a task that exceeds the Coast Guard's authorities. The Service must champion the issue and _partner with the executive and legislative branches to remove the legal, cultural, and fiscal barriers_ that impede information sharing of all kinds.

Prevent a Capabilities "Stern Chase"

Pursue Low-Risk Learning. The Coast Guard is playing an expanding role in the global competition for influence, which will call on the Service to _use assets and authorities in new, and untested ways, in high-stakes environments._ Robust participation in policy/war games, or establishment of a "Competition Center of Excellence," provide low-risk ways to identify gaps in capabilities and build vital expertise.

Create Future Informed Requirements. Fully incorporate futures—ranging from potential changes in overall mission demand to the impact of specific technologies—into the requirements process and _design with adaptation in mind._ Rather than developing capabilities to replace aging tools based on today's mission needs, a futures approach would add weight to emerging demands. _Said differently – "skate where the puck is going to be."_

Listen to Our Own Advice. The current innovation program tends to favor ideas that allow units to optimize their performance on current mission sets. Informed by low-risk learning and future requirements, senior leadership will be able to _set force development and experimentation priorities incorporating emerging demand_ rather than focusing on the lagging indicators such as tons of cocaine interdicted, buoys serviced, or inspections completed.

4

INTRODUCTION

PROJECT EVERGREEN

Project Evergreen is the Coast Guard's Strategic Foresight Initiative. Founded in 1996 as Project Longview, Project Evergreen has historically run in 4-year cycles; using scenario-based planning to identify strategic needs for incoming Commandants. In 2019, Evergreen restructured in order to best support executive leaders in their role as the Coast Guard's decision-making engines. After considering each Pinecone, Team Evergreen will produce a short report with emergent themes and initial analysis within 60 days, followed by a deeper dive report to develop and explain those themes. In the summer of 2021, Team Evergreen will begin a mixed-methods analysis of the Pinecones to identify strategic choices for the 27th Commandant of the Coast Guard's leadership team. SEMPTER ADAPTUS is the sixth of eight "pinecones" on the Project Evergreen tree.

SEMPER ADAPTUS

Whey SEMPER ADAPTUS? As Project Evergreen V kicked off, DCO-X engaged hundreds of Coast Guard personnel and experts as part of a rigorous process to identify the biggest drivers of change for the Service in the coming years. Then we led a workshop to identify the "most wicked" challenges those drivers might create. Those challenges shaped the next two years of Evergreen topics culminating in this final series of three workshops. They aim to understand future demands on the Service, identify strategic priorities for success, and then stress test those choices with rigor using game theory. SEMPER ADAPTUS was the first of this series of three workshops and revealed a key takeaway – whether the future brings fully autonomous barges to the Marine Transportation System or finds the Service enforcing new commercial regulations in space; partnerships, continuous iteration, and flexibility will enduring hallmarks of the World's Best Coast Guard.

URGENCY

Most of the ideas in this report are NOW ideas. In some cases, they are YESTERDAY ideas. Project Evergreen is charged with looking over the horizon. This distant focus was an important part of the process, but the road to that future is paved with the years that lie directly in front of us. The actions we take NOW will determine if the Coast Guard continues to matter a great deal to the Nation in the years ahead.

To join the conversation, contact the Project Evergreen Team or reach out to the Office of Emerging Policy (CG-DCO-X) at strategy@uscg.mil.

SEMPER PARATUS

PROJECT EVERGREEN

5

METHODOLOGY
Scenario-Based Planning | Multiple Futures | Rapid Iteration

On December 2-3, 2020, the Project Evergreen V Core Team convened for the "Semper Adaptus" virtual workshop sponsored by the Deputy Commandant for Capability. A cohort of 25 Coast Guard members ranking from E7 to O6 explored the future of mission demand and capabilities through the lens of four different futures.

Team Evergreen grounded all its activities in scenario-based planning. This is a classic strategic foresight practice applied by organizations ranging from the CIA to Disney. These scenarios included narratives around three divergent but plausible futures. The team applied the "design double diamond" in structuring this workshop and employed Human Centered Design-trained facilitators to drive each group through their scenario via predesigned workshop exercises. The team overlaid these group outputs to find common priorities and decisions among these teams. Those decisions that worked across multiple scenarios are robust. **Whether the Service will exist in a future with universal basic income and a gig economy or a new "war for food" and an end to the war on drugs, the choices highlighted in this document drive the Service toward success and hedge against future uncertainty.**

Semper Adaptus

By the end of Day 1, each team had identified discrete mission demands on the Service based on the range of factors in their scenarios. On Day 2 they addressed how the Coast Guard must meet those challenges demands and crafted strategic choices for addressing the gap. At the end of the design workshop, each group out briefed their findings and shared ideas for implementation to the Assistant Commandant for Capability, CG-7, RDML John Mauger. **While each team dealt with a unique future, their recommendations held consistent themes.**

Over the course of the engagement, participants generated hundreds of very specific ideas and proposals. They created narratives to explain their choices and explored the intersections of future cultural boundaries, economic forces, and emerging technologies on the Coast Guard's ability to effectively complete the future missions in their scenarios. This report contains a synthesis of their ideas, with additional research and consultation with experts, and makes high-level recommendations on where the Service should invest. This report is not a roadmap **– it is a call to action to choose** the most robust decisions **and to prioritize** those improvements that will leverage **the Service's competitive advantages in a world of accelerating change and unpredictability.**

6

SEMPER ADAPTUS analysis shows that while the specific capabilities the Service will need is unknown, glimpses emerged of a Coast Guard successful in both the domestic and international demands of safeguarding prosperity and life. Whether the future emphasized international engagement in the day-to-day with competitors and revisionist actors or domestic cyber and space-based capabilities and authorities, the Coast Guard must leverage its place as a collector, analyst, and broker of information in the wide space between the public it serves and the actions it seeks to influence – operationalizing it and sharing it with the American public, the interagency, and sometimes non-governmental agencies to shine a light on international spaces to affect behavior.

FUTURE CG CAPABILITIES

Infor-operable The Naval Service's strategic approach to countering revisionist states relies heavily on giving actionable information to vulnerable partners, with Coast Guard leading the way. As the competitive space expands, the range of partnerships and information the Service must share will likewise grow. Sharing information with interagency, international, private, & non-profit partners is critical to every mission, including disaster response, countering IUU fishing, and securing the cyber-MTS and the Arctic.

While the Service is rapidly growing its partnerships and positioning itself to continue being the "preferred partner" in the maritime space – the Service needs to expand its ability to share. This includes everything from open-source satellite imagery revealing revisionist state militia activities in the South China Sea, to (perhaps) Quad-Partner-Excepted-NOFORN classified feeds detailing artificial island building in the Antarctic.

Participants identified *information sharing* as a key capability the Service will increasingly need to be the nation's lynchpin in countering revisionist activities, and the Service has committed to a set of strategies with information at their core. This will require new collaborations and relationships both inside the Service and with the interagency. For instance – information sharing as a capability shifts enterprise responsibility to include more equities; participants suggested that information as capability will link CG-2 and CG-6 equities with a new CG-7 "Office of Information Operations" that would create policy and requirements to operationalize information.

There was a near-constant discussion of whether this type of information sharing should focus the Service on partnering with (and looking like) the DOD, with a focus on high-end capabilities and security more of that information, or more like DHS – with an emphasis on the interagency. The types information shared in a system meant to prioritize classified troop movements and would look very different from one meant to spread open-source information with as many stakeholders as possible.

Whether their future was one of an expansive and growing Coast Guard or a more inward-looking and domestically focused set of missions, being *infor*-operable, brokering and sharing information within itself, in the interagency, and in international fora was a critical need. Capabilities and practice must catch up.

Continuously Upgradable – Or Replaceable Leaders should expect long-lived or high cost assets – ranging from cutters to buildings to computer networks – to become obsolete earlier in their life spans than ever before. Just as "upgradeability" is a quality unto itself that should be seriously considered when acquiring assets. Whether it was cutters and aircraft with modularized pieces that could be swapped without complete overhaul of the asset, or simply creating an emphasis on software based designs over hardware, the ability to incrementally and frequently upgrade assets and capabilities was a critical enabler in the futures.

At the other end of the upgradability spectrum, the Service should also explore acquiring more capabilities as a service or purchasing "disposable" assets. Futures in which the Service divested these types of legacy risks were much more favorable to the Service than those in which the Service continued the status quo of expensive, exquisite, hardware intensive assets.

Persistently Resilient The Coast Guard has demonstrated the ability to continue meeting mission through challenges as diverse as an unprecedented terrorist attack, record storms, a prolonged government shutdown, and a global pandemic. That resilience could easily be traded away in pursuit of efficiency or out of enthusiasm for new technologies. While this principle was mostly discussed by participants in the abstract, some examples emerged – such as workforce enablers like remote work and alternate workplaces that would enable increased productiveness during normal operational periods, as well as flexibility for unit commanders and the workforce; but during surge periods or unexpected disruptions caused by natural or man-made crisis, it would increase the Service's ability to continue its mission and services; participants voiced that the current pandemic had forced the Service to accelerate baseline technologies like CVR Teams, Zoom for Government, and VPN/VDI access to workstations. The Service's ability to provide continuity of operations has been significantly improved. While this "dual use" capability is in retrospect a win-win in both steady state and surge/crisis, participants saw that some resilience improvements may not have the same usefulness in the steady state; but trading efficiency for resilience might be a choice the Service has to make

In most futures, state and non-state actors will be capable of degrading access to networks globally and holding some assets at physical risk. A Service that is called on to help state infrastructure recover from cyber attacks must itself be hardened and protected. This increase in cyber and information security might be worth the decrease in information efficiency in futures where the cyber infrastructure remains "offensive advantaged."

In addition to human-intended risks, the infrastructure that supports all Coast Guard operations will be subject to the stressors related to sea level rise and increasingly severe weather events. To remain viable and relevant, the Service must trade down its climate change risk to become climate adapted and resilient. Port infrastructure in Miami that has subsided while the sea level continues to rise must be moved or hardened against this threat.

Operating through these new challenges of calls for a deliberate investment in resilience.

Challenges and Opportunities

As SEMPER ADAPTUS teams examined futures with a wide range of economic, geopolitical, demographic, and environmental forces at play, it was evident that the missions the Service is required to perform will grow and change. Whether by congressional studies that adjust Service authorities or simply by public mandate, the Coast Guard will have increased, or at least changing, mission demand in 2030. Just as the pre-9/11 Coast Guard looked different than it does now, both trends and events indicate that the assets, capabilities, and authorities of the current Coast Guard will change – more rapidly than we may expect. By leveraging the value proposition that Coast Guard culture and doctrine provides, and prioritizing those common threads that will yield success among many different futures, the Service will be positioned to be ready and relevant in 2030.

8

HOW DO WE GET THERE?

Connect Innovation with Integration

Conduct Focused Integration Campaigns. The potential value of developments such as machine learning and unmanned systems are widely recognized. There was a general sense among Coast Guard participants, however, was that the adoption of such technologies was "bottom up," with advocates battling a hostile bureaucracy to gain acceptance. *Evergreen recommends a senior leader directed approach, in the form of "integration campaigns" to accelerate the successful adoption of such technology,* bringing in stakeholders from across the Coast Guard to generate holistic campaign plans and oversee their implementation.

Participants recognized the challenge in developing innovation and flexibility as a skillset throughout the Service. This means not only capitalizing on good ideas at all levels (which is also critical) but also to foster innovation and adaptability as a competency. "Innovation" efforts under existing Coast Guard structures favor low-risk incremental efficiencies to existing processes, often within the confines of traditional requirements development and acquisitions efforts.

Recognizing that historical Coast Guard budgets will not support sustained increases in mission demand, nor rapid technology adoption, the Service must invest its' limited resources in alliances and partnerships with other services and the private sector to capitalize on emerging ideas and technology. The Coast Guard needs to engage in a concerted effort to integrate lessons learned in this area by increasing detail, liaison, and industry training internships opportunities throughout the rank structure—from the deckplate to the officer corps—to inject perspective that propels the culture of the Service…and promotes retention of motivated and talented members. Closer ties to DoD and interagency acquisition, scientific, research and development initiatives (National Labs, DARPA, DIU, In-Q-Tel, AFWERX, SOFWERX, Army Futures Command, etc.) will allow the Coast Guard to act earlier and <u>partner in accepting reasonable risk</u> to capitalize on emerging technology in a timely manner. In order to remain resilient, the Coast Guard should prioritize interoperability of systems, both within the Service and across the interagency.

Match Form to Function. (Or Function to Form). In Clay Christianson's seminal work, *"The Innovator's Dilemma,"* he observes that market leaders are often the first to spot or create disruptive ideas. *They fail to reap the benefits of those disruptions because they are unwilling to alter their structures or processes.* The Coast Guard must reassess its organization, policies, and processes, and be willing to make significant change, to fully enjoy the benefits of emerging technology and concepts.

The proliferation of sensors and expansion of data-science capabilities creates opportunities to improve mission effectiveness and efficiencies (and threats in the hands of criminals and adversaries) through risk-based decision-making. The Coast Guard must embrace data as an enabler for success and to drive service transformation, considering it a function vs. collateral duty. To encourage this initiative and promote the data governance necessary for it to work, *the Coast Guard should establish data science as a competency and establish a data command headed by a Chief Data Officer (CDO) placed above the directorates*[1]. This would enable a centralized effort to champion data across the entire enterprise and ensure decision makers are equipped with the right data and tools. Traditional command structures, missions, and methods of executing them, may be challenged by this concept—but this is the type of change needed to 'match form to function' by effectively applying data science to efficient, risk-based, mission execution.

---

[1] Data Readiness Task Force and the Operations Research Community of Interest white papers on data governance, as well as open source case studies, highlight executive-level placement of the CDO as critical to building clear data governance and accountability.

The core team looked to see the CG use data analytics and AI to communicate requirements more holistically, facilitate policy change, and speed decision-making. Synchronizing those who develop requirements with those who write strategy will help the Service better adapt to change—with examples from planning for 'upgradability' of assets vs. focusing on procuring exquisite assets for today's needs. Working to shorten the timeline between development of requirements and fielding new capabilities will only further serve to allow the CG to better utilize scarce resources.

Create an Innovation "Risk" Budget. Many participants recommended an expansion of the Coast Guard's partnerships with R&D efforts at other departments and agencies, as well as increased investments in organic R&D. After examining the fate of many past Coast Guard R&D efforts, Evergreen assesses that *many ideas fall into the implementation gap, because most sponsors must take on the innovation out-of-hide* – with no allowance for potential drops in productivity or effectiveness as they onboard a new concept or technology. Each innovation should come with an initial "risk budget" to encourage adaptation of new ideas. This is compounded by the budgetary challenges of the Service, with the Coast Guard viewed differently by disparate external stakeholders whose perspective is shaped by their engagement with certain facets of the Service— maritime first responder, regulator of the MTS, law enforcement agency, or armed force.

Engineer methods to buy down risk in specific areas. One example of an area of specific that risk the CG currently absorbs is in the execution of gray zone strategic competition with adversary navies and coast guards. Gray zone operations stretches current CG capability to the edges of its traditional non-wartime missions, expertise, and current Service culture. Despite distributed or delegated decision-making being part of the DNA of the Coast Guard, from the days of remote lifesaving stations to the Revenue Cutter Service who set to sea with their paper patrol orders, today's advanced technology and C2 contribute to a higher level of strategic risk with immediate consequences at the tactical level.

Given the strategic risk to the nation inherent in such competition, the Coast Guard should establish Gray Zone TTPs as well as a "Maritime Gray Zone Center of Excellence" to institutionalize risk management of gray zone competition at the tactical, operational, and strategic levels. Having a better enterprise understanding of strategic competition and gray zone operations will help the Service shift the narrative from responding to demand signals to proactively shaping the conversation and directing limited CG resources towards regions, and countries, where the greatest impact can be made.

Recognize Decision Making and Information Sharing as an Operational Function
Information as a Service. The public, particularly *the maritime community, views sharing timely information as a vital government service.* "Information as a service," in the context of a government agency, is roughly the equivalent of "business intelligence" for the private sector—the concept of delivering enterprise data to the 'consumer' (internal, external, domestic and international) in a user-friendly format. The Coast Guard has been filling this role for centuries. Taken to its logical end, a buoy is a way to provide mariners with information about their environment. What has changed is the volume of information that the Coast Guard could collect, and the public's expectations for how they will receive it.

The volume of information held by the Coast Guard, and other agencies, is extensive often sitting in siloed databases, local personal files, and other inaccessible systems—information that is typically hard to access, hard to search, hard to share an only available in hard-to-understand formats.

Information as an Operational Resource The amount of data available to operational commanders and enterprise leaders will continue to grow as proliferating sensors provide information on everything from weather patterns and fish stocks to supply chains and drug flows. Bad actors, competitors, and adversaries will also have access to increased amount of data. *The ability to rapidly turn data from a variety of sources into knowledge is what will deliver competitive advantage*, enable effective planning, and empower real time decision making.

The Commandant has stated, our more-capable assets are not one-for-one replacements for the legacy assets they are replacing—this is not limited to NSC/OPC/FRCs, bur rather ranges to the advances of the Tech Revolution to appropriately provision Marine Inspectors and provide for a capable cyber workforce. With greater access to information, greater operational efficiencies can be achieved by delivering service (SAR, drug/migrant interdiction, fisheries enforcement, security escorts, or vessel inspections) at the *place, time and speed of need*.

Information as a Tool for Competition. Acting as an honest information broker in the maritime domain imparts the Coast Guard with the credibility *to protect rules and norms*. Information about illicit activities can be leveraged; when appropriate, to "apply sunlight" to deny malign actors the anonymity they seek.

For an operational example, with the increased focused on IUU fishing across the Indo-Pacific, the limited resources of a single NSC or LEDET aboard a U.S. Navy ship that offers intermittent patrol presence to help partner nations protect their resources can be amplified by providing shareable, and actionable, government or commercially procured information to partner nations that allow them to take action on their own.

This type of information sharing with international partners is often a two-way street, not only strengthening relationships with partners and allies but also giving the Coast Guard greater situational awareness and helping to remove blind spots in operating environments with less presence, sensors, and engagement.

With broad authority and strong existing network of international bilateral agreements, the Coast Guard is well-positioned to play a central role in strategic competition across the maritime domain. However, there are existing legal, policy, and cultural hurdles which would need to be addressed either via internal policy (e.g. Foreign Disclosure), improving broader Service literacy for the conduct of international operations (e.g. Global Coast Guard) or negotiation/renegotiation of bilateral or multilateral agreements in conjunction with interagency partners (e.g. specific information sharing agreements or holistic bilateral agreements).

Lead from the Middle. Or the Bottom. Building a seamless information-sharing ecosystem is a task that exceeds the Coast Guard's authorities. The Service must champion the issue and *partner with the executive and legislative branches to remove the legal, cultural, and fiscal barriers* that impede information sharing of all kind.

Building upon the concepts discussed for information as a tool for strategic competition, participants identified the theme of challenges within the U.S. interagency from law enforcement to the Intelligence Community as a self-imposed cultural barriers that prevent "whole-of-government" approaches to tackling our greatest national security challenges. The groups envisioned a seamless system where the U.S. interagency work more closely to facilitate 'nearer-to-real-time' decision-making regarding national and economic security interests threatened by transnational criminal or terrorist organizations. This concept will require legislation that mandates the development of an interagency law enforcement-intelligence sharing protocols, databases, and distribution methods that may only occur if there is strong leadership and a clearly articulated need.

As an honest information broker across a broad range of partners and constituents from the public to industry, interagency, international, and SLTT partners the Coast Guard can serve as a leader across all levels demonstrating best practices from the disparate stakeholders with which we engage and gaining consensus by validated success.

Prevent a Capabilities "Stern Chase" Participants identified several areas where the Service can, for relatively low cost, reduce its risk and build resilient, relevant capabilities.

Pursue Low-Risk Learning. The Coast Guard is playing an expanding role in the global competition for influence, which will call on the Service to *use assets and authorities in new and untested ways in high-stakes environments*. As the Service increasingly plays in this high-stakes space, it can pursue methods to explore and test its strategic choices and operational concepts before testing them in the real. The Service must commit to using analysis

11

tools like war games, tailored for its competitive space, to develop the right mix of assets, authorities, and capabilities needed to win.

When the Coast Guard signed the "Advantage at Sea" strategy, it committed to joining the Naval Services in defining and exploring key operational problems. But this will require the Coast Guard to acquire its own new analysis tools like gaming to gain tailored insights for its own set of risks. Robust participation in policy/war games, or perhaps establishment of a "Competition Center of Excellence," will provide low-risk ways to identify gaps in capabilities and build vital expertise.

Create Future Informed Requirements. Fully incorporate futures—ranging from potential changes in overall mission demand to the impact of specific technologies—into the requirements process and _design with adaptation in mind._ While the Service requires a fully integrated approach, the first step could be creating an "Office of Futures: Requirements and Capabilities" within CG-7, with the explicit task of creating common understandings of future requirements

> "Have we thought outside the box and tested our assumptions?"

among the various programs. Rather than developing capabilities to replace aging tools based on today's mission needs, a futures approach would add weight to emerging demands. As one participant stated – "we're going to have to sunset our aging H65 fleet; do we really want to just replace them with new helicopters? What if that option just gives us a really expensive portfolio of limited assets optimized for 2020? Have we thought outside the box and tested our assumptions?"

Examples of this abound – the most famous being the Army Futures Command. This is an entire enterprise led by a General dedicated to providing future warfighters with concepts, capabilities, and organizational structures needed to win. But as Army Undersecretary Ryan McCarthy said, relationships are its key to success[2]. Thus, a CG-7 Office of Futures would be connected to futures and innovation centers of excellence like Futures Command and Defense Innovation Unit and charged with informing Coast Guard requirements, blending a study of future Coast Guard needs with requirements. Connecting futures to the requirements making process is going to be more essential as the rate of technological change continues to accelerate. _Said differently – "skate where the puck is going to be."_

Similarly, these future informed requirements increasingly need to be designed with adaptation in mind. Increasing rates of change means systems and capabilities must be adapted to new and changing demands. A defense review recently stated, exquisite, single-use hardware platforms must be replaced with software solutions and apps. Just as the lifespan of a single class of cutters sees multiple stages of incremental systems improvement, by designing our platforms and systems knowing they will have modular updates, the Service can buy down its risk of obsolescence. In other words – we might need to spend less on the sensor, but more on a modular and upgradable software integration and analysis system.

Listen to Our Own Advice. The current innovation program tends to favor ideas that allow units to optimize their performance on current mission sets. This leads to preference for optimization for the present, but not necessarily to innovation for future readiness. Informed by low-risk learning and future requirements, senior leadership will be able to _set force development and experimentation priorities incorporating emerging demand_ rather than focusing on the lagging indicators such as tons of cocaine interdicted, buoys serviced, or inspections completed.

2

CONCLUSION

Thank you to the many members of SEMPER ADAPTUS and the Evergreen Core Team, along with partners from the interagency, academia, and industry who have contributed their valuable time and ideas to Project Evergreen. Thank you as well to the commands who shared their talented people with us, through the challenges of COVID constraints, so they could gain exposure to different parts of the Coast Guard enterprise and directly contribute to its future.

ABOUT PROJECT EVERGREEN & SEMPER ADAPTUS

Project Evergreen (EVG) employs Strategic Foresight to support executive leaders in their role as the Coast Guard's decision engines. To join the conversation, contact the Project Evergreen Team in the Office of Emerging Policy (CG-DCO-X) at foresight@uscg.mil.

PROJECT EVERGREEN

13

FLAG SPONSOR
Rear Admiral John Mauger, CG-7

FACILITATORS
LCDR Ryan Hawn, CG-DCO-X
CDR Aaron Delano-Johnson, CG-DCO-X
CDR Susana Lee, CG-DCO-X
LCDR Dan Crowley, CG-DCO-X

TEAM EVERGREEN
CDR Kate Higgins-Bloom
LCDR Ryan Hawn

PARTICPANTS – EVERGREEN V CORE TEAM

CAPT	Michael Sinclair	SEFP-Brookings
CAPT	Angelina Hidalgo	SEFP-CSIS
LCDR	Travis Thul	White House Fellow
LCDR	Tony Guido	PAE-1
LT	Brett Gayman	District Eleven
GS	Scott Craig	CG-926
OSC	Kyle Holbrook	District Eleven
CAPT	John Vann	SEFP-CFR
CDR	Jessica Behera	CG-761
CDR	Andy Goshorn	Sector N. New England
LCDR	Doug Eberly	PG, MPA, Syracuse
LT	Kumar Brunhart-McBratney	DCO-ES
CTR	Andy Howell	CG-791
LT	Kastriot Kastrati	USCGA, LDC, OCS
CAPT	Matthew Waldron	SEFP-ODNI
CDR	Jack Souders	SEFP-Hoover
LCDR	Joel Coito	CG-LMI
LCDR	Krysia Pohl	PAC
LT	Alyssa Milanese	FDCC
LT	Brittany Zirulnick	ICC
LTJG	Paige Holmes	C5IT
CAPT	Mark McDonnell	MIT Seminar XXI
CDR	Mike Courtney	ONA
LCDR	Denny Ernster	D11 DRAT
LCDR	Travis Noyes	Office of Maritime / Int'l Law
LT	Kimberlee Capp	CEU Oakland
CDR	Pedro Vazquez	CG-926
Ms.	Jen Ey	DCMS-5

14

F7. "Flash to Bang"

FLASH TO BANG

U.S. Coast Guard
Project Evergreen

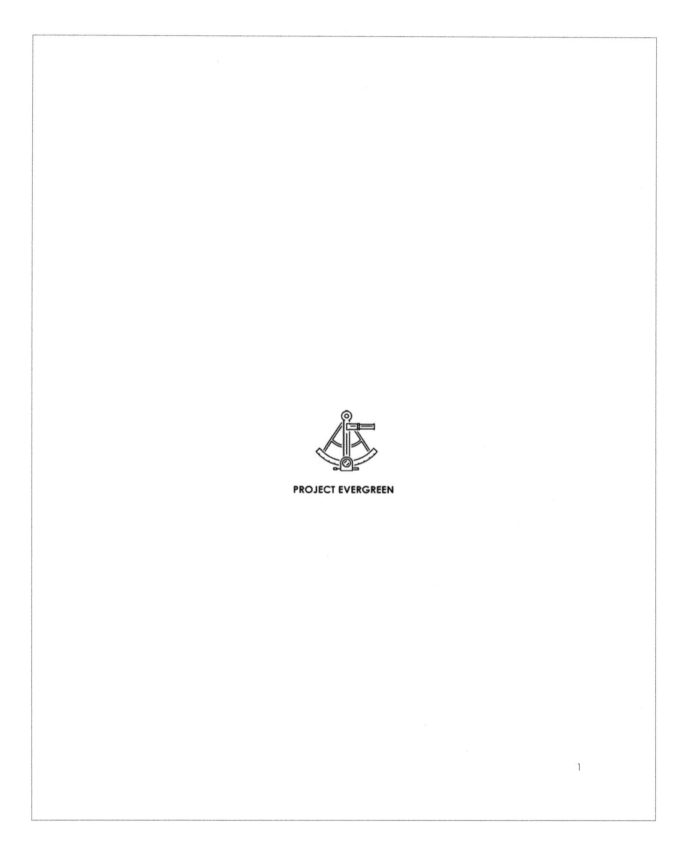

PROJECT EVERGREEN

Contents

PROJECT EVERGREEN

FLASH TO BANG – EXECUTIVE SUMMARY

The Coast Guard has always operated in a dynamic environment, requiring operational flexibility and strategic adaptation to fulfill national priorities and maintain pace with global trends. In the coming decades, emerging technologies, strategic competition, and environmental challenges will impel the Service adjust resources and investments with a nimbleness that will require even more responsive business rules.

METHODOLOGY

Scenario-Based Planning | Multiple Futures | Rapid Iteration

On February 23-25, 2021, the Project Evergreen V Core Team convened for the "Flash to Bang" virtual workshop sponsored by the Deputy Commandant for Materiel Readiness. A diverse cohort of 25 Coast Guard members ranking from E7 to O6, they formed four teams and explored the future of Coast Guard innovation, command and control, and mission support.

ATTRIBUTES OF A FASTER COAST GUARD

Modularity for Fungible Readiness. Just as *Semper Adaptus* highlighted a need for upgradability – or disposability – to be considered in requirements building and acquisitions, *Flash to Bang* teams identified modularity as a requirements and material strategy to more nimbly achieve readiness across the enterprise. Planned modularity allows pieces of investments to be "swapped" for upgrades or mission sets. The first National Security Cutter is already five years old – and in the 2035 future, it will already be old enough to be considered a "legacy" capital asset. By building modularity into new designs – just as Dutch Offshore Supply Vessels build containerized compartments into their stern to change capability from helicopter counter-narcotics support to medical relief missions – the Coast Guard can leverage modularity to keep legacy assets relevant.

Globally Engaged DNA. While the theater may change, all groups envisioned a Coast Guard influencing global norms in daily operations and day-to-day activities. While some futures focused on the Indo-Pacific as the location for the greatest impact, others saw it as a current model for understanding how the Service will thrive and remain relevant in other emerging theaters of strategic competition and great power cooperation. One key takeaway was a Service culture trained and organized around deployability rather than domestic geographic basing.

Innovation as a Cultural and Operational Imperative. All groups recognized the dire need to get change to implementation. While some identified properly resourcing the Coast Guard Research and Development Center (RDC) as core to this, they also recognized "connective tissue" missing between R&D outputs and implementation into programs. Some groups identified a Future Capabilities shop as central to creating an institutional "pull" for innovation, as well as cultural nudges to emphasize an "innovation risk and reward" cycle to incentivize programmatically taking innovation risk.

DIVERGING DEMANDS

Flash to Bang teams recognized explicit and increasing global demands on Coast Guard services across all future scenarios. Global competition will require forces that can operate with DoD in any theater. Simultaneously, increasingly severe and unpredictable storms will impact aging maritime infrastructure and densely populated communities – driving up domestic demand for response capabilities.

COMMON THREADS

USCG COCOM

Delegating Down Layers

Institutionalizing the "Pull" of the Future

Consolidated vs. Distributed

THE BALANCING ACT

- **Working with the Coast Guard of 1990** Some futures called for globally deployed law enforcement and training teams. Others called for more teams to surge domestically to respond to severe disasters or cyber-attacks. Some required both. Navigating an increase of services home and abroad held hints of how the future Coast Guard may need to be organized, with implications to everything from GFM to EDM.
- **DOD vs...Everyone Else** A pillar of the Service's value proposition is its ability to bridge between lethality and diplomacy. As DOD acquires increasingly high-end tech while international, federal, state, and local partners acquire less capable systems, the gap Coast Guard needs to bridge is getting wider.
- **Robustness vs Efficiency** A key element of Coast Guard success has been its ability to deliver results in times of crisis. But when the hazards are not hurricanes, ice storms, and flooding, but rather malign actors, strategic competitors, and contested regions, traditionally efficient means of supporting operations and delivering mission support may not work... and FEDEX may not be an option to get engine parts to the cutter.

HOW DO WE GET THERE?

Building on Progress. The findings below presuppose continued progress and commitment to recommendations found in previous Evergreen products. Namely, a transformation of the Coast Guard's talent management system and establishment of a service wide data culture.

Structure a 2040 Coast Guard. Where *Semper Adaptus* saw increasing demand for Coast Guard services abroad, *Flash to Bang* forced participants to understand implications for quick organizational response to those demands. *Echoes of the Past.* Many participants laid out a case to tailor Coast Guard organizational structure to these emerging strategic pulls. These discussions contained hints of the "OPCOM" and "FORCECOM" model and suggested a range of options for more globally-responsive operations

Expanding Roles and New Service Structure. From Districts operating more like Combatant Commands with authority to liaise directly with foreign allies and partners, Evergreen participants saw a future with dynamic operations abroad that implied faster C2 decision making and partner building.

Layers and Delayers. To offset growth abroad, leaner or fewer layers of traditional C2 may be required. Evergreen players saw gains in information automation and filtering as enablers that can enable restructuring force employment and force generation to balance domestic and abroad operations.

Innovation Integration. Most participants saw innovation as a crucial attribute of the future Service that integrates innovation with institutional processes.

Pull Innovation into Service Culture. As Workforce 2030 pointed out – the Service must cultivate what it wants to grow. All groups saw a need to make innovation a trait to incentivize. Some groups built an "Innovation" block into the OER; another provided a day of each week for employees to work on innovative solutions within their program (a la Google). All identified successful futures in integrating innovation into Service culture.

Institutionalize Operational Innovation into the "System." Participants agreed that "institution" and "innovation" are often at odds. They identified "program saturation" as a key reason that innovations fail to be absorbed. To get at this problem, they proposed "connective tissue" between the USCG RDC and the DCO and DCMS directorates as a "Future Requirements" nexus. Much of this involved a CG-7 Futures Capabilities shop with roles that cut across the traditional directorate programs, and there were echoes of a similar empowered shop within DCMS.

Prepare New Models for Relevance. The Service is acquiring more new capabilities and assets than at any point in its history. An NSC is not just a new WHEC, and a FRC is not merely a 110. These assets fill roles an entire class above what they were original envisioned. Traditional USCG capabilities and authorities – like aerial and surface interdiction, Captain of the Port Authorities, and foreign affairs roles like attaches, liaisons, and IPSLOs take on new significance in strategic competition. Evergreen participants saw the need to develop models for understanding what this means. This was seen as so critical to relevance in 2035, that the next workshop – CONOP 2035 – is partly structured to elaborate and feed the final Evergreen V year's "Serious Game."

Indo-Pacific Operations as a Global Template. While each Evergreen group has unique geographic hotspots that drove their thinking, the Indo-Pacific was unique. One group saw a need to articulate Concepts of Operations that highlighted the critical role of foreign partnerships and new types of USCG training and liaison teams to strengthen governance and build gray-zone resistant networks. Another proposed a hub-and-spoke model of mission support abroad and "modularity" as a mission support concept critical to making the Coast Guard capabilities more fungible.

Information Activities as a Core Function. For the American public, sharing timely and accurate information to achieve domestic and international outcomes is a vital government service, and one the Coast Guard has fulfilled for centuries. What has changed are the methods and volume of receiving this information – and who it is shared with. In the after-analysis of Flash to Bang, it was clear that the Service has experienced an unmeasured growth in need to share information with partners and the public. Whether facilitating safe navigation of coastal waterways or discovering and shining a light on exclusionary fishing practices on the high seas, information sharing was a universal force multiplier.

4

INTRODUCTION

PROJECT EVERGREEN

Project Evergreen is the Coast Guard's Strategic Foresight Initiative. Founded in 1996 as Project Longview, Project Evergreen has historically run in 4-year cycles; using scenario-based planning to identify strategic needs for incoming Commandants. In 2019, Evergreen restructured in order to best support executive leaders in their role as the Coast Guard's decision-making engines. After considering each Pinecone, Team Evergreen will produce a short report with emergent themes and initial analysis within 60 days, followed by a deeper dive report to develop and explain those themes. In the summer of 2021, Team Evergreen will begin a mixed-methods analysis of the Pinecones to identify strategic choices for the 27th Commandant of the Coast Guard's leadership team. FLASH TO BANG is the seventh of eight "pinecones" on the Project Evergreen tree.

From FLASH TO BANG

Whey FLASH TO BANG? As Project Evergreen V kicked off, DCO-X engaged hundreds of Coast Guard personnel and experts as part of a rigorous process to identify the biggest drivers of change for the Service in the coming years. Then we led a workshop to identify the "most wicked" challenges those drivers might create. Those challenges shaped the next two years of Evergreen topics culminating in this final series of three workshops. They aim to understand future demands on the Service, identify strategic priorities for success, and then stress test those choices with rigor using game theory. FLASH TO BANG was the second of this series of three workshops and revealed key takeaways – whether the future brings fully autonomous barges to the Marine Transportation System or finds the Service enforcing new commercial regulations in space; uniquely distributed and deep operational partnerships, continuously integrating innovation into culture, and flexibile iteration will be enduring hallmarks of the World's Best Coast Guard.

URGENCY

In many ways this product is the next step past SEMPER ADAPTUS. FLASH TO BANG assumes many of those recommendations will have occurred, or are critical to success, and explores what might be required to *do* them. Most of the ideas in this report are NOW ideas. In some cases, they are YESTERDAY ideas. Project Evergreen is charged with looking over the horizon, but we realize we must be adaptive in our approach. The distant focus was an important part of the process, but the road to that future is paved with the years that lie directly in front of us. The actions we take NOW will determine if the Coast Guard continues to matter a great deal to the Nation in the years ahead.

To join the conversation, contact the Project Evergreen Team or reach out to the Office of Emerging Policy (CG-DCO-X) at strategy@uscg.mil.

SEMPER PARATUS

PROJECT EVERGREEN

METHODOLOGY
Scenario-Based Planning | Multiple Futures | Rapid Iteration

On February 23-25, 2021, the Project Evergreen V Core Team convened for the "Flash to Bang" virtual workshop sponsored by the Deputy Commandant for Materiel Readiness. A diverse cohort of 25 Coast Guard members ranking from E7 to O6, they formed four teams and explored the future of Coast Guard innovation, command and control, and mission support.

Team Evergreen grounded all its activities in scenario-based planning. This is a classic strategic foresight practice applied by organizations ranging from the CIA to Disney. These scenarios included narratives around three divergent but plausible futures. The team applied the "design double diamond" in structuring this workshop and employed Human Centered Design-trained facilitators to drive each group through their scenario via predesigned workshop exercises. The team overlaid these group outputs to find common priorities and decisions among these teams. Those decisions that worked across multiple scenarios are robust. **Whether the Service will exist in a future with universal basic income and a gig economy or a new "war for food" and an end to the war on drugs, the choices highlighted in this document drive the Service toward success and hedge against future uncertainty.**

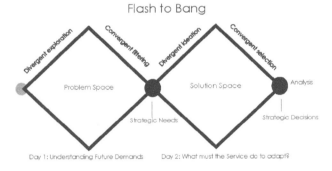

Flash to Bang

By the end of Day 1, each team had identified discrete mission demands on the Service based on the range of factors in their scenarios. On Day 2 they addressed how the Coast Guard must meet those challenges demands and crafted strategic choices for addressing the gap. At the end of the design workshop, each group out briefed their findings and shared ideas for implementation with the team, and passed along their initial findings to the Assistant Commandant for Material Readiness, DP-M, RADM Kevin Lunday. **While each team dealt with a unique future with different recommendations, but many consistent themes.**

Over the course of the engagement, participants generated hundreds of very specific ideas and proposals. They created narratives to explain their choices and explored the intersections of future cultural boundaries, economic forces, and emerging technologies on the Coast Guard's ability to effectively complete the future missions in their scenarios. This report contains a synthesis of their ideas, with additional research and consultation with experts, and makes high-level recommendations on where the Service should invest. This report is not a roadmap – it is an analysis of robust decisions from a comprehensive range of future scenarios designed to leverage the **Service's competitive advantages in a world of accelerating change and unpredictability.**

6

FLASH TO BANG analysis shows that while the specific capabilities the Service will need is unknown, value proposition in each future scenario lay in the balance between current and future readiness. There was an inherent tension between resourcing to provide forces ready "now" and updating those forces and capabilities to be more ready "tomorrow." While some groups emphasized strategic investment of current resources, others focused on strategically "reprogramming" requirements, acquisitions, and logistics to be more flexible and future informed. Whether the future emphasized international engagement in the day-to-day with competitors and revisionist actors or domestic cyber and space-based capabilities and authorities, all groups agreed that the Service and its people excel at flexible, iterative, and creative *operational* solutions; their recommendations across all future scenarios and solutions emphasized building an organization more responsive to current and future demands; their solutions included institutionalizing iteration and innovation into the supporting and enabling enterprise.

Attributes of a Faster Coast Guard

Modularity for Fungible Readiness. Fungible readiness is a term that participants have begun to use during this Evergreen cycle. It refers to the ability to take an operational resource from one mission and apply it to another – or to delay using an operational resource now and preserve it for a future use.

Just as *Semper Adaptus* highlighted a need for upgradability – or disposability – to be considered in requirements building and acquisitions, *Flash to Bang* teams identified modularity as a requirements and material strategy to more nimbly achieve readiness across the enterprise and make it more fungible.

Planned modularity allows pieces of investments to be "swapped" for upgrades or more relevant modules – this makes capability readiness fungible across mission sets and platforms. The first National Security Cutter is already five years old – and in the 2035 future, it will already be old enough to be considered a "legacy" capital asset. By building modularity into new designs – just as Dutch Offshore Supply Vessels build containerized compartments into their stern to change capability from helicopter counter-narcotics support to medical relief missions – the Coast Guard can leverage modularity to keep legacy assets relevant.

But this does not end with modularizing operational assets[1] - it might transform physical infrastructure by trading current readiness for a more risk-balanced future. For example - modularized Sector Miami physical infrastructure could be reconstituted near Sector Jacksonville in advance of a Category V hurricane, allowing it to "stay in the game" from a new location. Participants envisioned building in some capacity for this type of continuity of operations into planning and resourcing units; and rather than duplicating equipment in a locker to only be used in a reconstitution effort, they envisioned fielding fully capable command center packages that were used daily during normal operations and were containerized for pre-positioning to avoid inundation zones and in preparation for major surge events.

Groups understood building fungible readiness would distribute multi-mission capabilities and provide balance when future readiness outweighs current readiness, and this was especially

---

[1] Modularity as an operational asset enabler is common in small asset standardization in the Coast Guard – small boats and smaller cutters are increasingly standardized to simplify training and maintenance, and Coast Guard aviation is uses completely standardized equipment in each of its fleet aircraft and, increasingly, among fixed and rotary aircraft sensors, displays, and interfaces. http://www.modular.org/htmlPage.aspx?name=MILITARY#:~:text=This%20shift%20in%20operations%20has,to%20help%20meet%20this%20need

7

important in their considerations of future events in which events like low-level regions experienced more frequent flooding during hurricanes or changes behaviors of adversaries like TCTOs forced rapid adaptation of sensors and cyber-hardened systems.

Innovation as a Cultural and Operational Imperative. All groups recognized the dire need to get the right changes implemented. They identified getting enterprise assets and capabilities "out the door" faster as critical to being relevant. Per SEMPER ADAPTUS work they didn't merely view "enterprise assets and capabilities" as ships and aircraft, but enabling apps and increasingly software based systems – this could be charts and navigation updates, cyber hardened comms and data that can keep pace in less permissive environments, and AI enabled visualizations to assist in mission prioritization like boardings and intel collection. They viewed getting both evolutionary and innovative products to the field as an imperative that needed to go beyond operational innovation, which tends to be grass roots (i.e. Fish Tactic and many Innovation Awards products), and making enterprise culture and institutional processes more innovative.

They envisioned a demand-cycle for mission capabilities that is and will continue to accelerate, with a growing gap between adopted enterprise capabilities and those identified needs.

While some identified properly resourcing the Coast Guard RDC as core to this, they also identified "connective tissue" missing between R&D outputs and implementation into programs.

Some groups saw a Future Capabilities shop as central to creating an institutional "pull" for what R&D produces, to create a virtuous cycle of Service requirements and needs informed by emerging demands.

Globally Engaged DNA. While the theater may change, all groups envisioned a Coast Guard influencing global norms in daily operations and day-to-day activities.

While some futures focused on the Indo-Pacific as the location for the greatest impact, others saw it as a current model for understanding how the Service will thrive and remain relevant in other emerging theaters of both strategic competition and operational cooperation. Workshop participants looked at key drivers for this outward expansion, and *a resounding theme in all scenarios was that the Service is increasing its capabilities and will be expected to exercise them*. The three most impactful were: first, an increase in domestic and international partnerships enables Coast Guard missions, but it is also growing external requests for Coast Guard assistance. This is a demand signal that the public, legislators, and administration will certainly hear.

Second, the development and fielding of extremely capable and long-legged physical assets like ships that *will likely not be sitting off the port of Boston* but increasingly used to influence the global commons.

Third, an increase of enabling presence like international training teams and liaisons with partners and allies. One key takeaway was the likelihood of a Service organization and culture that will incrementally become arranged around deploy-ability. Being "abroad" as a cultural norm will grow beyond cutter and deployable specialized forces (DSF) communities, with fewer expectations of domestic geographic basing. More people and assets, further deployed, more often.

8

As FLASH TO BANG teams examined futures with a wide range of economic, geopolitical, demographic, and environmental forces at play, it was evident that the missions the Service is required to perform will grow and change. Whether by congressional studies that adjust Service authorities or simply by public mandate, the Coast Guard will have increased, or at least changing, mission demand in 2030. Just as the pre-9/11 Coast Guard looked different than it does now, both trends and events indicate that the assets, capabilities, and authorities of the current Coast Guard will change – more rapidly than we may expect. The Coast Guard can leverage advantages of culture and doctrine, prioritizing those common threads that will yield success among many different futures, to positioned itself to be ready and relevant in 2030.

How Do We Get There?

Building on progress. The findings below presuppose continued progress and commitment to recommendations found in previous Evergreen products. Namely, a transformation of the Coast Guard's talent management system[2], establishment of a service-wide data culture[3], an information-operable Service[4], and futures-informed requirements[5].

Structure a 2040 Coast Guard. Where Semper Adaptus saw increasing demand for Coast Guard services abroad, Flash to Bang forced participants to understand implications for quick organizational response to those demands while balancing domestic responsibilities—from more-frequent surge operations (hurricanes, wildfires or Western Rivers flooding) to burgeoning offshore wind and commercial space operations. How does the Service balance potentially-flat budgets to increasing demand signals for global engagement, steady state operations (SAR, Inspections, etc.) and more-frequent surge operations without the benefit of a garrison force?

Echoes of the Past. Many participants laid out a case to tailor Coast Guard organizational structure to these emerging strategic pulls. These discussions contained hints of the "OPCOM" and "FORCECOM" model and suggested a range of options for more globally-responsive operations. The capability to better developing nimble, tailored force packages in support of national priorities, COCOMs, task forces or organically to the Coast Guard may demand greater centralization—especially when the Coast Guard's interests may not 100% align with that of the COCOM or when the Service should work to drive narratives vs. simply responding to demand signals in its' own best interest.

Expanding Roles and New Service Structure. From Areas, and some Districts, operating more like Combatant Commands with both the necessity, and authority, to liaise directly with foreign allies and partners, the Evergreen core team saw a future with dynamic operations abroad that implied faster C2 decision-making, domestic and international partnership-building.

Layers and Delayers. To appropriately respond to growing demand for a Global Coast Guard, leaner or fewer layers of traditional C2 may be required—this concept builds upon the idea that the structural design of today's Coast Guard C2 is what the Service needed to be successful 30+ years ago; with built-in redundancies across operational layers[6]. With continuous advances in technology the Evergreen core team saw the ability for gains in information automation

---

[2] See DCO-X Evergreen products Workforce 2030 and Total Workforce 2030
[3] Ibid, Risks to the Maritime Transportation System in 2040
[4] Ibid, SEMPER ADAPTUS
[5] Ibid
[6] As highlighted in Coast Guard Pub 3-0 (Operations), page 16-17

9

and data filtering as enablers that can facilitate restructuring force employment and force generation to balance domestic needs and demand for Global Coast Guard operations.

Participants identified that better methods are needed for more rapidly and effectively allocating, deploying, and performing command and control of operational assets across missions and Districts in order to adapt and respond to changing mission drivers and priorities—which challenges the status quo of Station, Sector, District, Area and National Command Centers; perhaps some Sectors need to be run by a Flag officer which may negate the need for the traditional District as currently envisioned.

If appropriately leveraged, technology and operational decision-making can help eliminate redundant organizational layers and legacy resources could be reprogrammed for expanding or prioritizing missions across geographical "boundaries."

**Innovation Integration.** Most participants saw innovation as a crucial attribute of the future Service. They recognized that reprogramming innovation to be integrated into the organization – as opposed to an "add-on" function attached to it – will be required to produce adaptive and transformative value to the enterprise.

Pull Innovation into Service Culture. As Workforce 2030 pointed out – the Service must cultivate what it wants to grow. All groups saw a need to make innovation a trait to incentivize. Some groups built an "Innovation" block into the OER; another provided a day of each week for employees to work on innovative solutions within their program (a la Google). All identified successful futures in integrating innovation into Service culture.

Just as SEMPER ADAPTUS recommended an innovation "risk" budget for task-saturated programs to have capacity to take on an innovative change, FLASH TO BANG participants saw cultural barriers to more rapid procurement of innovative systems. They suggested that advocating for a rapid procurement authorization for mission-critical technology or adapting the Navy development squadron concept[7]. This would involve changing policy and practices to allow new technologies to be incorporated as new systems are developed, rather than locking into tech solutions during the development phase. Those participants with CG-9 experience pointed out that this is not just policy change – it is cultural, as it requires _adopting an acquisition risk position_ to bridge technology gaps more rapidly.

Institutionalize Innovation into the "System." The Service must aggressively create disruption in its current pace of change management. Participants agreed that "institution" and "innovation" are often at odds, and that change will require reprogramming of the "system." For example, they identified "program saturation" as a key reason that innovations fail to be absorbed. To get at this problem, they proposed "connective tissue" between the USCG RDC and the DCO and DCMS directorates as a "Future Requirements" nexus. Much of this involved a CG-7 Futures Capabilities shop with roles that cut across the traditional directorate programs, and there were hints of a similarly empowered shop within DCMS.

---

[7] The Pentagon acquisition directorate's Adaptive Acquisition Framework and Contracting Cone describe adaptive steps to use alternative authorities for acquisitions and contracting. These include "other transactional authorities," middle-tier acquisitions, rapid prototyping and rapid fielding, and specialized routes for software acquisition.

10

328

This harkened back to SEMPER ADAPTUS, and built on that CG-7 Future Capabilities (CG-7FC). As an example of a recommendation, one team created a CG-7FC function connected to three places in the enterprise to drive a virtuous cycle of iteration and innovation:

- CG-7FC workshop-driven deliverables would generate input directly to Coast Guard RDC, to inform their research projects as well as identify programs and offices primarily within CG-7 to receive them. They would also provide accountability for not just R&D delivery but would also advocate for sustained placement and resourcing within a CG-7 program.

- Program Analysis and Evaluation (CG-PAE) would be connected to review, from a PAE-1 futures perspective and with a PAE-2 evaluation review, the value proposition of the CG-7FC future requirements.

- CG-6 enterprise, leveraging its nascent Artificial Intelligence Division experience, provide input regarding AI-enabled solutions, per recommendations from GAO and the National Security Commission on Artificial Intelligence (NSCAI)[8,9].

All groups understood well that the Service will not have the resources to build the innovation and R&D models that DOD enjoys, like Army Futures Command or Naval Research Labs – so they proposed "reprogramming" pieces of the USCG enterprise, especially those pieces that drive capabilities and requirements, to smartly drive, inform, and receive those resources the Service does have.

Prepare New Models for Relevance. The Service is acquiring more new capabilities and assets than at any point in its history. An NSC is not just a new WHEC, and a FRC is not merely a 110. These assets fill roles an entire class above what they were original envisioned. Traditional USCG capabilities and authorities – like aerial and surface interdiction, Captain of the Port Authorities, and foreign affairs roles like attaches, liaisons, and IPSLOs take on new significance in strategic competition. Evergreen participants saw the need to develop models for understanding what this means. This was seen as so critical to relevance in 2035, that the next workshop – CONOP 2035 – is partly structured to elaborate on this gap and feed the final Evergreen V year's "Serious Game."

Indo-Pacific Operations as a Global Template. While each Evergreen group had unique geographic hotspots that drove their thinking, the Indo-Pacific was unique. One group saw a need to articulate Concepts of Operations that highlighted the critical role of foreign partnerships and new types of USCG training and liaison teams to strengthen governance and build gray-zone resistant networks.

While researching whether this would be a new product or simply improve upon an old one, two groups referenced U.S. Coast Guard Publication 3, "Operations" as a helpful place to begin. They built an example concept for operating abroad, called "Global & Domestic Force Packages" that envisioned an integrated operations package approach to organizing force to apply to domestic missions while being ready for global deploy-ability. This envisioned a shift from looking Coast Guard assets like ships and aircraft to looking at "effects," and building types of force packages that would deliver these effects.

For example - to compete in the day-to-day against IUUF in both the western hemisphere and abroad, these force packages would be optimized with specialized collection as well as unclassified collections to find and fix illegally fishing targets off Ecuador and might include a persistently present surface vessel, some type of fast interdiction aircraft to deliver some type of effect and expand the reach of the surface asset, with C2 occurring from PACAREA retaining operational control of

---

[8] See https://www.nscai.gov/2021-final-report/ for recommendations
[9] See War On The Rocks, "Oh My, AI" for use cases and NSCAI recommendations on placing AI requirements into future systems and software acquisitions https://warontherocks.com/2021/05/oh-my-ai/

packages south of Panama. Coupled with targeted placements of liaisons and training teams, they would build capacity with partners to conduct fisheries enforcement while modeling and conducting operations at sea.

Another group proposed a hub-and-spoke model of mission support abroad, leveraging "modularity" as a mission support concept critical to making the Coast Guard capabilities more fungible. Their vision of modularity treated cube-satellites, produced and fielded at relatively low-cost, providing service during their useful life or technological relevance; they would then be disposed of and replaced with new state of the art technology. Incorporating excess defense articles and foreign military sales into acquisition lifecycles would also help.

Most groups saw operational innovation, or at least adaptation, happening in the Indo-Pacific, with the Service adopting new operational models to maximize its impact in strategic competition. The Coast Guard is finding new demands and urgency to strengthen governance in international spaces to limit revision, and this was evident in many futures – even ones in which the People's Republic of China experienced national decline. But they also recognized this must be balanced with domestic responsibilities and demands in other regions.

Whether in the Arctic or off the coast of Africa, the Service's place in strengthening governance meant fielding similar capabilities adapted to new locations; and the Indo-Pacific was a testbed for new operational models.

Build Information Activities as a Core Function. For the American public, sharing timely and accurate information to achieve domestic and international outcomes is a vital government service, and one the Coast Guard has fulfilled since its inception. SEMPER ADAPTUS highlighted this need as a capability to execute mission, FLASH TO BANG saw it as a core function required for ever activity and mission in 2030.

Information activities were seen as a core function of the Coast Guard in 2030 – with the Weather Service being one analogy for the type of service provided to the public. For example – products might be automatically collected and show patterns of congestion on inland waterways to highlight a need for more Marine Transportation System infrastructure; or they might directly target activities – brokering information between Non-Governmental Agencies collecting commercial satellite data on vessel traffic and activity to "shine a light" on bad maritime behavior.

Whether as an enabler or a broker, there is a niche to fill with Information Activities in 2030 that does not overlap DOD's high-end defense-related information space.

What has changed and will accelerate in 2030 are the increasingly automated methods that will drive the volume of information. The costs of collection are rapidly dropping, the amount collected will climb, and this will require more automation to make sense of these massive datasets. It is both a challenge – to understand how to build and employ operational data governance – and an opportunity – to both create better insights while removing burden of collection off members employed in missions.

In the after-analysis of Flash to Bang, it was clear that the Service has experienced an unmeasured growth in need to share information with partners and the public. Whether facilitating safe navigation of coastal waterways or discovering and shining a light on exclusionary fishing practices on the high seas, information sharing was a universal force multiplier in each 2030 scenario.

12

Conclusion

This pinecone was in many ways an extension of SEMPER ADAPTUS. It confirmed insights while exploring ways to accelerate changes that SEMPER ADAPTUS discovered. The next and final pinecone – CONCEPT 2035 – will explore new models operationalizing themes from both workshops. A series of "serious games" will stress test the ideas, and the results will be placed into a "Final Report" to inform the next Commandant of the Coast Guard's transition team.

Thank you to the many members of FLASH TO BANG and the Evergreen Core Team, along with partners from the interagency, academia, and industry who have contributed their valuable time and ideas to Project Evergreen. Thank you as well to the commands who shared their talented people with us, through the challenges of COVID constraints, so they could gain exposure to different parts of the Coast Guard enterprise and directly contribute to its future.

ABOUT PROJECT EVERGREEN & SEMPER ADAPTUS

Project Evergreen (EVG) employs Strategic Foresight to support executive leaders in their role as the Coast Guard's decision engines. To join the conversation, contact the Project Evergreen Team in the Office of Emerging Policy (CG-DCO-X) at foresight@uscg.mil.

PROJECT EVERGREEN

FLAG SPONSOR
Rear Admiral Kevin Lunday, DCMS-DMR

FACILITATORS
LCDR Ryan Hawn, CG-DCO-X
CDR Aaron Delano-Johnson, CG-DCO-X
CDR David Vicks, CG-DCO-X
LCDR Dan Crowley, CG-DCO-X

TEAM EVERGREEN
LCDR Ryan Hawn
CDR Aaron Delano-Johnson

PARTICPANTS – EVERGREEN V CORE TEAM

CAPT	Michael Sinclair	SEFP-Brookings
CAPT	Angelina Hidalgo	SEFP-CSIS
LCDR	Travis Thul	White House Fellow
LCDR	Tony Guido	PAE-1
LT	Brett Gayman	District Eleven
GS	Scott Craig	CG-926
OSC	Kyle Holbrook	District Eleven
CAPT	John Vann	SEFP-CFR
CDR	Jessica Behera	CG-761
CDR	Andy Goshorn	Sector N. New England
LCDR	Doug Eberly	PG, MPA, Syracuse
LT	Kumar Brunhart-McBratney	DCO-ES
CTR	Andy Howell	CG-791
LT	Kastriot Kastrati	USCGA, LDC, OCS
CAPT	Matthew Waldron	SEFP-ODNI
CDR	Jack Souders	SEFP-Hoover
LCDR	Joel Coito	CG-LMI
LCDR	Krysia Pohl	PAC
LT	Alyssa Milanese	FDCC
LT	Brittany Zirulnick	ICC
LTJG	Paige Holmes	C5IT
CAPT	Mark McDonnell	MIT Seminar XXI
CDR	Mike Courtney	ONA
LCDR	Denny Ernster	D11 DRAT
LCDR	Travis Noyes	Office of Maritime / Int'l Law
LT	Kimberlee Capp	CEU Oakland
CDR	Pedro Vazquez	CG-926
Ms.	Jen Ey	DCMS-5

14

References

Adams, David, Jeff Cares, Brett Morah, Albert Nofi, Antonio Sordia, and David Soldow, "SSG Served as an Innovation Incubator," *US Naval Proceedings*, Vol. 143, No. 4, April 2017. As of August 26, 2022:
https://www.usni.org/magazines/proceedings/2017/april/ssg-served-innovation-incubator

"Aftershock," PAXSims.Wordpress, webpage, undated. As of June 2, 2021:
https://paxsims.wordpress.com/aftershock/

American Red Cross, "The Disaster Game, or 'Lights Out!'" webpage, undated. As of August 26, 2022:
https://www.redcross.org/content/dam/redcross/atg/PDF_s/Chapters/Denver/disastergamecards.pdf

Arup International Development, *City Resilience Framework*, prepared for the Rockefeller Foundation, April 2014, updated December 2015. As of June 26, 2019:
https://www.rockefellerfoundation.org/report/city-resilience-framework/

Bryant, Benjamin P., and Robert J. Lempert, "Thinking Inside the Box: A Participatory, Computer-Assisted Approach to Scenario Discovery," *Technological Forecasting and Social Change*, Vol. 77, No. 1, January 2010, pp. 34–49.

Brynen, Rex, and Gary Milante, "Peacebuilding with Games and Simulations," *Gaming & Simulation*, Vol. 44, No. 1, 2012, pp. 27–35.

Center for Strategic and International Studies, "Gray Zone Project," webpage, undated. As of August 26, 2022:
https://www.csis.org/grayzone

Cyber and Innovative Policy Institute, *Defend Forward: Critical Infrastructure War Game 2019 Game Report*, Newport, R.I.: U.S. Naval War College, 2019.

Dalkey, N. C., *The Delphi Method: An Experimental Study of Group Opinion*, Santa Monica, Calif.: RAND Corporation, RM-5888-PR, 1969; As of August 26, 2022:
https://www.rand.org/pubs/research_memoranda/RM5888.html

Dalkey, N. C., and O. Helmer, *An Experimental Application of the Delphi Method to the Use of Experts*, Santa Monica, Calif.: RAND Corporation, RM-721/1, July 1962. As of August 26, 2022:
https://www.rand.org/pubs/research_memoranda/RM727z1.html

Delahunty, Stephen, "Banking Comms' 'Significant Role' Revealed in Cyber-Attack 'War-Game,'" *PRWeek*, October 30, 2019.

Drees, Simon, Karin Geffer, and Rex Brynen, "Crisis on the Board Game—A Novel Approach to Teach Medical Students About Disaster Medicine," *GMS Journal for Medical Education*, Vol. 35, No. 4, 2018.

Duffin, Erin, "Median Age of the Resident Population of the United States from 1960 to 2020," Statista, webpage, undated. As of September 30, 2022:
https://www.statista.com/statistics/241494/median-age-of-the-us-population/

"Evergreen V: Project Management Plan," Homeland Security Operational Analysis Center, Strategy, Policy, and Operations Program, prepared for U.S. Department of Homeland Security, U.S. Coast Guard, Office of Emerging Policy (DCO-X), Modification 10, Santa Monica, Calif.: RAND Corporation, April 2021. Not available to public.

Federal Emergency Management Agency, "Cyber Ready Community Game," webpage, 2020. As of June 2, 2021:
https://www.fema.gov/emergency-managers/national-preparedness/exercises/tools

Federal Reserve Bank of San Francisco, "Chair the Fed," webpage, 2020. As of June 2, 2020:
https://www.frbsf.org/education/teacher-resources/chair-federal-reserve-economy-simulation-game/

Fitch, Kathryn, Steven J. Bernstein, Maria Dolores Aguilar, Bernard Burnand, Juan Ramon LaCalle, Pablo Lazaro, Mirjam van het Loo, Joseph McDonnell, Janneke Vader, and James P. Kahan, *The RAND/UCLA Appropriateness Method User's Manual*, Santa Monica, Calif.: RAND Corporation, MR-1269-DG-XII/RE, 2001. As of August 26, 2022:
https://www.rand.org/pubs/monograph_reports/MR1269.html

Gordon, T., and O. Helmer, *Report on Long-Range Forecasting Study*, Santa Monica, Calif.: RAND Corporation, P-2982, 1964. As of August 26, 2022:
https://www.rand.org/pubs/papers/P2982.html

Greenblott, Joseph M., Thomas O'Farrell, Robert Olson, and Beth Burchard, "Strategic Foresight in the Federal Government: A Survey of Methods, Resources, and Institutional Arrangements," *World Futures Review*, Vol. 11, No. 3, 2019, pp. 245–266.

Hall, Charlie, "The Art and Craft of Making Board Games for the CIA," *Polygon*, webpage, June 22, 2017. As of August 26, 2022:
https://www.polygon.com/2017/6/22/15730254/cia-board-game-volko-ruhnke-coin-series-gmt-games

Horn, John, "Playing War Games to Win," *McKinsey Quarterly*, March 2011. As of September 14, 2022:
https://www.mckinsey.com/business-functions/strategy-and-corporate-finance/our-insights/playing-war-games-to-win

Kanter, Rosabeth Moss, John J. Kao, and Frederik Derk Wiersema, eds., *Innovation: Breakthrough Thinking at 3M, DuPont, GE, Pfizer, and Rubbermaid*, New York: Harper Business, 1997.

Khodyakov, Dmitry, and Christine Chen, *Nature and Predictors of Response Changes in Modified-Delphi Panels*, Santa Monica, Calif.: RAND Corporation, EP-68427, 2020. As of August 26, 2022:
https://www.rand.org/pubs/external_publications/EP68427.html

Knopman, Debra, Susan Resetar, Parry Norling, and Irene Bramakulam, *Innovation and Change Management in Public and Private Organizations: Case Studies and Options for the EPA*, RAND Corporation, Santa Monica, CA, DB-393, April 2003. As of August 26, 2022:
https://www.rand.org/pubs/documented_briefings/DB393.html

Kotter, John P., *Leading Change*, Cambridge, Mass.: Harvard Business School Press, 1996.

Lane, Sylvan, "'Chair the Fed' Makes Monetary Policy a Video Game," *The Hill*, September 15, 2016.

Mandiant, "Tabletop Exercise: Test Your Organization's Cyber Response Plan with Scenario Gameplay," FireEye, webpage, undated. As of June 2, 2021:
https://www.fireeye.com/content/dam/fireeye-www/services/pdfs/pf/ms/ds-tabletop-exercise.pdf

Marchau, Vincent A. W. J., Warren E. Walker, Pieter J. T. M. Bloemen, and Steven W. Popper, eds., *Decision Making Under Deep Uncertainty: From Theory to Practice*, New York: Springer, 2019.

Morris, Lyle J., Michael J. Mazarr, Jeffrey W. Hornung, Stephanie Pezard, Anika Binnendijk, and Marta Kepe, *Gaining Competitive Advantage in the Gray Zone: Response Options for Coercive Aggression Below the Threshold of Major War*, Santa Monica, Calif.: RAND Corporation, RR-2942-OSD, 2019. As of June 27, 2021:
https://www.rand.org/pubs/research_reports/RR2942.html

Mural.com, webpage, undated. As of May 16, 2022:
https://www.mural.co

Normand, S. L.-T., B. J. McNeil, L. E. Peterson, and R. H. Palmer, "Eliciting Expert Opinion Using the Delphi Technique: Identifying Performance Indicators for Cardiovascular Disease," *International Journal for Quality in Health Care*, Vol. 3, No. 2, 1998, pp. 247–260. As of August 26, 2022:
https://pubmed.ncbi.nlm.nih.gov/9661064/

Office of Management and Budget, "Circular No. A-11: Preparation, Submission, and Execution of the Budget," Washington, D.C.: Executive Office of the President, 2017.

Perla, Peter, *Peter Perla's The Art of Wargaming: A Guide for Professionals and Hobbyists*, John Curry, ed., Morrisville, N.C.: Lulu Press, 2012.

Resetar, Susan A., Michelle D. Ziegler, Aaron C. Davenport, and Melissa Bauman, *U.S. Coast Guard Workforce 2040: Better Management Through Transparency*, Santa Monica, Calif.: RAND Corporation, PE-358-DHS, 2020. As of June 2, 2021:
https://www.rand.org/pubs/perspectives/PE358.html

Rohrbeck, René, and Jan Oliver Schwarz, "The Value Contribution of Strategic Foresight: Insights from an Empirical Study of Large European Companies," *Technological Forecasting and Social Change*, Vol. 80, No. 8, 2013, pp. 1593–1606.

Savitz, Scott, Aaron C. Davenport, and Michelle D. Ziegler, *The Marine Transportation System, Autonomous Technology, and Implications for the U.S. Coast Guard*, Santa Monica, Calif.: RAND Corporation, PE-359-DHS, 2020. As of June 2, 2021:
https://www.rand.org/pubs/perspectives/PE359.html

Savitz, Scott, Miriam Matthews, and Sarah Weilant, *Assessing Impact to Inform Decisions: A Toolkit on Measures for Policymakers*, Santa Monica, Calif.: RAND Corporation, TL-263-OSD, 2017. As of August 26, 2022:
https://www.rand.org/pubs/tools/TL263.html

Scoblic, Peter, "Learning from the Future," *Harvard Business Review*, July–August 2020. As of September 14, 2022:
https://hbr.org/2020/07/learning-from-the-future

Smith, Julia, Nathan Sears, Ben Taylor, and Madeline Johnson, "Serious Games for Serious Crises: Reflections from an Infectious Disease Outbreak Matrix Game," *Globalization and Health*, Vol. 16, Article 18, 2020.

Solomon, Dan, and Paula Forbes, "Inside the Story of How H-E-B Planned for the Pandemic," *Texas Monthly*, March 26, 2020. As of September 14, 2022:
https://www.texasmonthly.com/food/heb-prepared-coronavirus-pandemic/

Tingstad, Abbie, Scott Savitz, Kristin Van Abel, Dulani Woods, Katherine Anania, Michelle D. Ziegler, Aaron C. Davenport, and Katherine Costello, *Identifying Potential Gaps in U.S. Coast Guard Arctic Capabilities*, Santa Monica, Calif.: RAND Corporation, RR-2310-DHS, 2018. As of May 20, 2021:
https://www.rand.org/pubs/research_reports/RR2310.html

Tingstad, Abbie, Michael T. Wilson, Katherine Anania, Jordan R. Fischbach, Susan A. Resetar, Scott Savitz, Kristin Van Abel, R. J. Briggs, Aaron C. Davenport, Stephanie Pezard, Kristin Sereyko, Jonathan Theel, Marc Thibault, and Edward Ulin, *Developing New Future Scenarios for the U.S. Coast Guard's Evergreen Strategic Foresight Program*, Santa Monica, Calif.: RAND Corporation, RR-3147-DHS, 2020. As of May 21, 2021: https://www.rand.org/pubs/research_reports/RR3147.html

Tingstad, Abbie, Yuna Huh Wong, and Scott Savitz, *How Can the Coast Guard Use Gaming?* Santa Monica, Calif.: RAND Corporation, PE-A148-1, 2020. As of May 20, 2021: https://www.rand.org/pubs/perspectives/PEA148-1.html

U.S. Army Command and General Staff College, *Master of Military Science and Art (MMSA) Program Information*, Fort Leavenworth, Kans., undated.

U.S. Coast Guard, "Creating and Sustaining Strategic Intent in the U.S. Coast Guard," Version 3.0, September 2013. As of August 26, 2022: https://www.uscg.mil/Portals/0/Strategy/Report%20Evergreen%20III%20Blue%20Book.pdf

———, *Coast Guard Strategic Plan: 2018–2022*, 2018. As of August 26, 2022: https://www.uscg.mil/Portals/0/seniorleadership/alwaysready/USCG_Strategic%20Plan __LoResReaderSpreads_20181115_vFinal.pdf?ver=2018-11-14-150015-323

"U.S. Maritime Strategy: Advantage at Sea," *USNI News*, December 17, 2020. As of August 26, 2022: https://news.usni.org/2020/12/17/u-s-maritime-strategy-advantage-at-sea

Wilkinson, Angela, and Roland Kupers, "Living in the Futures," *Harvard Business School Magazine*, May 2013. As of September 14, 2022: https://hbr.org/2013/05/living-in-the-futures

Wong, Yuna Huh, Sebastian Joon Bae, Elizabeth M. Bartels, and Benjamin Michael Smith, *Next-Generation Wargaming for the U.S. Marine Corps: Recommended Courses of Action*, Santa Monica, Calif.: RAND Corporation, RR-2227-USMC, 2019. As of May 20, 2021: https://www.rand.org/pubs/research_reports/RR2227.html

Zegers, Antony, *Matrix Game Methodology: Support to V2010 Olympic Maritime Security Planners*, Defence R&D Canada, Technical Report DRDC CORA TR 2011-016, February 2011.

Zigler, Michelle D., Aaron C. Davenport, Susan A. Resetar, Scott Savitz, Katherine Anania, Melissa Bauman, and Karishma Patel, *Shaping Coast Guard Culture to Enhance the Future Workforce*, Santa Monica, Calif: RAND Corporation, PE-A872-1, 2021. As of September 9, 2022: https://www.rand.org/pubs/perspectives/PEA872-1.html

Lightning Source UK Ltd.
Milton Keynes UK
UKHW051936110123
415204UK00013B/82

9 781977 410238